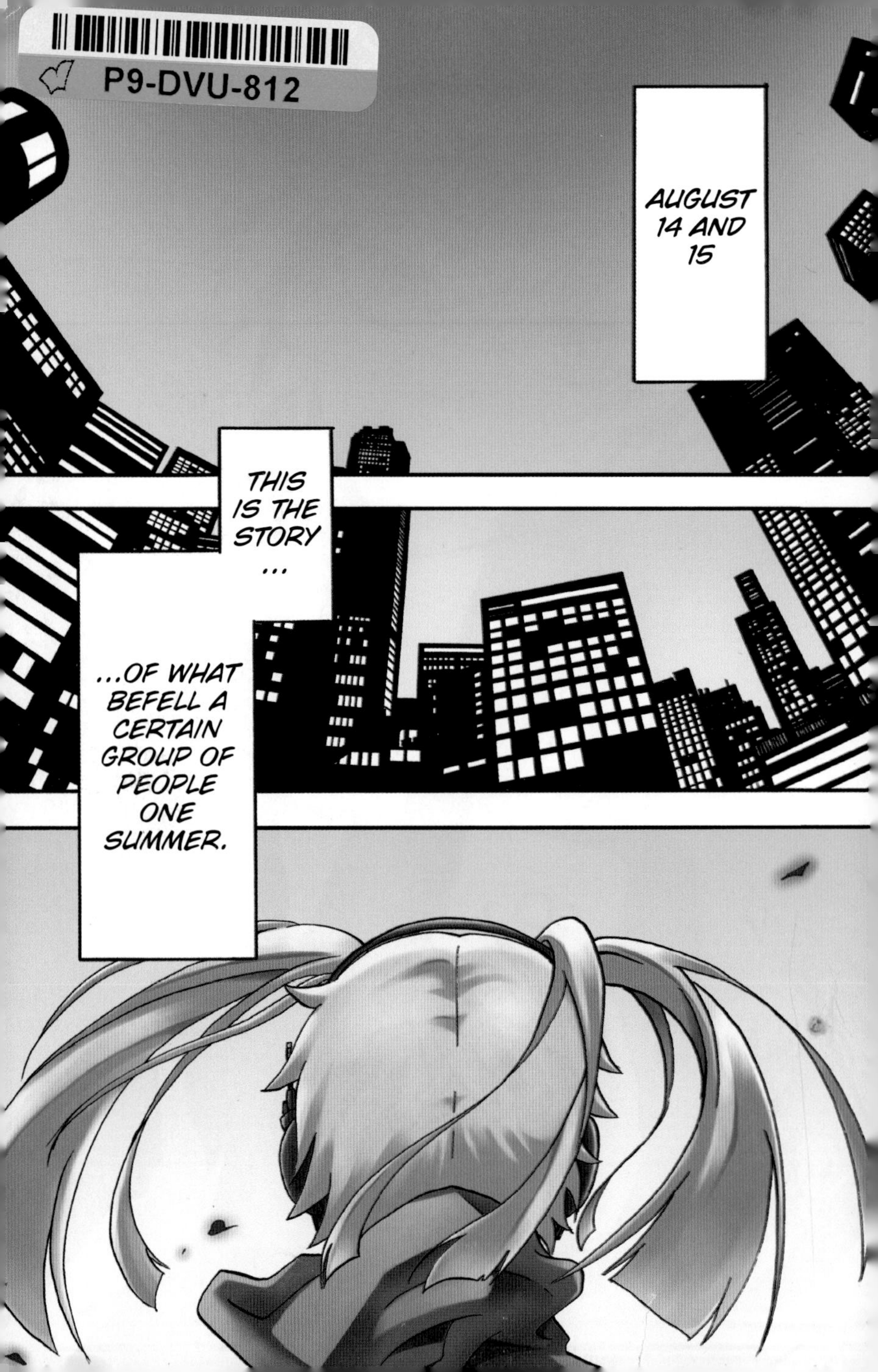
AUGUST 14 AND 15
THIS IS THE STORY ...
...OF WHAT BEFELL A CERTAIN GROUP OF PEOPLE ONE SUMMER.

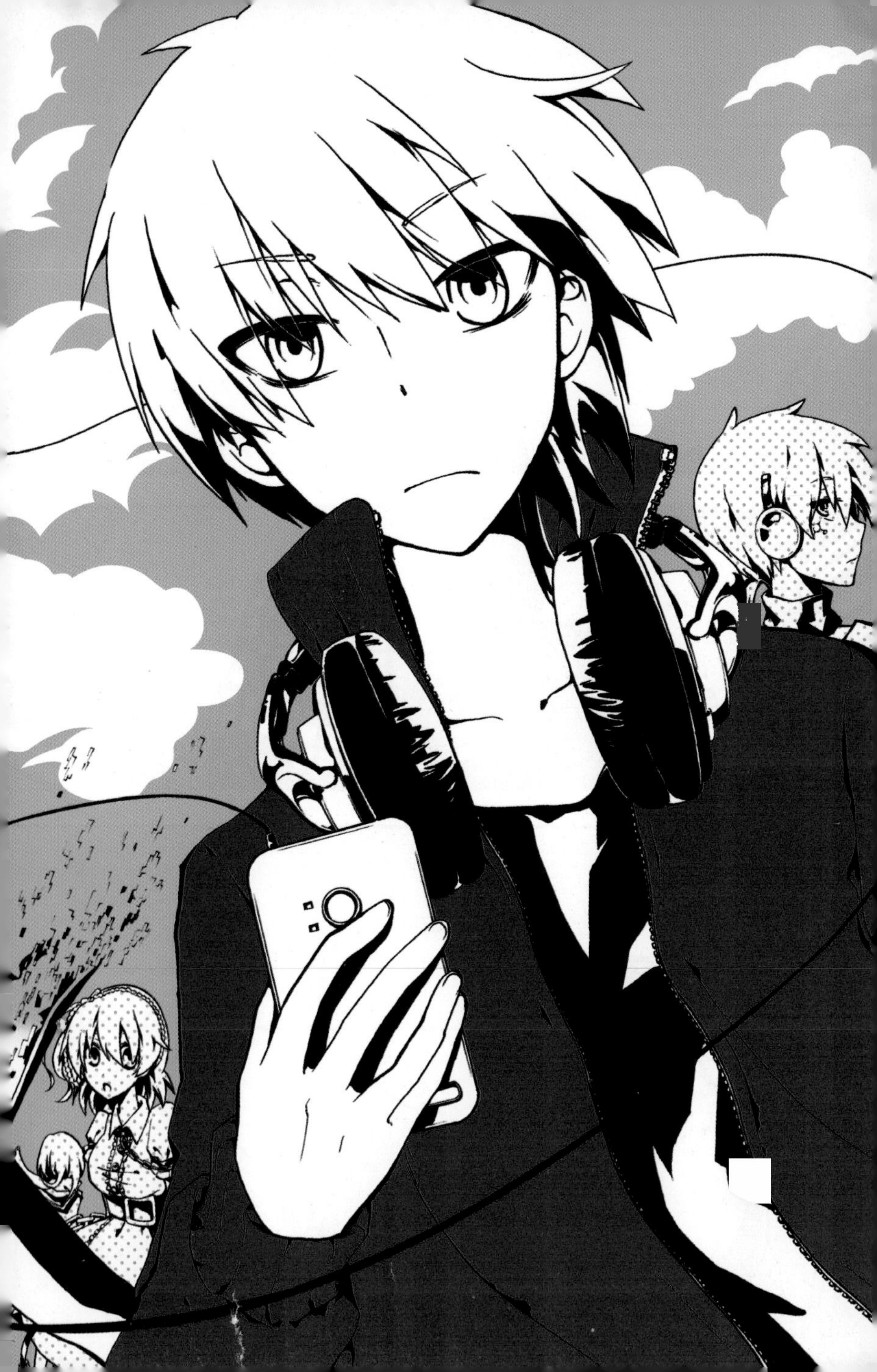

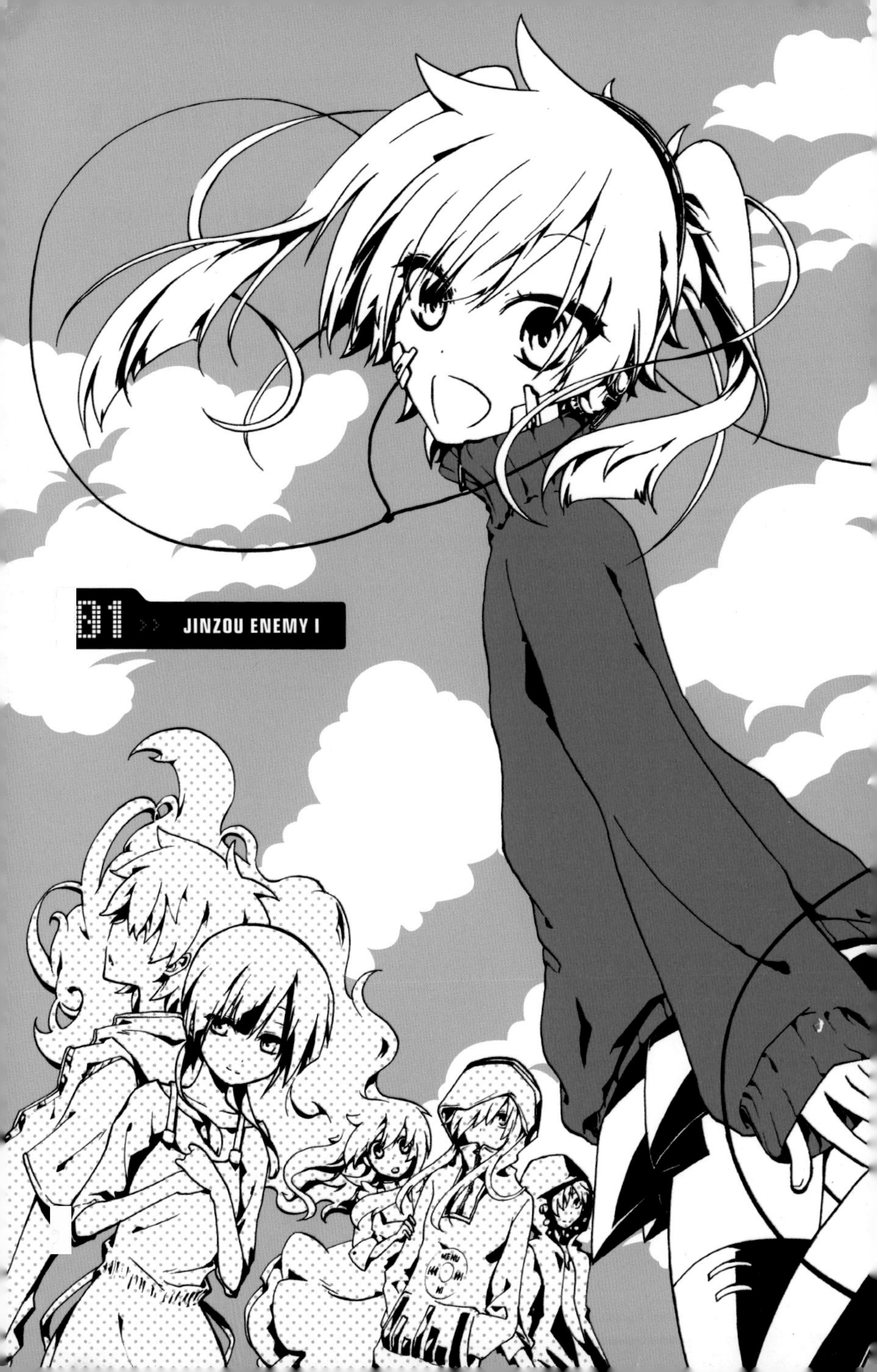
01 >> JINZOU ENEMY I
MENU

KAGEROU DAZE 1

CONTENTS

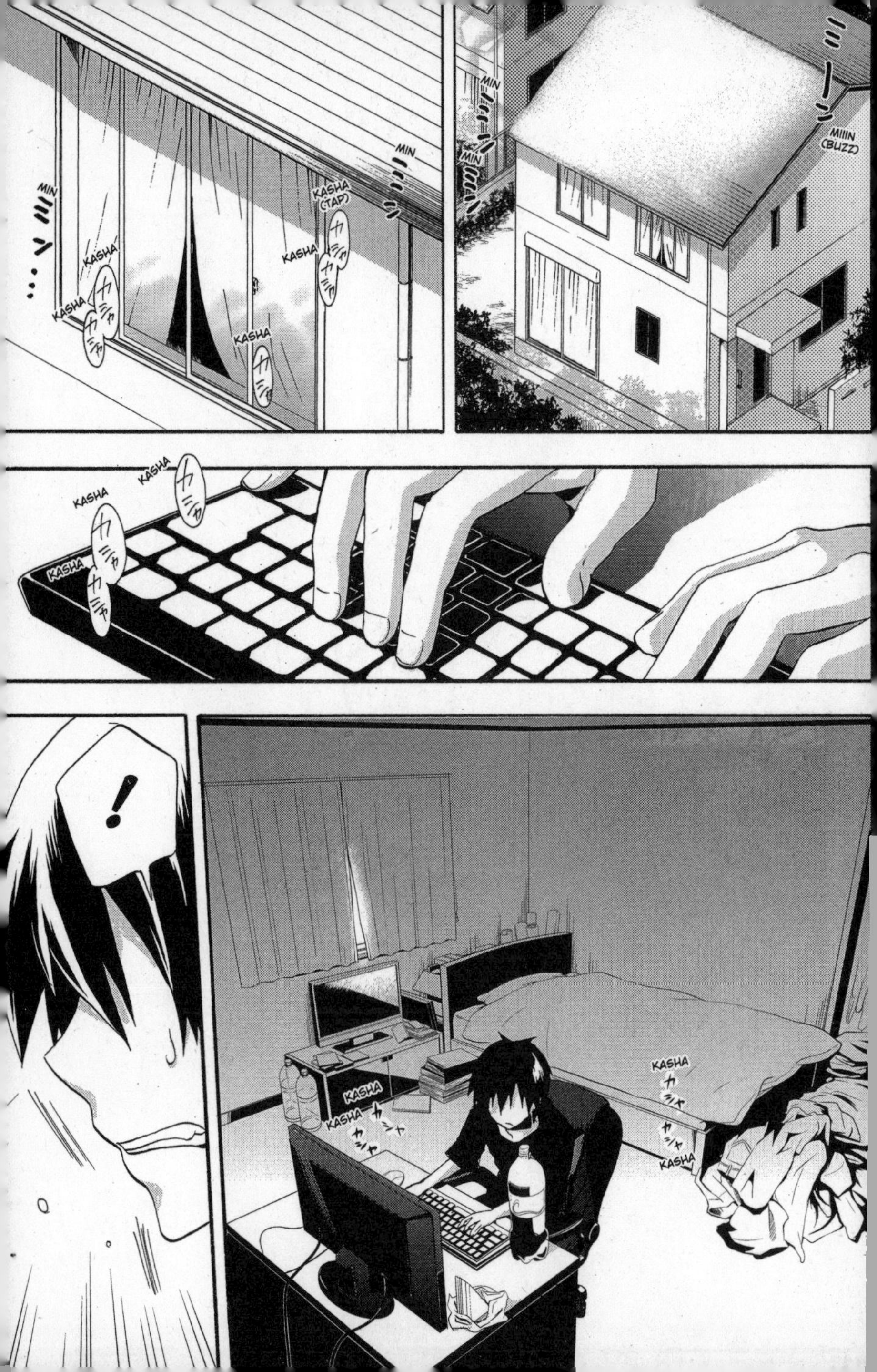
MIIIN (BUZZ)
MIN
MIN
MIN
KASHA (TAP)
KASHA
MIN
KASHA
KASHA
KASHA
KASHA
KASHA
KASHA
KASHA
KASHA
KASHA
KASHA
!

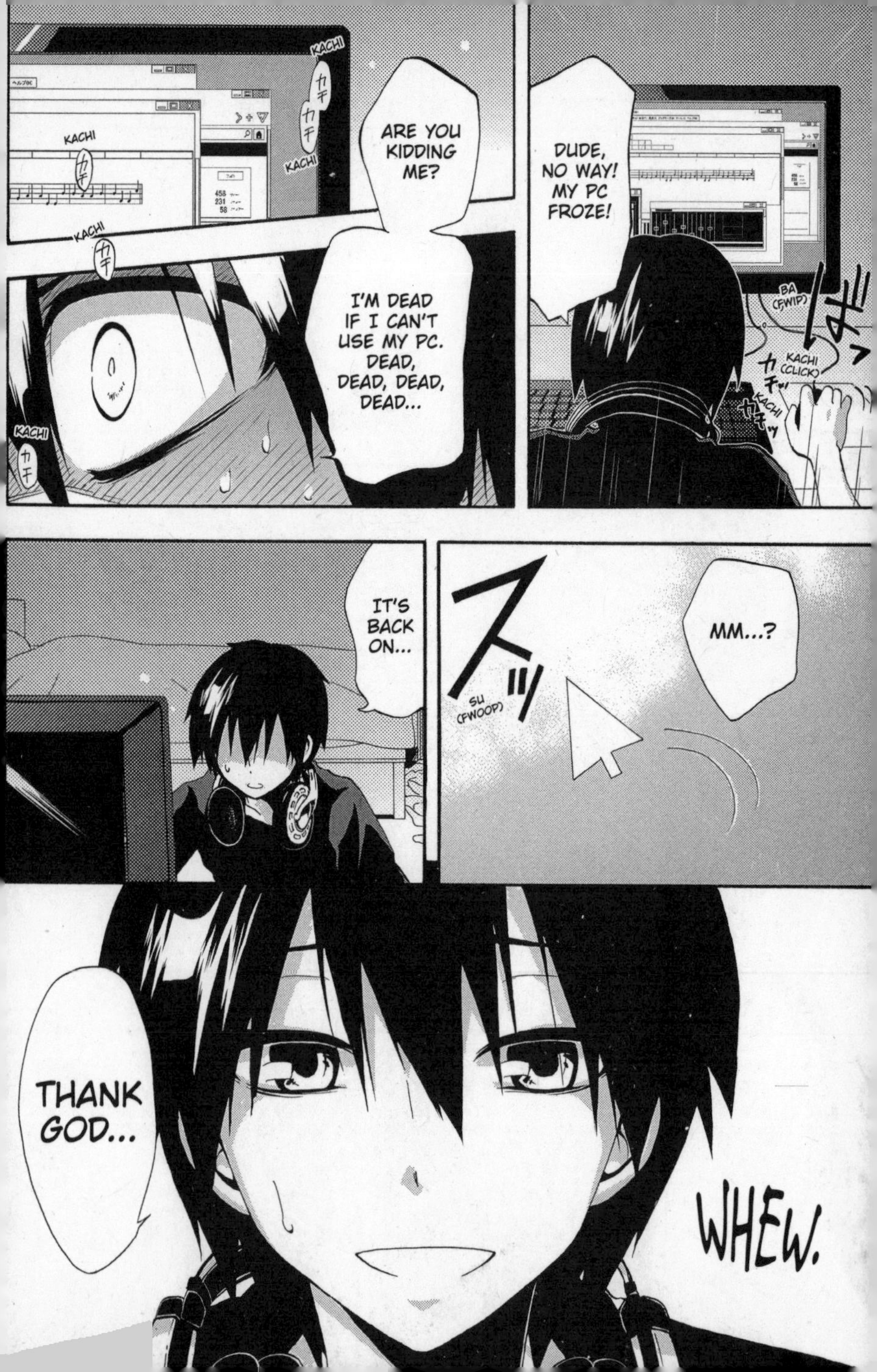
DUDE, NO WAY! MY PC FROZE!
BA (FWIP)
KACHI (CLICK)
KACHI
KACHI
KACHI
KACHI
ARE YOU KIDDING ME?
KACHI
I'M DEAD IF I CAN'T USE MY PC. DEAD, DEAD, DEAD, DEAD...
KACHI
MM...?
SU (FWOOP)
IT'S BACK ON...
THANK GOD...
WHEW.

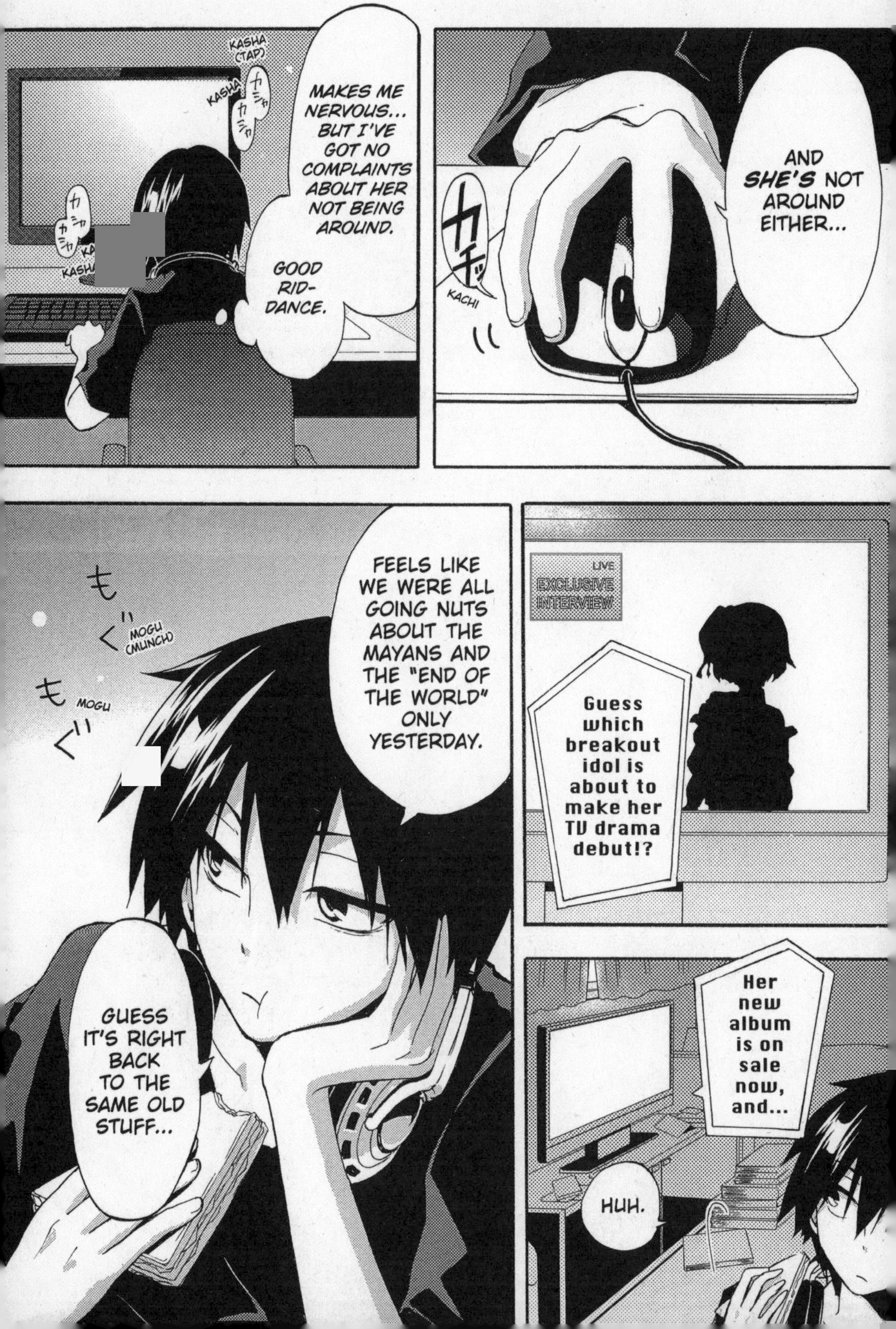

カチッ
KACHI
AND SHE'S NOT AROUND EITHER...
KASHA (TAP)
KASHA
KASHA
MAKES ME NERVOUS... BUT I'VE GOT NO COMPLAINTS ABOUT HER NOT BEING AROUND.
GOOD RID-DANCE.
LIVE
EXCLUSIVE INTERVIEW
Guess which breakout idol is about to make her TV drama debut!?
Her new album is on sale now, and...
HUH.
もぐ
MOGU (MUNCH)
もぐ
MOGU
FEELS LIKE WE WERE ALL GOING NUTS ABOUT THE MAYANS AND THE "END OF THE WORLD" ONLY YESTERDAY.
GUESS IT'S RIGHT BACK TO THE SAME OLD STUFF...

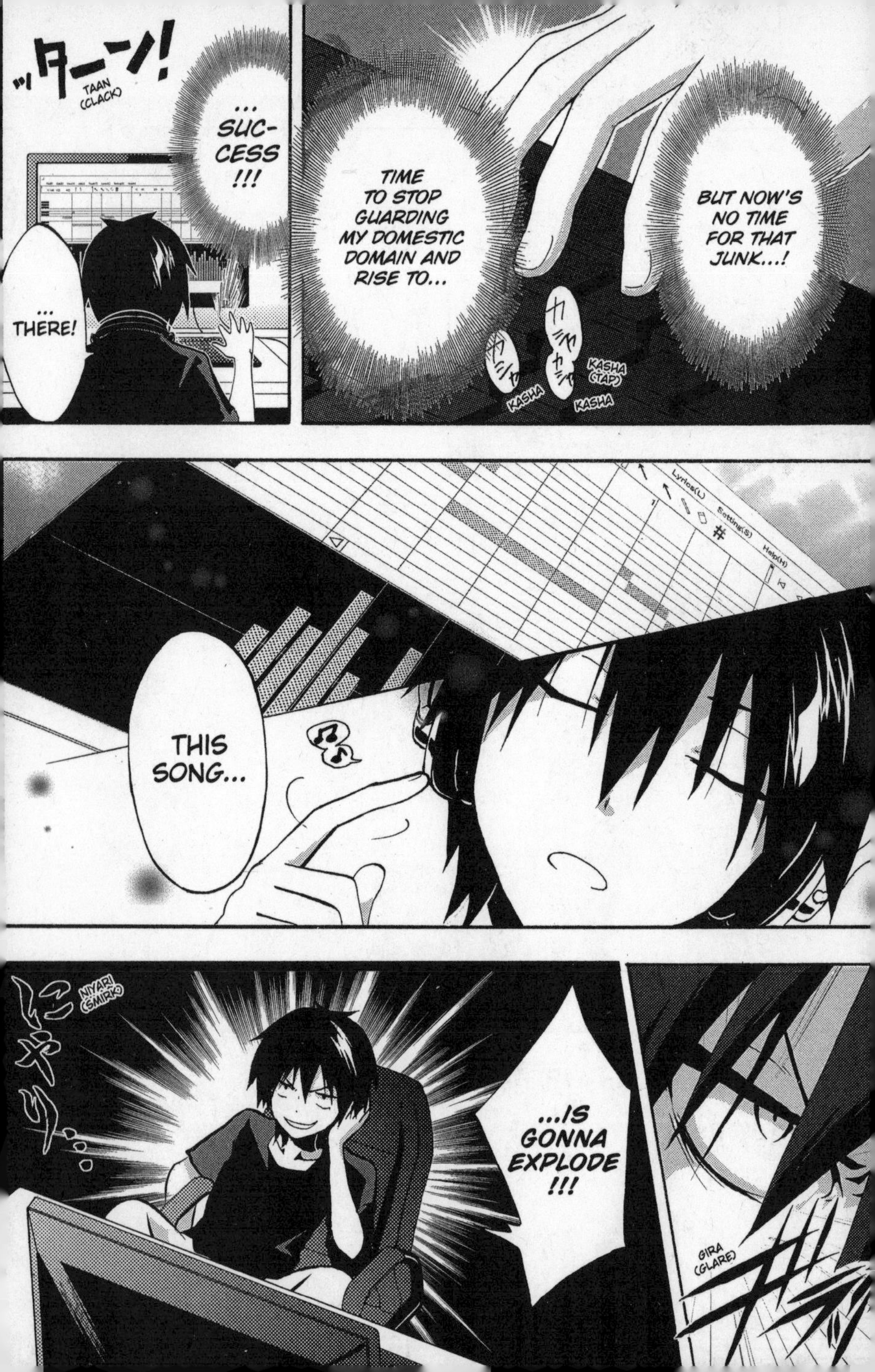
BUT NOW'S NO TIME FOR THAT JUNK...!
TIME TO STOP GUARDING MY DOMESTIC DOMAIN AND RISE TO...
KASHA (TAP)
KASHA
KASHA
TAAN (CLACK)
...SUCCESS!!!
...THERE!
Setting(S)
Help(H)
THIS SONG...
GIRA (GLARE)
NIYARI (SMIRK)
...IS GONNA EXPLODE!!!

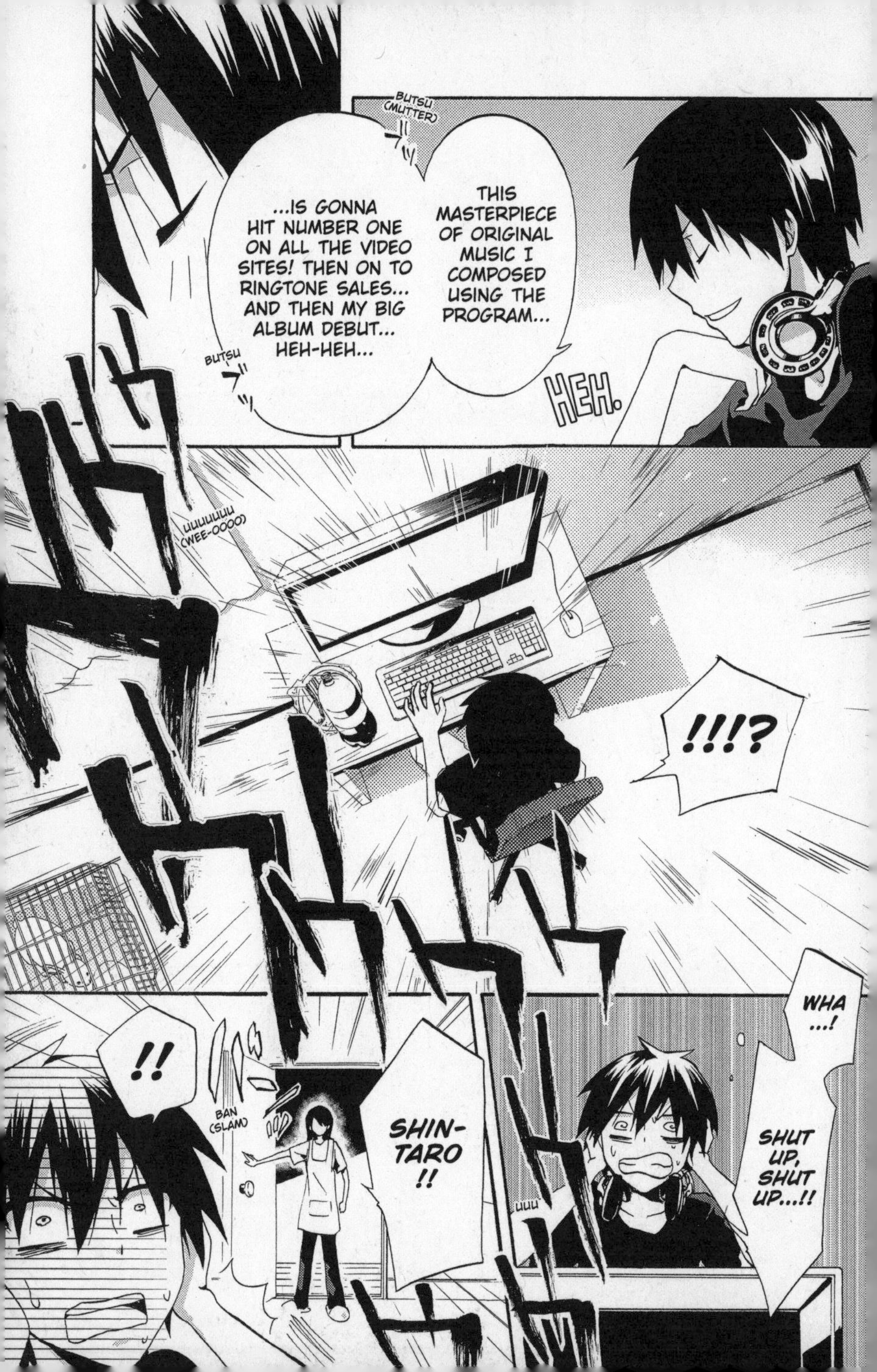
BUTSU (MUTTER)
THIS MASTERPIECE OF ORIGINAL MUSIC I COMPOSED USING THE PROGRAM...
...IS GONNA HIT NUMBER ONE ON ALL THE VIDEO SITES! THEN ON TO RINGTONE SALES... AND THEN MY BIG ALBUM DEBUT... HEH-HEH...
BUTSU
HEH.
UUUUUUU (WEE-OOOO)
!!!?
WHA ...!
SHUT UP, SHUT UP...!!
UUU
SHIN-TARO !!
BAN (SLAM)
!!

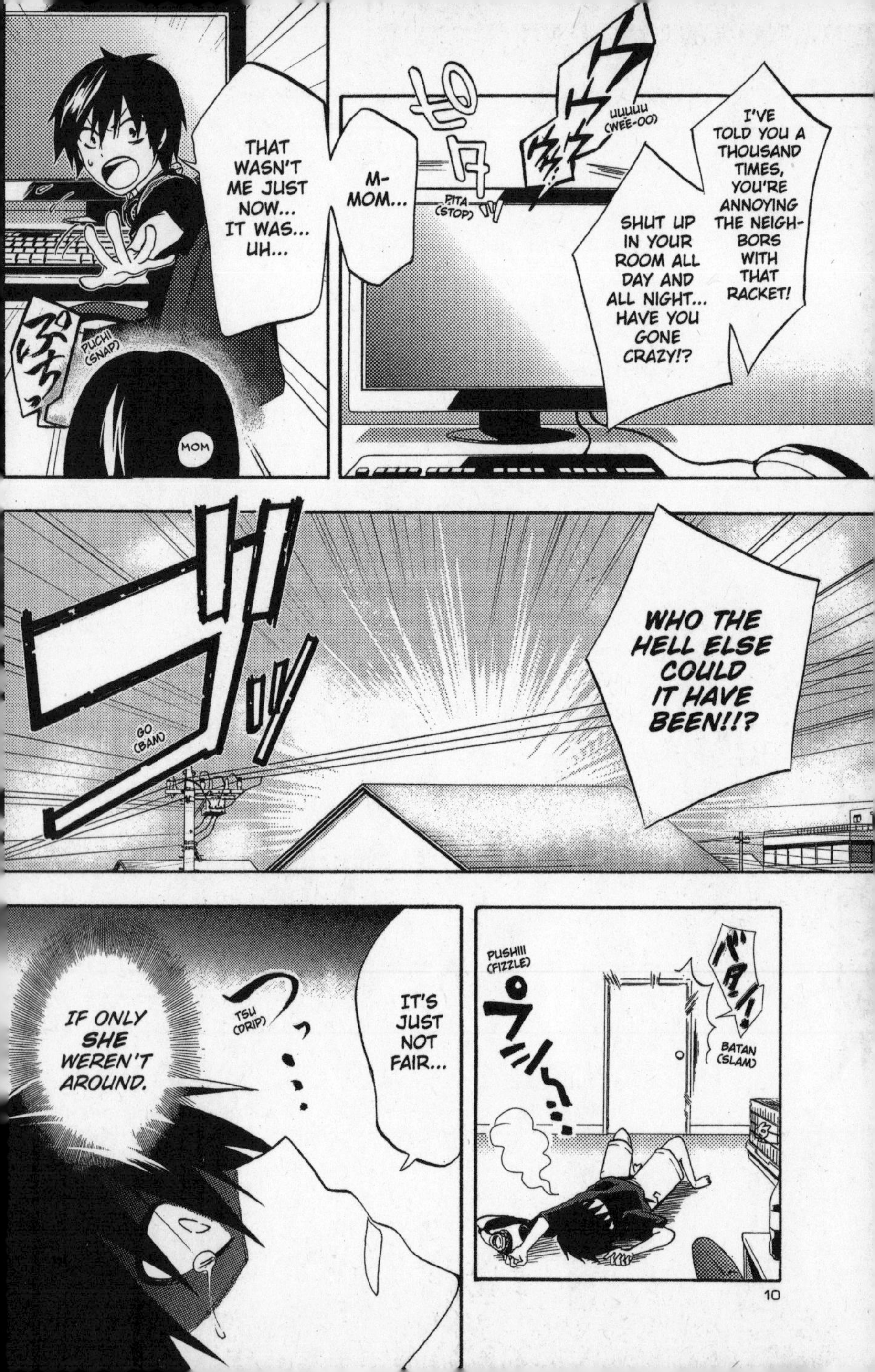
UUUUU (WEE-OO)
I'VE TOLD YOU A THOUSAND TIMES, YOU'RE ANNOYING THE NEIGHBORS WITH THAT RACKET!
SHUT UP IN YOUR ROOM ALL DAY AND ALL NIGHT... HAVE YOU GONE CRAZY!?
PITA (STOP)
M-MOM...
THAT WASN'T ME JUST NOW... IT WAS... UH...
PUCHI (SNAP)
MOM
WHO THE HELL ELSE COULD IT HAVE BEEN!!?
GO (BAM)
BATAN (SLAM)
PUSHIII (FIZZLE)
IT'S JUST NOT FAIR...
TSU (DRIP)
IF ONLY SHE WEREN'T AROUND.

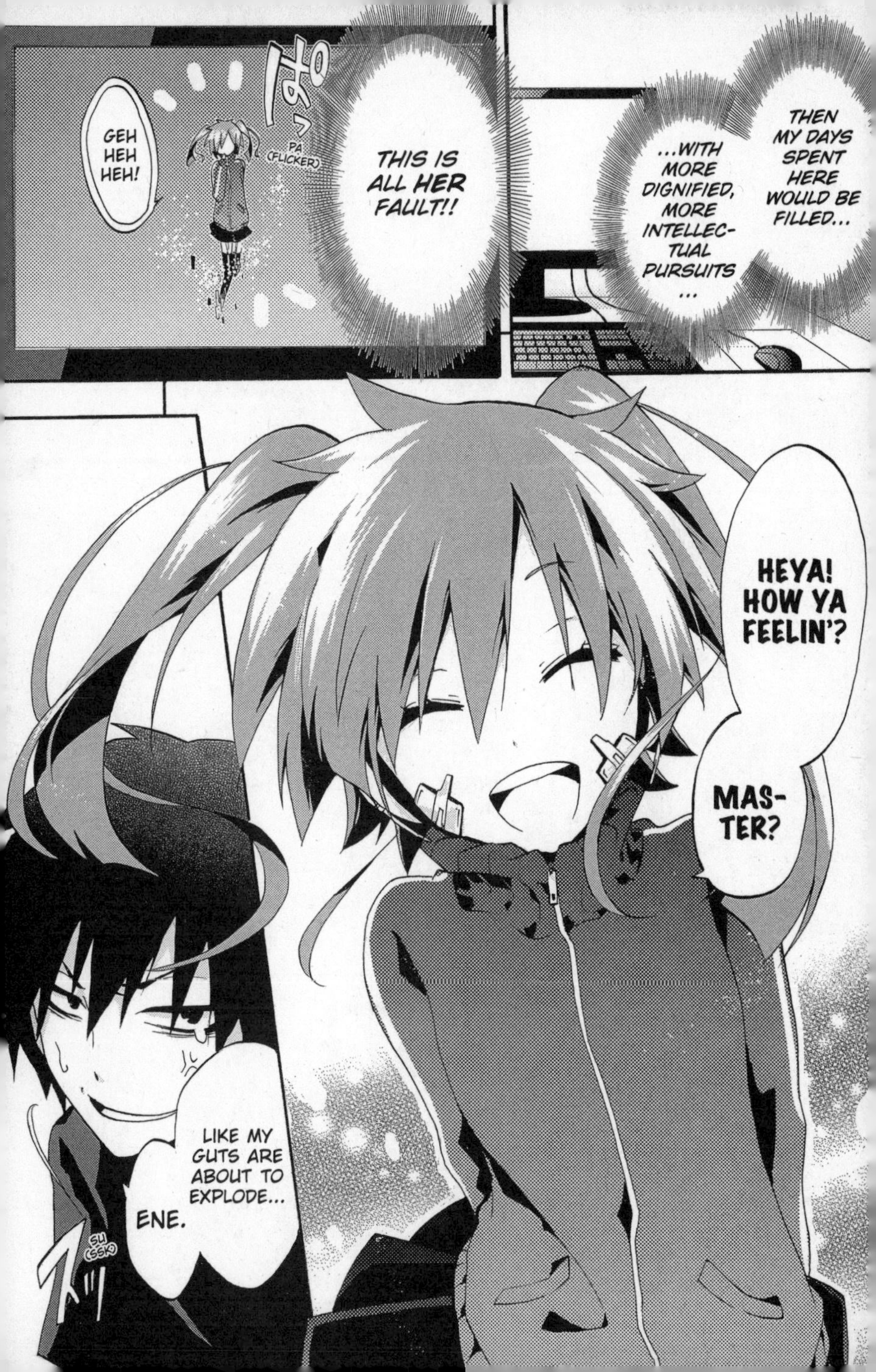
THEN MY DAYS SPENT HERE WOULD BE FILLED...
...WITH MORE DIGNIFIED, MORE INTELLEC-TUAL PURSUITS ...
THIS IS ALL HER FAULT!!
ぱっ
PA (FLICKER)
GEH HEH HEH!
HEYA! HOW YA FEELIN'?
MAS-TER?
LIKE MY GUTS ARE ABOUT TO EXPLODE...
ENE.
スッ
SU (SSK)

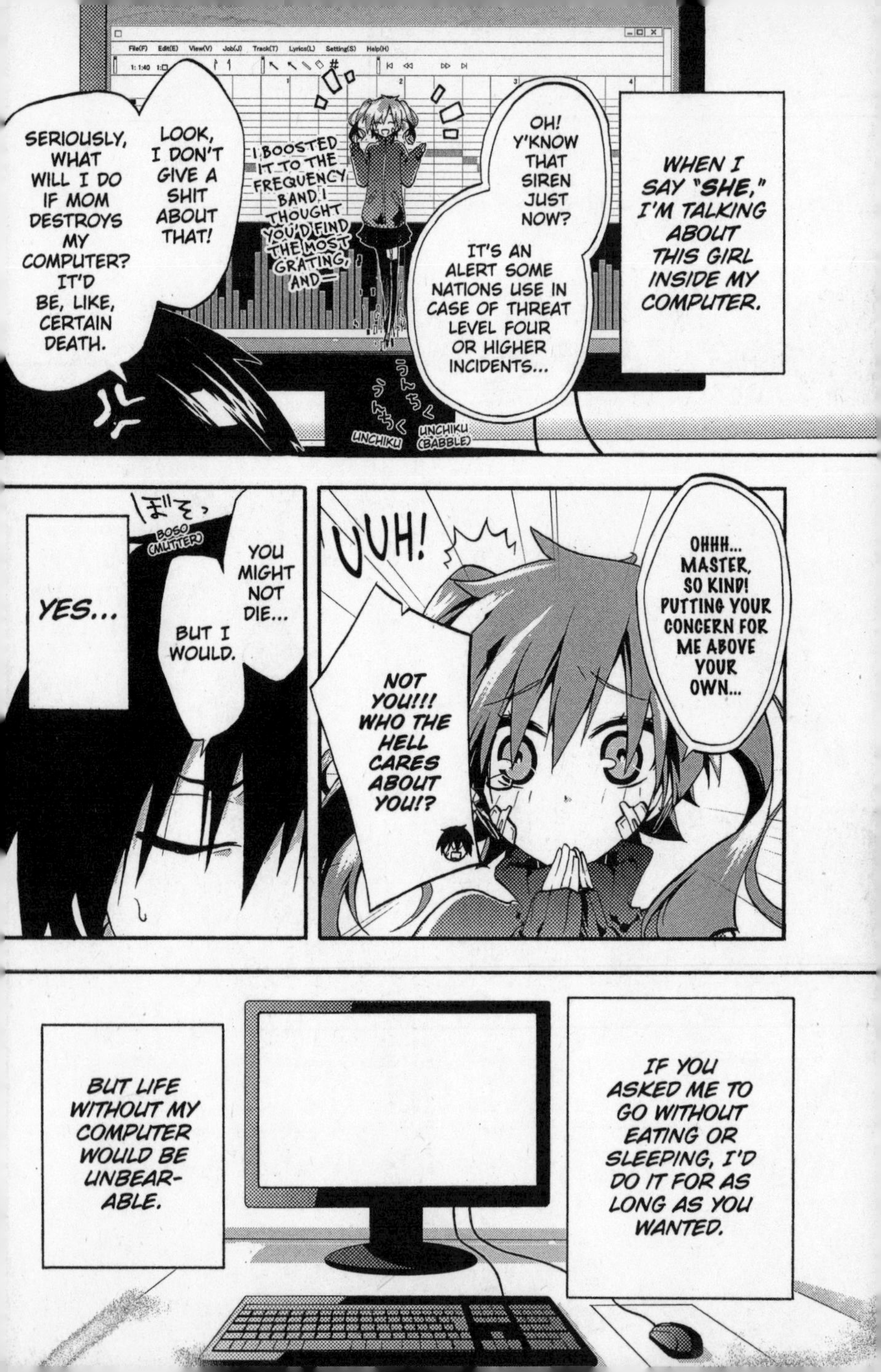
File(F) Edit(E) View(V) Job(J) Track(T) Lyrics(L) Setting(S) Help(H)
WHEN I SAY "SHE," I'M TALKING ABOUT THIS GIRL INSIDE MY COMPUTER.
OH! Y'KNOW THAT SIREN JUST NOW?
IT'S AN ALERT SOME NATIONS USE IN CASE OF THREAT LEVEL FOUR OR HIGHER INCIDENTS...
うんちく
UNCHIKU (BABBLE)
うんちく
UNCHIKU
I BOOSTED IT TO THE FREQUENCY BAND I THOUGHT YOU'D FIND THE MOST GRATING, AND—
LOOK, I DON'T GIVE A SHIT ABOUT THAT!
SERIOUSLY, WHAT WILL I DO IF MOM DESTROYS MY COMPUTER? IT'D BE, LIKE, CERTAIN DEATH.
OHHH... MASTER, SO KIND! PUTTING YOUR CONCERN FOR ME ABOVE YOUR OWN...
UUH!
NOT YOU!!! WHO THE HELL CARES ABOUT YOU!?
ぼそっ
BOSO (MUTTER)
YOU MIGHT NOT DIE...
BUT I WOULD.
YES...
IF YOU ASKED ME TO GO WITHOUT EATING OR SLEEPING, I'D DO IT FOR AS LONG AS YOU WANTED.
BUT LIFE WITHOUT MY COMPUTER WOULD BE UNBEAR-ABLE.

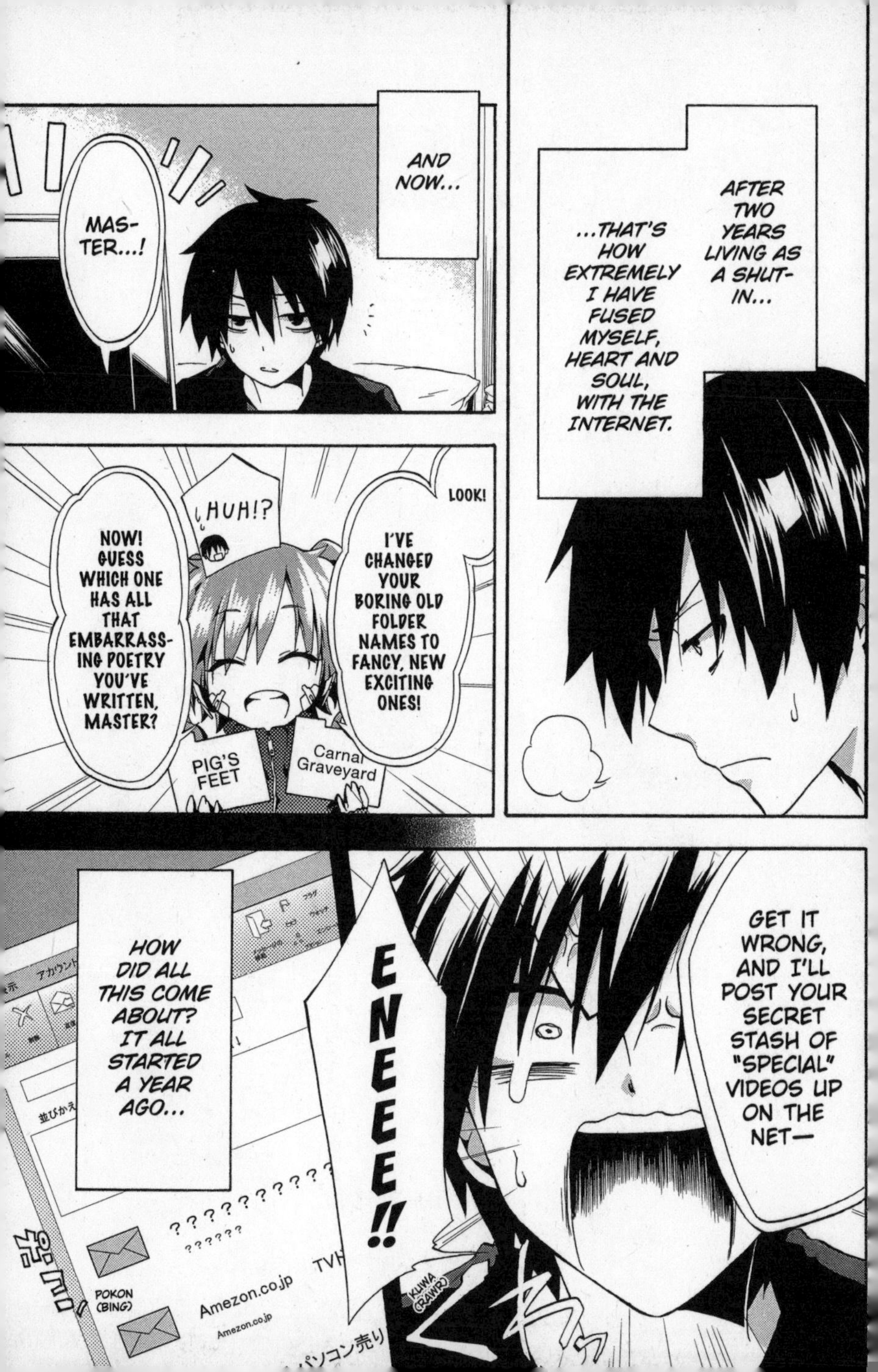
AFTER TWO YEARS LIVING AS A SHUT-IN...
...THAT'S HOW EXTREMELY I HAVE FUSED MYSELF, HEART AND SOUL, WITH THE INTERNET.
AND NOW...
MASTER...!
LOOK!
I'VE CHANGED YOUR BORING OLD FOLDER NAMES TO FANCY, NEW EXCITING ONES!
HUH!?
NOW! GUESS WHICH ONE HAS ALL THAT EMBARRASSING POETRY YOU'VE WRITTEN, MASTER?
Carnal Graveyard
PIG'S FEET
GET IT WRONG, AND I'LL POST YOUR SECRET STASH OF "SPECIAL" VIDEOS UP ON THE NET—
ENEEEE!!
KUWA (RAWR)
HOW DID ALL THIS COME ABOUT? IT ALL STARTED A YEAR AGO...
アカウント
並びかえ
POKON (BING)
Amezon.co.jp
Amezon.co.jp
パソコン売り

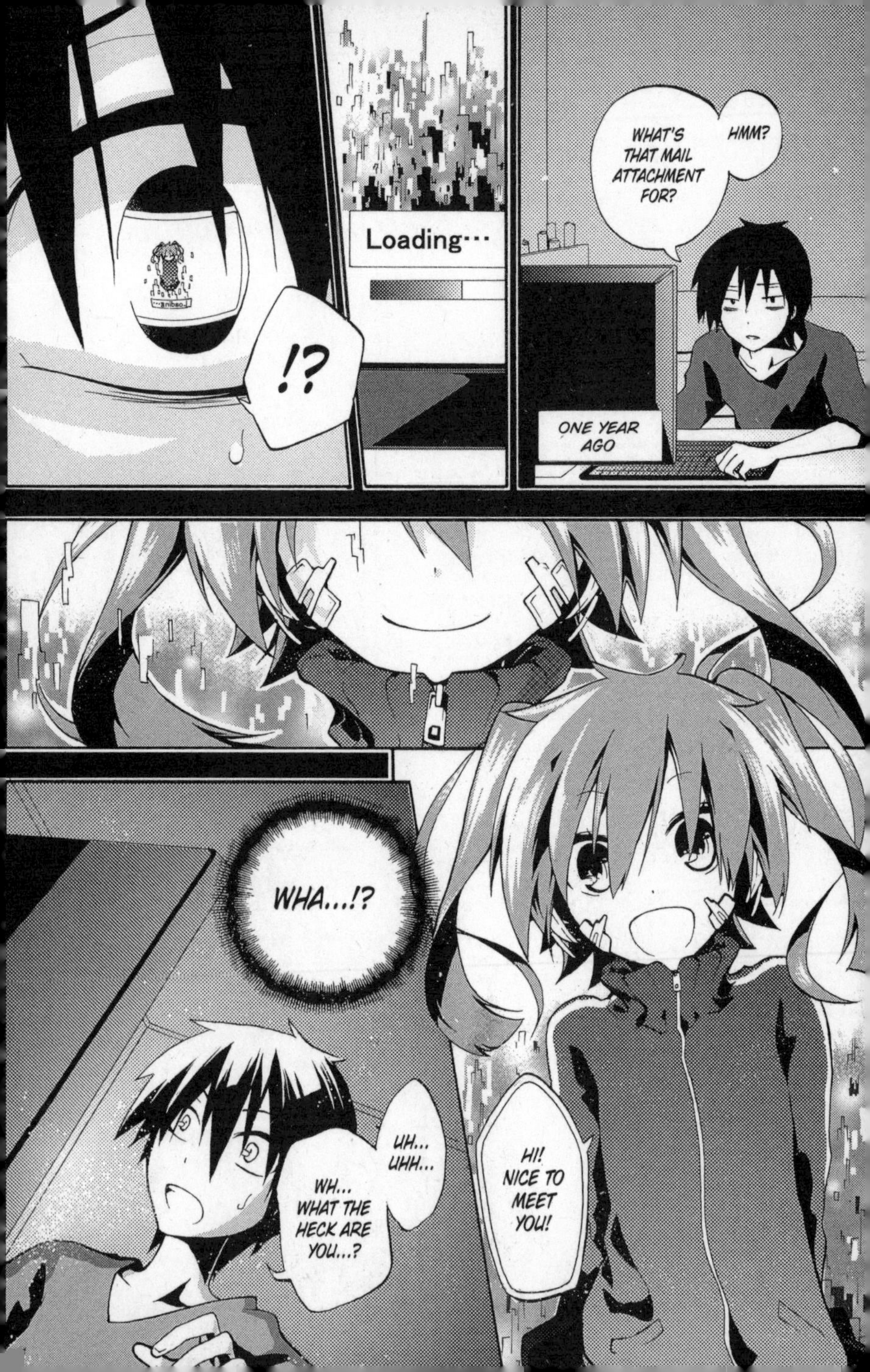
HMM?
WHAT'S THAT MAIL ATTACHMENT FOR?
ONE YEAR AGO
Loading…
!?
WHA...!?
HI! NICE TO MEET YOU!
UH... UHH...
WH... WHAT THE HECK ARE YOU...?

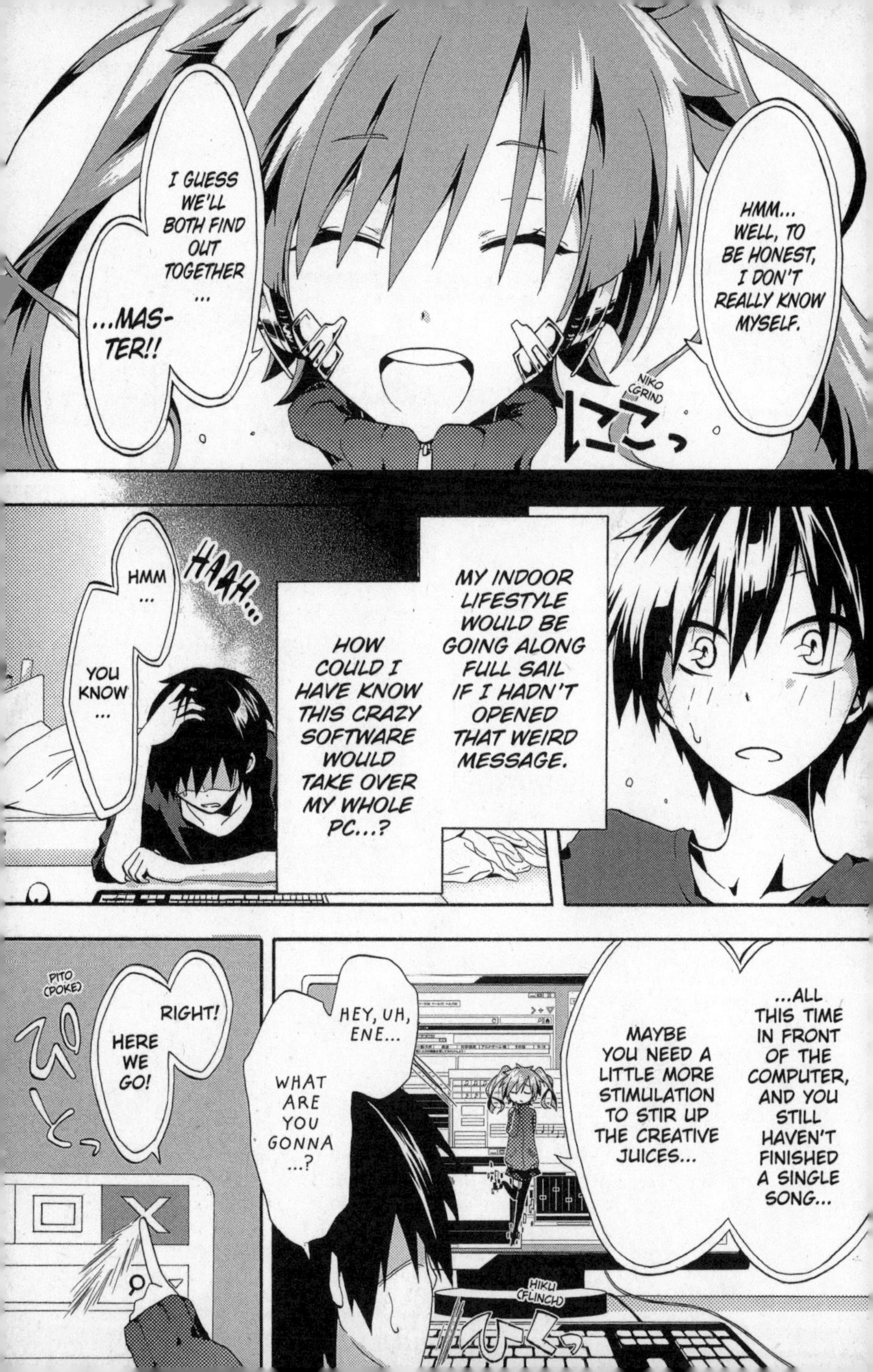
HMM... WELL, TO BE HONEST, I DON'T REALLY KNOW MYSELF.
NIKO (GRIN)
I GUESS WE'LL BOTH FIND OUT TOGETHER ...
...MASTER!!
MY INDOOR LIFESTYLE WOULD BE GOING ALONG FULL SAIL IF I HADN'T OPENED THAT WEIRD MESSAGE.
HOW COULD I HAVE KNOW THIS CRAZY SOFTWARE WOULD TAKE OVER MY WHOLE PC...?
HAAAH...
HMM ...
YOU KNOW ...
...ALL THIS TIME IN FRONT OF THE COMPUTER, AND YOU STILL HAVEN'T FINISHED A SINGLE SONG...
MAYBE YOU NEED A LITTLE MORE STIMULATION TO STIR UP THE CREATIVE JUICES...
HEY, UH, ENE...
WHAT ARE YOU GONNA ...?
HIKU (FLINCH)
PITO (POKE)
RIGHT!
HERE WE GO!

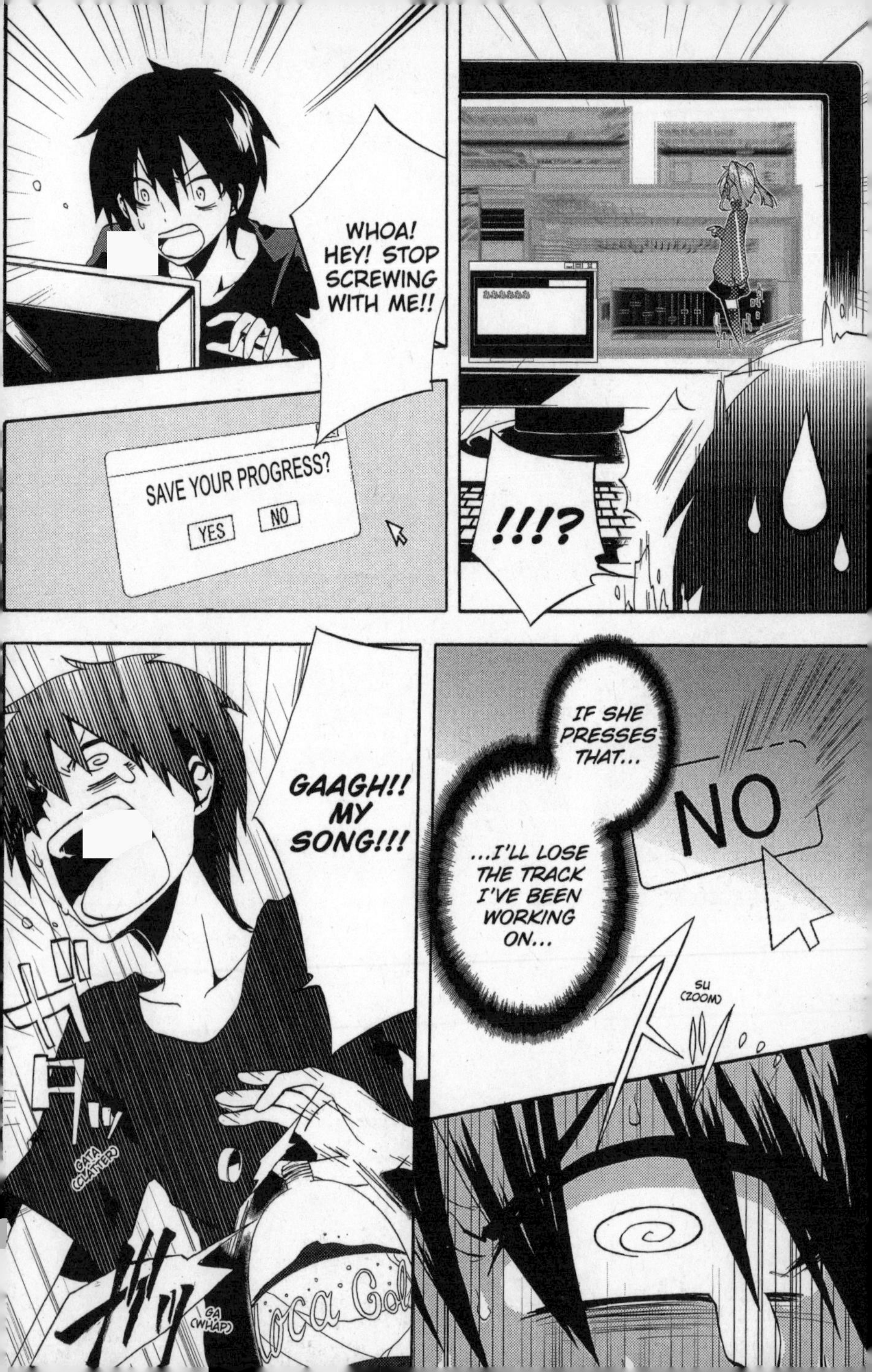
!!!?
WHOA! HEY! STOP SCREWING WITH ME!!
SAVE YOUR PROGRESS?
YES
NO
IF SHE PRESSES THAT...
...I'LL LOSE THE TRACK I'VE BEEN WORKING ON...
NO
SU (ZOOM)
GAAGH!! MY SONG!!!
GATA (CLATTER)
GA (WHAP)

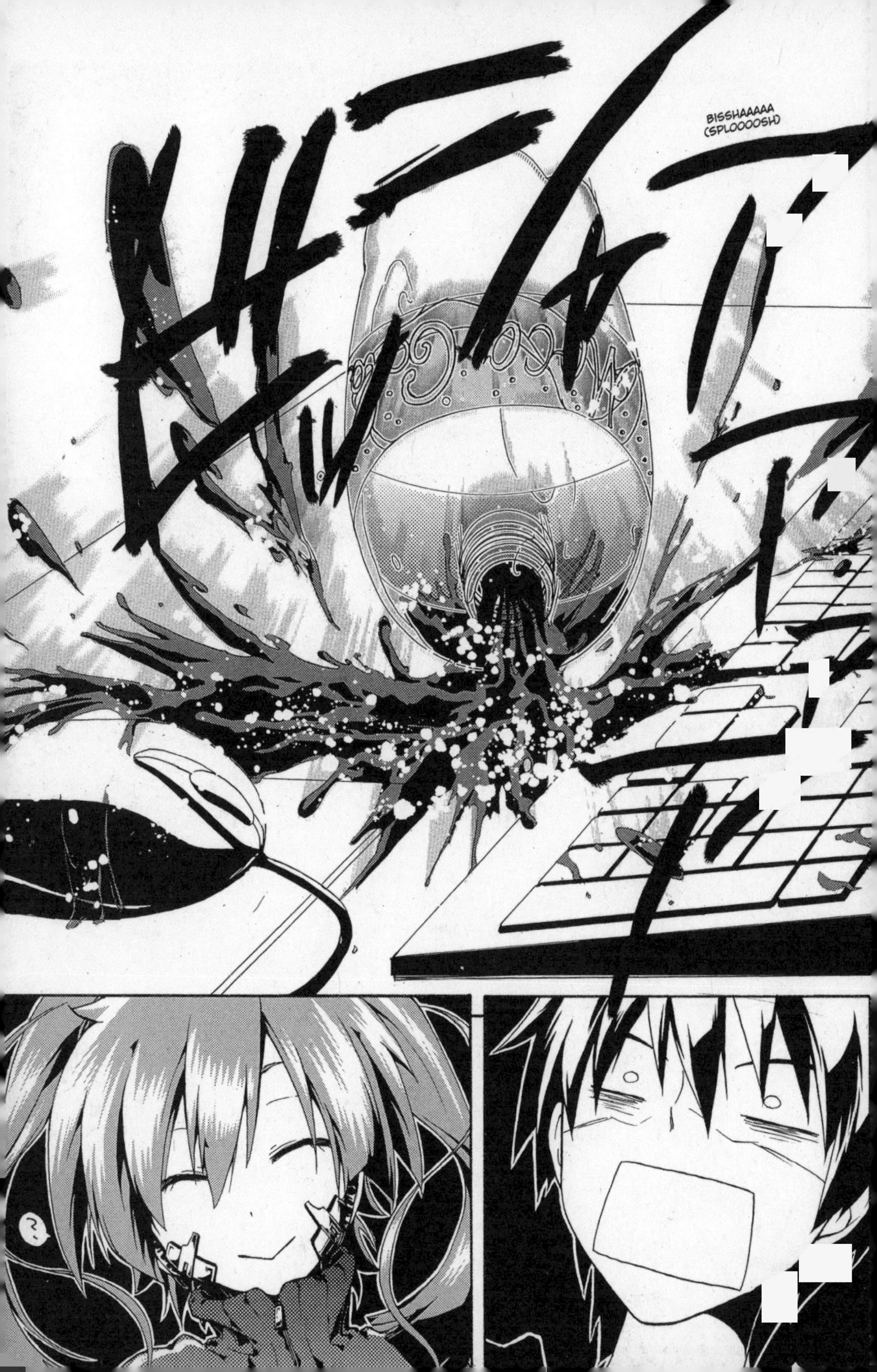
BISSHAAAAA
(SPLOOOOSH)
?

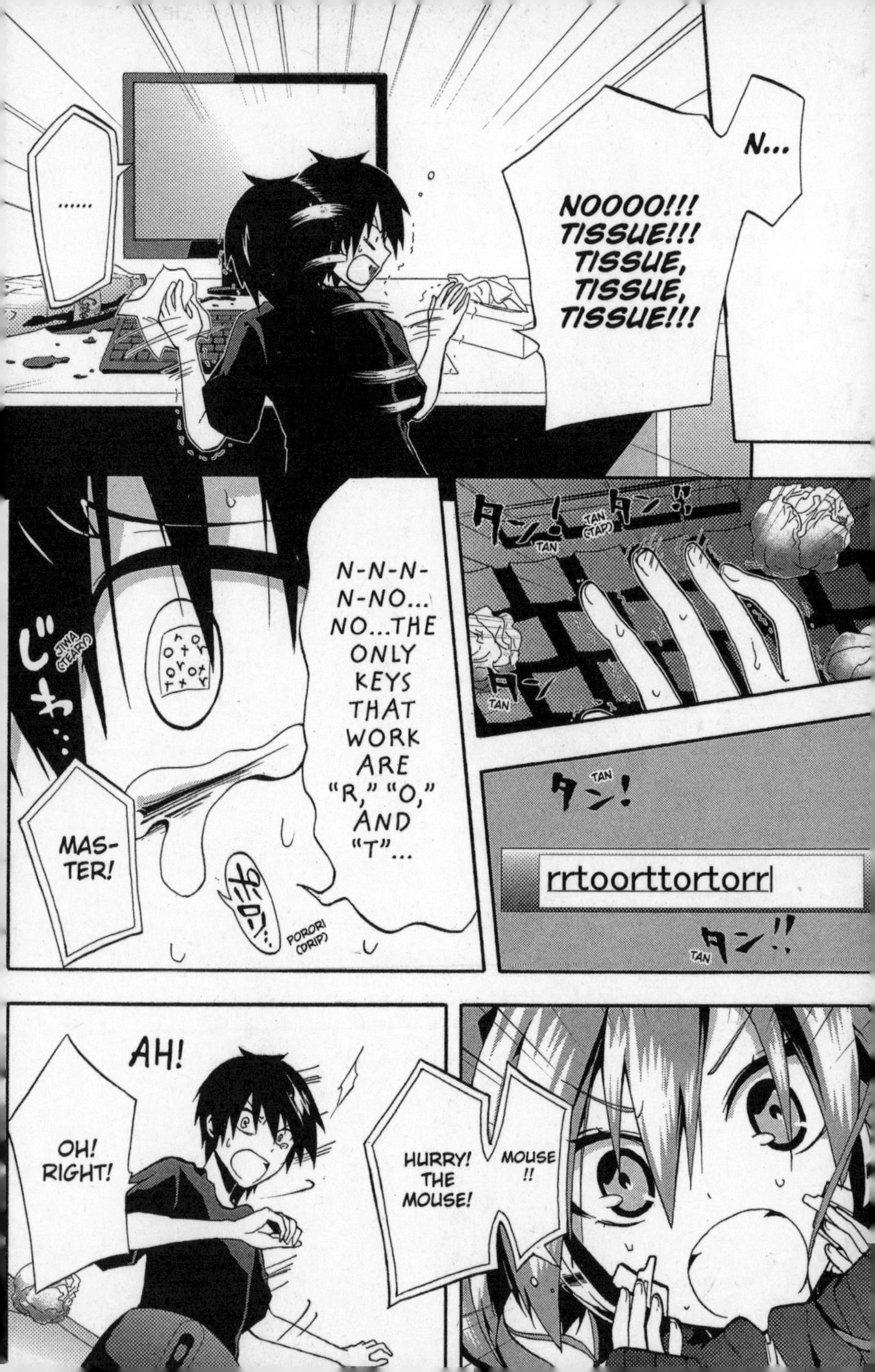

N...
NOOOO!!! TISSUE!!! TISSUE, TISSUE, TISSUE!!!
......
タン! TAN
タン!! TAN (TAP)
TAN
タン! TAN
rrtoorttortorr
タン!! TAN
N-N-N-N-NO... NO...THE ONLY KEYS THAT WORK ARE "R," "O," AND "T"...
JIWA (TEARY)
MAS-TER!
POROR I (DRIP)
MOUSE !!
HURRY! THE MOUSE!
AH!
OH! RIGHT!

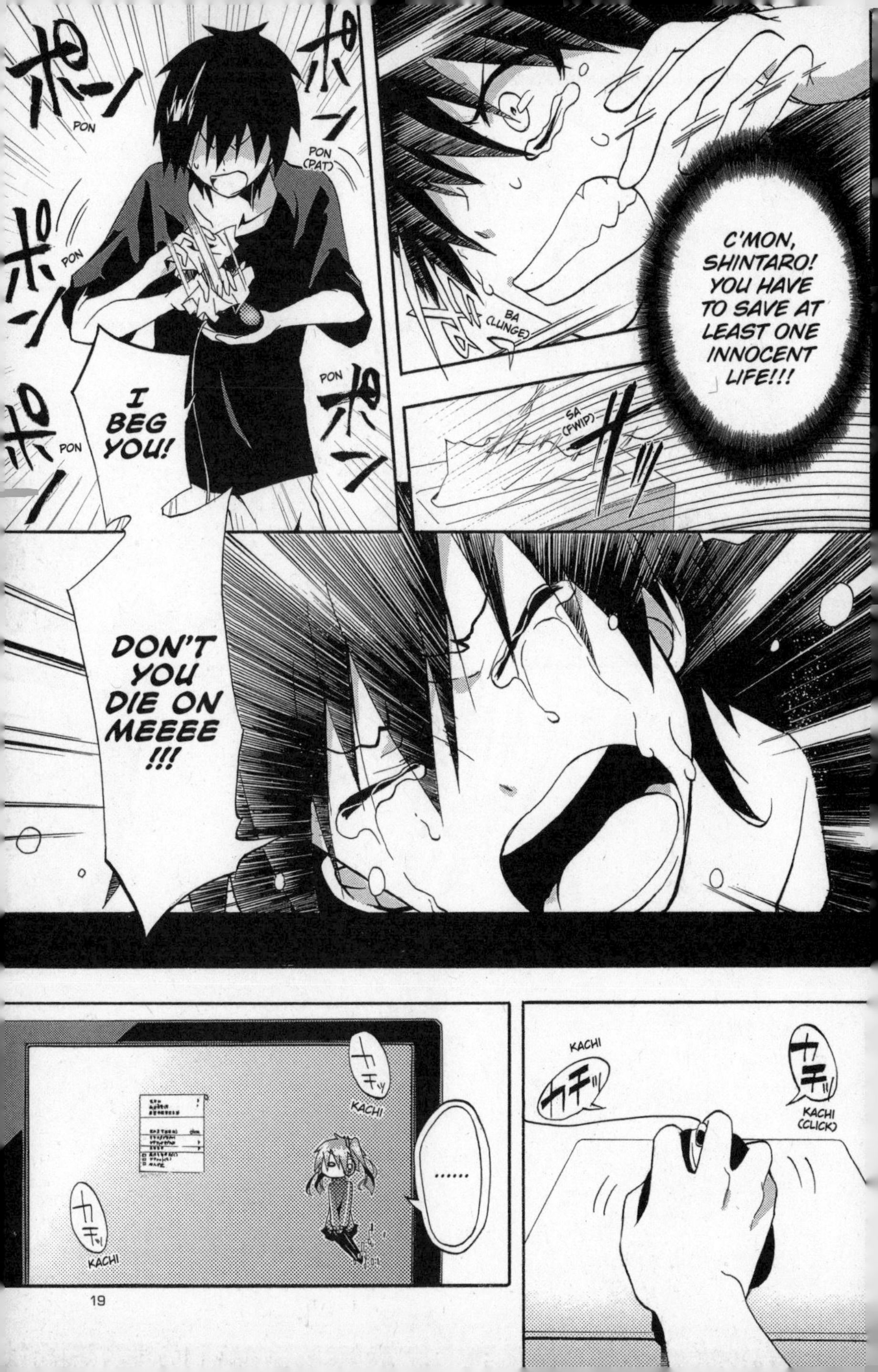
BA (LUNGE)
C'MON, SHINTARO! YOU HAVE TO SAVE AT LEAST ONE INNOCENT LIFE!!!
SA (FWIP)
PON (PAT)
PON
PON
I BEG YOU!
PON
PON
DON'T YOU DIE ON MEEEE!!!
KACHI
KACHI (CLICK)
KACHI
......
KACHI

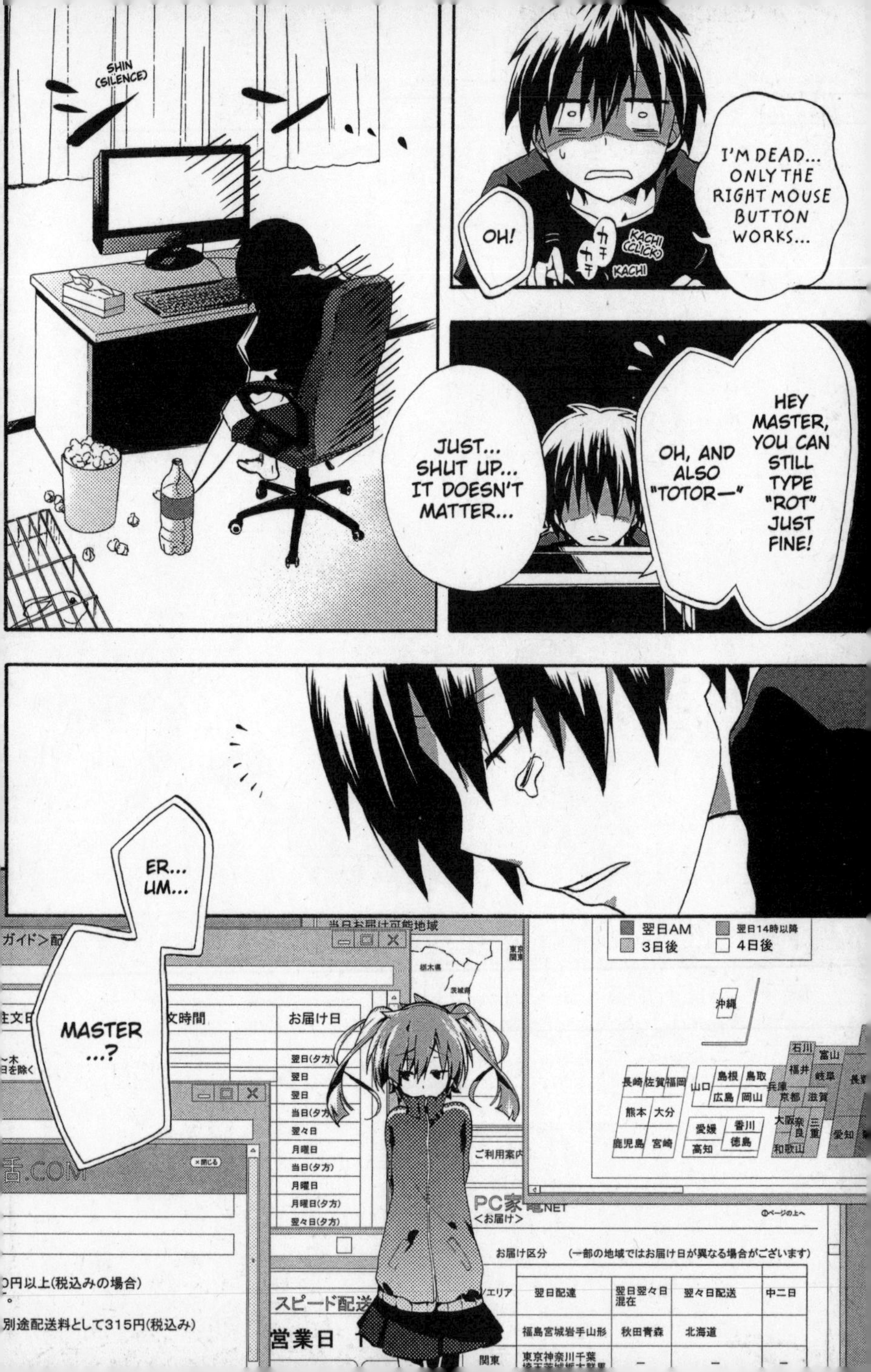
I'M DEAD... ONLY THE RIGHT MOUSE BUTTON WORKS...
KACHI (CLICK) KACHI
OH!
HEY MASTER, YOU CAN STILL TYPE "ROT" JUST FINE!
OH, AND ALSO "TOTOR—"
JUST... SHUT UP... IT DOESN'T MATTER...
SHIN (SILENCE)
ER... UM...
MASTER ...?

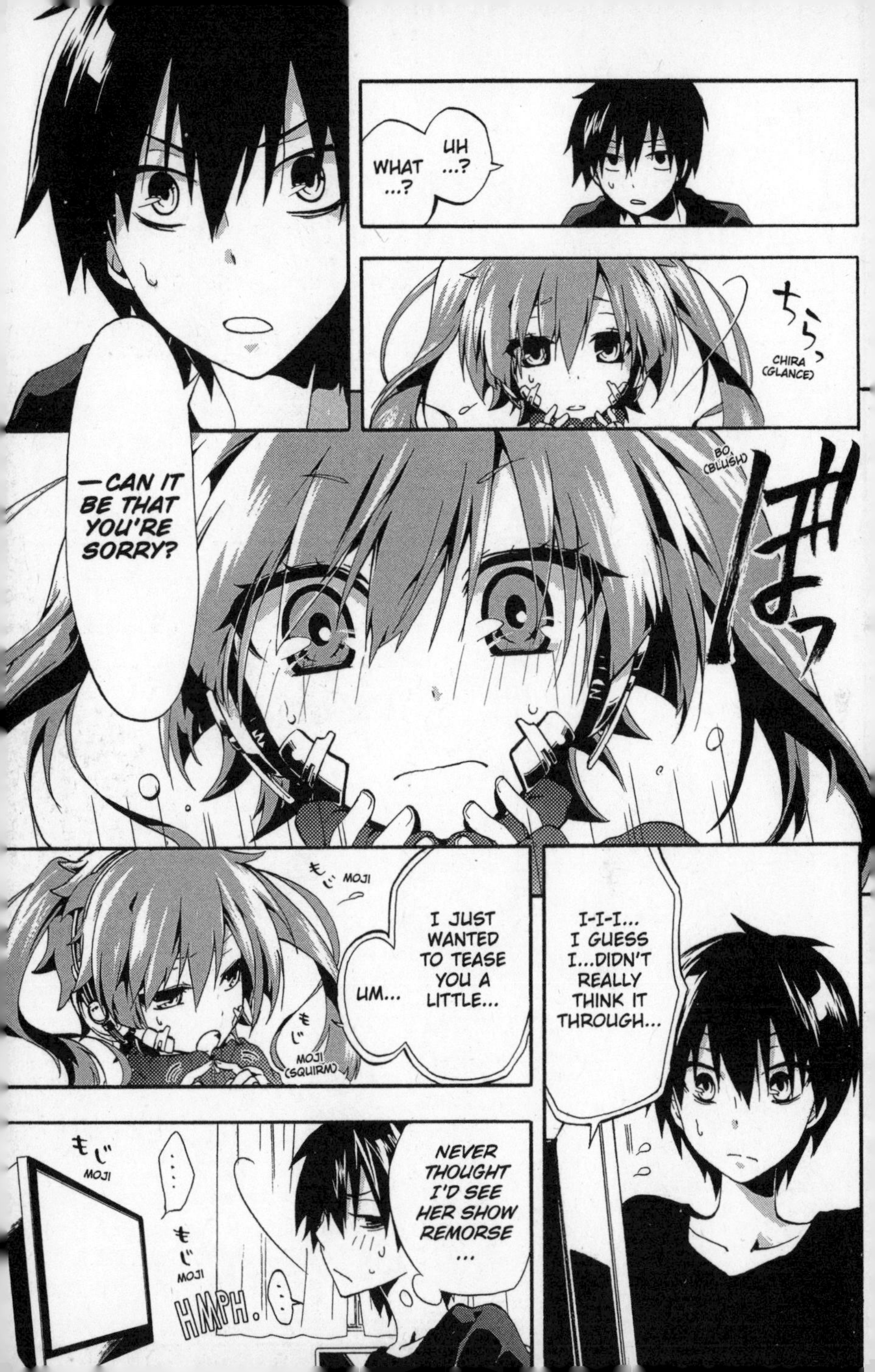
UH ...?
WHAT ...?
ちらっ
CHIRA (GLANCE)
—CAN IT BE THAT YOU'RE SORRY?
ぼっ
BO (BLUSH)
I-I-I... I GUESS I...DIDN'T REALLY THINK IT THROUGH...
もじ
MOJI
I JUST WANTED TO TEASE YOU A LITTLE...
UM...
もじ
MOJI (SQUIRM)
NEVER THOUGHT I'D SEE HER SHOW REMORSE ...
....
...
もじ
MOJI
もじ
MOJI
HMPH.

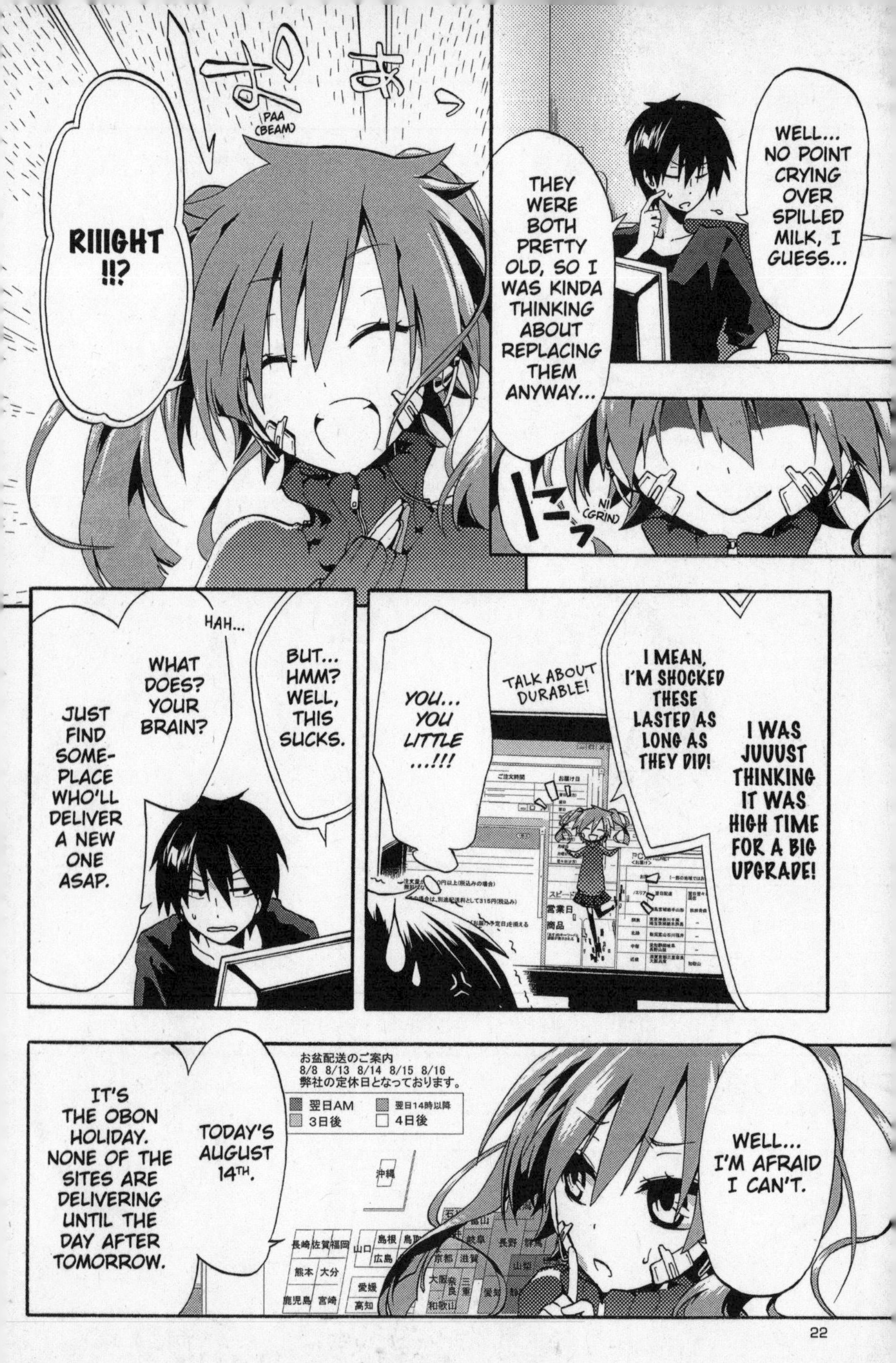
WELL... NO POINT CRYING OVER SPILLED MILK, I GUESS...
THEY WERE BOTH PRETTY OLD, SO I WAS KINDA THINKING ABOUT REPLACING THEM ANYWAY...
NI (GRIN)
PAA (BEAM)
RIIIGHT !!?
I WAS JUUUST THINKING IT WAS HIGH TIME FOR A BIG UPGRADE!
I MEAN, I'M SHOCKED THESE LASTED AS LONG AS THEY DID!
TALK ABOUT DURABLE!
YOU... YOU LITTLE ...!!!
BUT... HMM? WELL, THIS SUCKS.
HAH...
WHAT DOES? YOUR BRAIN?
JUST FIND SOME-PLACE WHO'LL DELIVER A NEW ONE ASAP.
WELL... I'M AFRAID I CAN'T.
お盆配送のご案内
8/8 8/13 8/14 8/15 8/16
弊社の定休日となっております。
翌日AM
翌日14時以降
3日後
4日後
TODAY'S AUGUST 14TH.
IT'S THE OBON HOLIDAY. NONE OF THE SITES ARE DELIVERING UNTIL THE DAY AFTER TOMORROW.

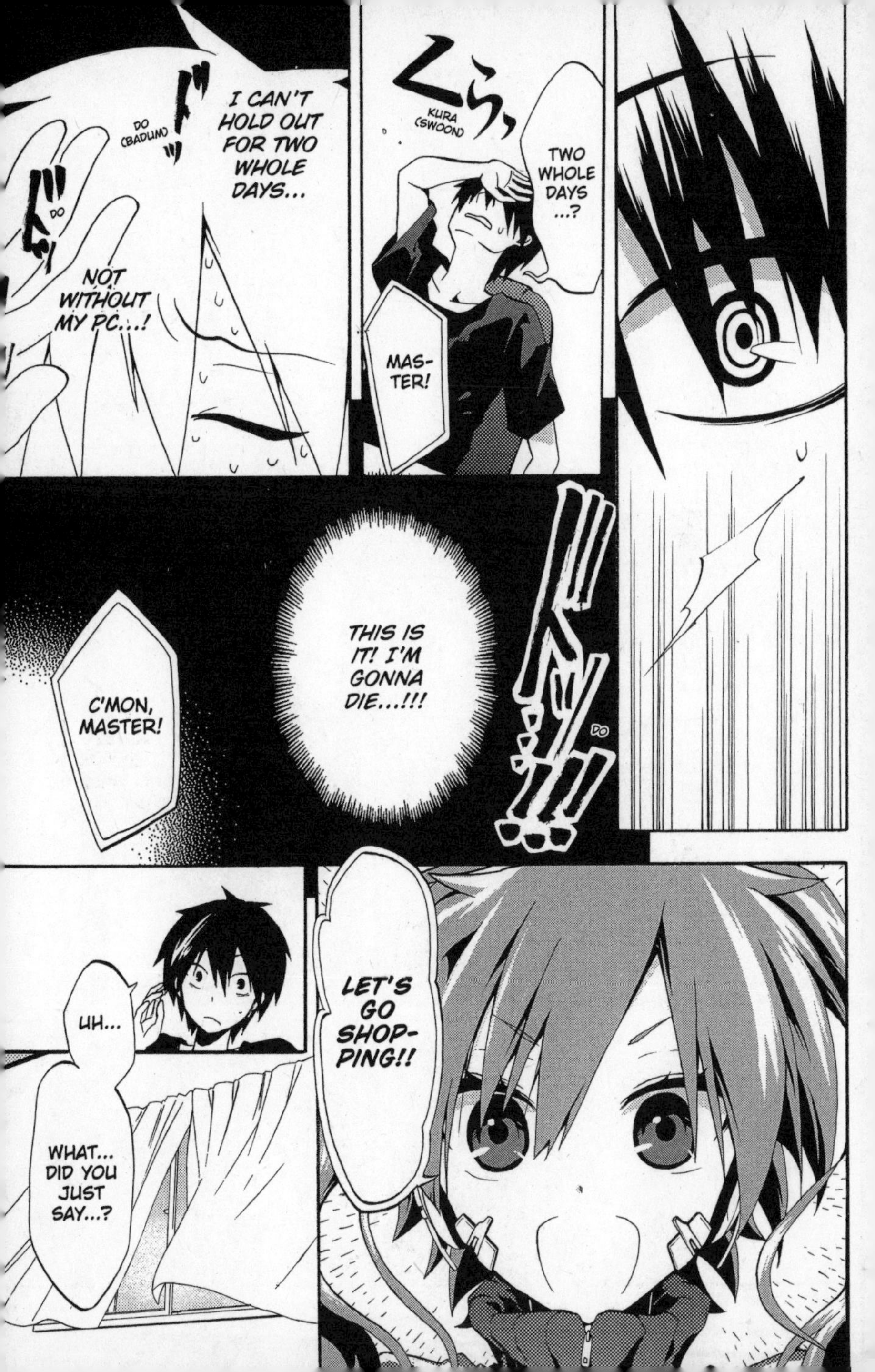
くらっ
KURA (SWOON)
TWO WHOLE DAYS ...?
MASTER!
DO (BADUM)
I CAN'T HOLD OUT FOR TWO WHOLE DAYS...
DO
NOT WITHOUT MY PC...!
DO
THIS IS IT! I'M GONNA DIE...!!!
C'MON, MASTER!
LET'S GO SHOPPING!!
UH...
WHAT... DID YOU JUST SAY...?

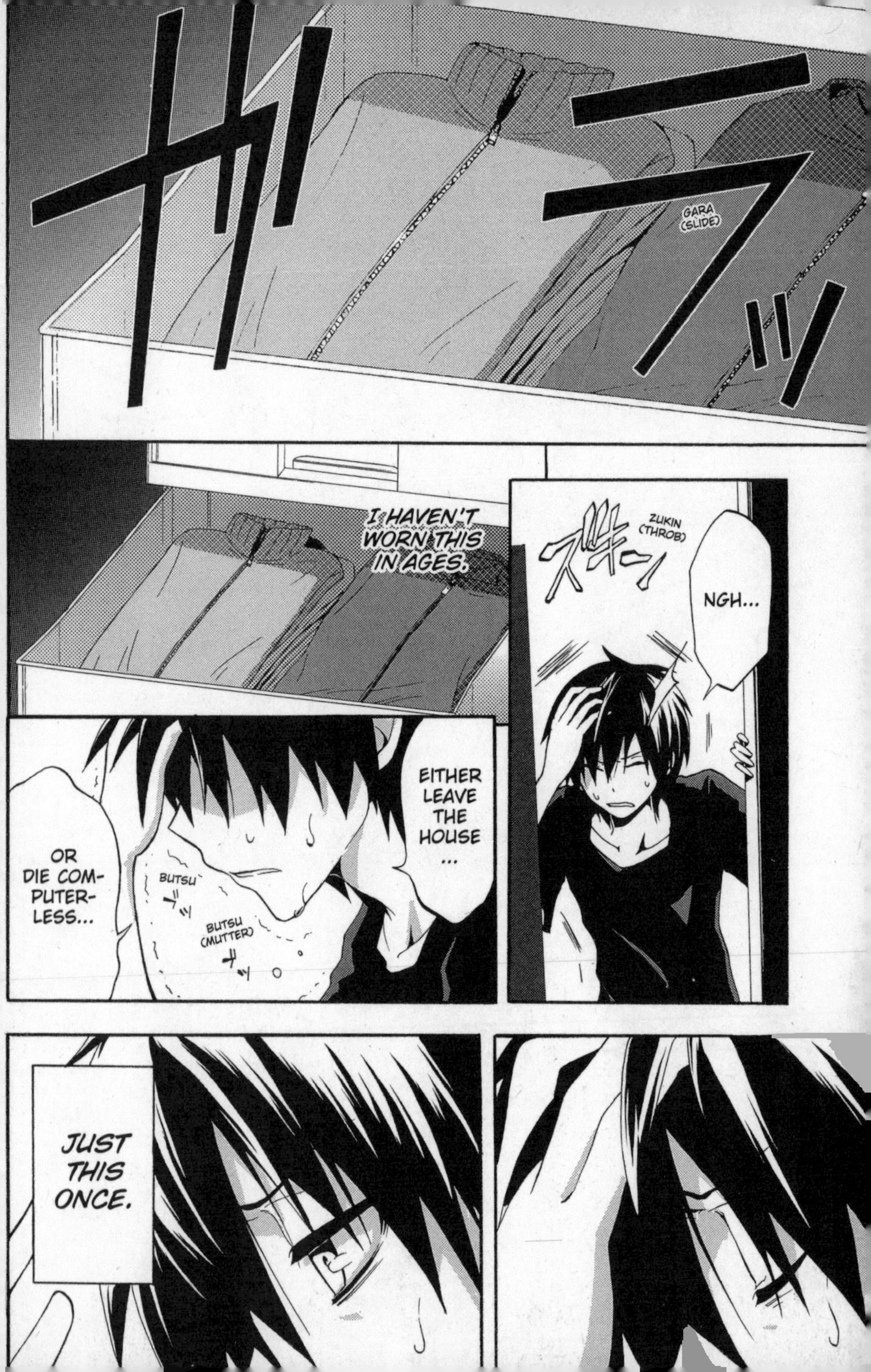
GARA (SLIDE)
ZUKIN (THROB)
NGH...
I HAVEN'T WORN THIS IN AGES.
EITHER LEAVE THE HOUSE ...
OR DIE COM-PUTER-LESS...
BUTSU
BUTSU (MUTTER)
JUST THIS ONCE.

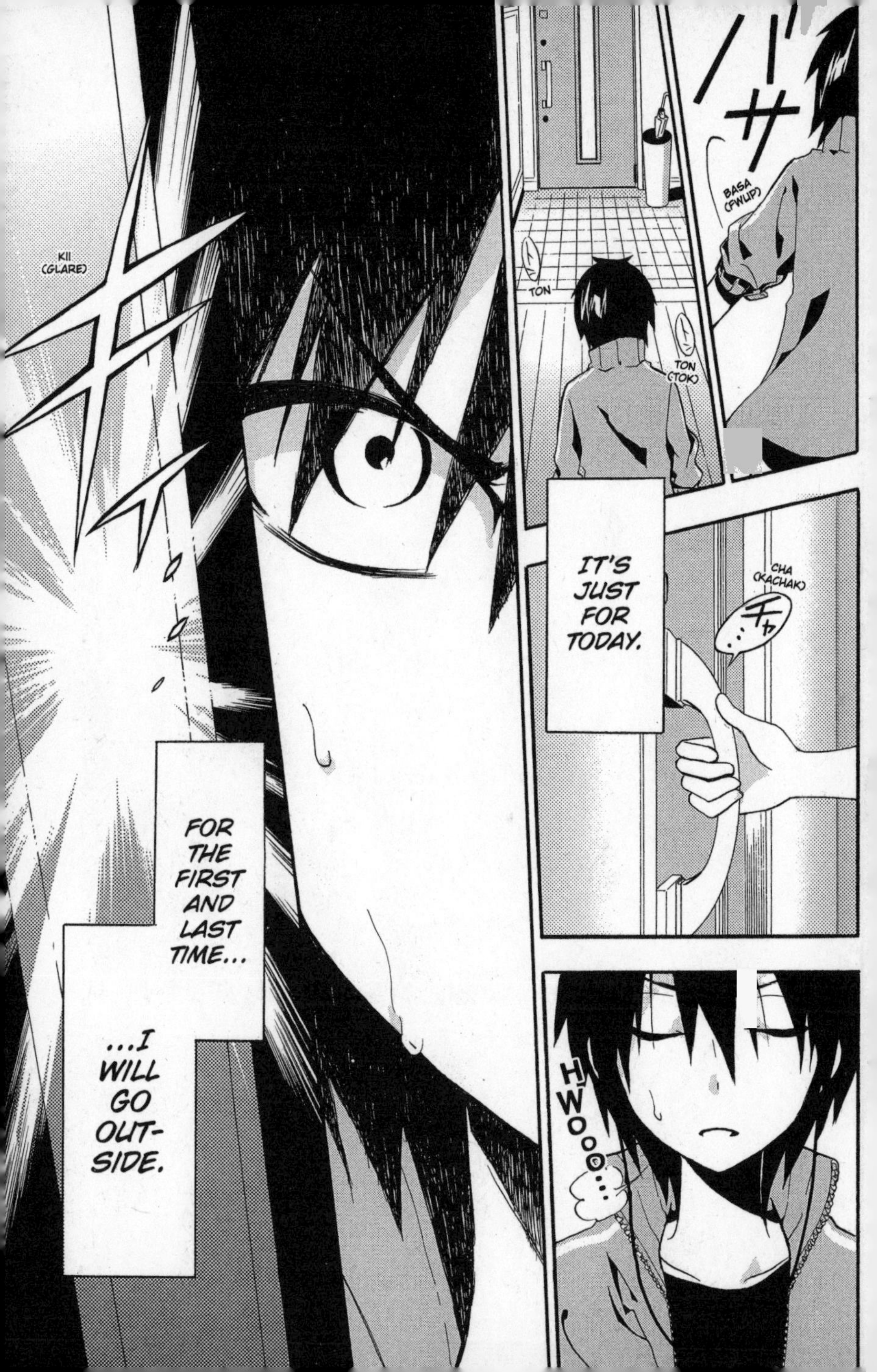
BASA (FWUP)
TON
TON (TOK)
IT'S JUST FOR TODAY.
CHA (KACHAK)
HWOOO...
KII (GLARE)
FOR THE FIRST AND LAST TIME...
...I WILL GO OUTSIDE.

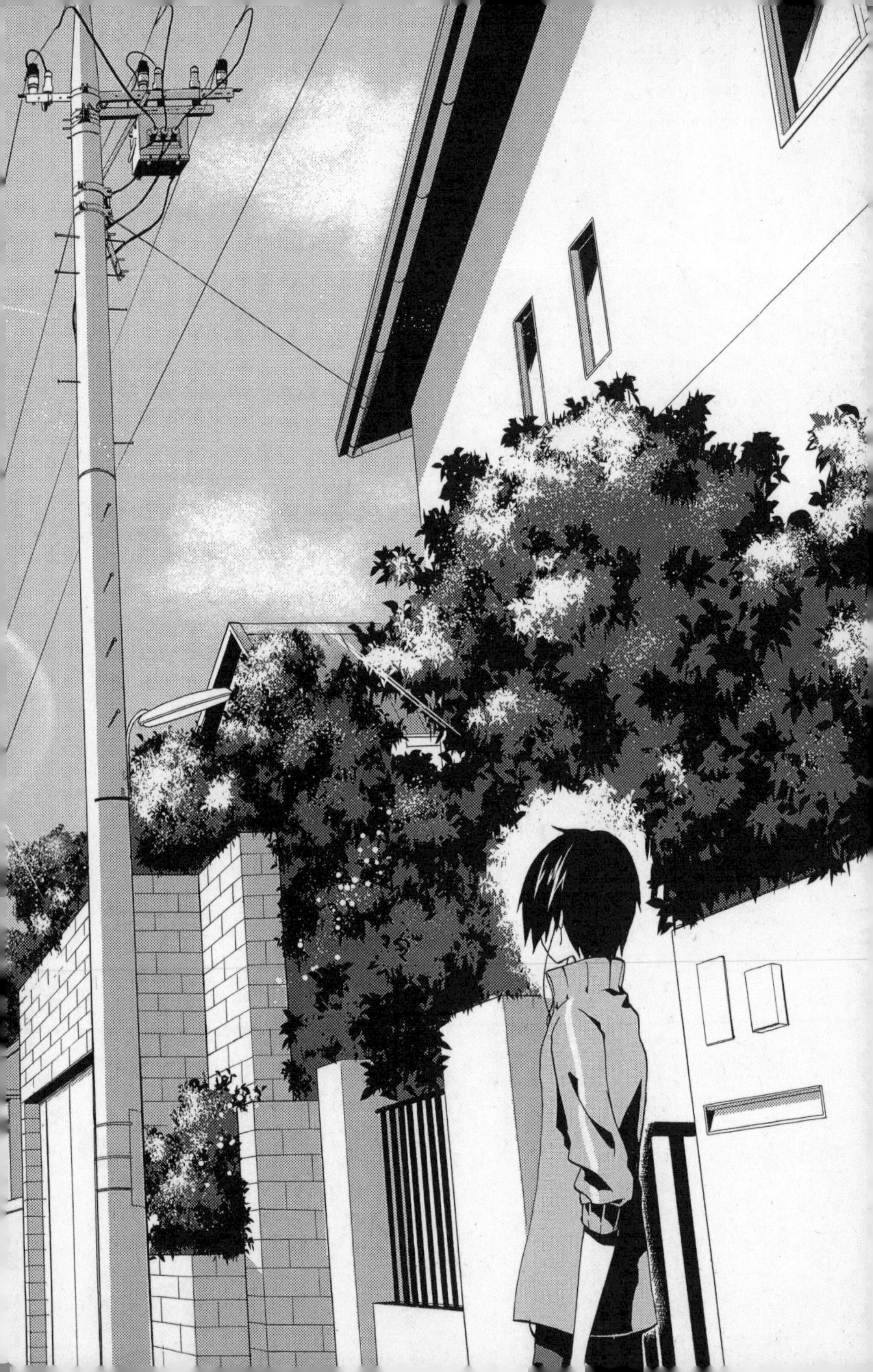

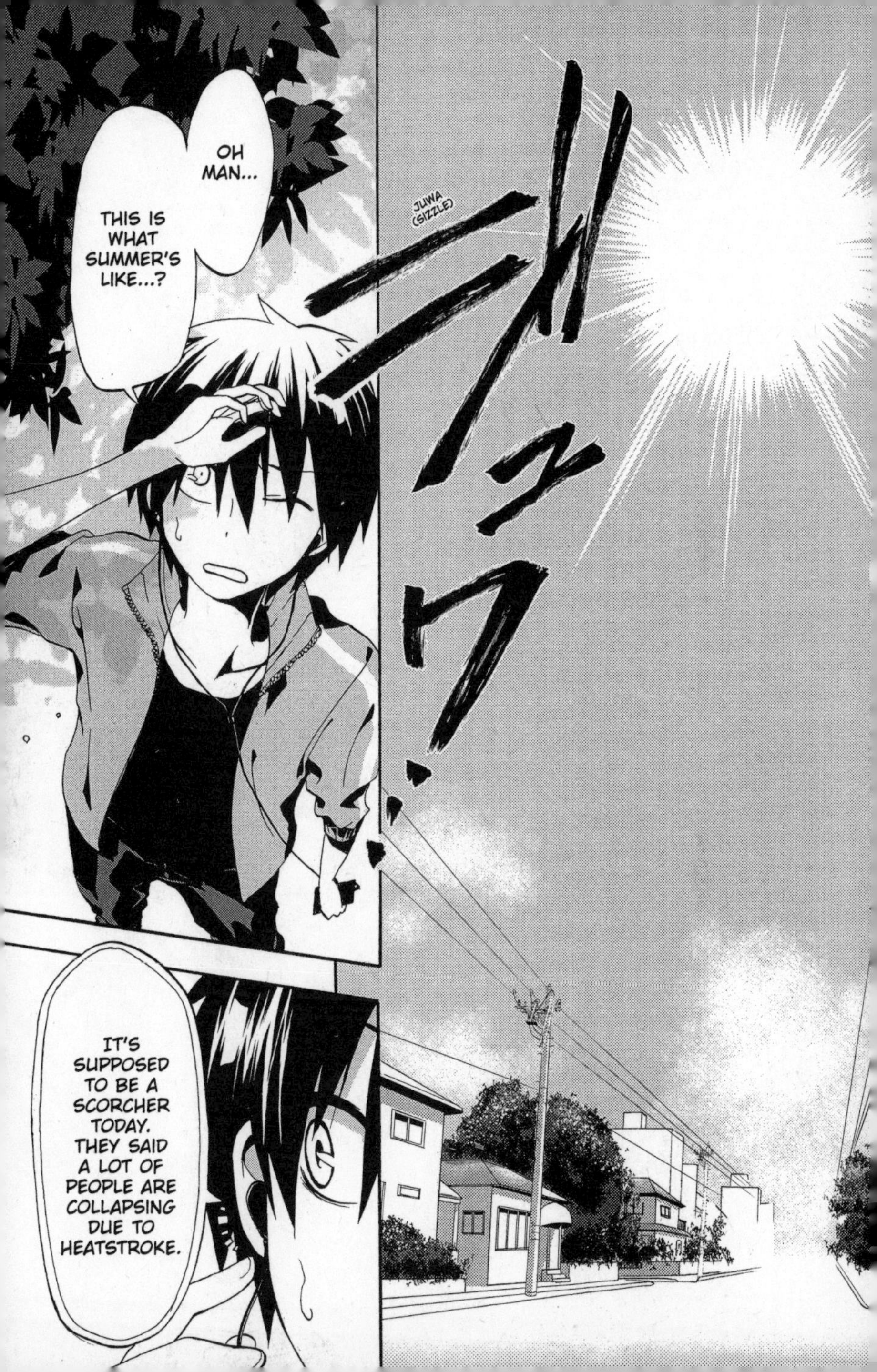
JUWA (SIZZLE)
OH MAN...
THIS IS WHAT SUMMER'S LIKE...?
IT'S SUPPOSED TO BE A SCORCHER TODAY. THEY SAID A LOT OF PEOPLE ARE COLLAPSING DUE TO HEATSTROKE.

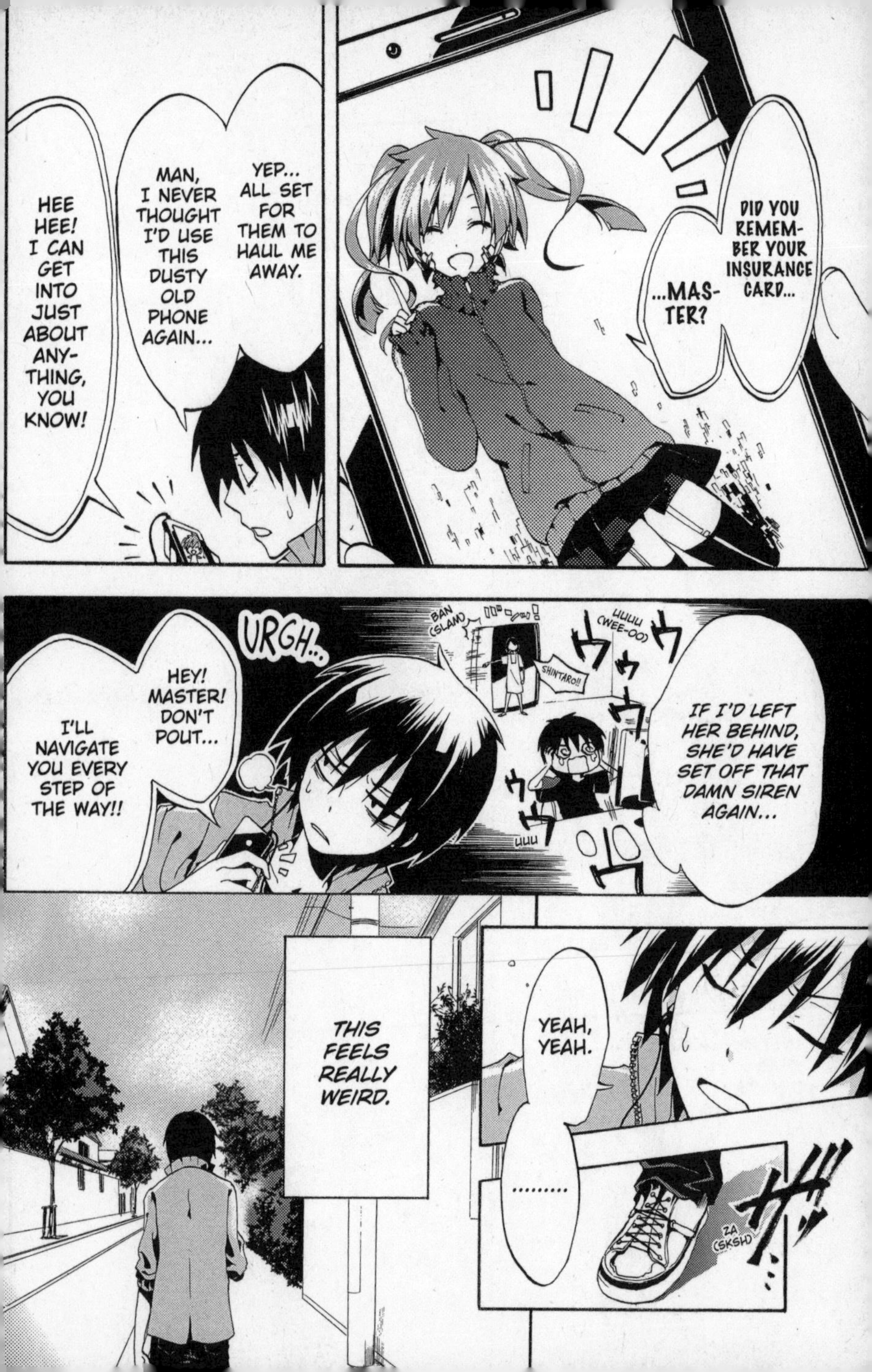
DID YOU REMEMBER YOUR INSURANCE CARD...
...MASTER?
YEP... ALL SET FOR THEM TO HAUL ME AWAY.
MAN, I NEVER THOUGHT I'D USE THIS DUSTY OLD PHONE AGAIN...
HEE HEE! I CAN GET INTO JUST ABOUT ANYTHING, YOU KNOW!
IF I'D LEFT HER BEHIND, SHE'D HAVE SET OFF THAT DAMN SIREN AGAIN...
UUUU (WEE-OO)
BAN (SLAM)
SHINTARO!!
UUU
URGH...
HEY! MASTER! DON'T POUT...
I'LL NAVIGATE YOU EVERY STEP OF THE WAY!!
YEAH, YEAH.
....
ZA (SKSH)
THIS FEELS REALLY WEIRD.

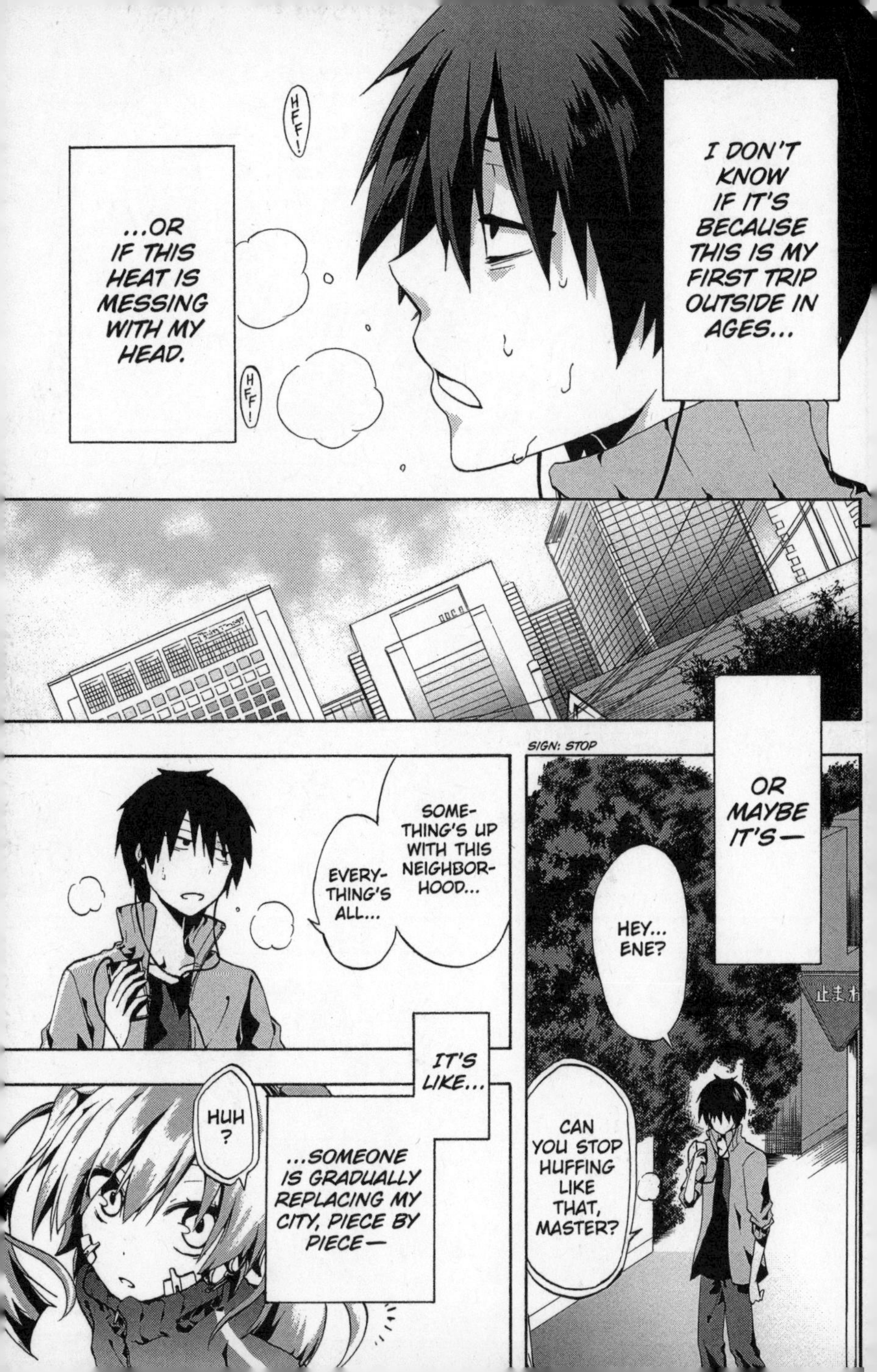
I DON'T KNOW IF IT'S BECAUSE THIS IS MY FIRST TRIP OUTSIDE IN AGES...
HFF!
...OR IF THIS HEAT IS MESSING WITH MY HEAD.
HFF!
OR MAYBE IT'S—
SIGN: STOP
HEY... ENE?
CAN YOU STOP HUFFING LIKE THAT, MASTER?
SOME-THING'S UP WITH THIS NEIGHBOR-HOOD...
EVERY-THING'S ALL...
IT'S LIKE...
HUH?
...SOMEONE IS GRADUALLY REPLACING MY CITY, PIECE BY PIECE—

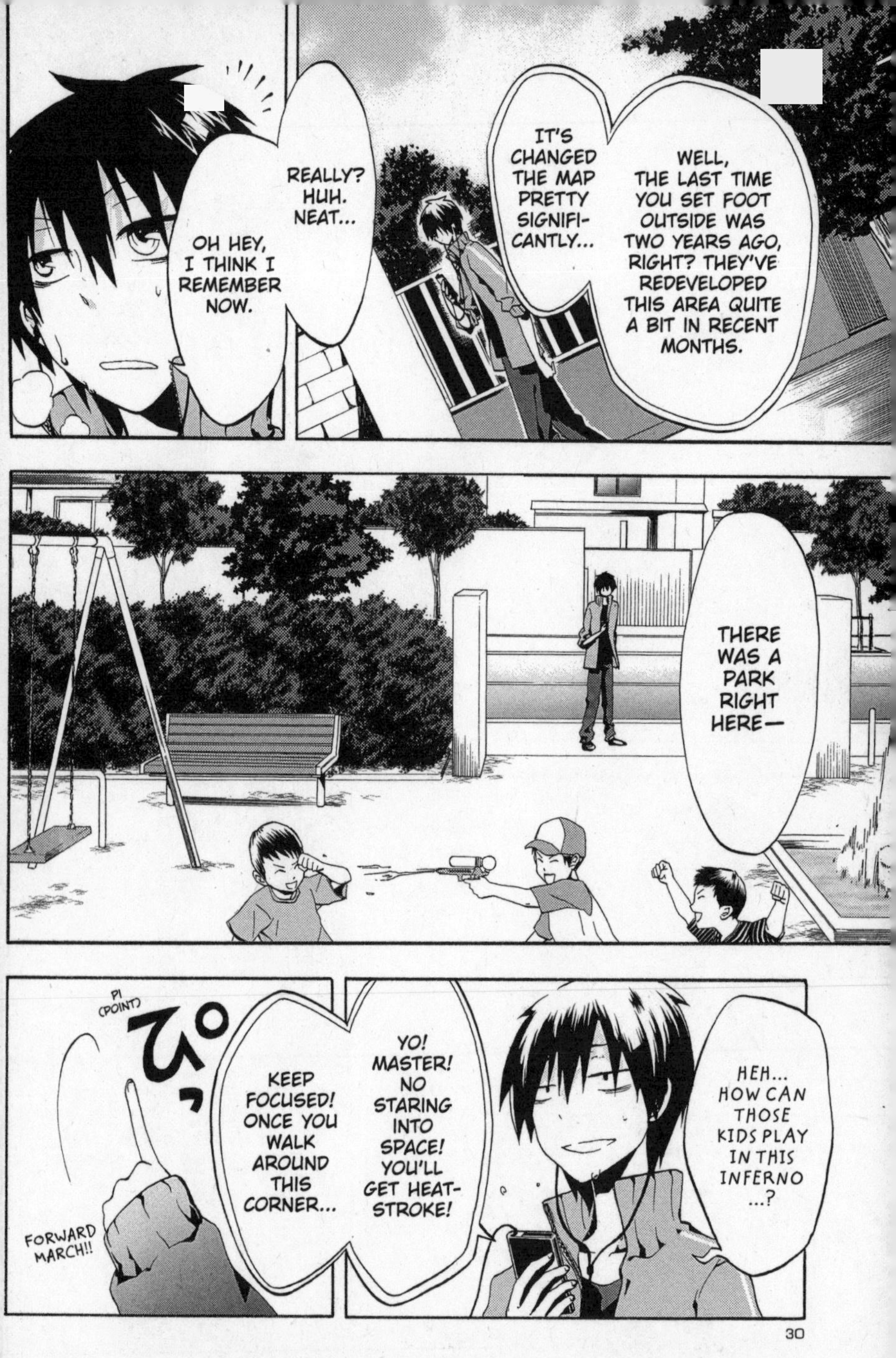
WELL, THE LAST TIME YOU SET FOOT OUTSIDE WAS TWO YEARS AGO, RIGHT? THEY'VE REDEVELOPED THIS AREA QUITE A BIT IN RECENT MONTHS.
IT'S CHANGED THE MAP PRETTY SIGNIFI-CANTLY...
REALLY? HUH. NEAT...
OH HEY, I THINK I REMEMBER NOW.
THERE WAS A PARK RIGHT HERE—
HEH... HOW CAN THOSE KIDS PLAY IN THIS INFERNO ...?
YO! MASTER! NO STARING INTO SPACE! YOU'LL GET HEAT-STROKE!
KEEP FOCUSED! ONCE YOU WALK AROUND THIS CORNER...
PI (POINT)
ぴっ
FORWARD MARCH!!

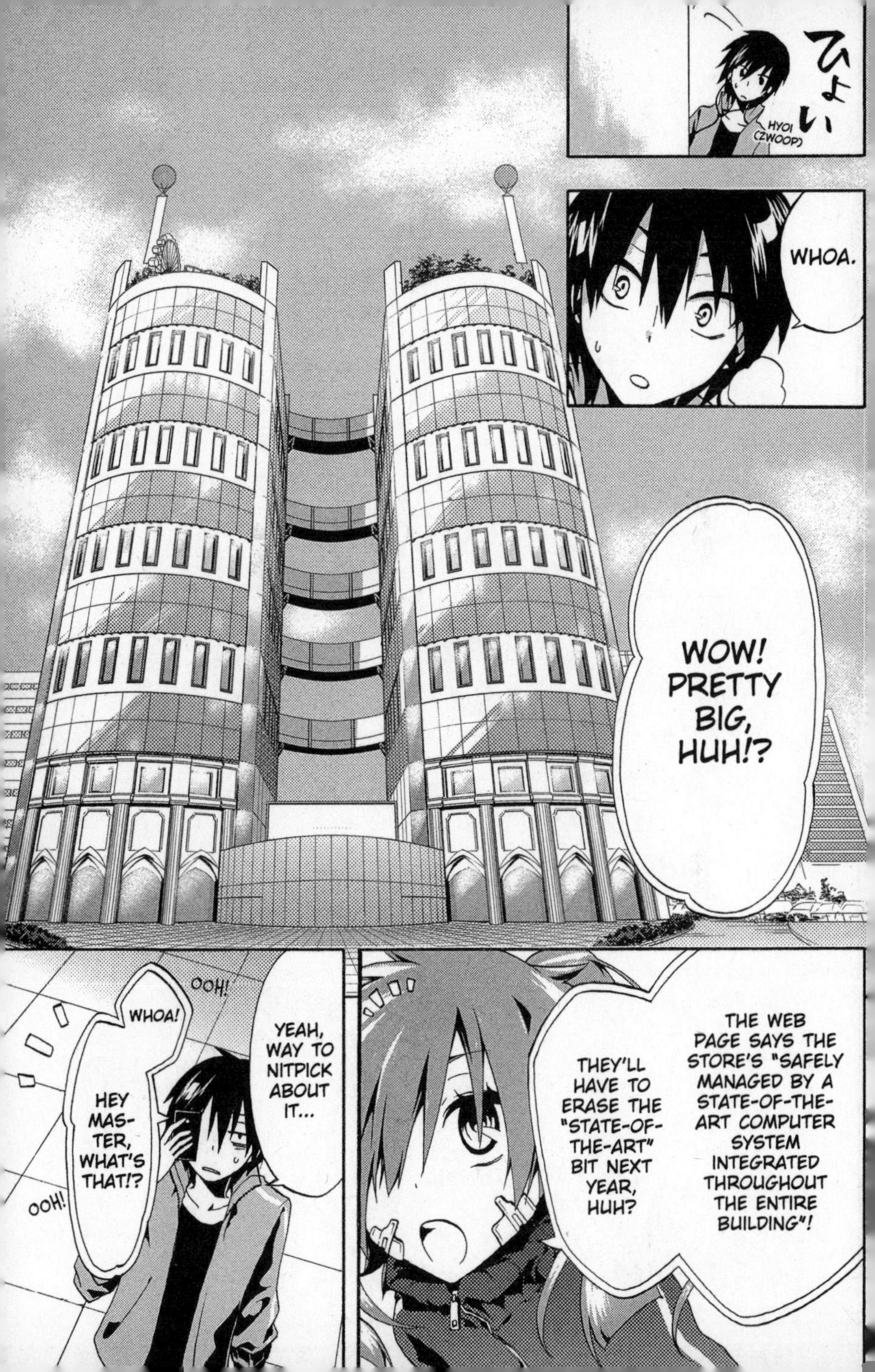
ひょい
HYOI (ZWOOP)
WHOA.
WOW! PRETTY BIG, HUH!?
THE WEB PAGE SAYS THE STORE'S "SAFELY MANAGED BY A STATE-OF-THE-ART COMPUTER SYSTEM INTEGRATED THROUGHOUT THE ENTIRE BUILDING"!
THEY'LL HAVE TO ERASE THE "STATE-OF-THE-ART" BIT NEXT YEAR, HUH?
YEAH, WAY TO NITPICK ABOUT IT...
OOH!
WHOA!
HEY MAS-TER, WHAT'S THAT!?
OOH!

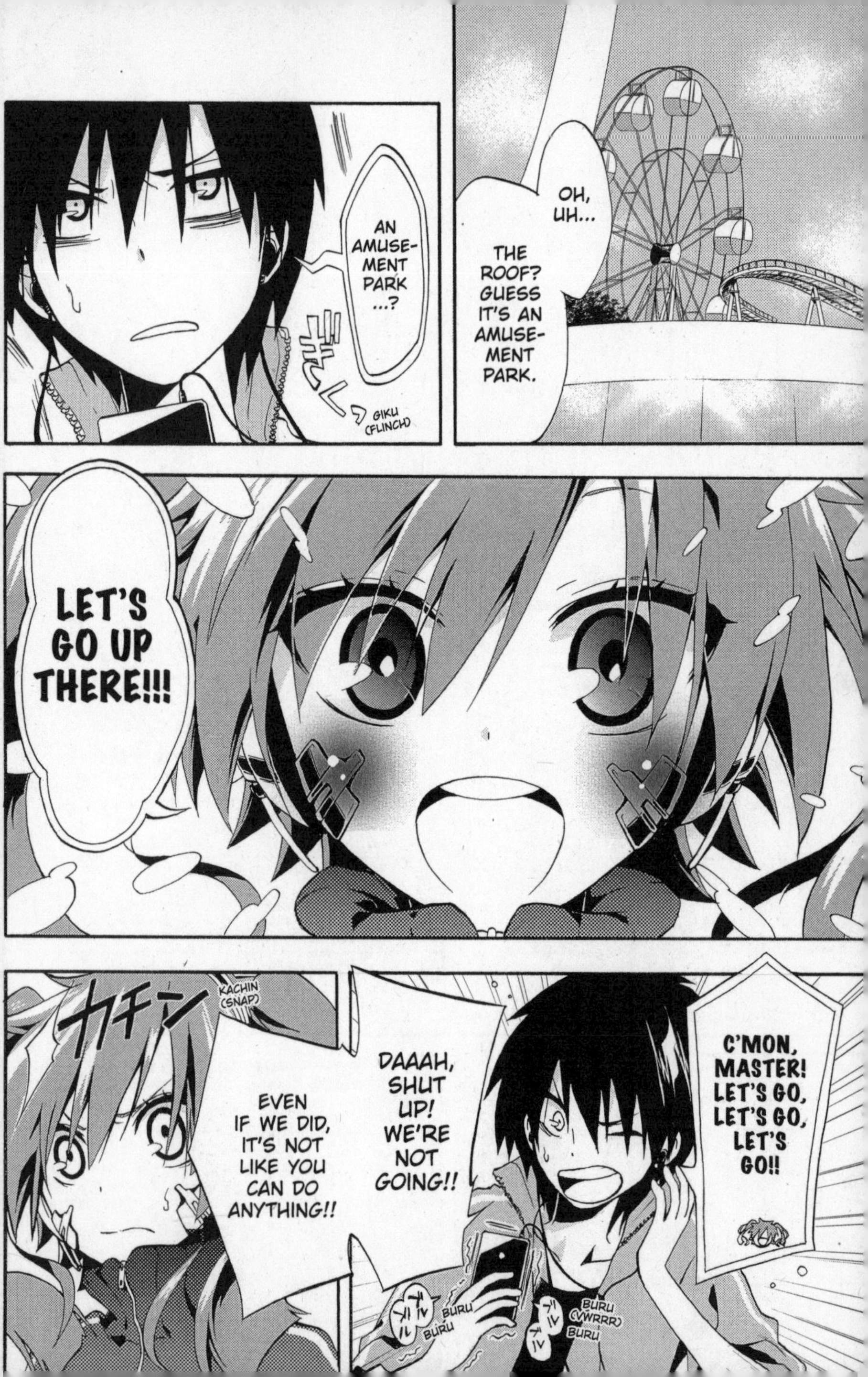
OH, UH...
THE ROOF? GUESS IT'S AN AMUSEMENT PARK.
AN AMUSEMENT PARK ...?
GIKU (FLINCH)
LET'S GO UP THERE!!!
C'MON, MASTER! LET'S GO, LET'S GO, LET'S GO!!
DAAAH, SHUT UP! WE'RE NOT GOING!!
KACHIN (SNAP)
EVEN IF WE DID, IT'S NOT LIKE YOU CAN DO ANYTHING!!
BURU (VWRRR) BURU
BURU BURU

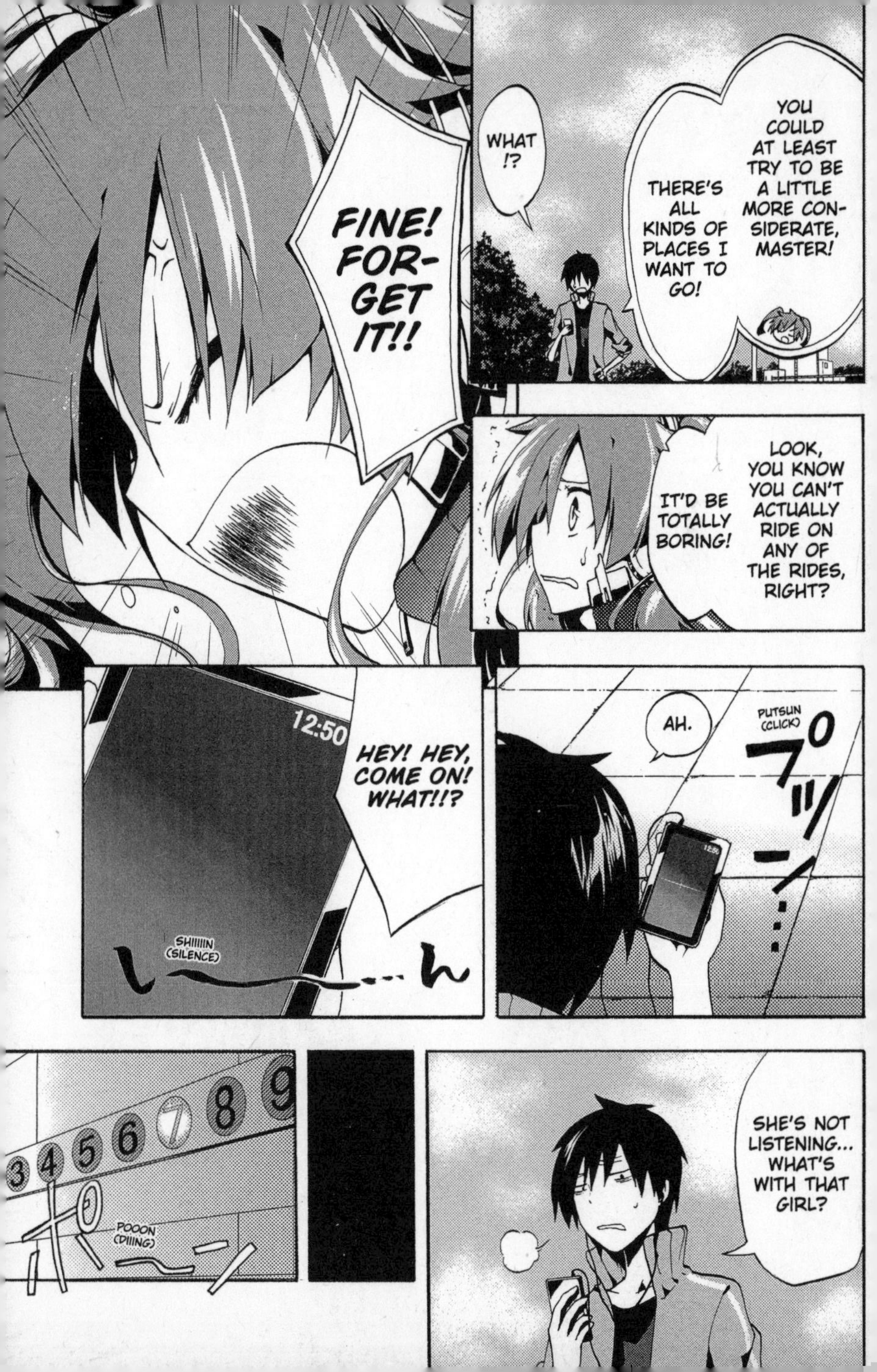

YOU COULD AT LEAST TRY TO BE A LITTLE MORE CON-SIDERATE, MASTER!
THERE'S ALL KINDS OF PLACES I WANT TO GO!
WHAT!?
LOOK, YOU KNOW YOU CAN'T ACTUALLY RIDE ON ANY OF THE RIDES, RIGHT?
IT'D BE TOTALLY BORING!
FINE! FOR-GET IT!!
AH.
PUTSUN (CLICK)
12:50
HEY! HEY, COME ON! WHAT!!?
SHIIIIN (SILENCE)
SHE'S NOT LISTENING... WHAT'S WITH THAT GIRL?
3 4 5 6 7 8 9
POOON (DIIING)

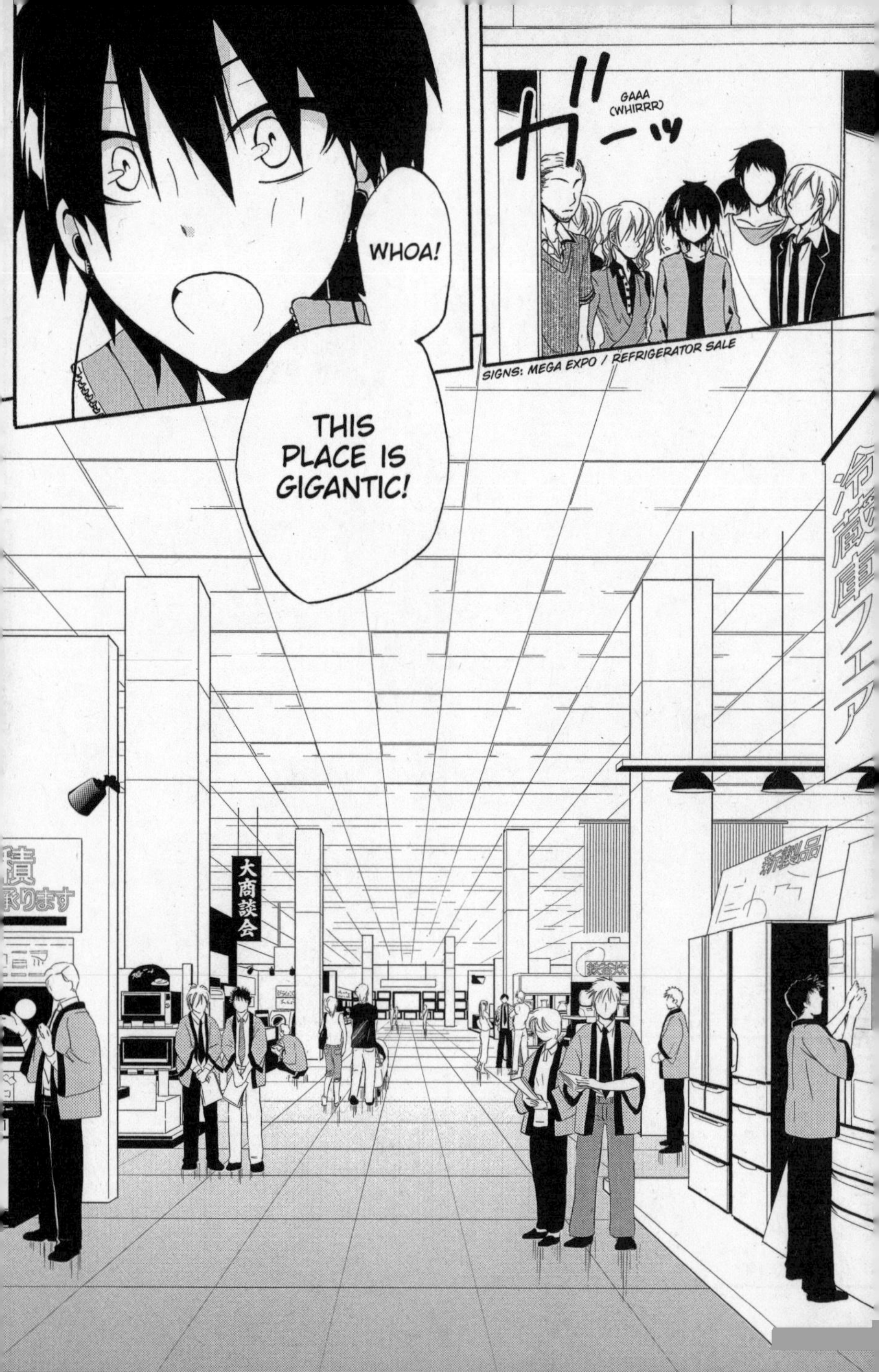

ガーッ
GAAA (WHIRRR)
WHOA!
THIS PLACE IS GIGANTIC!
SIGNS: MEGA EXPO / REFRIGERATOR SALE
冷蔵庫フェア
新製品
大商談会

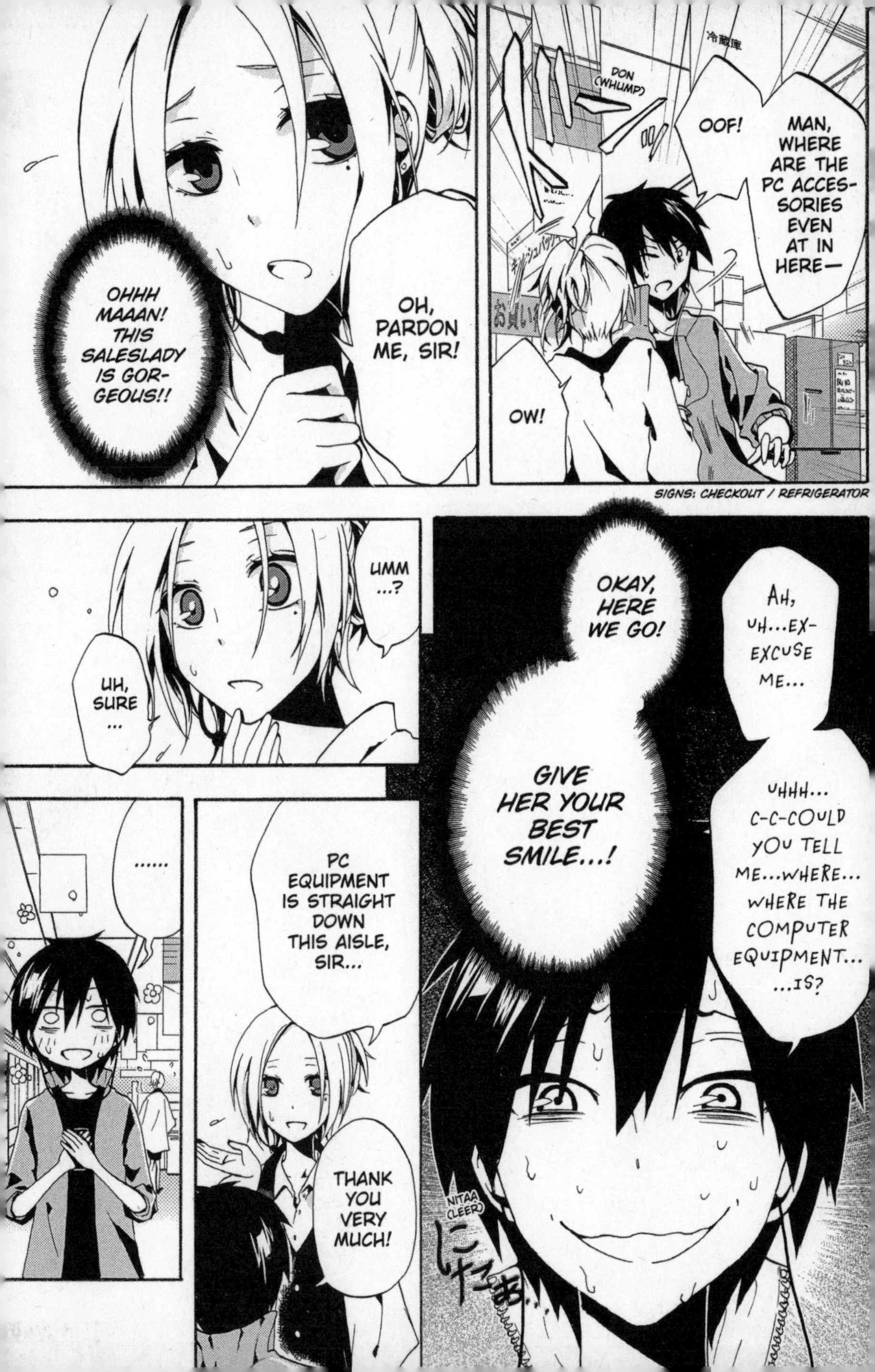
冷蔵庫
DON (WHUMP)
MAN, WHERE ARE THE PC ACCES-SORIES EVEN AT IN HERE—
OOF!
OW!
OH, PARDON ME, SIR!
OHHH MAAAN! THIS SALESLADY IS GOR-GEOUS!!
SIGNS: CHECKOUT / REFRIGERATOR
AH, UH...EX-EXCUSE ME...
OKAY, HERE WE GO!
UHHH... C-C-COULD YOU TELL ME...WHERE... WHERE THE COMPUTER EQUIPMENT... ...IS?
GIVE HER YOUR BEST SMILE...!
NITAA (LEER)
UMM ...?
UH, SURE ...
PC EQUIPMENT IS STRAIGHT DOWN THIS AISLE, SIR...
THANK YOU VERY MUCH!
......

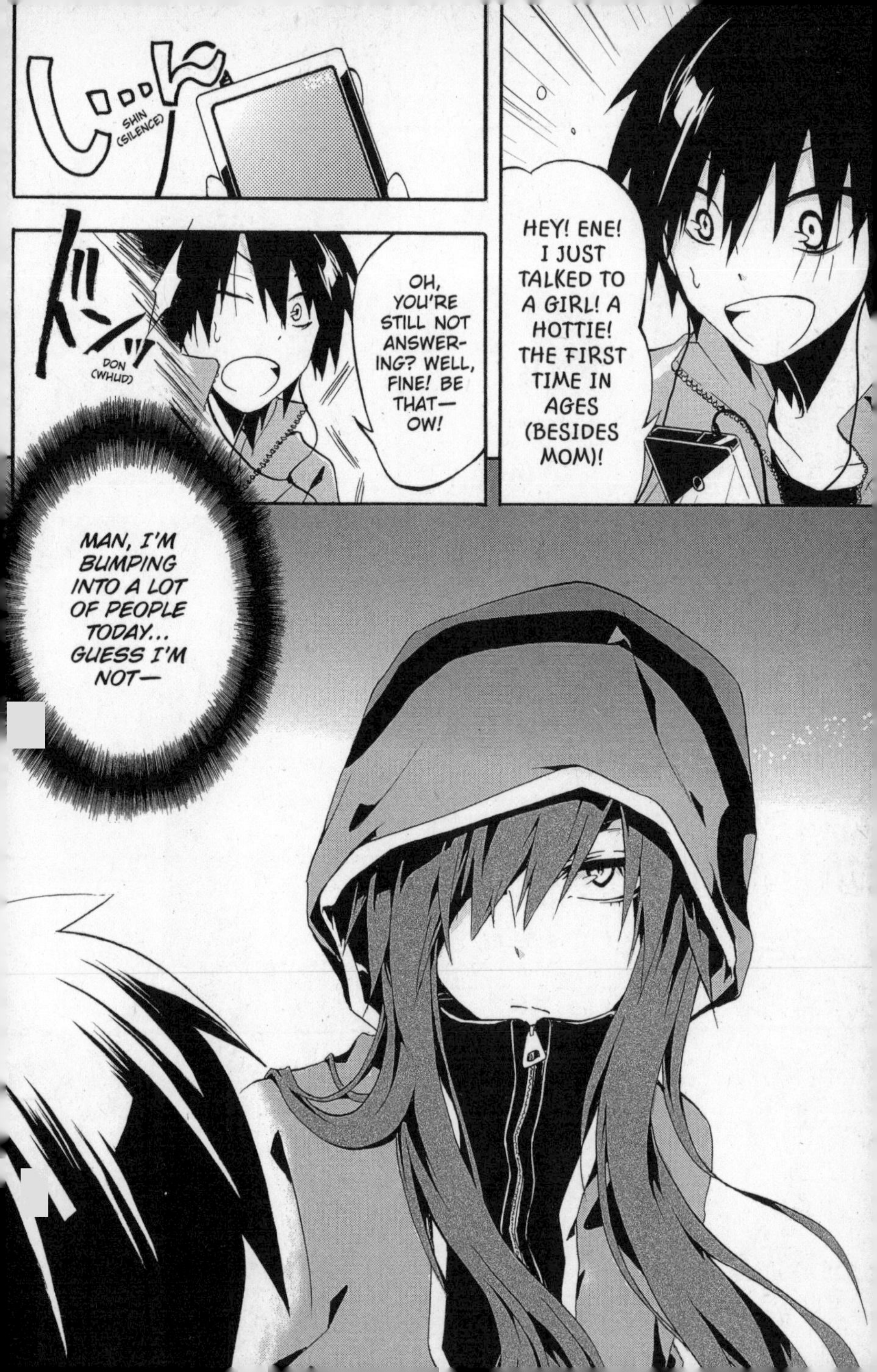
HEY! ENE! I JUST TALKED TO A GIRL! A HOTTIE! THE FIRST TIME IN AGES (BESIDES MOM)!
SHIN (SILENCE)
OH, YOU'RE STILL NOT ANSWER-ING? WELL, FINE! BE THAT— OW!
DON (WHUD)
MAN, I'M BUMPING INTO A LOT OF PEOPLE TODAY... GUESS I'M NOT—

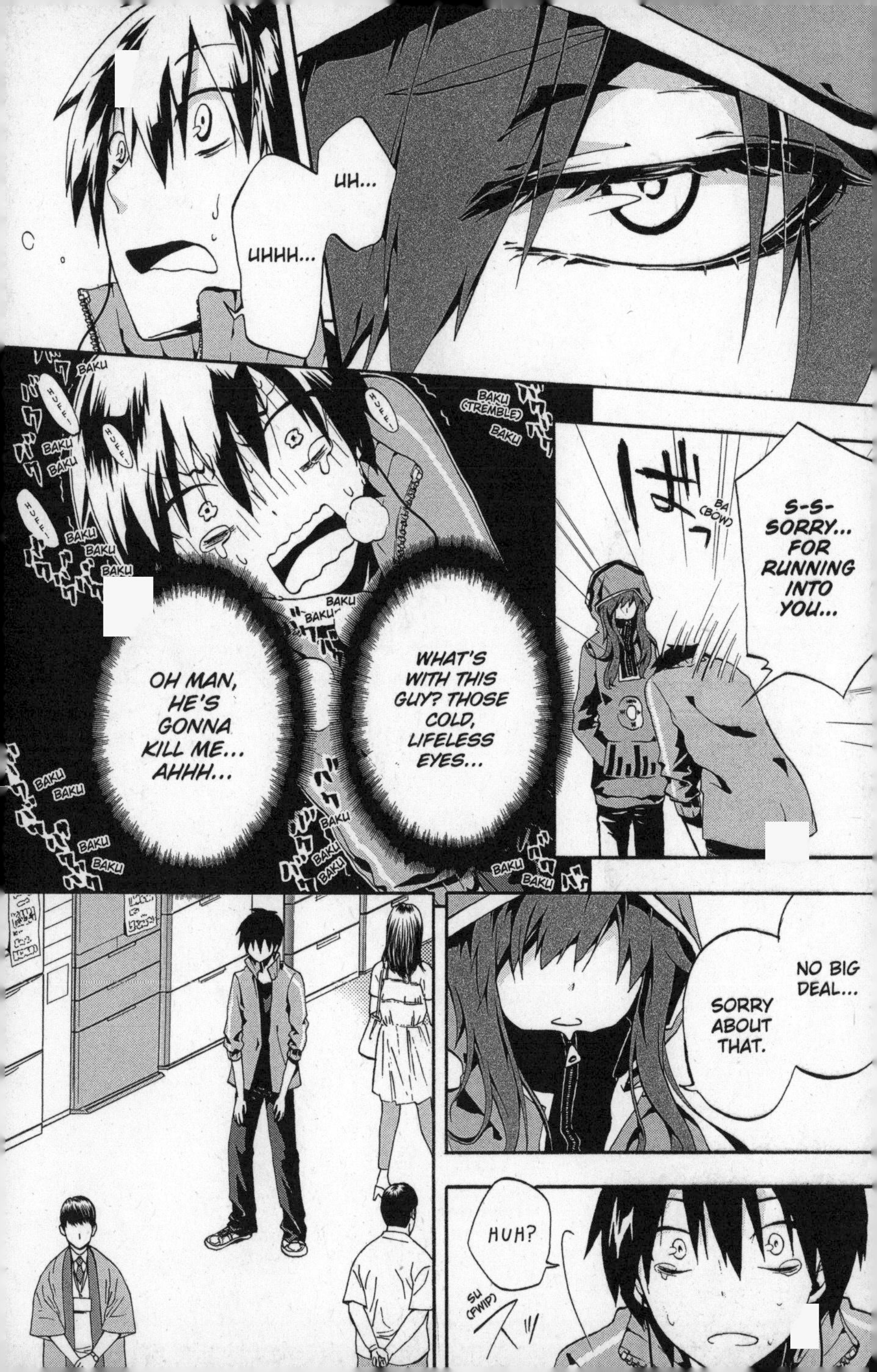
UH...
UHHH...
BA (BOW)
S-S-SORRY... FOR RUNNING INTO YOU...
BAKU (TREMBLE) BAKU
HUFF!
HUFF!
BAKU
BAKU BAKU
HUFF!
BAKU BAKU BAKU
BAKU BAKU
WHAT'S WITH THIS GUY? THOSE COLD, LIFELESS EYES...
OH MAN, HE'S GONNA KILL ME... AHHH...
BAKU BAKU
BAKU BAKU
BAKU BAKU BAKU
BAKU BAKU
NO BIG DEAL...
SORRY ABOUT THAT.
HUH?
SU (FWIP)

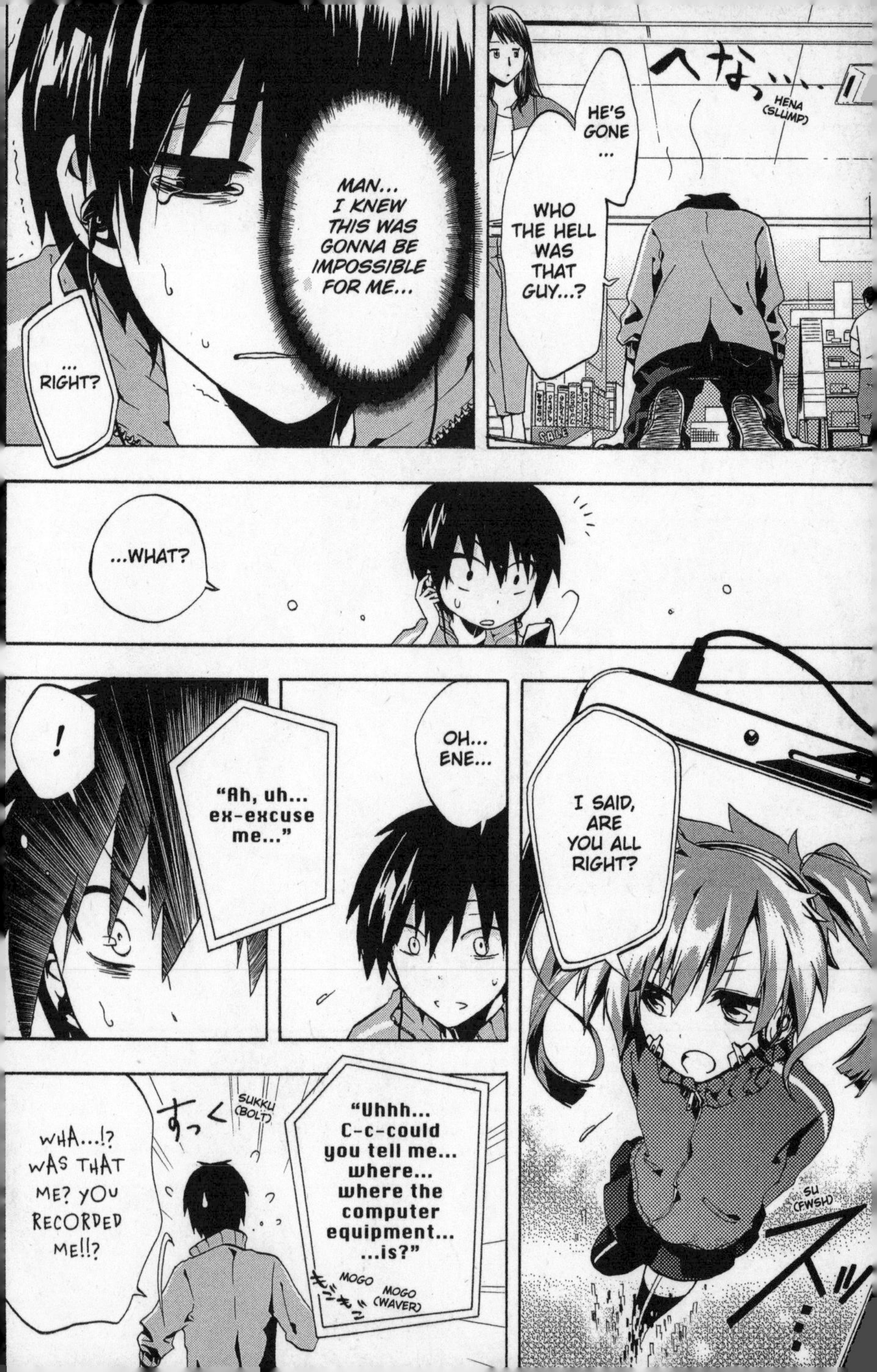
へな…
HENA (SLUMP)
HE'S GONE ...
WHO THE HELL WAS THAT GUY...?
MAN... I KNEW THIS WAS GONNA BE IMPOSSIBLE FOR ME...
... RIGHT?
...WHAT?
I SAID, ARE YOU ALL RIGHT?
SU (FWSH)
OH... ENE...
"Ah, uh... ex-excuse me..."
!
すっく
SUKKU (BOLT)
"Uhhh... C-c-could you tell me... where... where the computer equipment... ...is?"
MOGO MOGO (WAVER)
WHA...!? WAS THAT ME? YOU RECORDED ME!!?

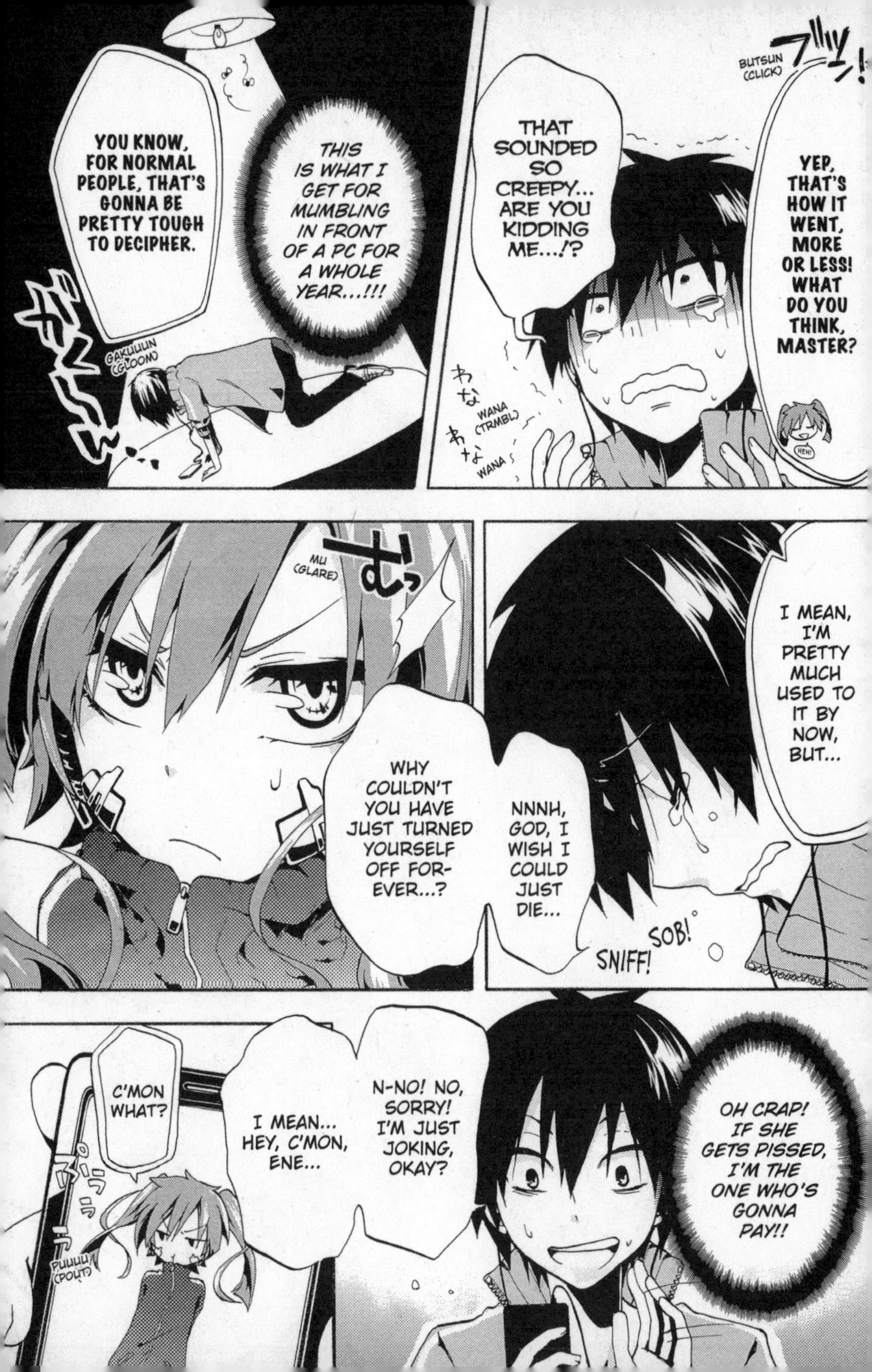
BUTSUN (CLICK)
YEP, THAT'S HOW IT WENT, MORE OR LESS! WHAT DO YOU THINK, MASTER?
THAT SOUNDED SO CREEPY... ARE YOU KIDDING ME...!?
WANA (TRMBL) WANA
HEH!
THIS IS WHAT I GET FOR MUMBLING IN FRONT OF A PC FOR A WHOLE YEAR...!!!
YOU KNOW, FOR NORMAL PEOPLE, THAT'S GONNA BE PRETTY TOUGH TO DECIPHER.
GAKUUUN (GLOOM)
I MEAN, I'M PRETTY MUCH USED TO IT BY NOW, BUT...
NNNH, GOD, I WISH I COULD JUST DIE...
SOB!
SNIFF!
MU (GLARE)
WHY COULDN'T YOU HAVE JUST TURNED YOURSELF OFF FOR-EVER...?
OH CRAP! IF SHE GETS PISSED, I'M THE ONE WHO'S GONNA PAY!!
N-NO! NO, SORRY! I'M JUST JOKING, OKAY?
I MEAN... HEY, C'MON, ENE...
C'MON WHAT?
PUUUU (POUT)

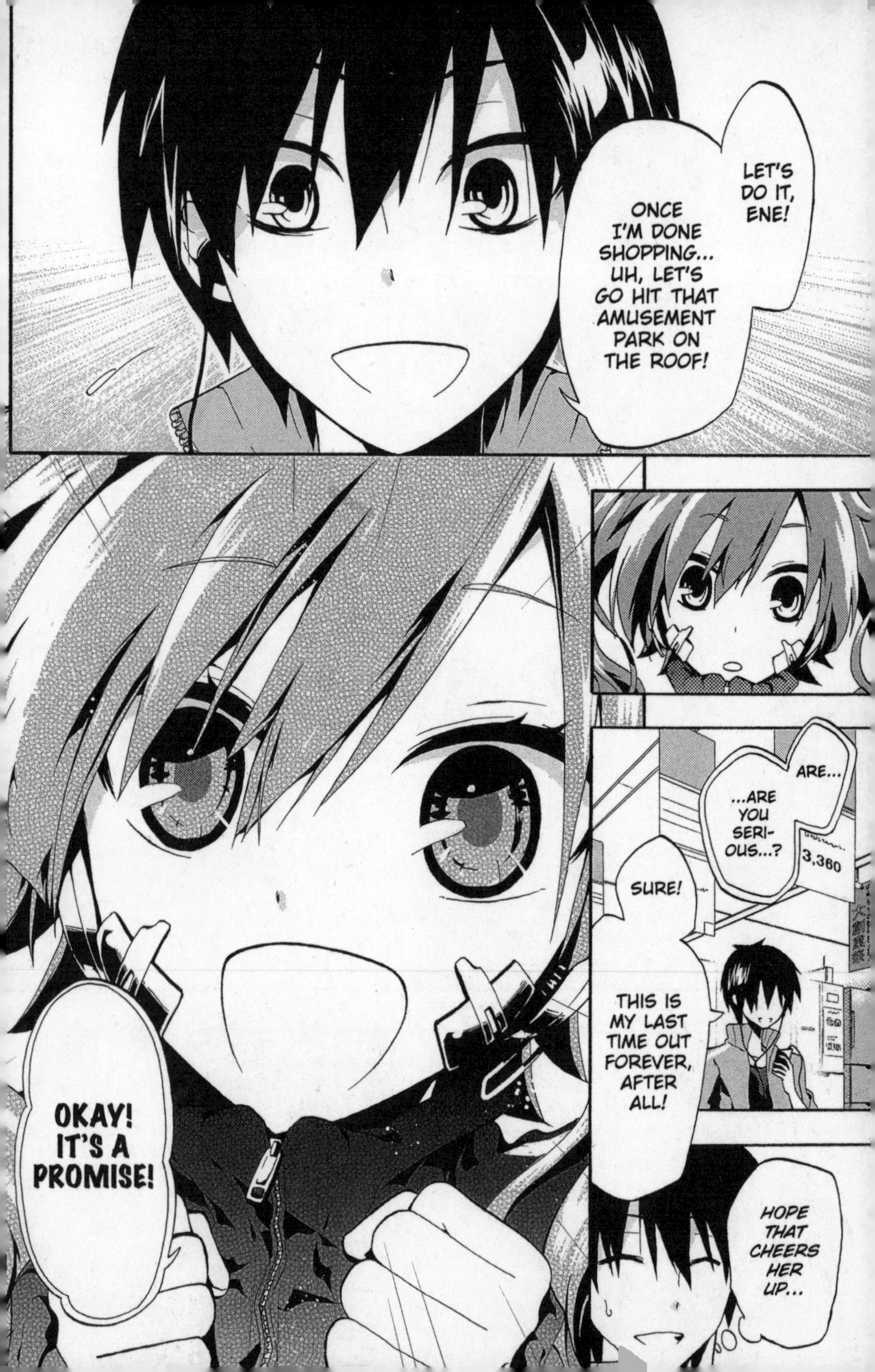
LET'S DO IT, ENE!
ONCE I'M DONE SHOPPING... UH, LET'S GO HIT THAT AMUSEMENT PARK ON THE ROOF!
ARE...
...ARE YOU SERI-OUS...?
3,360
SURE!
THIS IS MY LAST TIME OUT FOREVER, AFTER ALL!
HOPE THAT CHEERS HER UP...
OKAY! IT'S A PROMISE!

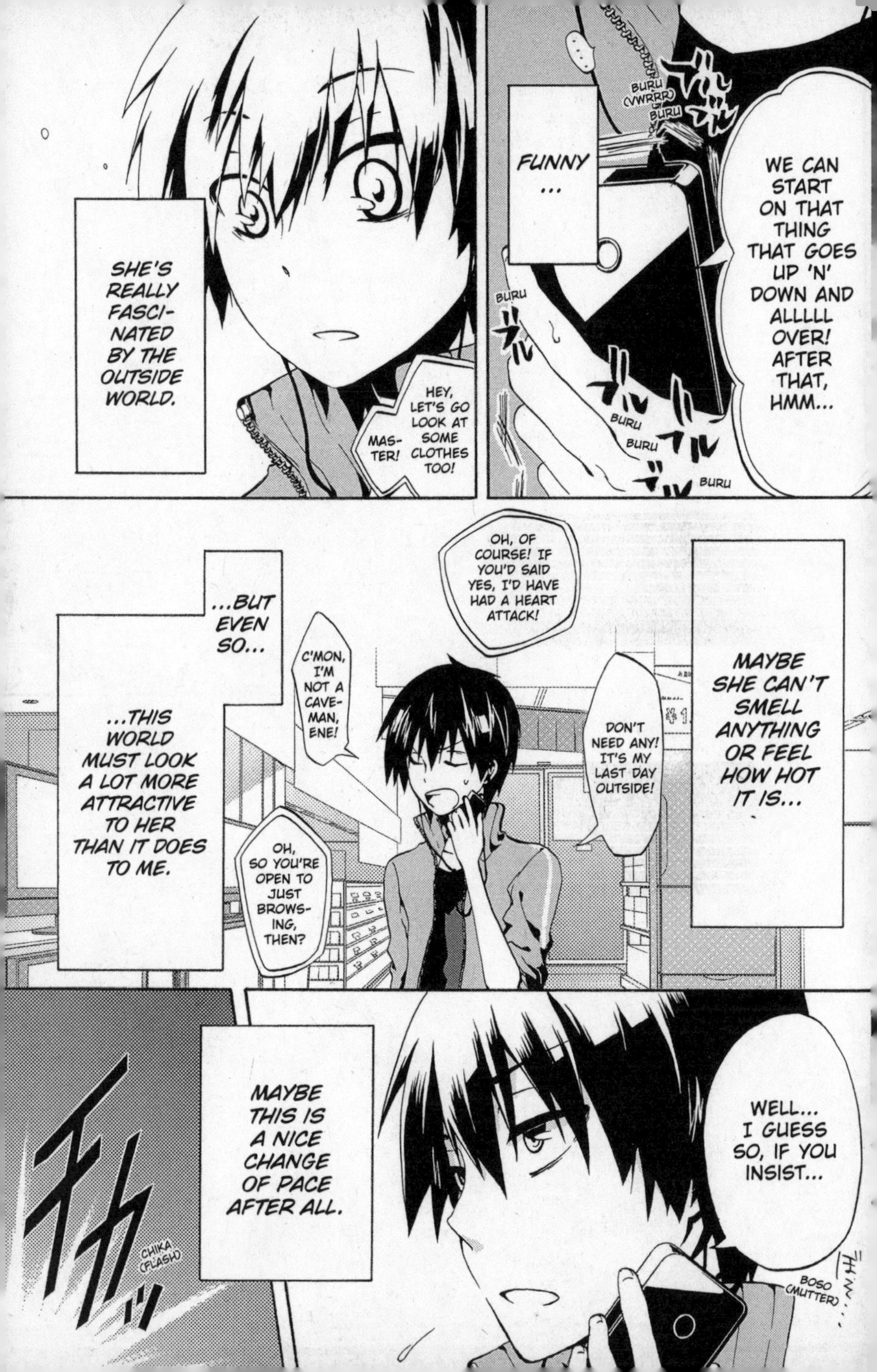
WE CAN START ON THAT THING THAT GOES UP 'N' DOWN AND ALLLLL OVER! AFTER THAT, HMM...
BURU (VWRRR) BURU
FUNNY ...
BURU
BURU
BURU
BURU
HEY, LET'S GO LOOK AT SOME CLOTHES TOO! MASTER!
SHE'S REALLY FASCINATED BY THE OUTSIDE WORLD.
MAYBE SHE CAN'T SMELL ANYTHING OR FEEL HOW HOT IT IS...
DON'T NEED ANY! IT'S MY LAST DAY OUTSIDE!
OH, OF COURSE! IF YOU'D SAID YES, I'D HAVE HAD A HEART ATTACK!
...BUT EVEN SO...
C'MON, I'M NOT A CAVEMAN, ENE!
OH, SO YOU'RE OPEN TO JUST BROWSING, THEN?
...THIS WORLD MUST LOOK A LOT MORE ATTRACTIVE TO HER THAN IT DOES TO ME.
WELL... I GUESS SO, IF YOU INSIST...
BOSO (MUTTER)
MAYBE THIS IS A NICE CHANGE OF PACE AFTER ALL.
CHIKA (FLASH)

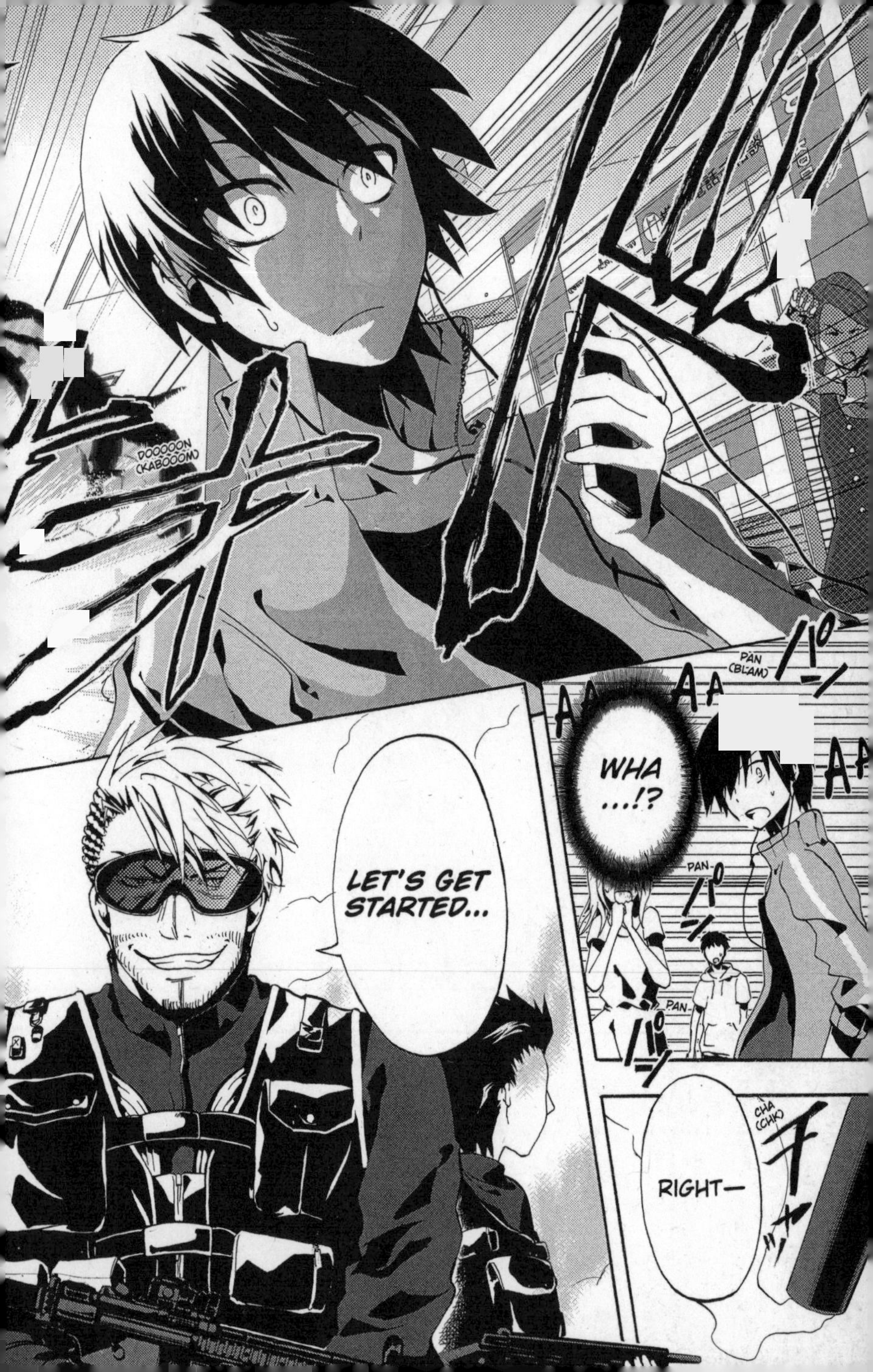
DOOOOON (KABOOOM)
PAN (BLAM)
AA AA AA
WHA ...!?
PAN-
PAN-
CHA (CHK)
RIGHT—
LET'S GET STARTED...

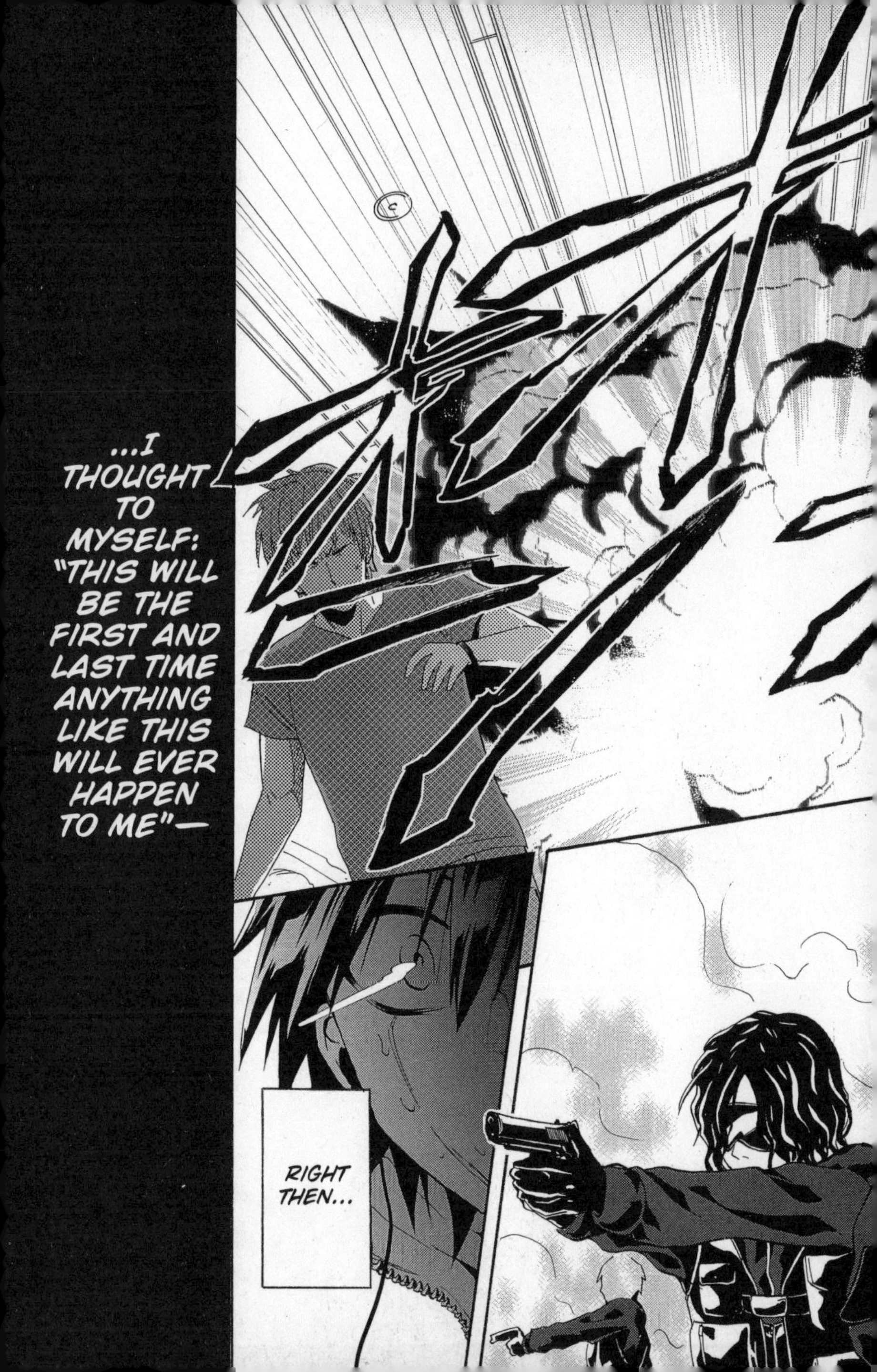
...I THOUGHT TO MYSELF: "THIS WILL BE THE FIRST AND LAST TIME ANYTHING LIKE THIS WILL EVER HAPPEN TO ME"—
RIGHT THEN...

KAGEROU DAZE

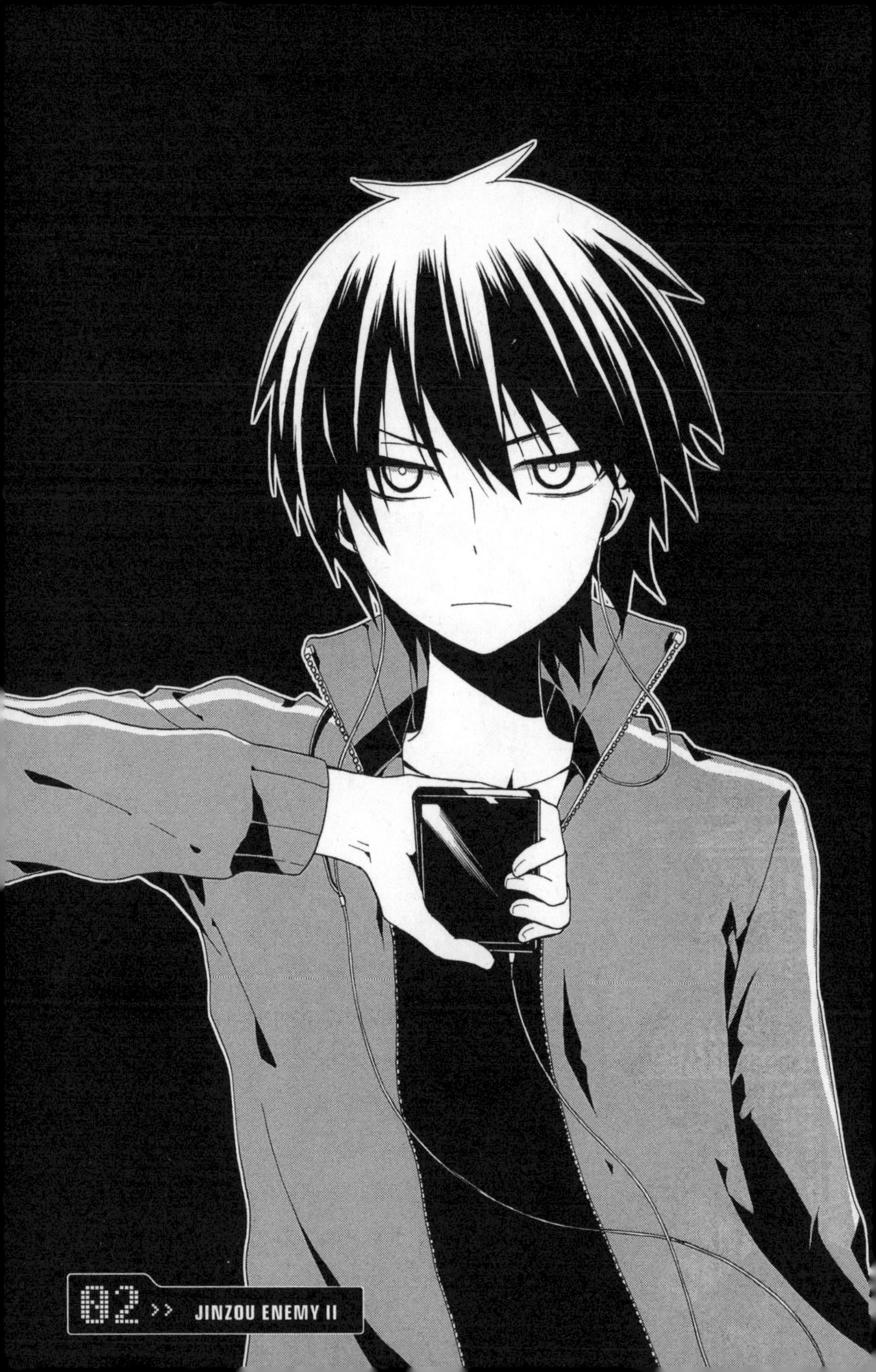
02 >> JINZOU ENEMY II

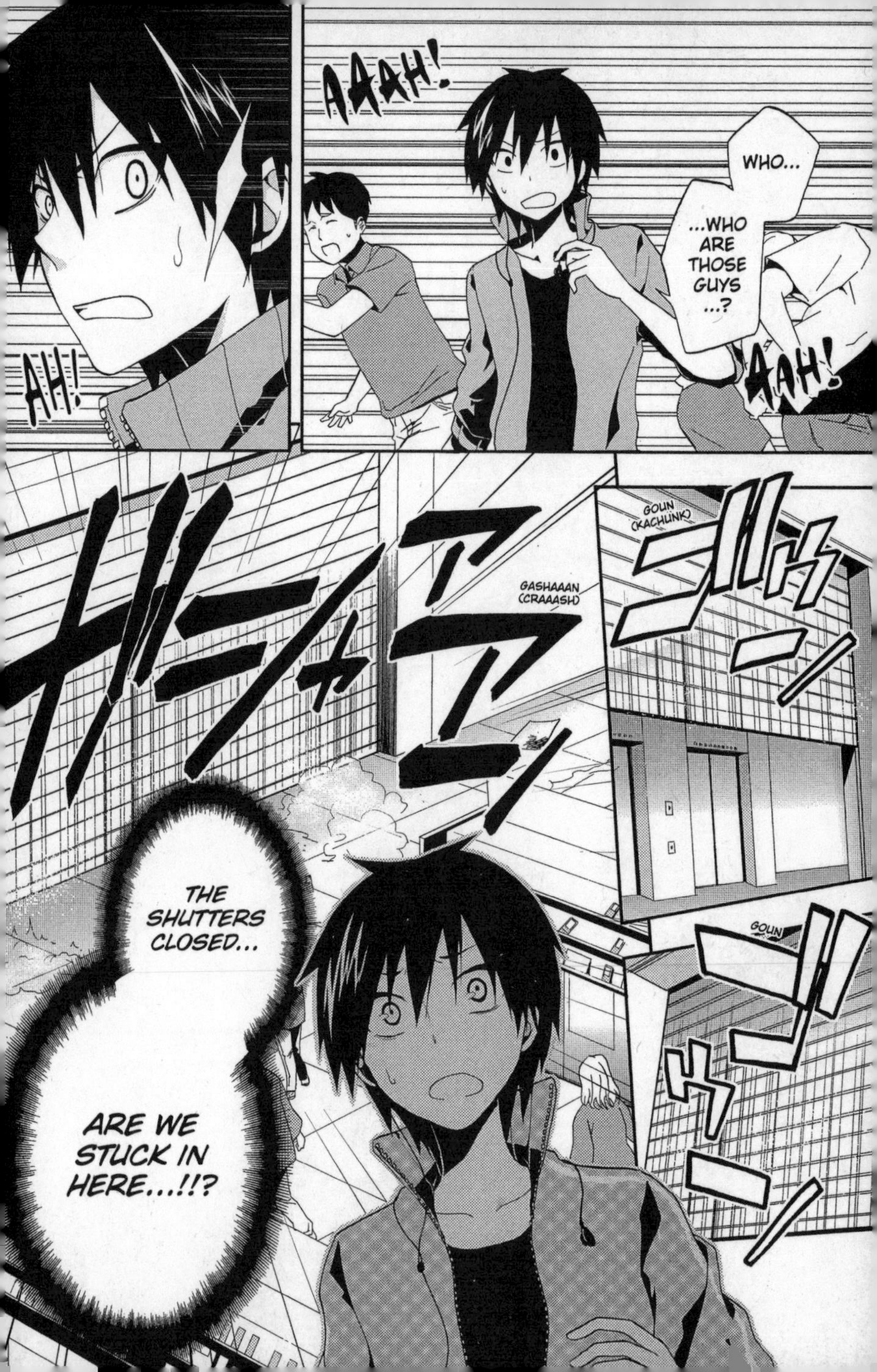
AAAH!
WHO...
...WHO ARE THOSE GUYS ...?
AAH!
AH!
GOUN (KACHUNK)
GOUN
GASHAAAN (CRAAASH)
THE SHUTTERS CLOSED...
ARE WE STUCK IN HERE...!!?

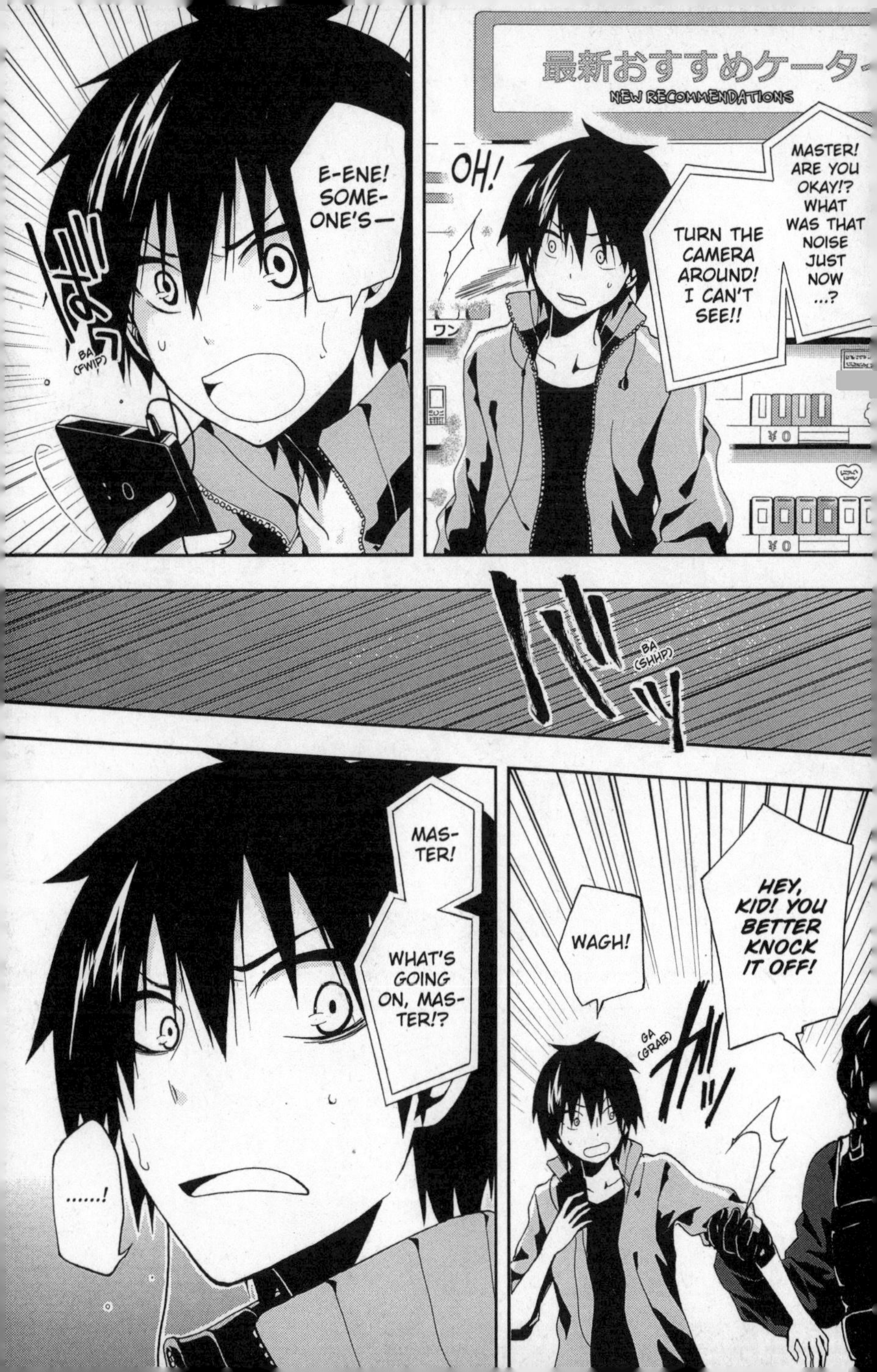

最新おすすめケータ
NEW RECOMMENDATIONS
OH!
MASTER! ARE YOU OKAY!? WHAT WAS THAT NOISE JUST NOW ...?
TURN THE CAMERA AROUND! I CAN'T SEE!!
¥0
E-ENE! SOME-ONE'S—
BA (FWIP)
BA (SHHP)
HEY, KID! YOU BETTER KNOCK IT OFF!
WAGH!
GA (GRAB)
MAS-TER!
WHAT'S GOING ON, MAS-TER!?
......!

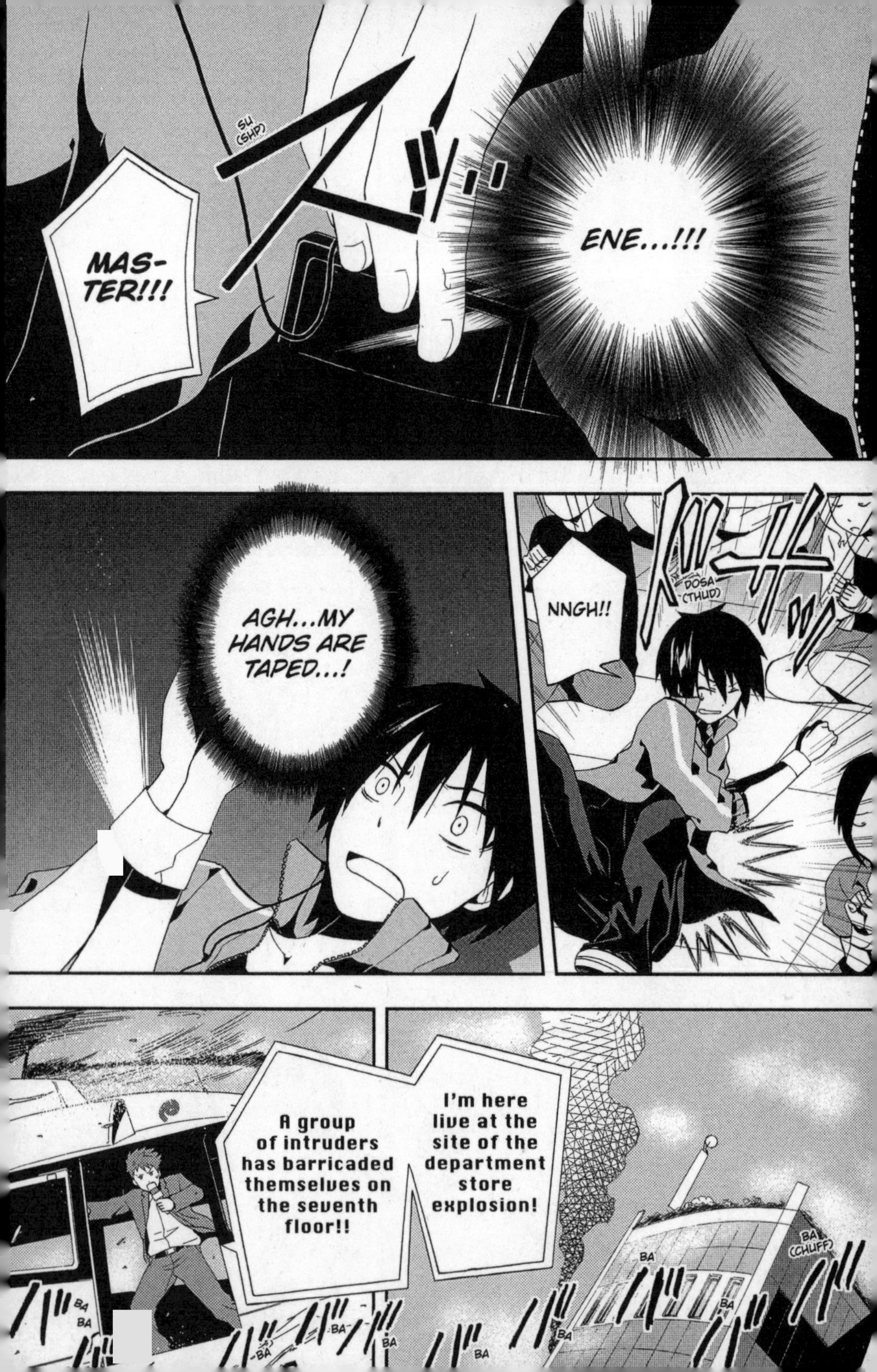
ENE...!!!
SU (SHP)
MAS-TER!!!
DOSA (THUD)
NNGH!!
AGH...MY HANDS ARE TAPED...!
BA (CHUFF)
BA
I'm here live at the site of the department store explosion!
A group of intruders has barricaded themselves on the seventh floor!!
BA
BA
BA
BA
BA
BA
BA

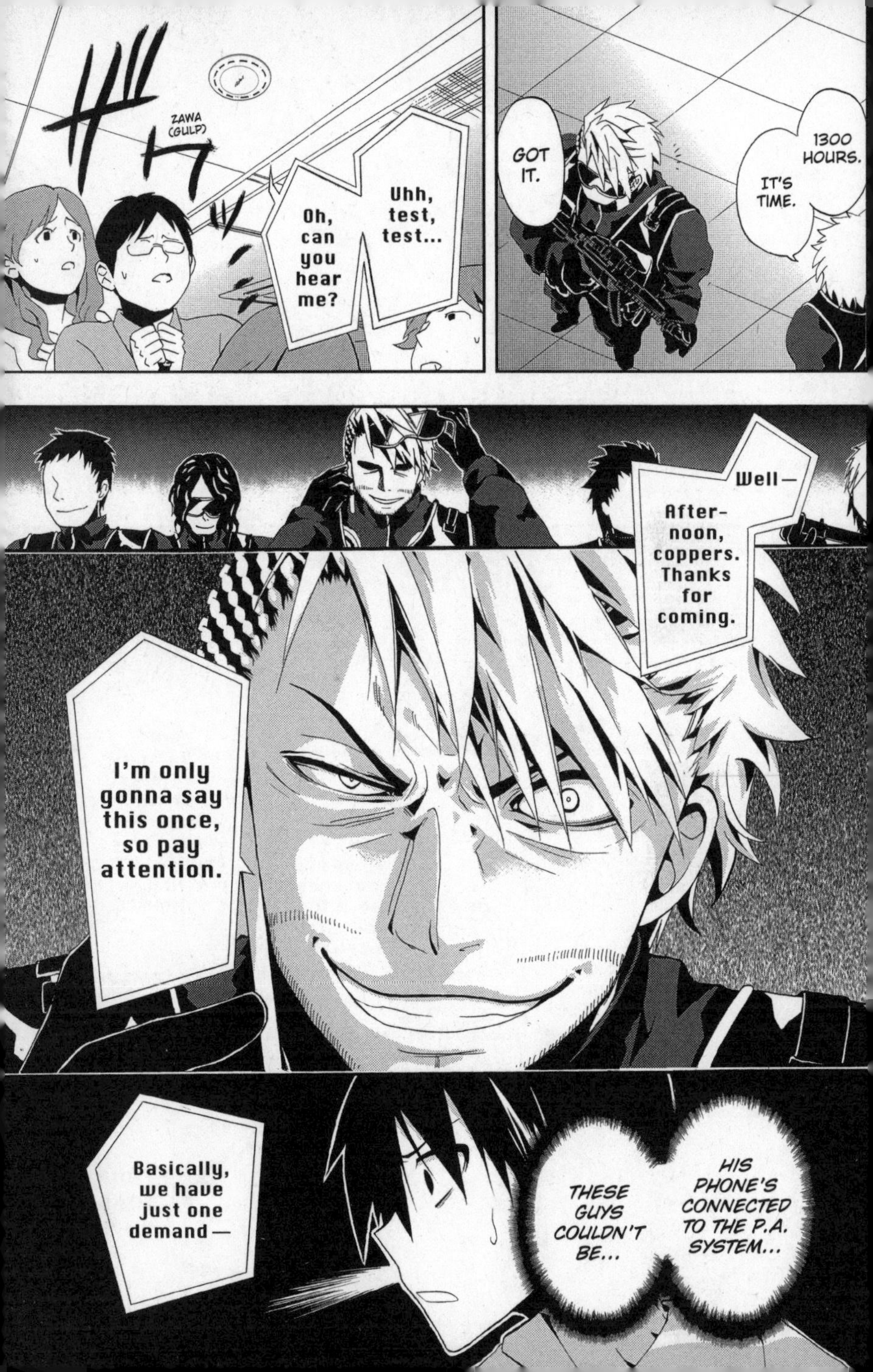

1300 HOURS. IT'S TIME.
GOT IT.
Uhh, test, test...
Oh, can you hear me?
ZAWA (GULP)
Well—
Afternoon, coppers. Thanks for coming.
I'm only gonna say this once, so pay attention.
HIS PHONE'S CONNECTED TO THE P.A. SYSTEM...
THESE GUYS COULDN'T BE...
Basically, we have just one demand—

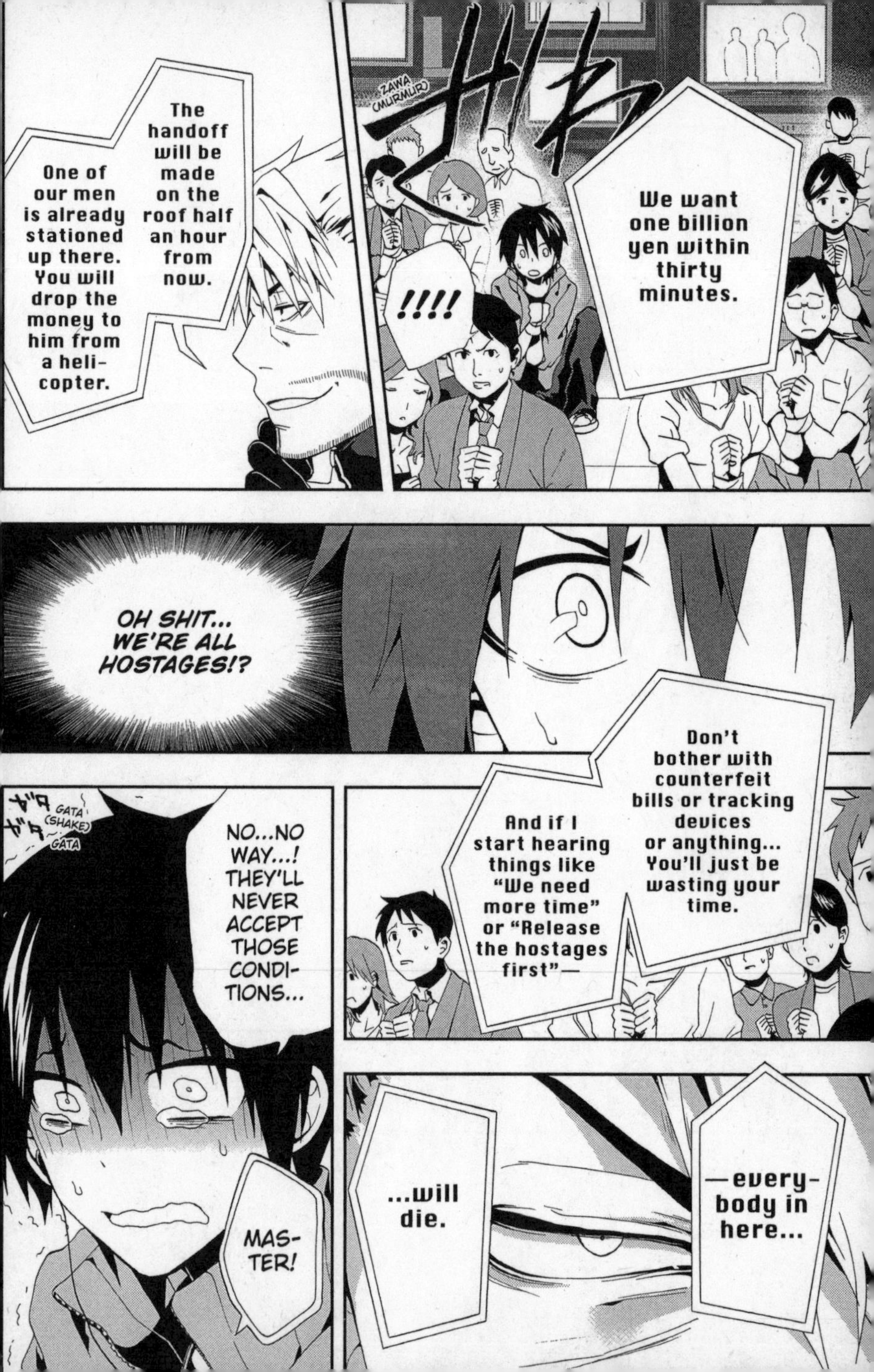
We want one billion yen within thirty minutes.
ZAWA (MURMUR)
!!!!
The handoff will be made on the roof half an hour from now.
One of our men is already stationed up there. You will drop the money to him from a heli-copter.
OH SHIT... WE'RE ALL HOSTAGES!?
Don't bother with counterfeit bills or tracking devices or anything... You'll just be wasting your time.
And if I start hearing things like "We need more time" or "Release the hostages first"—
—every-body in here...
...will die.
NO...NO WAY...! THEY'LL NEVER ACCEPT THOSE CONDI-TIONS...
GATA (SHAKE) GATA
MAS-TER!

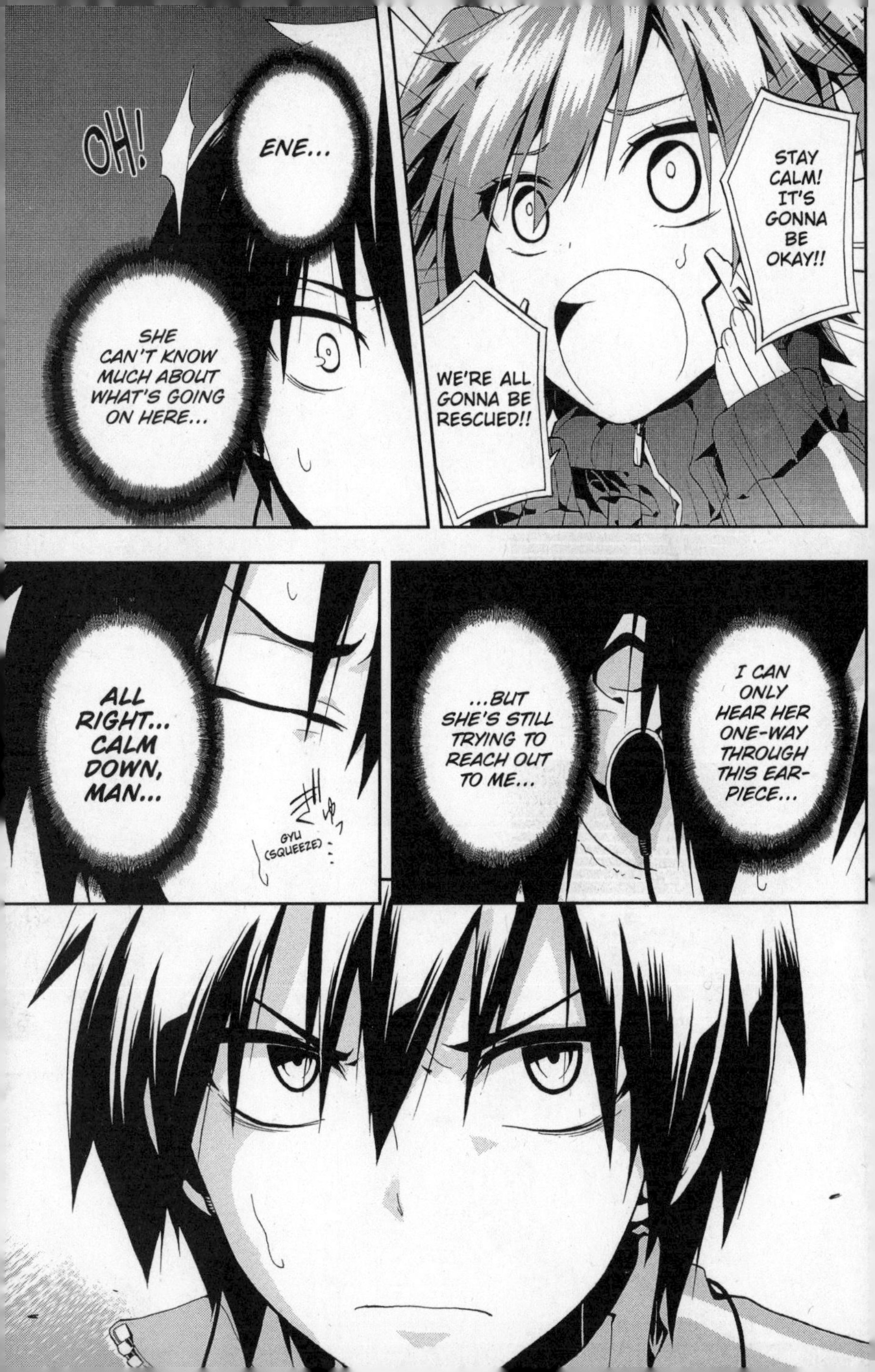
STAY CALM! IT'S GONNA BE OKAY!!
WE'RE ALL GONNA BE RESCUED!!
OH!
ENE...
SHE CAN'T KNOW MUCH ABOUT WHAT'S GOING ON HERE...
I CAN ONLY HEAR HER ONE-WAY THROUGH THIS EAR-PIECE...
...BUT SHE'S STILL TRYING TO REACH OUT TO ME...
ALL RIGHT... CALM DOWN, MAN...
GYU (SQUEEZE)

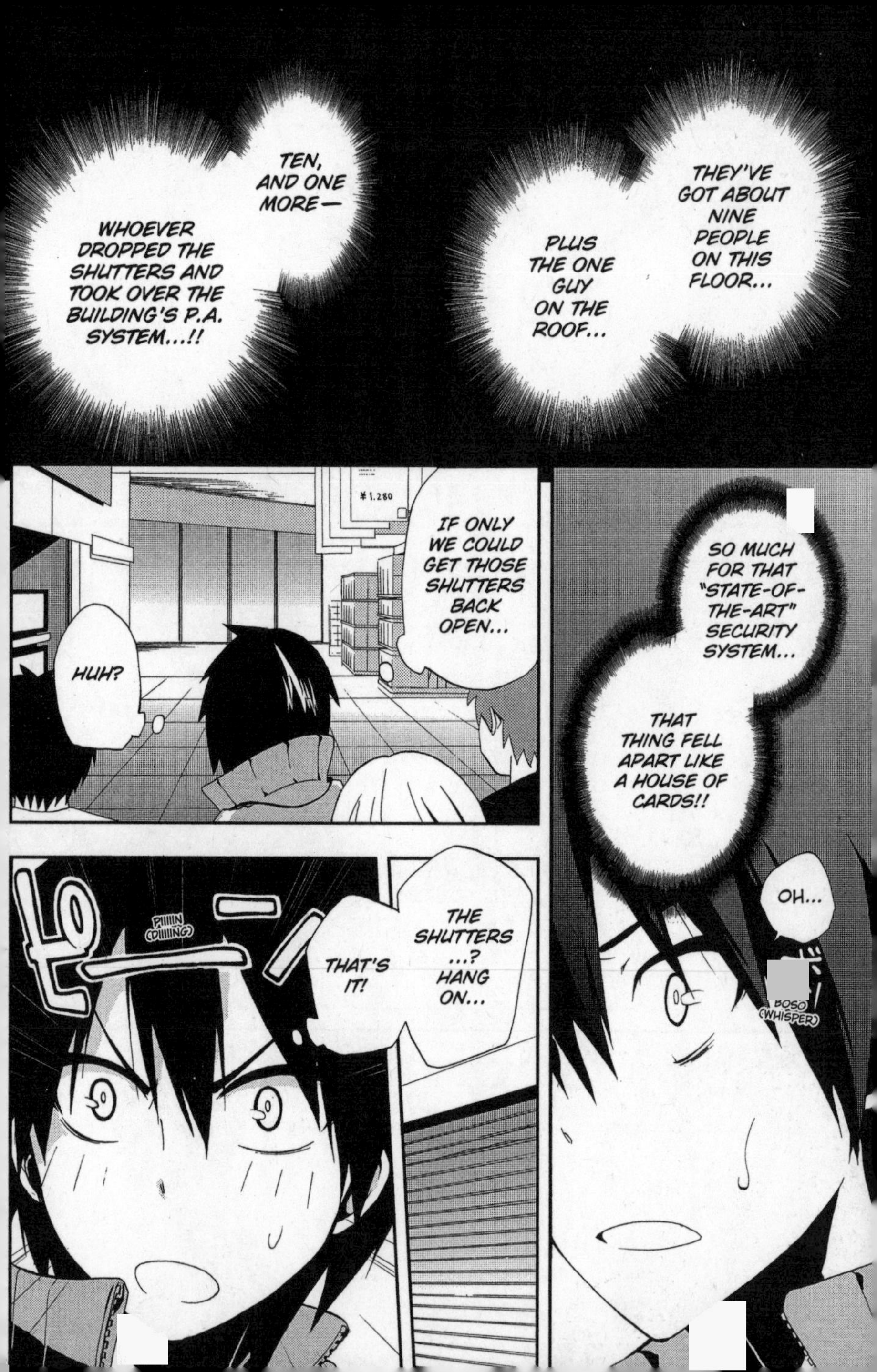
THEY'VE GOT ABOUT NINE PEOPLE ON THIS FLOOR...
PLUS THE ONE GUY ON THE ROOF...
TEN, AND ONE MORE—
WHOEVER DROPPED THE SHUTTERS AND TOOK OVER THE BUILDING'S P.A. SYSTEM...!!
SO MUCH FOR THAT "STATE-OF-THE-ART" SECURITY SYSTEM...
THAT THING FELL APART LIKE A HOUSE OF CARDS!!
OH...
BOSO (WHISPER)
IF ONLY WE COULD GET THOSE SHUTTERS BACK OPEN...
HUH?
THE SHUTTERS ...? HANG ON...
THAT'S IT!
PIIIIN (DIIIING)

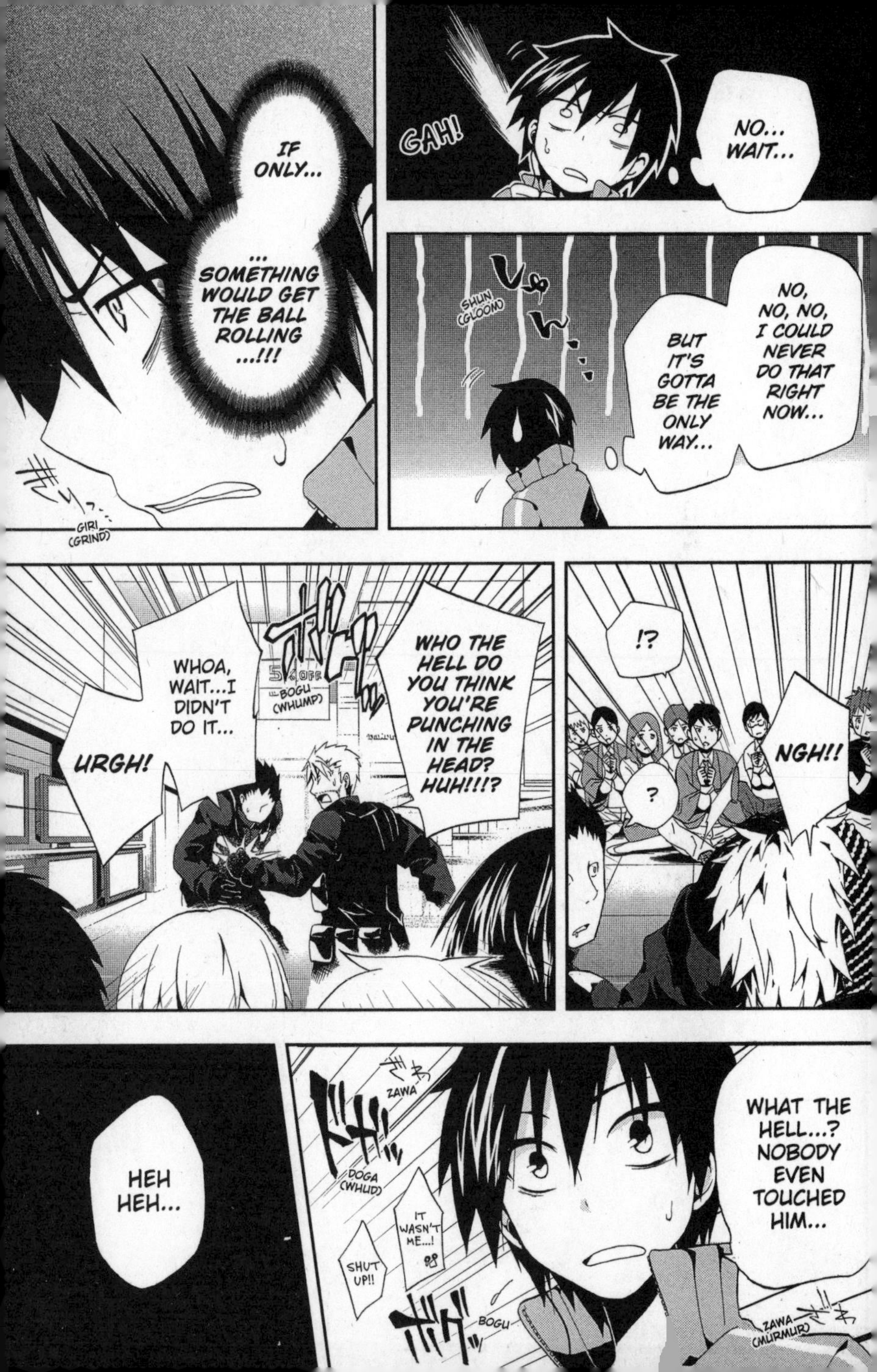
NO... WAIT...
GAH!
NO, NO, NO, I COULD NEVER DO THAT RIGHT NOW...
BUT IT'S GOTTA BE THE ONLY WAY...
SHUN (GLOOM)
IF ONLY...
...SOMETHING WOULD GET THE BALL ROLLING ...!!!
GIRI (GRIND)
!?
NGH!!
?
WHO THE HELL DO YOU THINK YOU'RE PUNCHING IN THE HEAD? HUH!!!?
BOGU (WHUMP)
WHOA, WAIT...I DIDN'T DO IT...
URGH!
WHAT THE HELL...? NOBODY EVEN TOUCHED HIM...
ZAWA
DOGA (WHUD)
IT WASN'T ME...!
SHUT UP!!
BOGU
ZAWA (MURMUR)
HEH HEH...

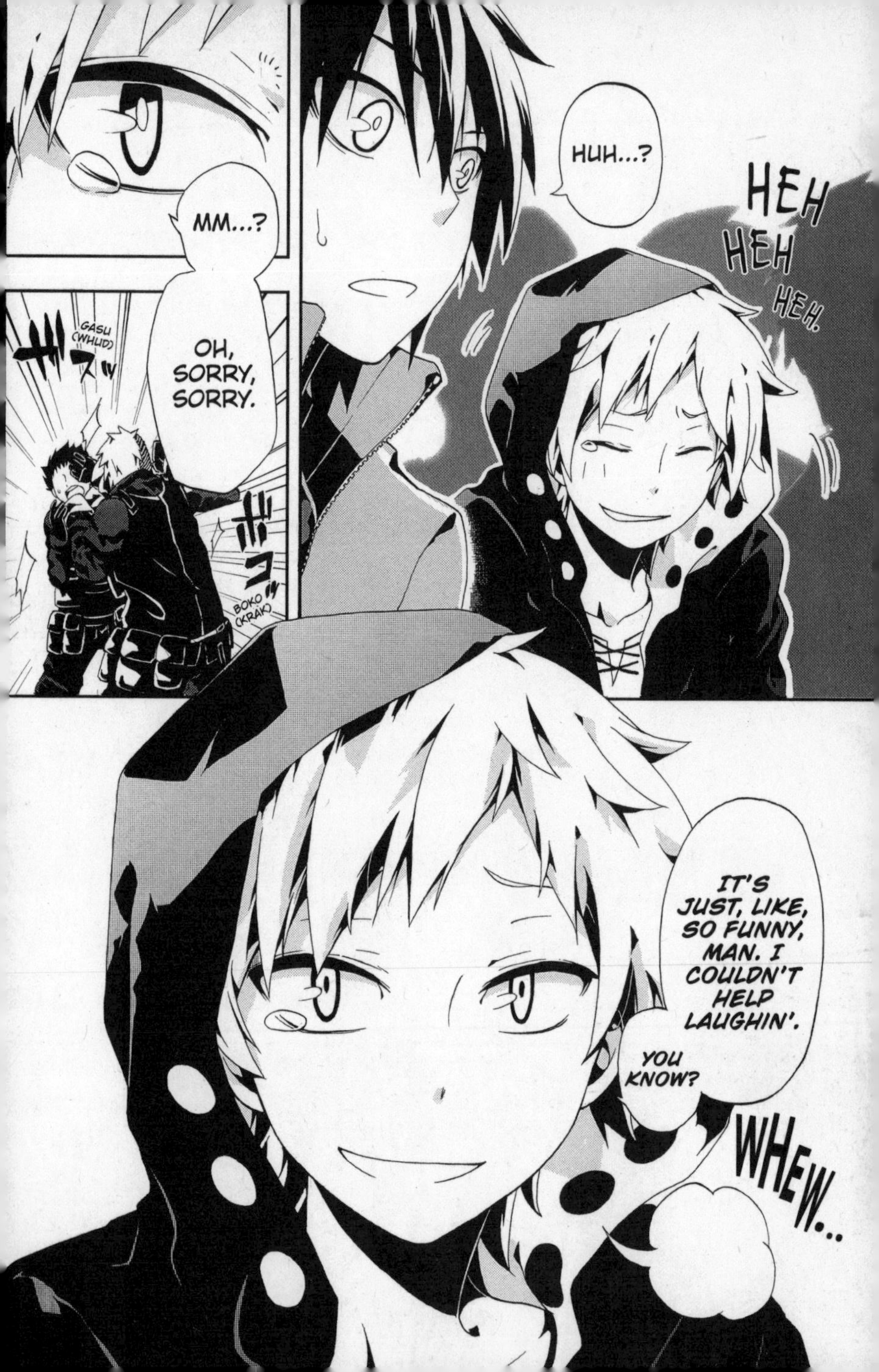
HUH...?
HEH HEH HEH.
MM...?
OH, SORRY, SORRY.
GASU (WHUD)
BOKO (KRAK)
IT'S JUST, LIKE, SO FUNNY, MAN. I COULDN'T HELP LAUGHIN'.
YOU KNOW?
WHEW...

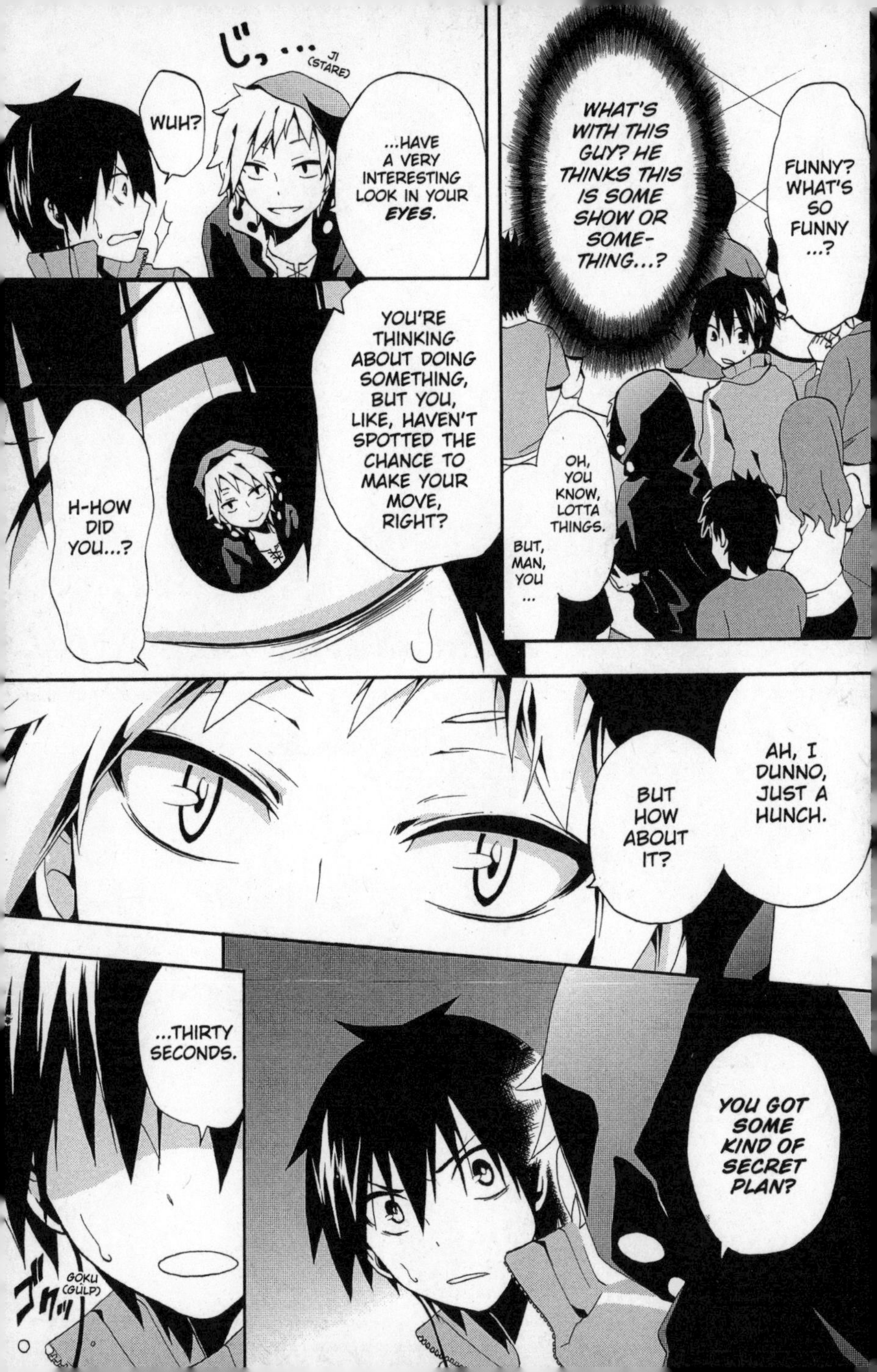
FUNNY? WHAT'S SO FUNNY ...?
WHAT'S WITH THIS GUY? HE THINKS THIS IS SOME SHOW OR SOME-THING...?
OH, YOU KNOW, LOTTA THINGS.
BUT, MAN, YOU ...
じっ…
JI (STARE)
...HAVE A VERY INTERESTING LOOK IN YOUR EYES.
WUH?
YOU'RE THINKING ABOUT DOING SOMETHING, BUT YOU, LIKE, HAVEN'T SPOTTED THE CHANCE TO MAKE YOUR MOVE, RIGHT?
H-HOW DID YOU...?
AH, I DUNNO, JUST A HUNCH.
BUT HOW ABOUT IT?
YOU GOT SOME KIND OF SECRET PLAN?
...THIRTY SECONDS.
ゴクッ
GOKU (GULP)

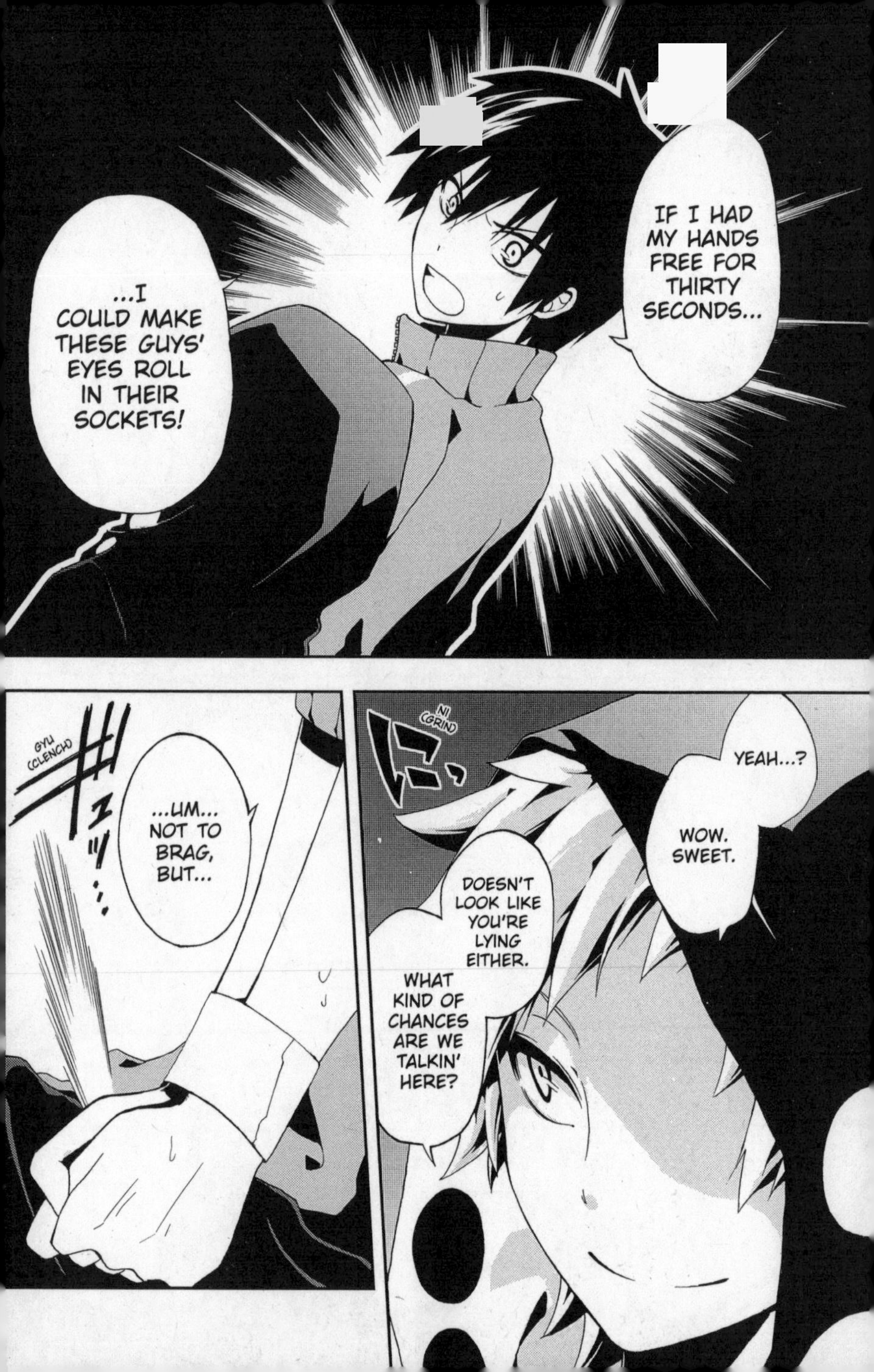
IF I HAD MY HANDS FREE FOR THIRTY SECONDS...
...I COULD MAKE THESE GUYS' EYES ROLL IN THEIR SOCKETS!
NI (GRIND)
YEAH...?
WOW. SWEET.
DOESN'T LOOK LIKE YOU'RE LYING EITHER.
WHAT KIND OF CHANCES ARE WE TALKIN' HERE?
GYU (CLENCH)
...UM... NOT TO BRAG, BUT...

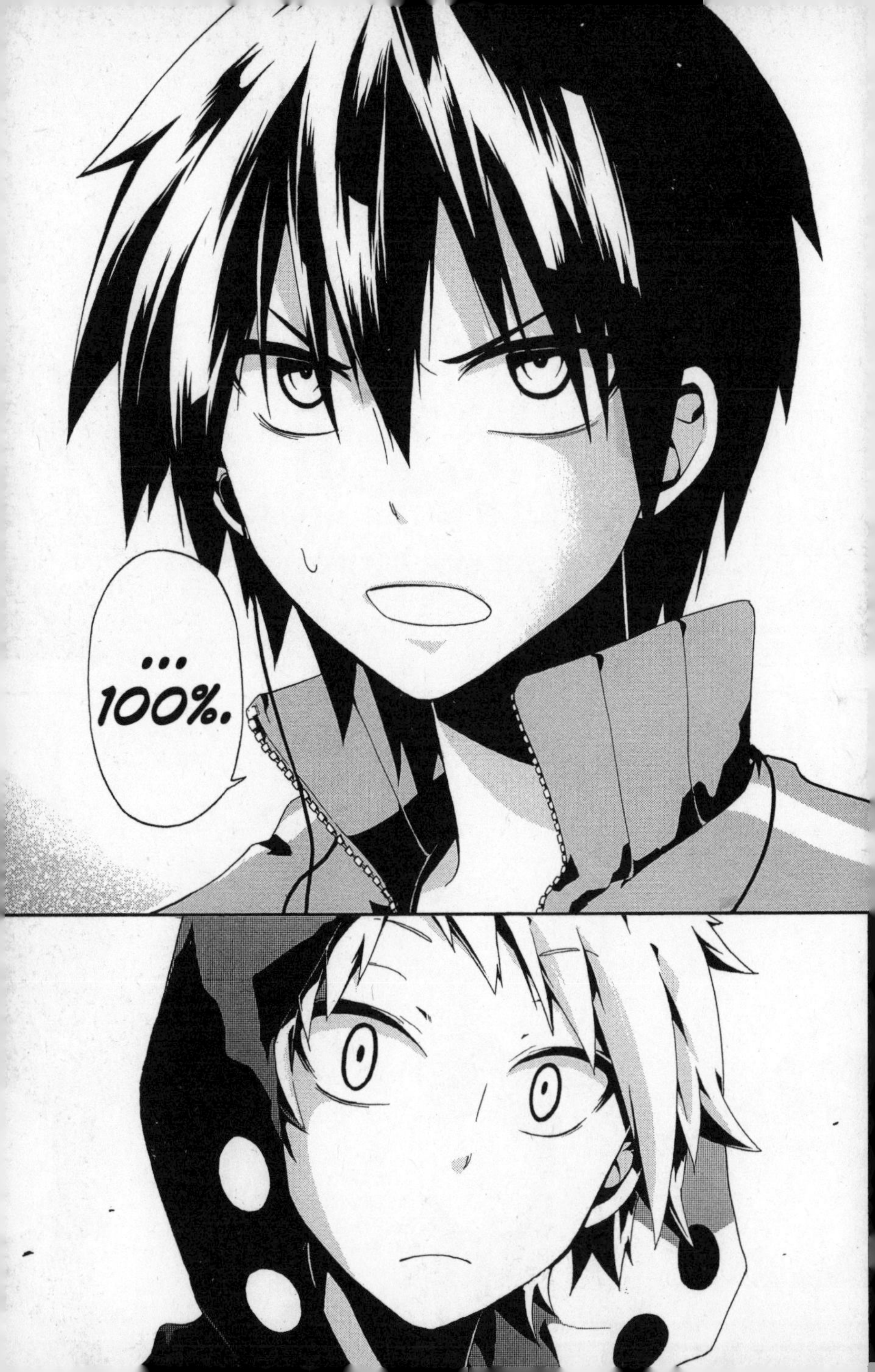
...
100%.

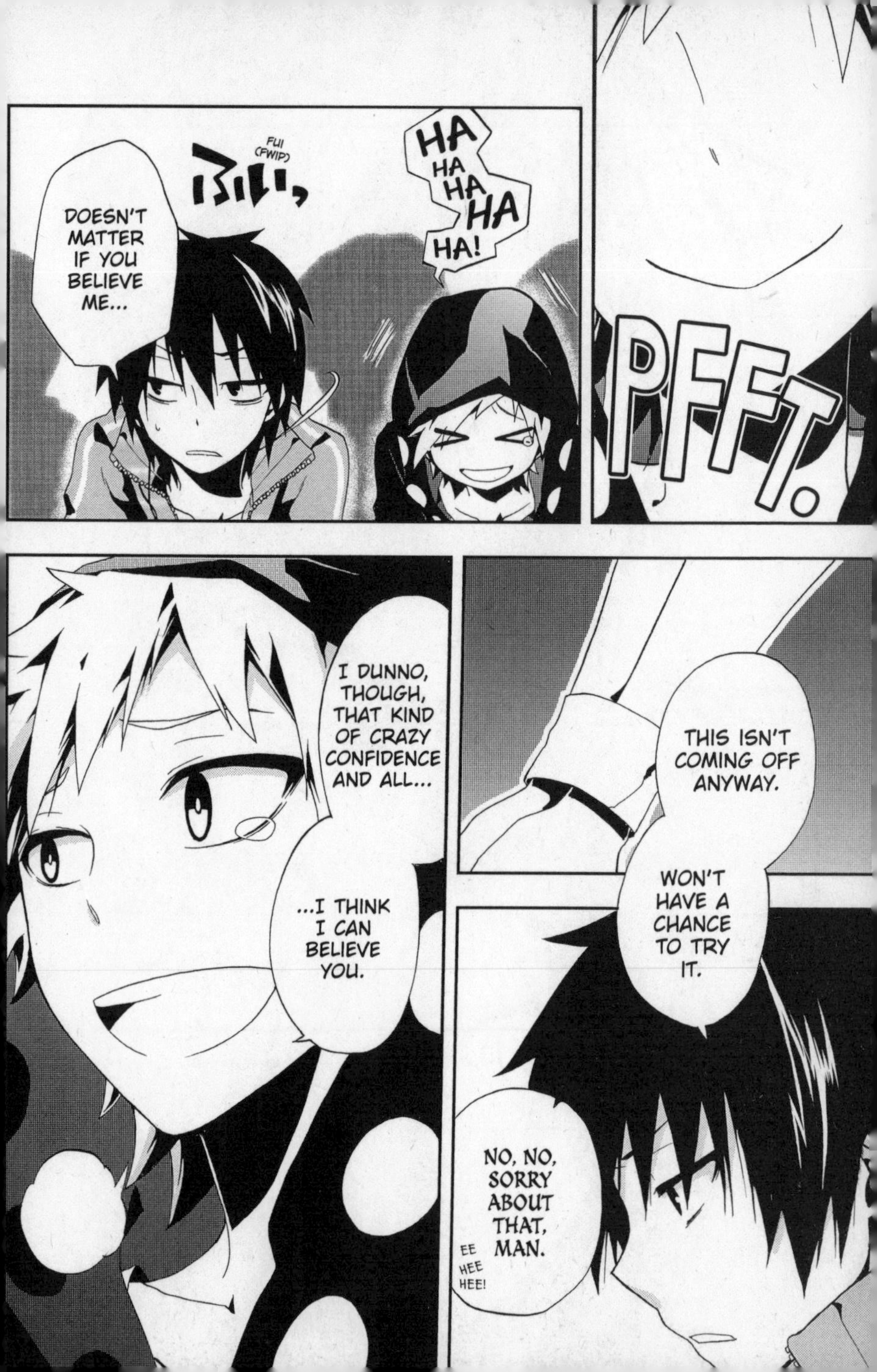
PFFT.
HA HA HA HA HA!
ふい
FUI (FWIP)
DOESN'T MATTER IF YOU BELIEVE ME...
THIS ISN'T COMING OFF ANYWAY.
WON'T HAVE A CHANCE TO TRY IT.
NO, NO, SORRY ABOUT THAT, MAN.
EE HEE HEE!
I DUNNO, THOUGH, THAT KIND OF CRAZY CONFIDENCE AND ALL...
...I THINK I CAN BELIEVE YOU.

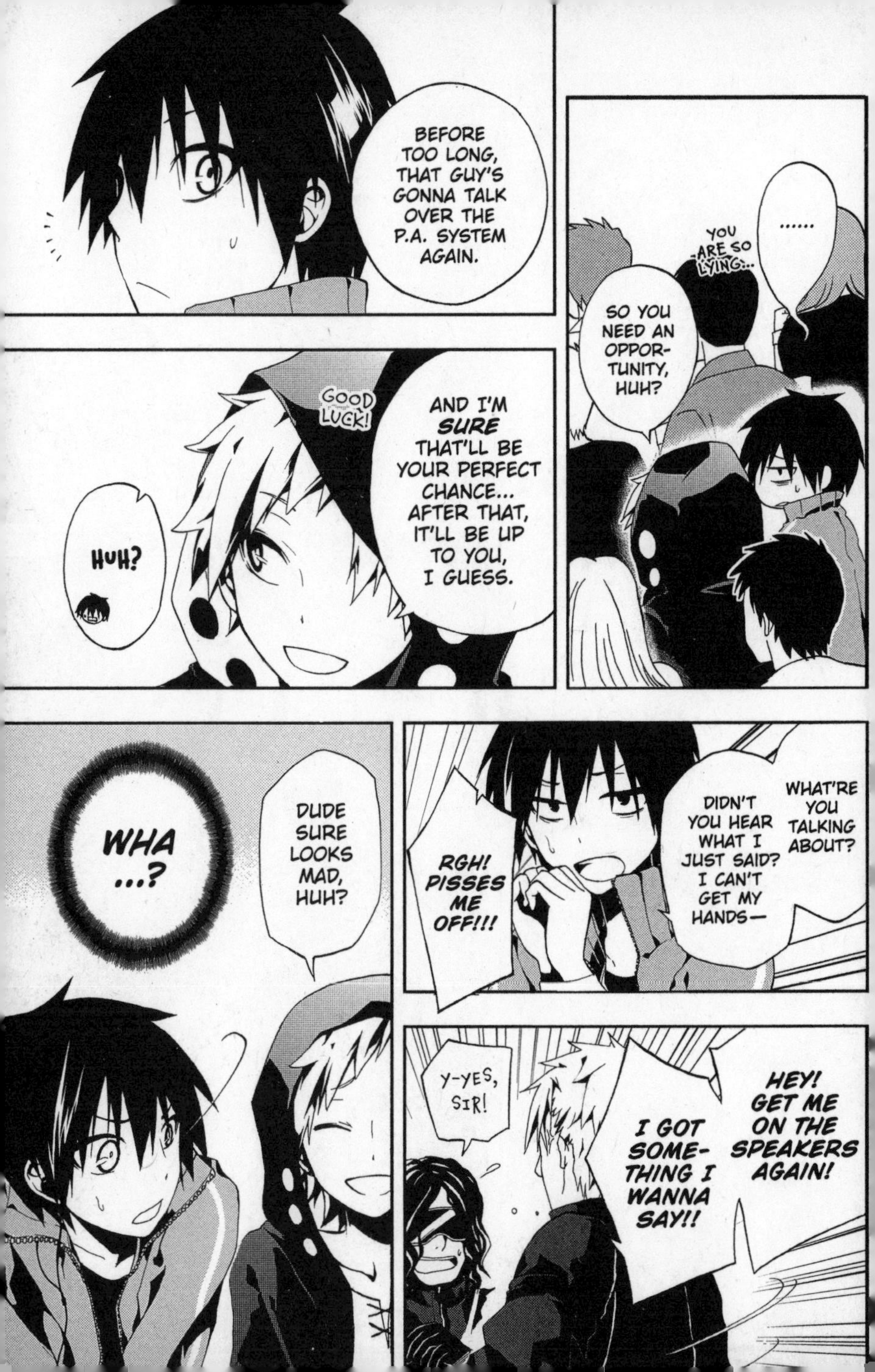
......
YOU ARE SO LYING...
SO YOU NEED AN OPPOR-TUNITY, HUH?
BEFORE TOO LONG, THAT GUY'S GONNA TALK OVER THE P.A. SYSTEM AGAIN.
AND I'M *SURE* THAT'LL BE YOUR PERFECT CHANCE... AFTER THAT, IT'LL BE UP TO YOU, I GUESS.
GOOD LUCK!
HUH?
WHAT'RE YOU TALKING ABOUT?
DIDN'T YOU HEAR WHAT I JUST SAID? I CAN'T GET MY HANDS—
RGH! PISSES ME OFF!!!
HEY! GET ME ON THE SPEAKERS AGAIN!
I GOT SOME-THING I WANNA SAY!!
Y-YES, SIR!
DUDE SURE LOOKS MAD, HUH?
WHA ...?

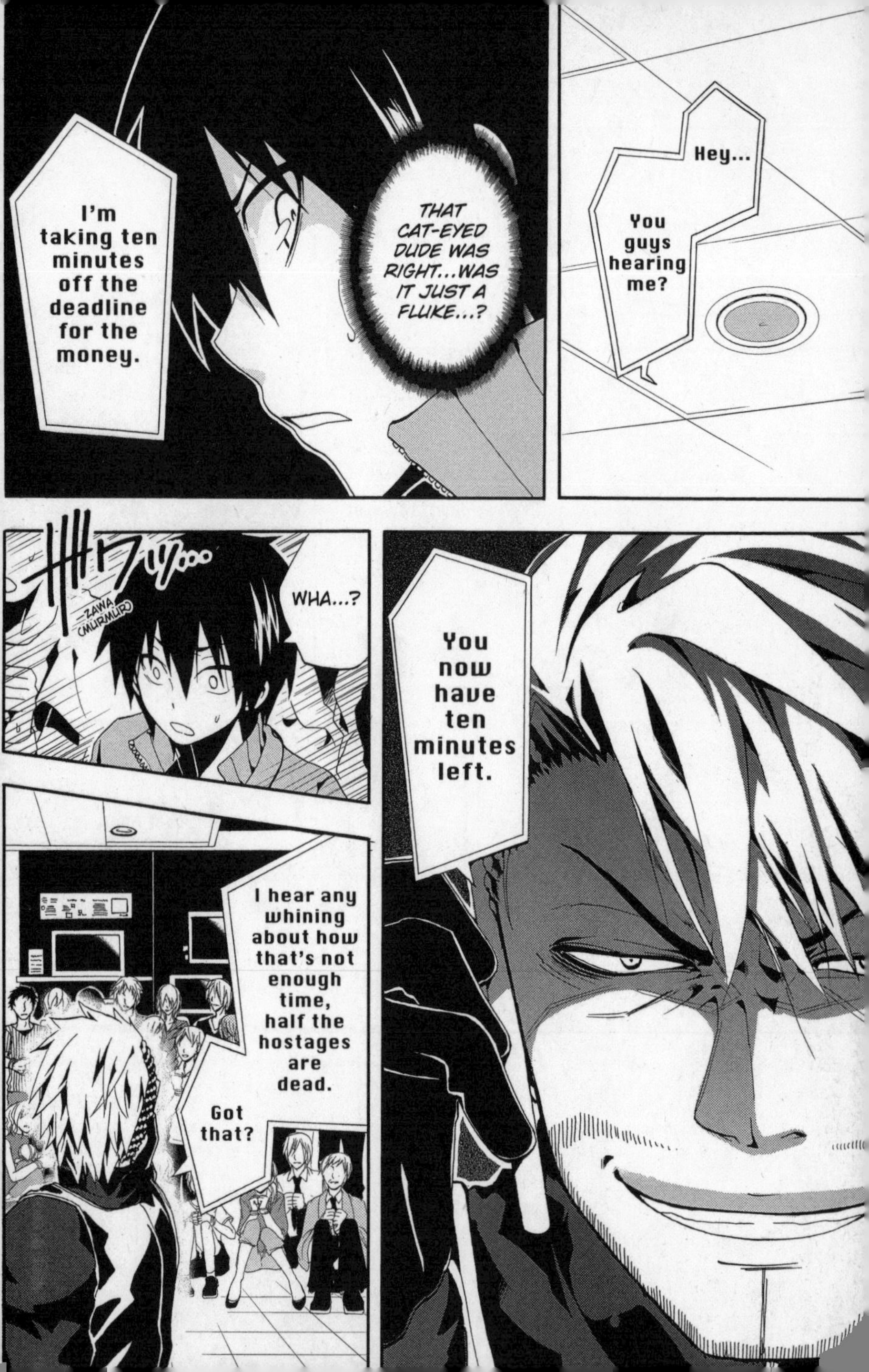

Hey...
You guys hearing me?
THAT CAT-EYED DUDE WAS RIGHT...WAS IT JUST A FLUKE...?
I'm taking ten minutes off the deadline for the money.
You now have ten minutes left.
WHA...?
ZAWA (MURMUR)
I hear any whining about how that's not enough time, half the hostages are dead.
Got that?

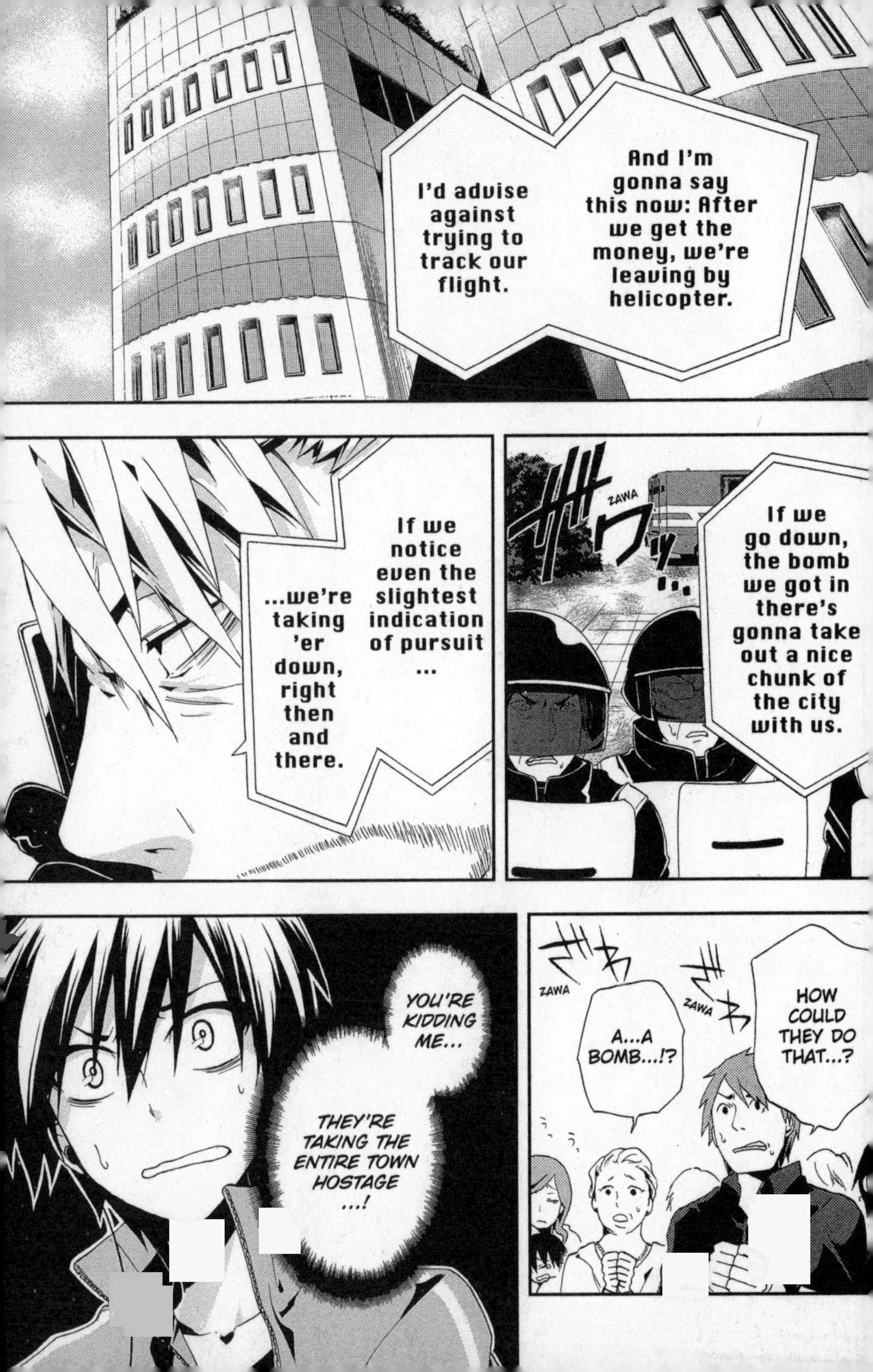
And I'm gonna say this now: After we get the money, we're leaving by helicopter.
I'd advise against trying to track our flight.
ZAWA
If we go down, the bomb we got in there's gonna take out a nice chunk of the city with us.
If we notice even the slightest indication of pursuit...
...we're taking 'er down, right then and there.
ZAWA
ZAWA
HOW COULD THEY DO THAT...?
A...A BOMB...!?
YOU'RE KIDDING ME...
THEY'RE TAKING THE ENTIRE TOWN HOSTAGE...!

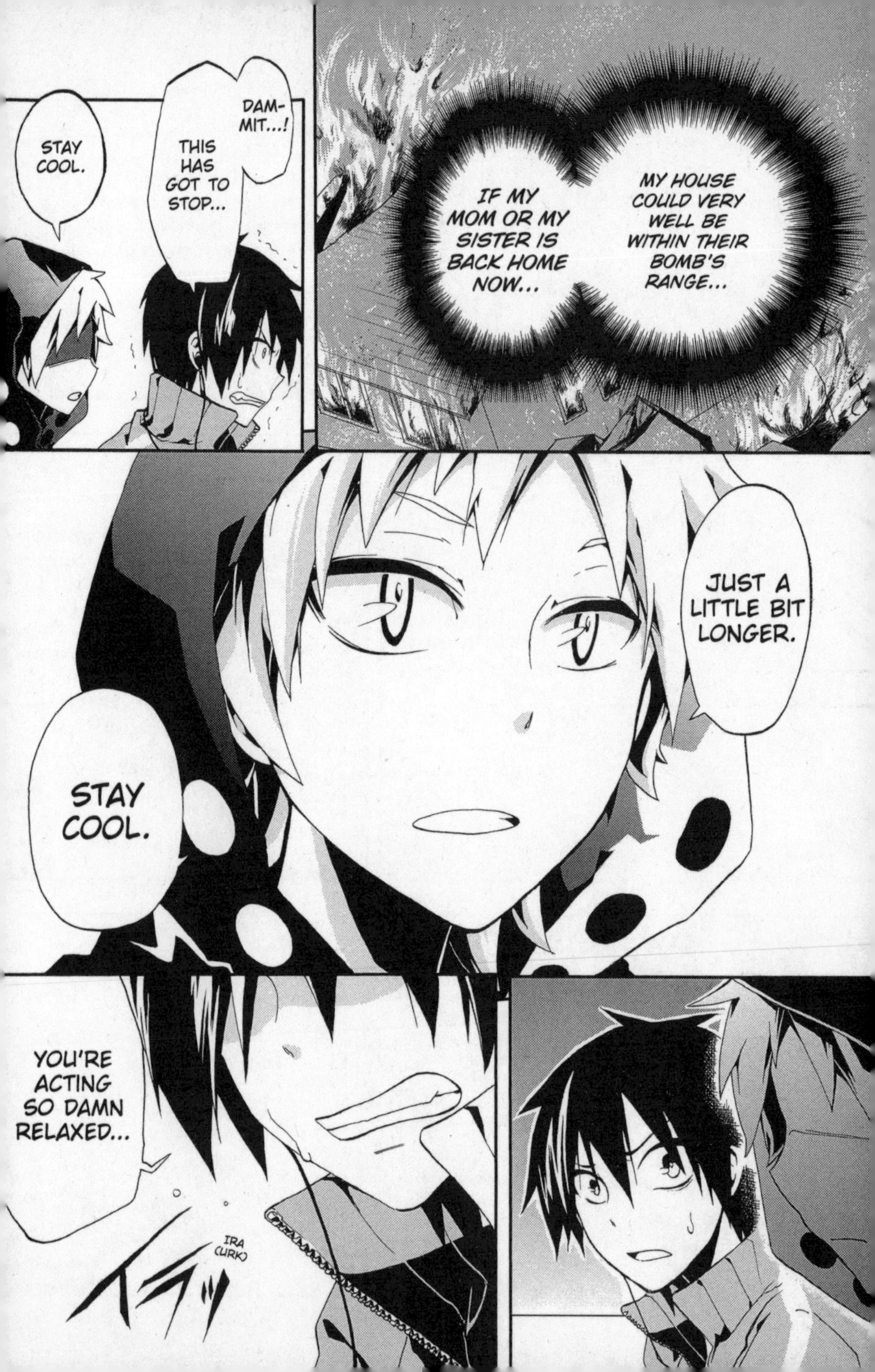
MY HOUSE COULD VERY WELL BE WITHIN THEIR BOMB'S RANGE...
IF MY MOM OR MY SISTER IS BACK HOME NOW...
DAM-MIT...!
THIS HAS GOT TO STOP...
STAY COOL.
JUST A LITTLE BIT LONGER.
STAY COOL.
YOU'RE ACTING SO DAMN RELAXED...
IRA (URK)

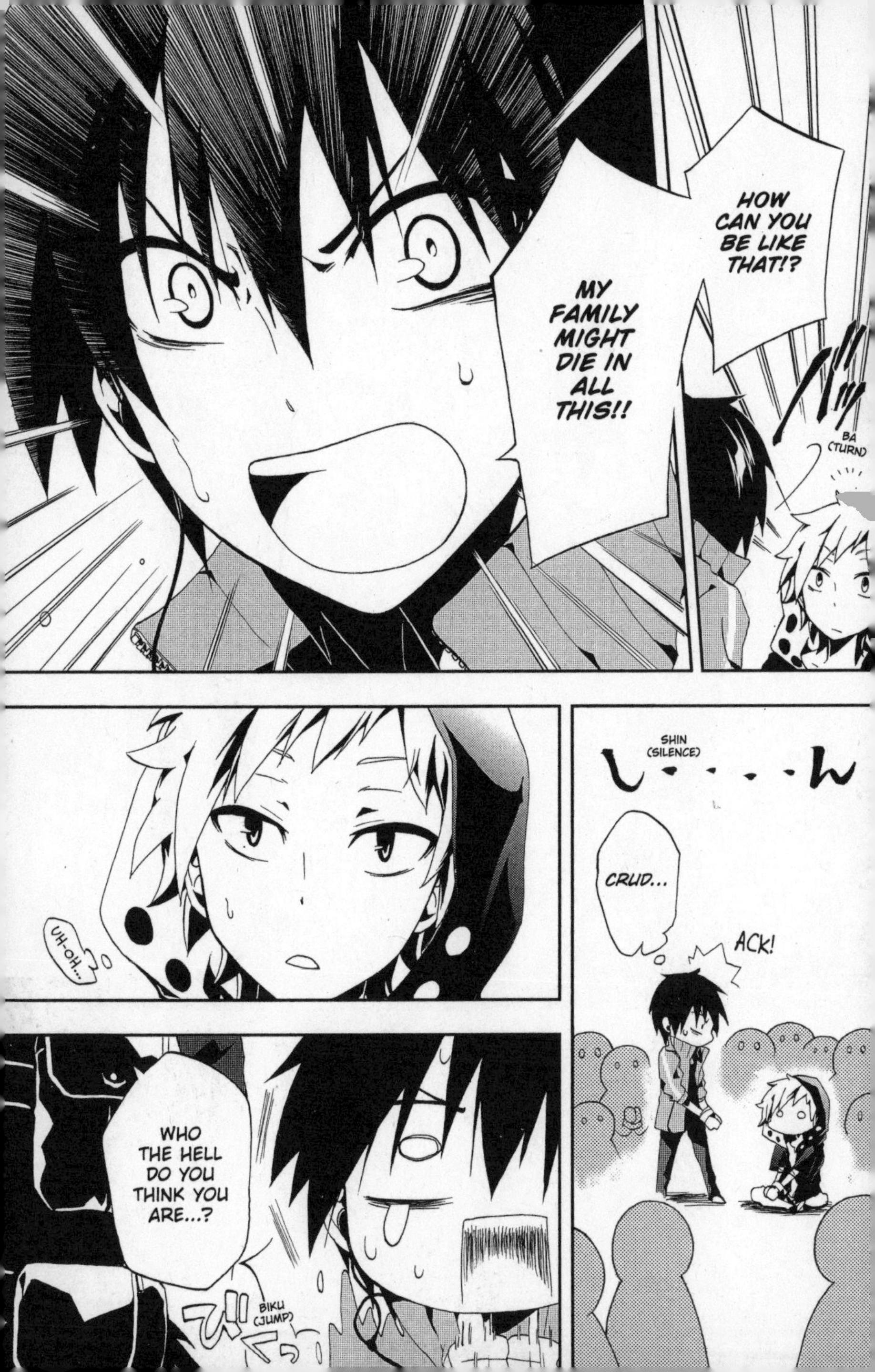
HOW CAN YOU BE LIKE THAT!?
MY FAMILY MIGHT DIE IN ALL THIS!!
BA (TURN)
SHIN (SILENCE)
CRUD...
ACK!
UH-OH...
WHO THE HELL DO YOU THINK YOU ARE...?
BIKU (JUMP)

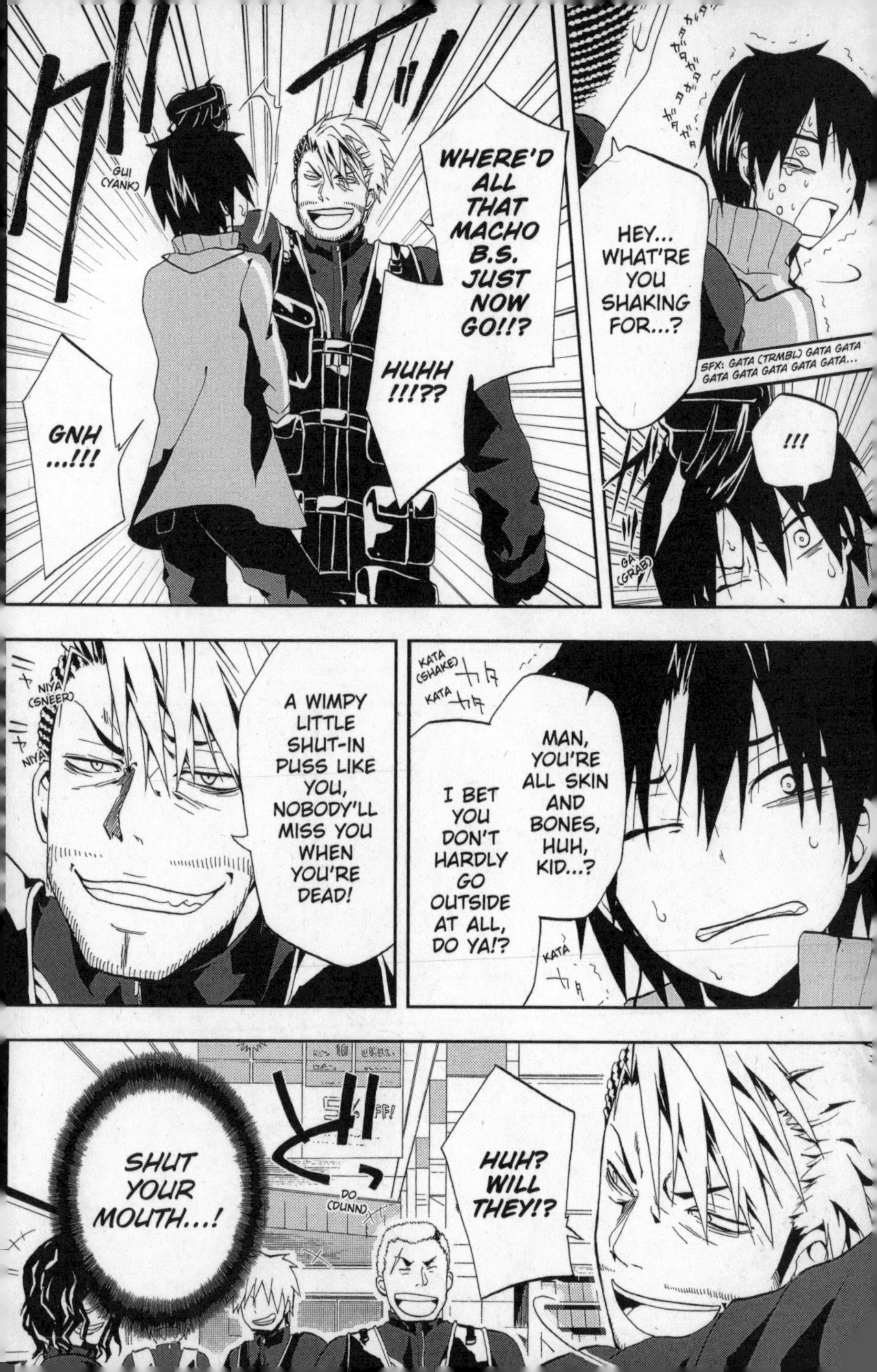
SFX: GATA (TRMBL) GATA GATA GATA GATA GATA GATA...
HEY... WHAT'RE YOU SHAKING FOR...?
!!!
GA (GRAB)
WHERE'D ALL THAT MACHO B.S. JUST NOW GO!!?
HUHH !!!??
GUI (YANK)
GNH ...!!!
KATA (SHAKE)
KATA
MAN, YOU'RE ALL SKIN AND BONES, HUH, KID...?
I BET YOU DON'T HARDLY GO OUTSIDE AT ALL, DO YA!?
KATA
A WIMPY LITTLE SHUT-IN PUSS LIKE YOU, NOBODY'LL MISS YOU WHEN YOU'RE DEAD!
NIYA (SNEER)
NIYA
HUH? WILL THEY!?
DO (DUNNN)
SHUT YOUR MOUTH...!

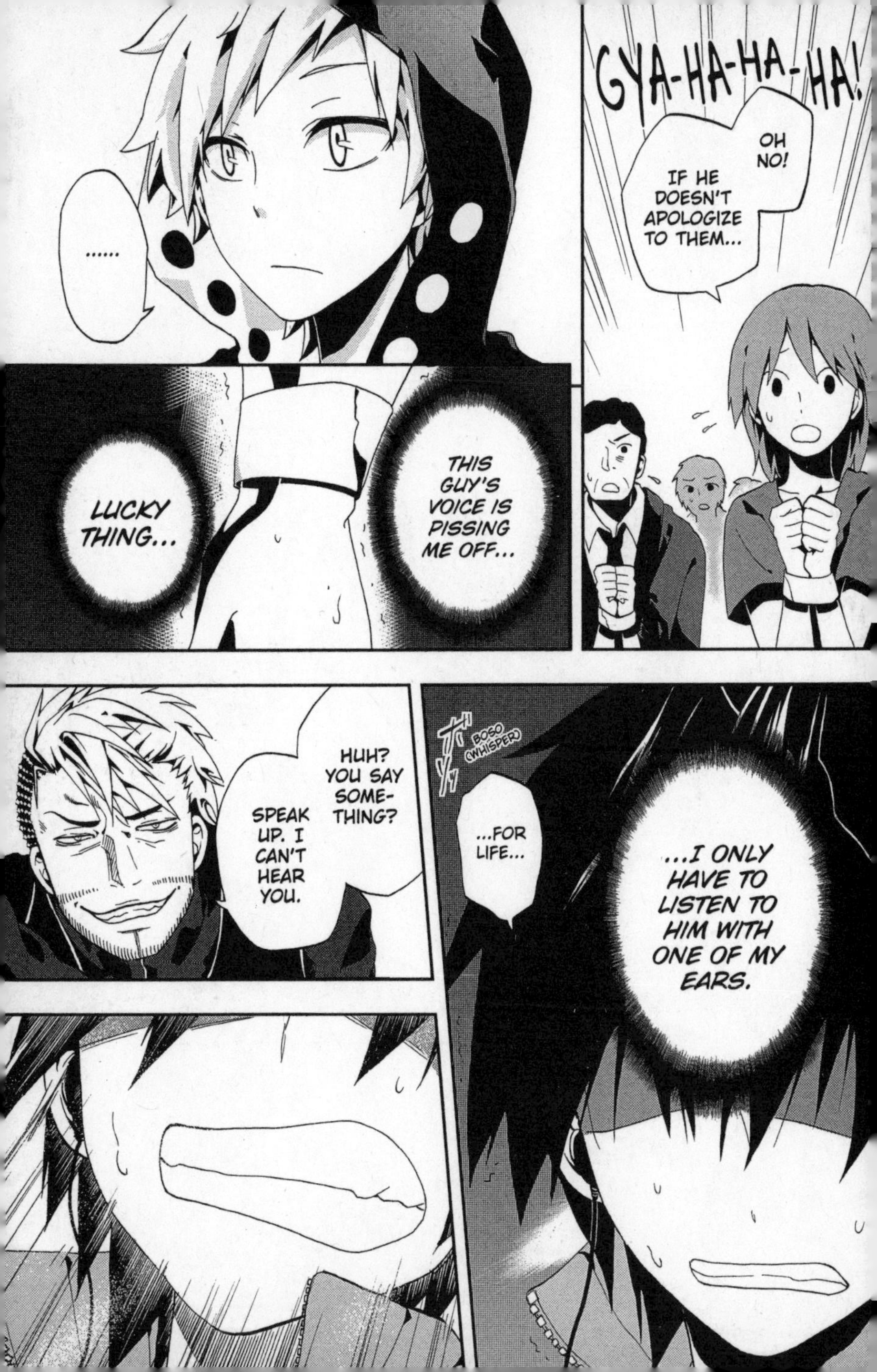
GYA-HA-HA-HA!
OH NO!
IF HE DOESN'T APOLOGIZE TO THEM...
......
THIS GUY'S VOICE IS PISSING ME OFF...
LUCKY THING...
BOSO (WHISPER)
...FOR LIFE...
...I ONLY HAVE TO LISTEN TO HIM WITH ONE OF MY EARS.
HUH? YOU SAY SOMETHING?
SPEAK UP. I CAN'T HEAR YOU.

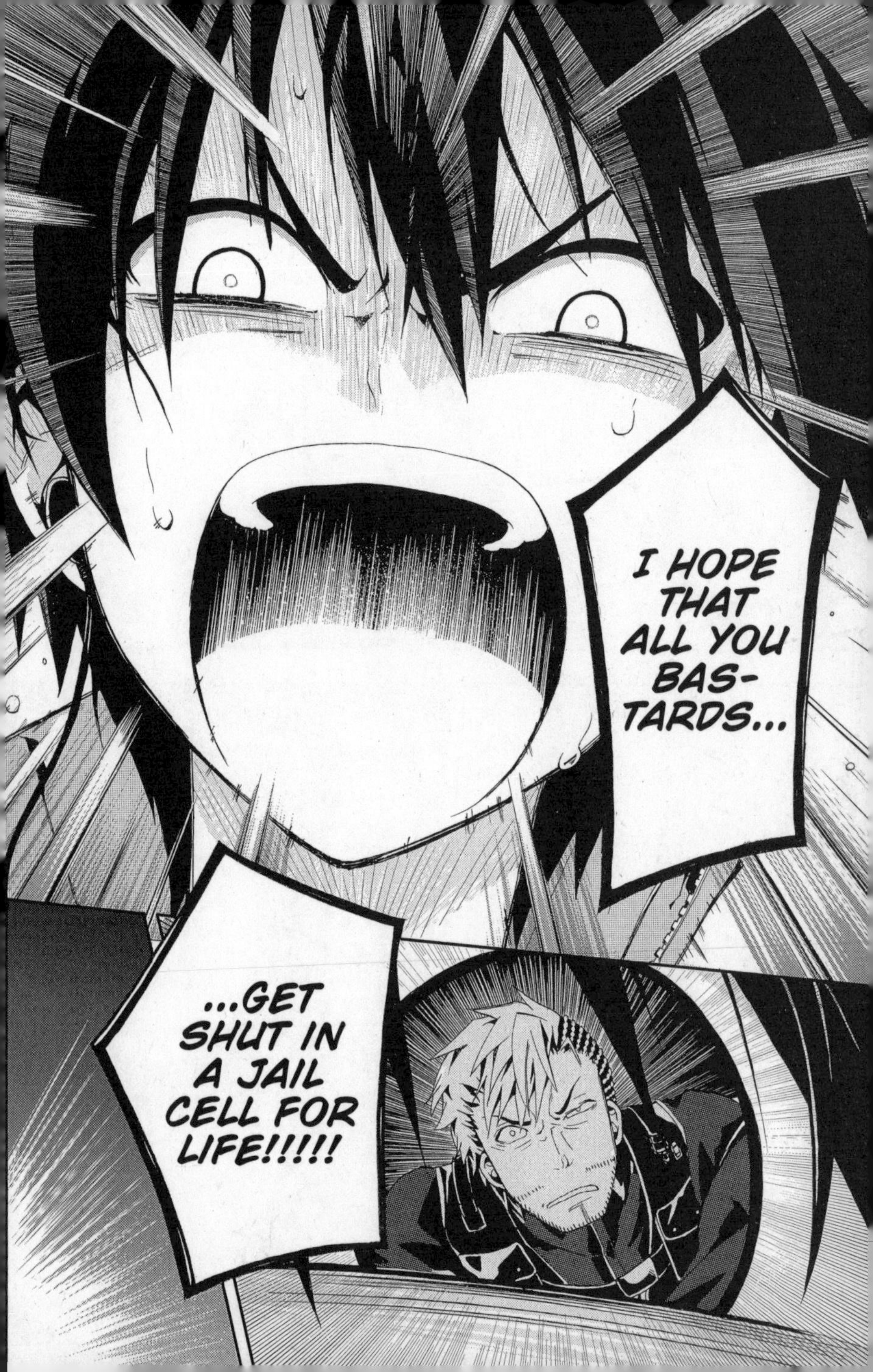
I HOPE THAT ALL YOU BAS-TARDS...
...GET SHUT IN A JAIL CELL FOR LIFE!!!!!

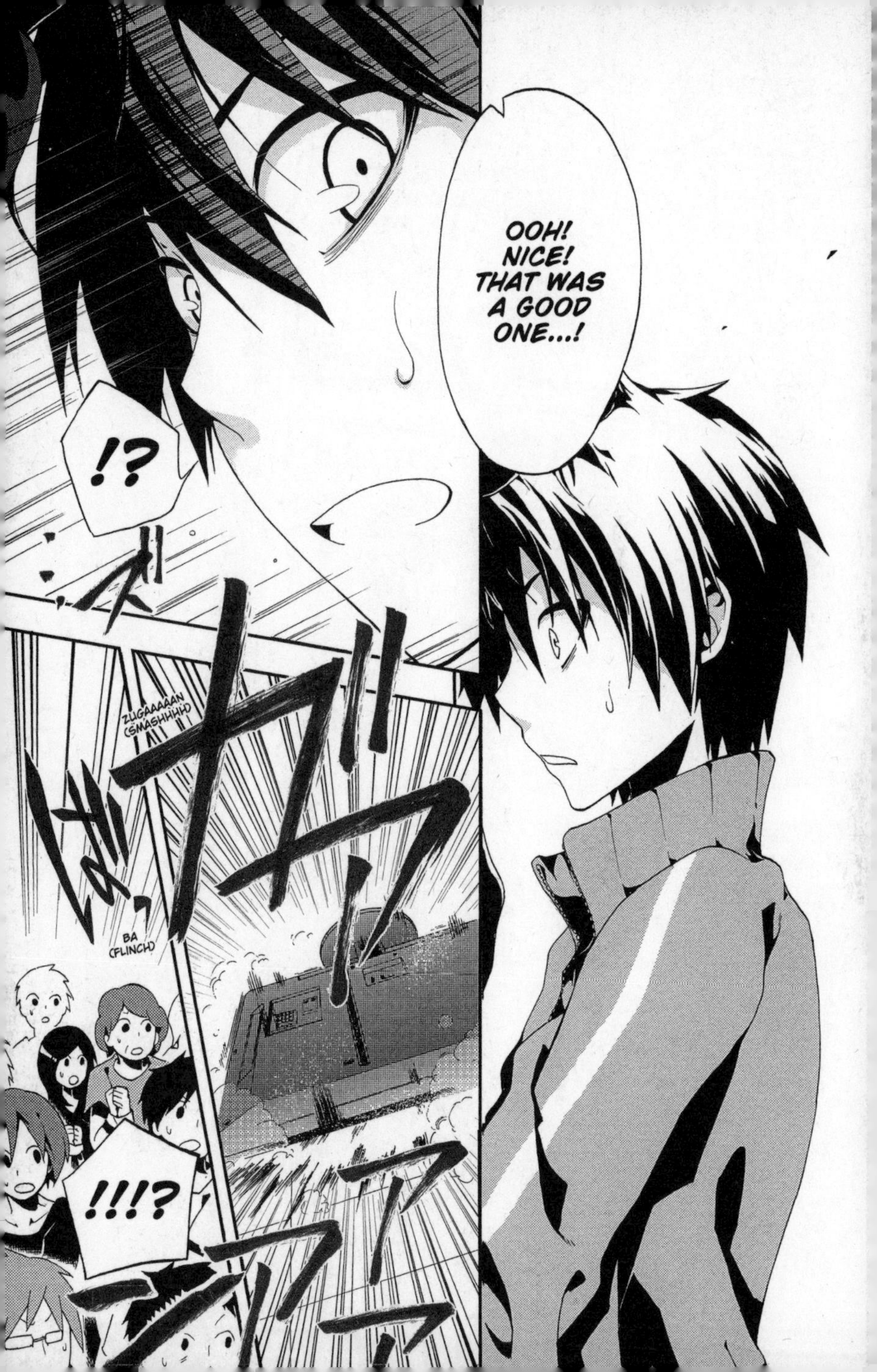
OOH! NICE! THAT WAS A GOOD ONE...!
!?
ZUGAAAAAN (SMASHHHH)
BA (FLINCH)
!!!?

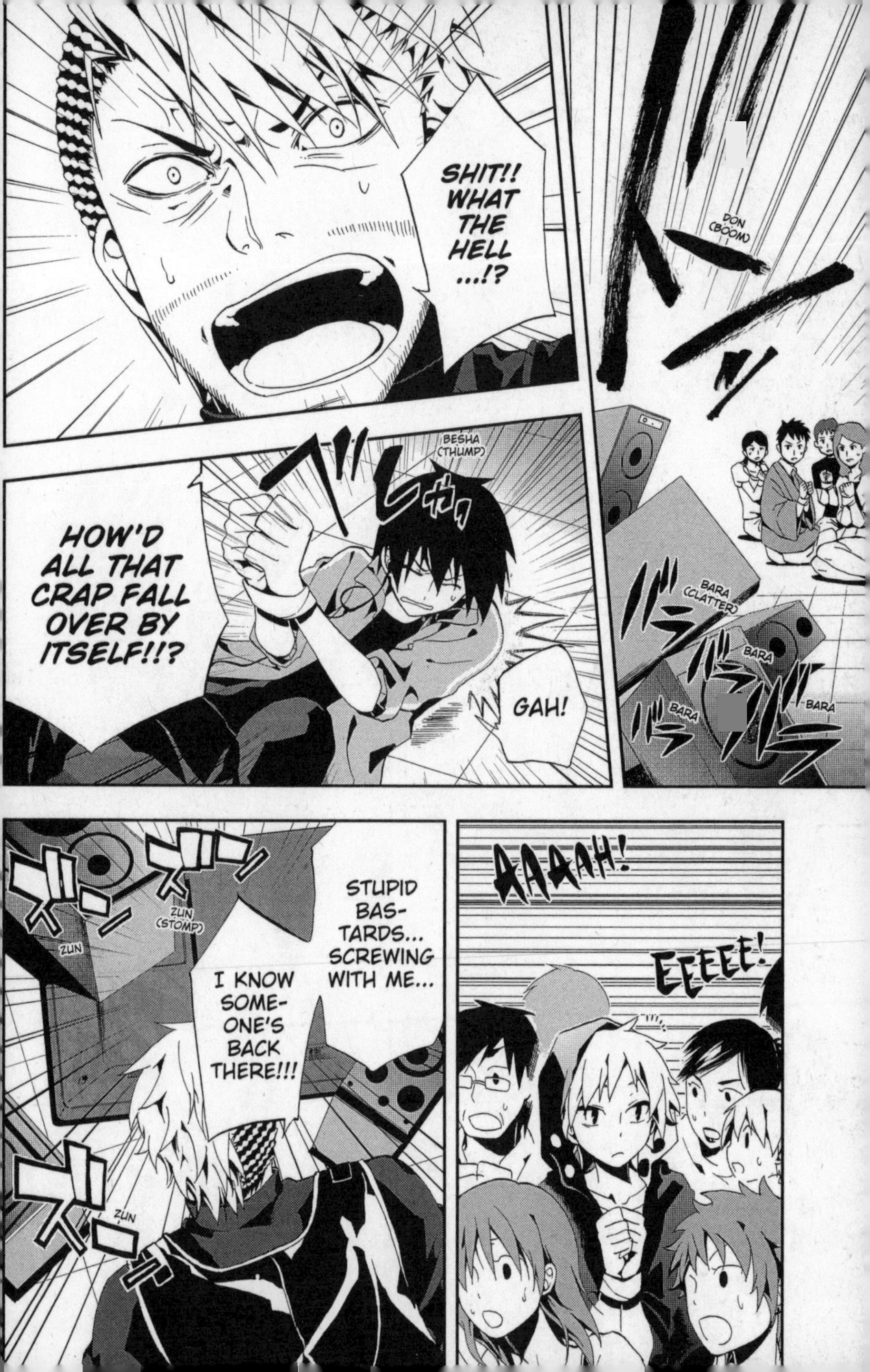
DON (BOOM)
BARA (CLATTER)
BARA
BARA
BARA
SHIT!! WHAT THE HELL ...!?
BESHA (THUMP)
HOW'D ALL THAT CRAP FALL OVER BY ITSELF!!?
GAH!
AAAAH!
EEEEE!
STUPID BAS-TARDS... SCREWING WITH ME...
I KNOW SOME-ONE'S BACK THERE!!!
ZUN (STOMP)
ZUN
ZUN

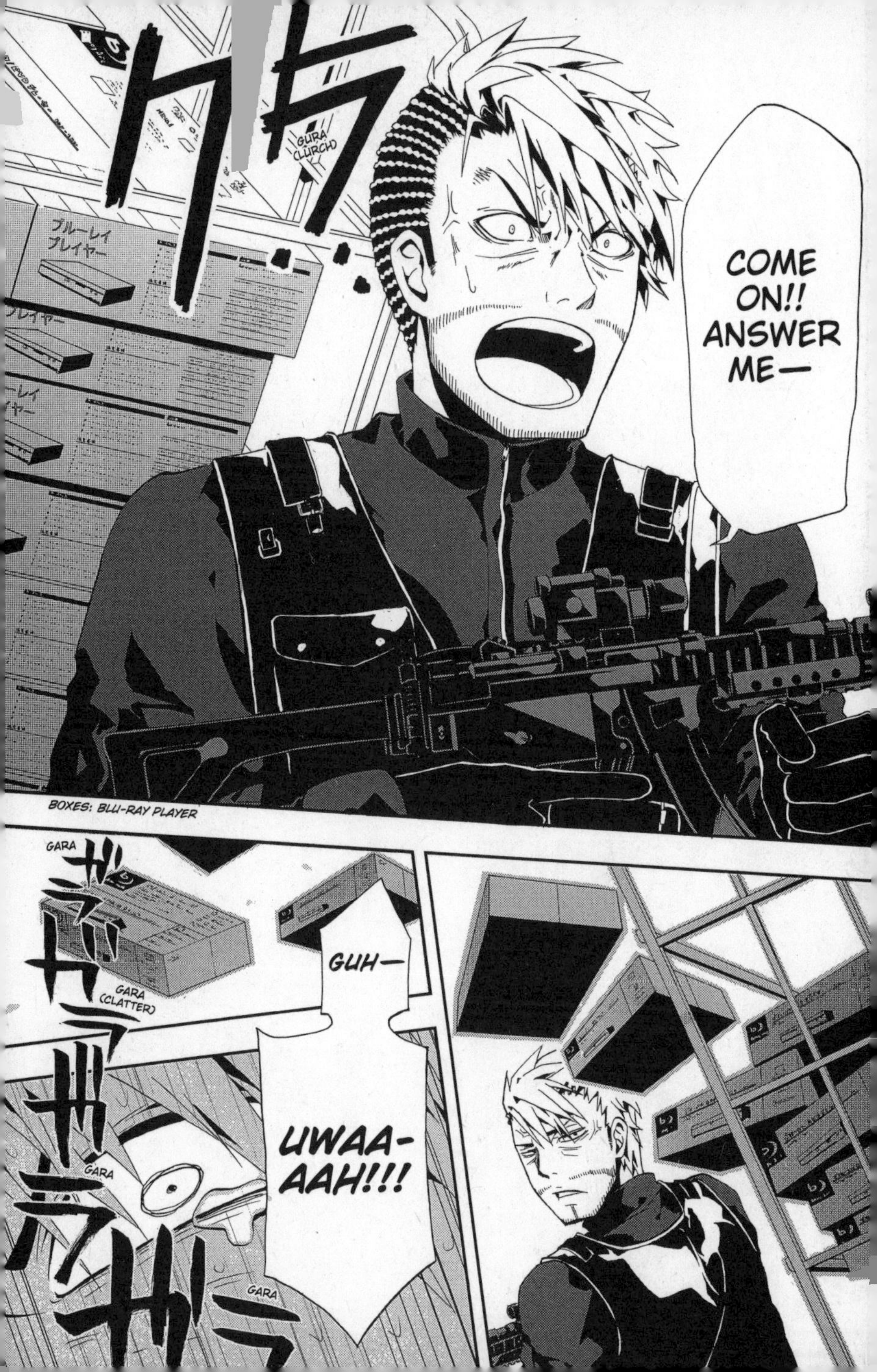
GURA (CLURCH)
ブルーレイ
プレイヤー
COME ON!! ANSWER ME—
GARA
GARA (CLATTER)
GARA
GARA
GUH—
UWAA-AAH!!!
BOXES: BLU-RAY PLAYER

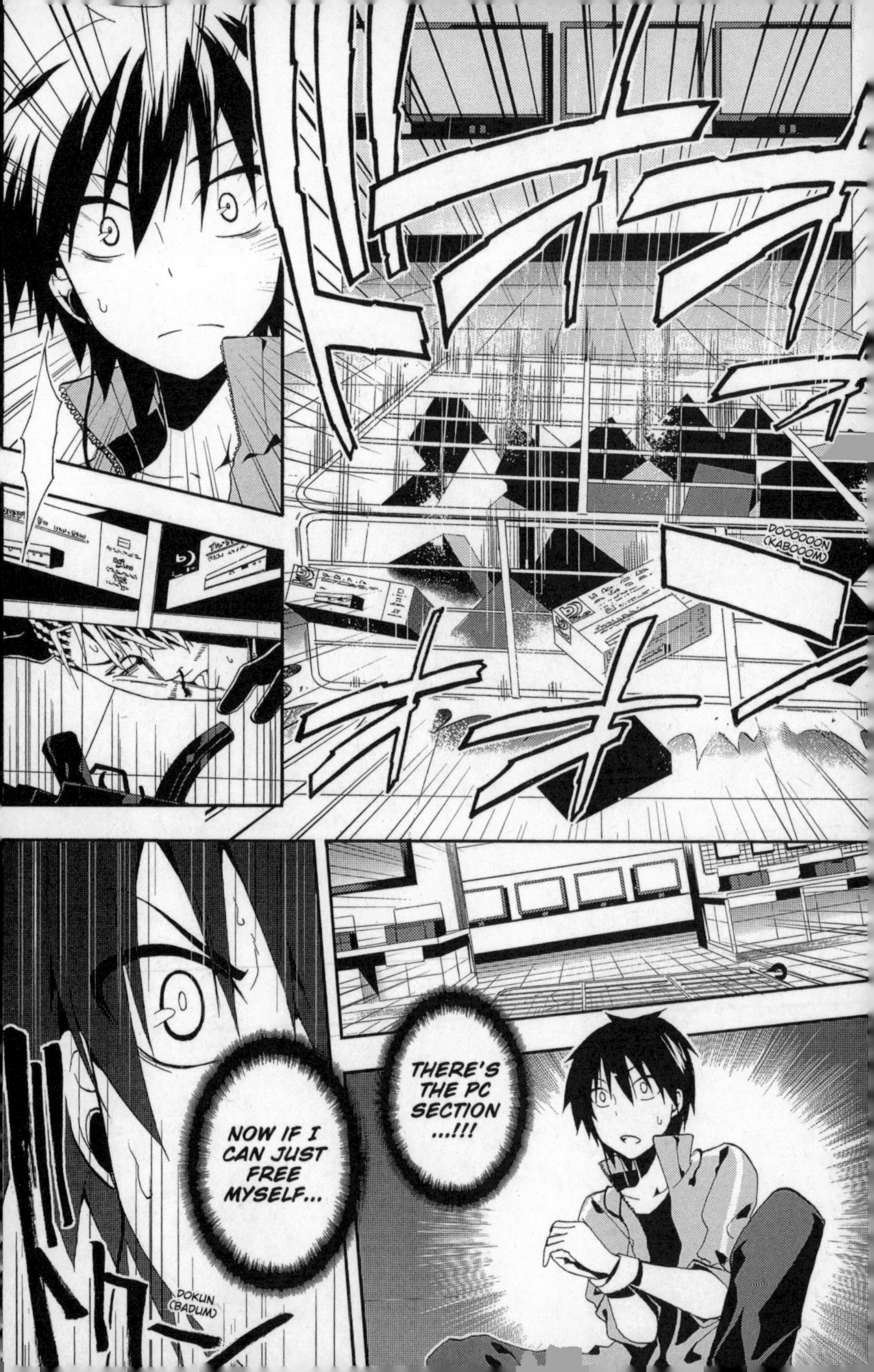
DOOOOOON
(KABOOOM)
THERE'S THE PC SECTION ...!!!
NOW IF I CAN JUST FREE MYSELF...
DOKUN
(BADUM)

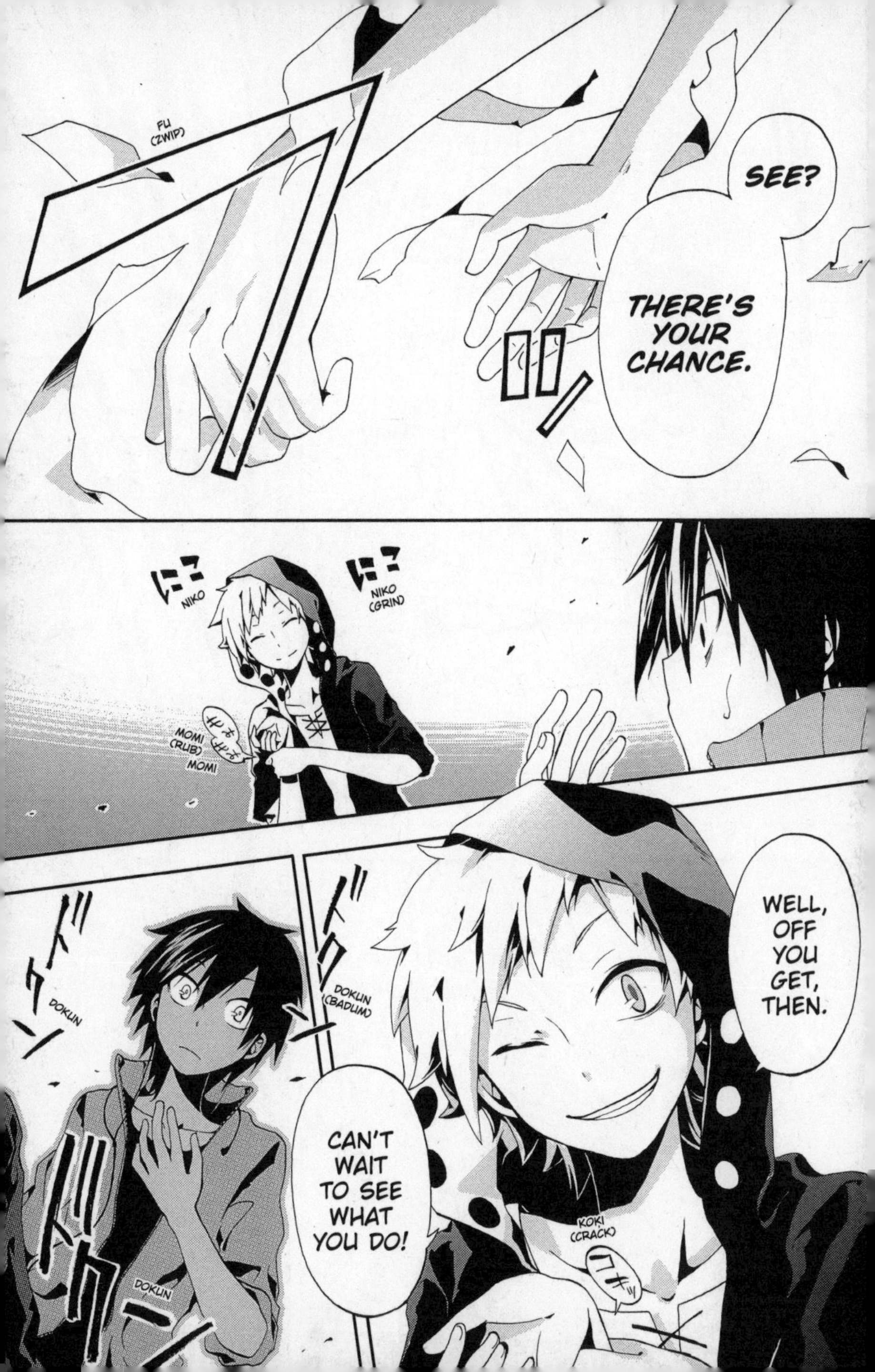
SEE?
THERE'S YOUR CHANCE.
FU (ZWIP)
NIKO (GRIN)
NIKO
MOMI (RUB) MOMI
WELL, OFF YOU GET, THEN.
CAN'T WAIT TO SEE WHAT YOU DO!
KOKI (CRACK)
DOKUN (BADUM)
DOKUN
DOKUN

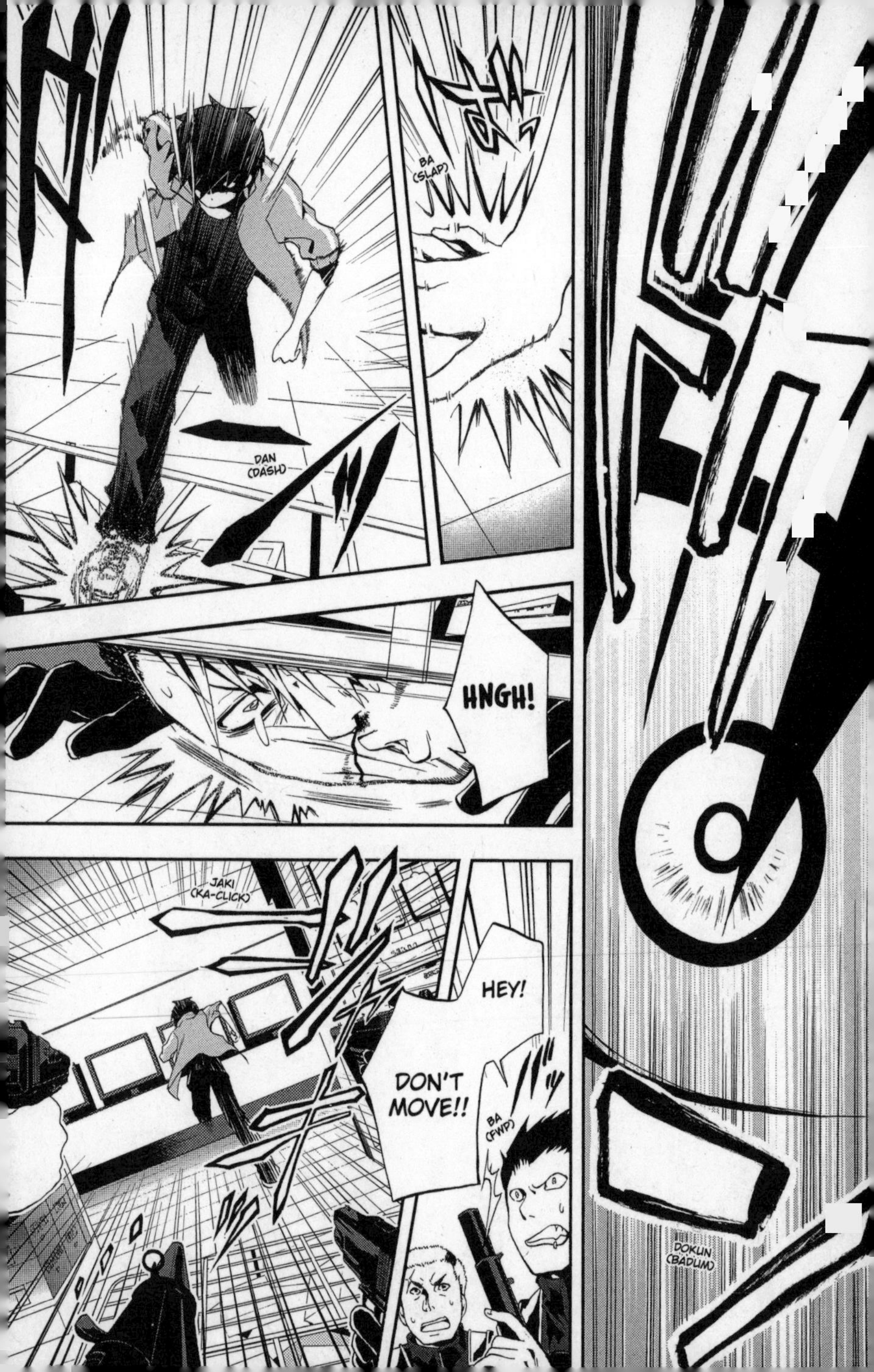
DOKUN (BADUM)
BA (SLAP)
DAN (DASH)
HNGH!
JAKI (KA-CLICK)
HEY!
DON'T MOVE!!
BA (FWP)

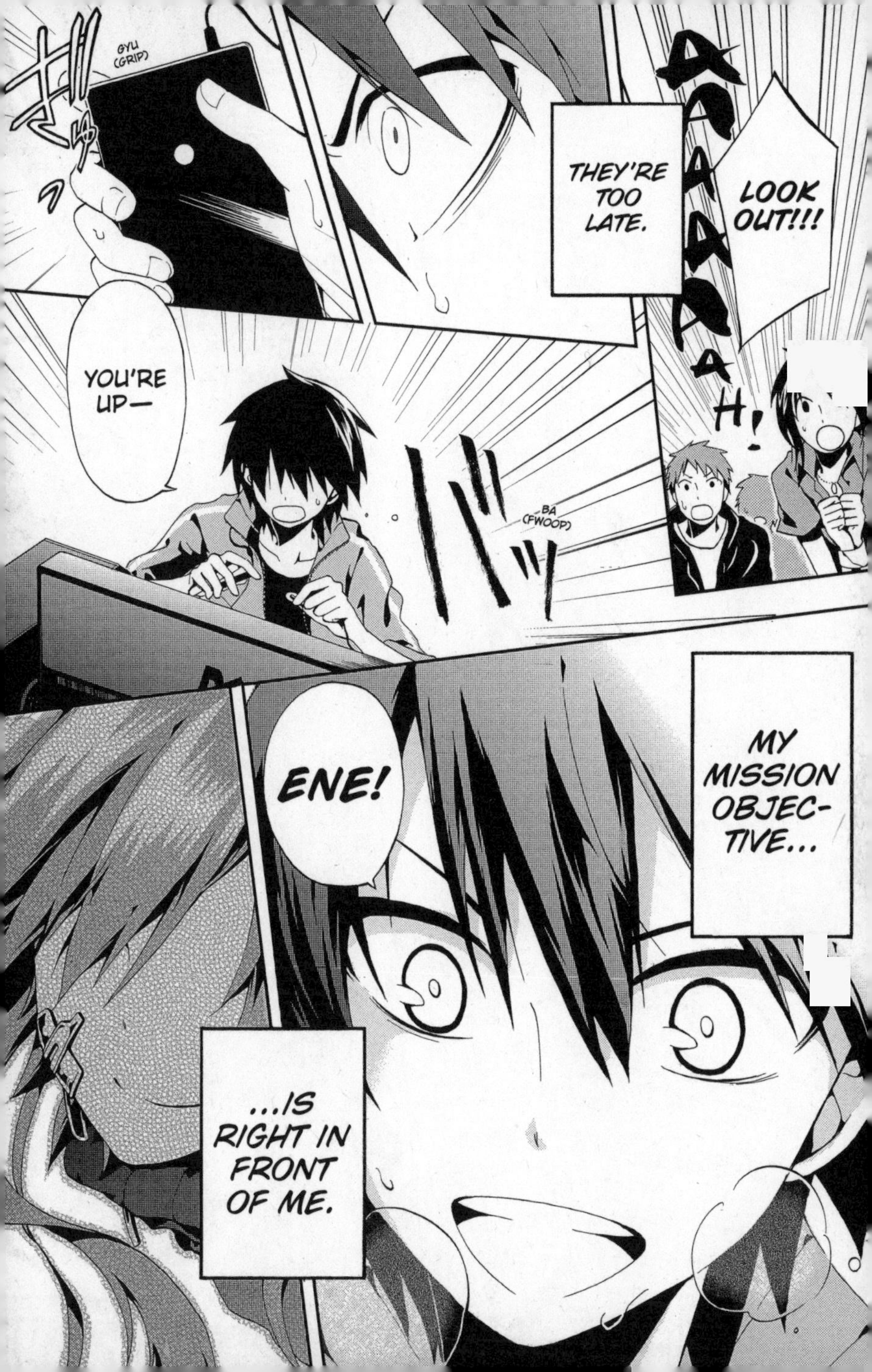
LOOK OUT!!!
AAAAAAH!
THEY'RE TOO LATE.
GYU (GRIP)
YOU'RE UP—
BA (FWOOP)
MY MISSION OBJEC-TIVE...
ENE!
...IS RIGHT IN FRONT OF ME.

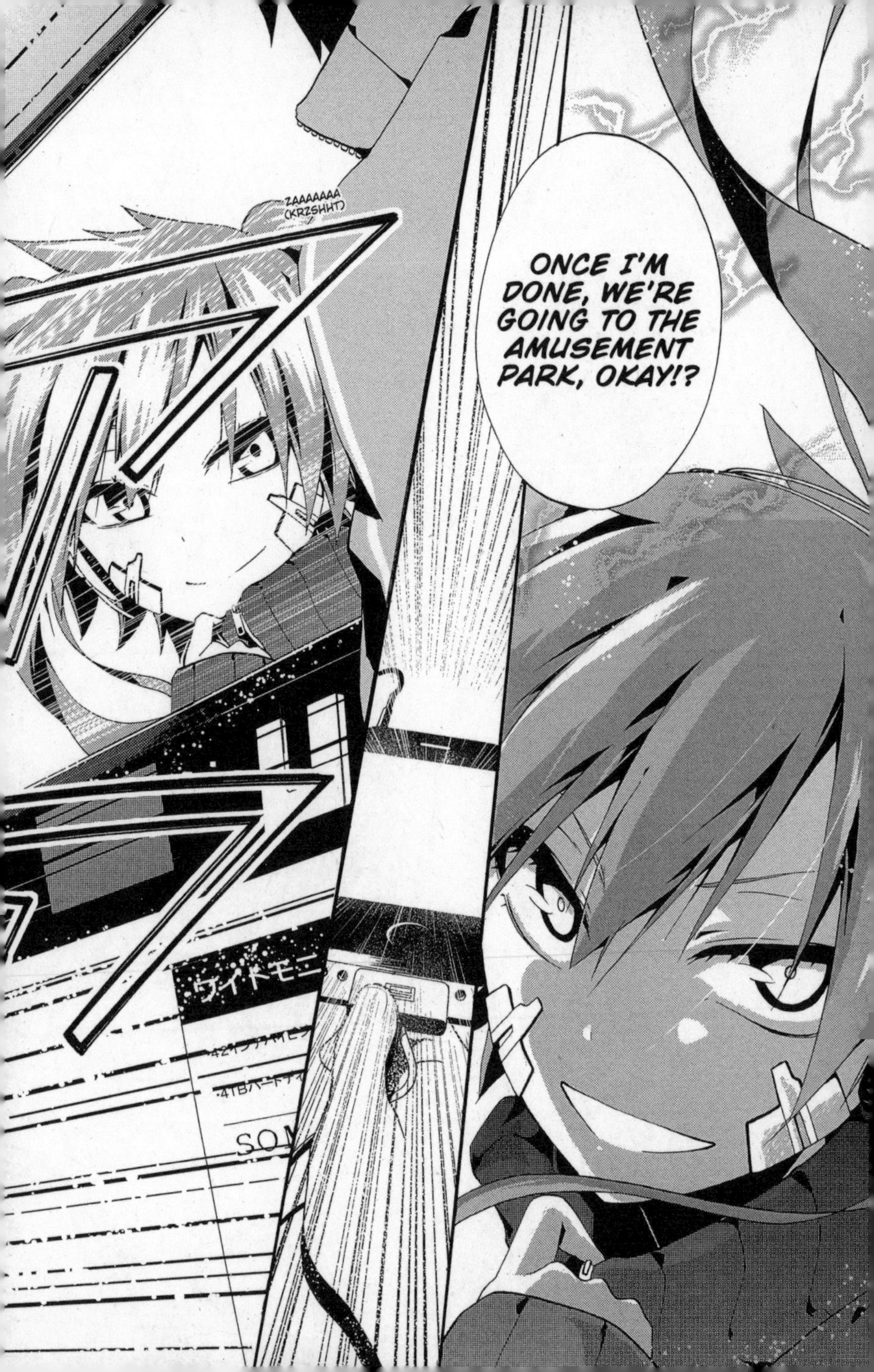
ONCE I'M DONE, WE'RE GOING TO THE AMUSEMENT PARK, OKAY!?
ZAAAAAAA (KRZSHHT)

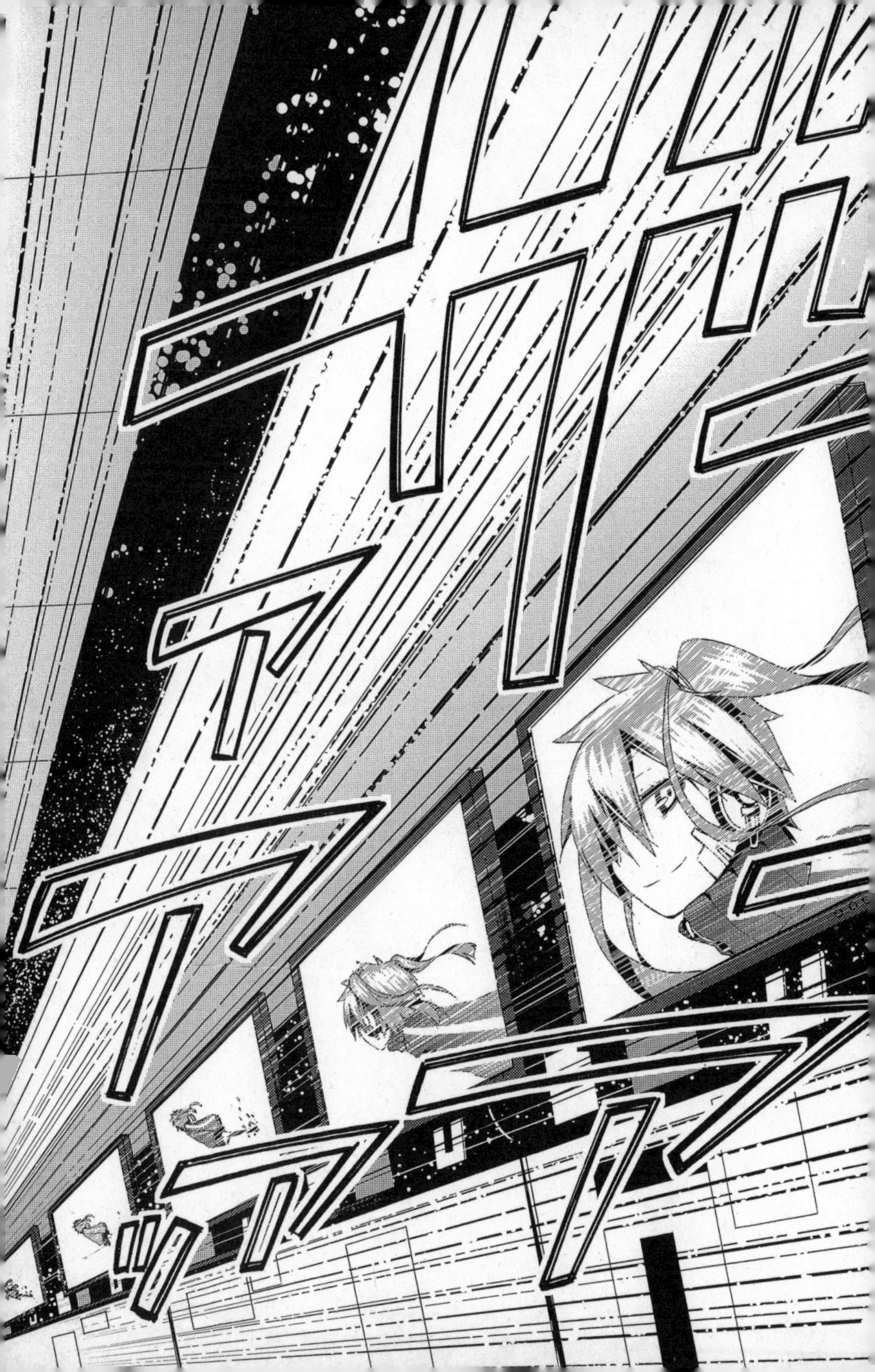

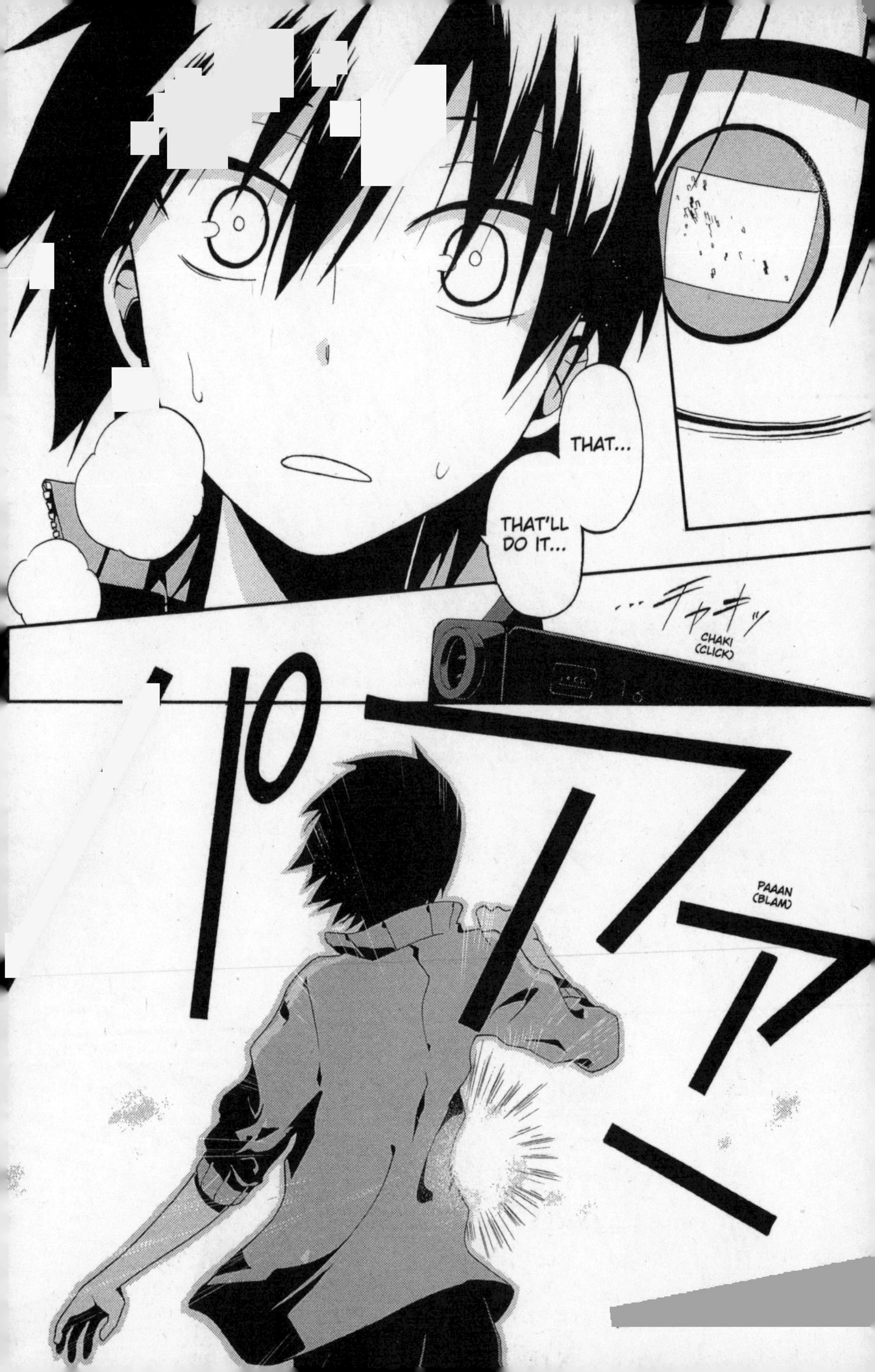
THAT...
THAT'LL DO IT...
…チャキッ
CHAKI (CLICK)
PAAAN (BLAM)

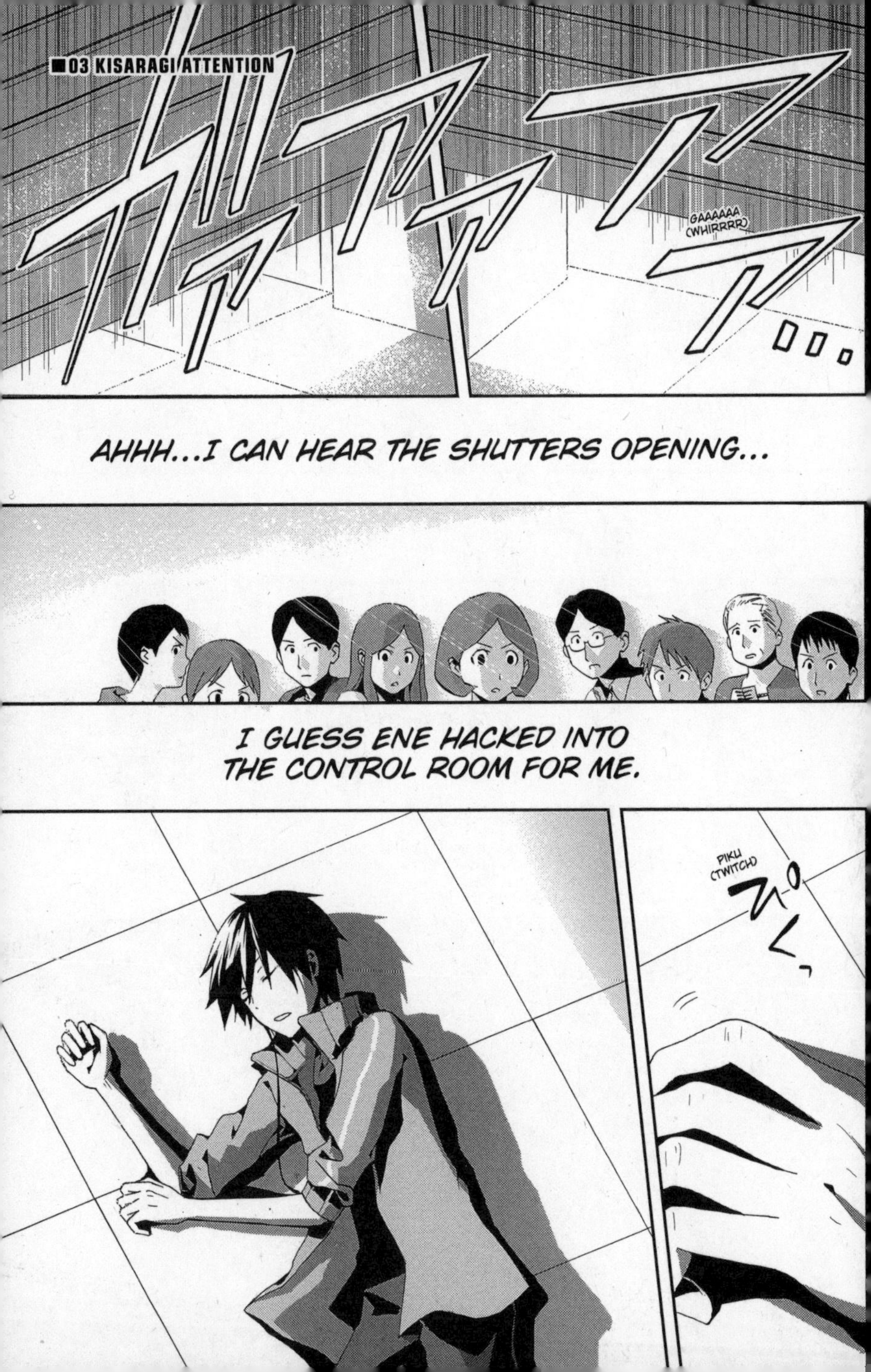
GAAAAAA
(WHIRRRR)
AHHH...I CAN HEAR THE SHUTTERS OPENING...
I GUESS ENE HACKED INTO THE CONTROL ROOM FOR ME.
PIKU
(TWITCH)

BUT I CAN'T...I...

...I'M LOSING CONSCIOUSNESS......

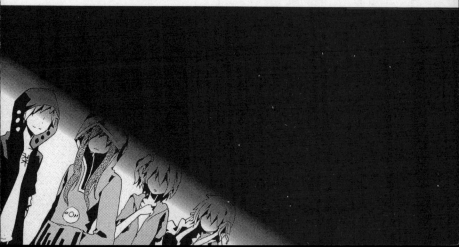

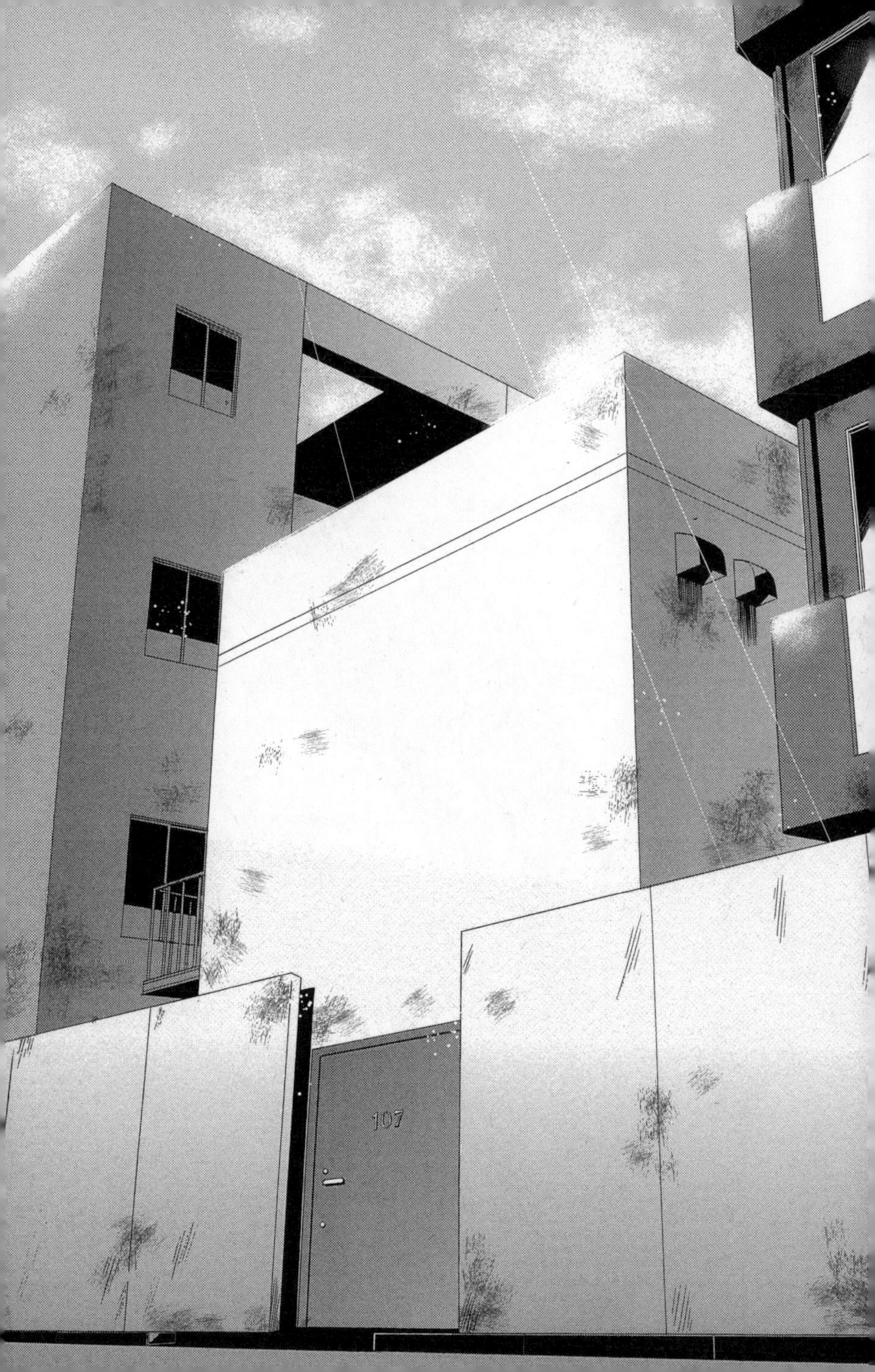
107

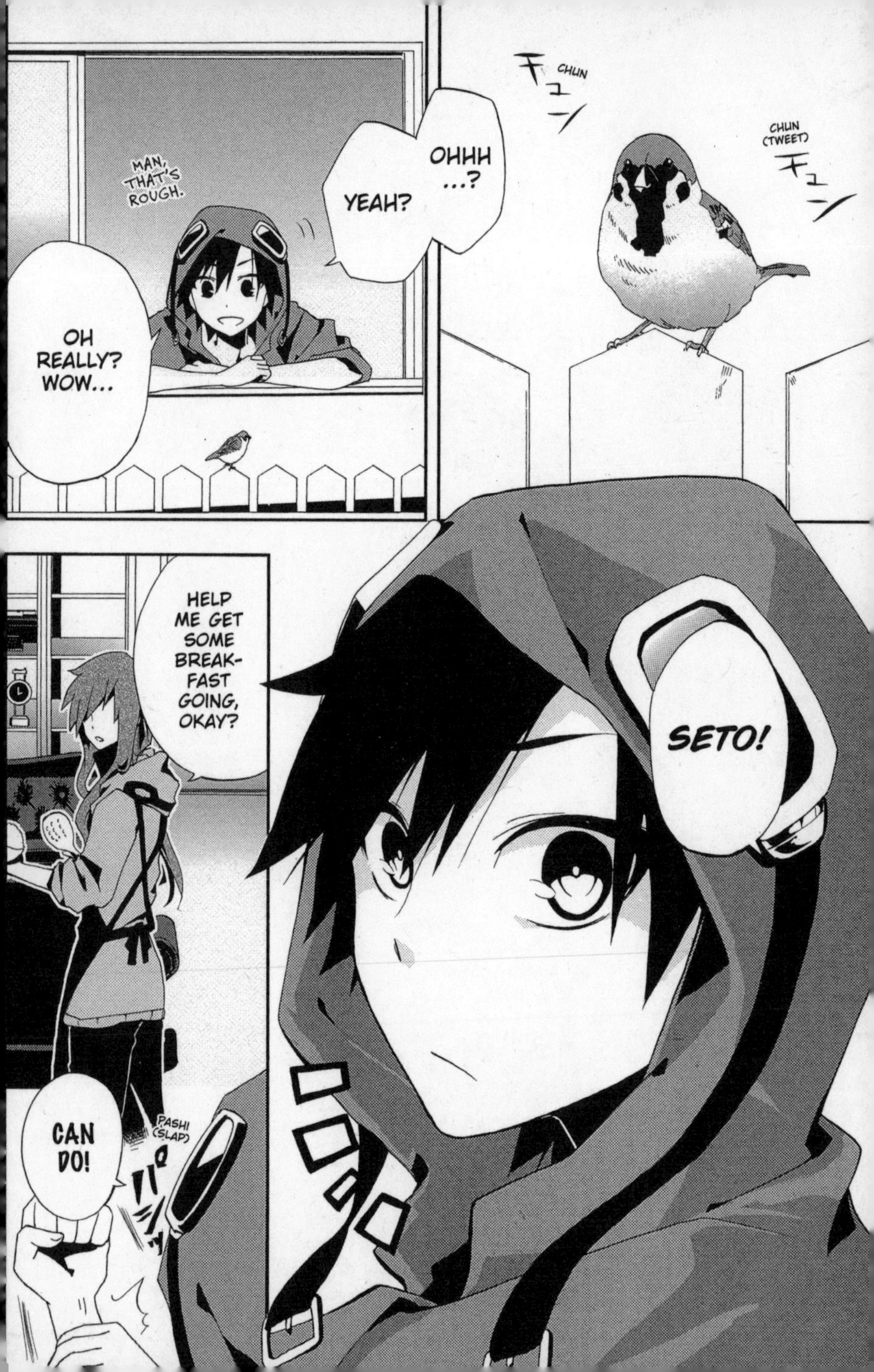
チュン
CHUN
CHUN (TWEET)
チュン
OHHH ...? YEAH?
MAN, THAT'S ROUGH.
OH REALLY? WOW...
SETO!
HELP ME GET SOME BREAK-FAST GOING, OKAY?
CAN DO!
PASHI (SLAP)

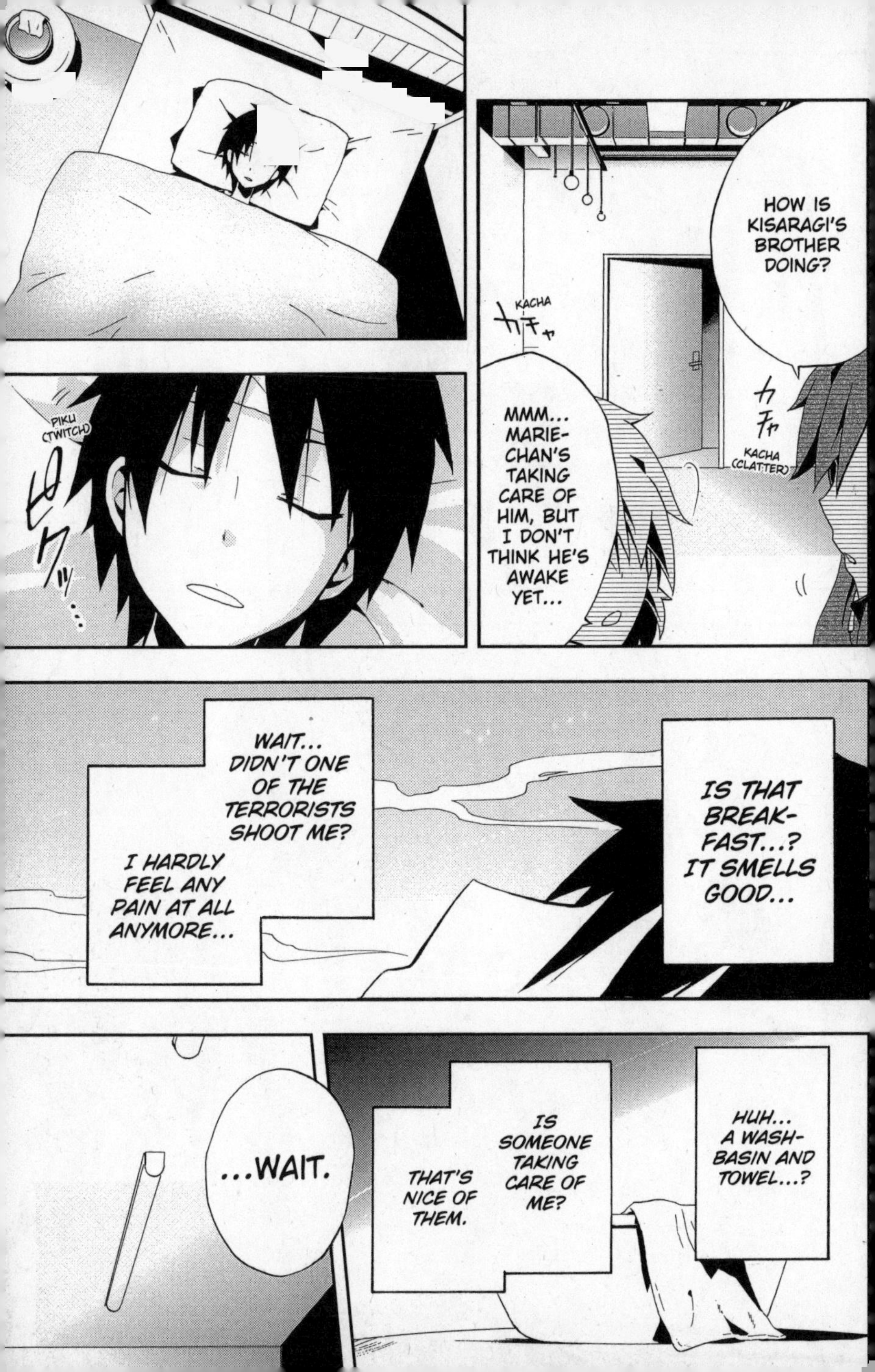
HOW IS KISARAGI'S BROTHER DOING?
KACHA
KACHA (CLATTER)
MMM... MARIE-CHAN'S TAKING CARE OF HIM, BUT I DON'T THINK HE'S AWAKE YET...
PIKU (TWITCH)
IS THAT BREAK-FAST...? IT SMELLS GOOD...
WAIT... DIDN'T ONE OF THE TERRORISTS SHOOT ME?
I HARDLY FEEL ANY PAIN AT ALL ANYMORE...
HUH... A WASH-BASIN AND TOWEL...?
IS SOMEONE TAKING CARE OF ME?
THAT'S NICE OF THEM.
...WAIT.

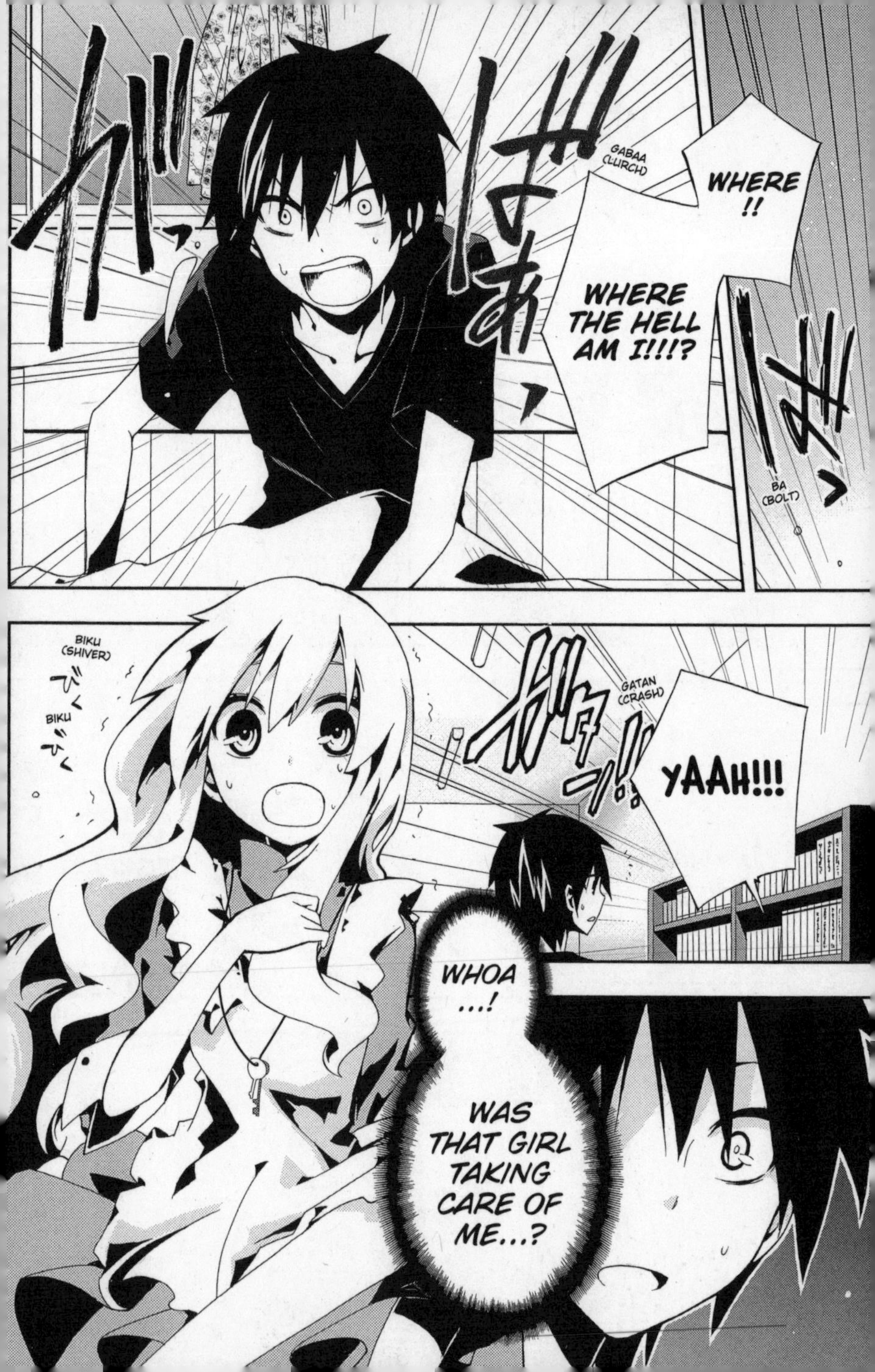
WHERE !!
GABAA (LURCH)
WHERE THE HELL AM I!!!?
BA (BOLT)
YAAH!!!
GATAN (CRASH)
BIKU (SHIVER)
BIKU
WHOA ...!
WAS THAT GIRL TAKING CARE OF ME...?

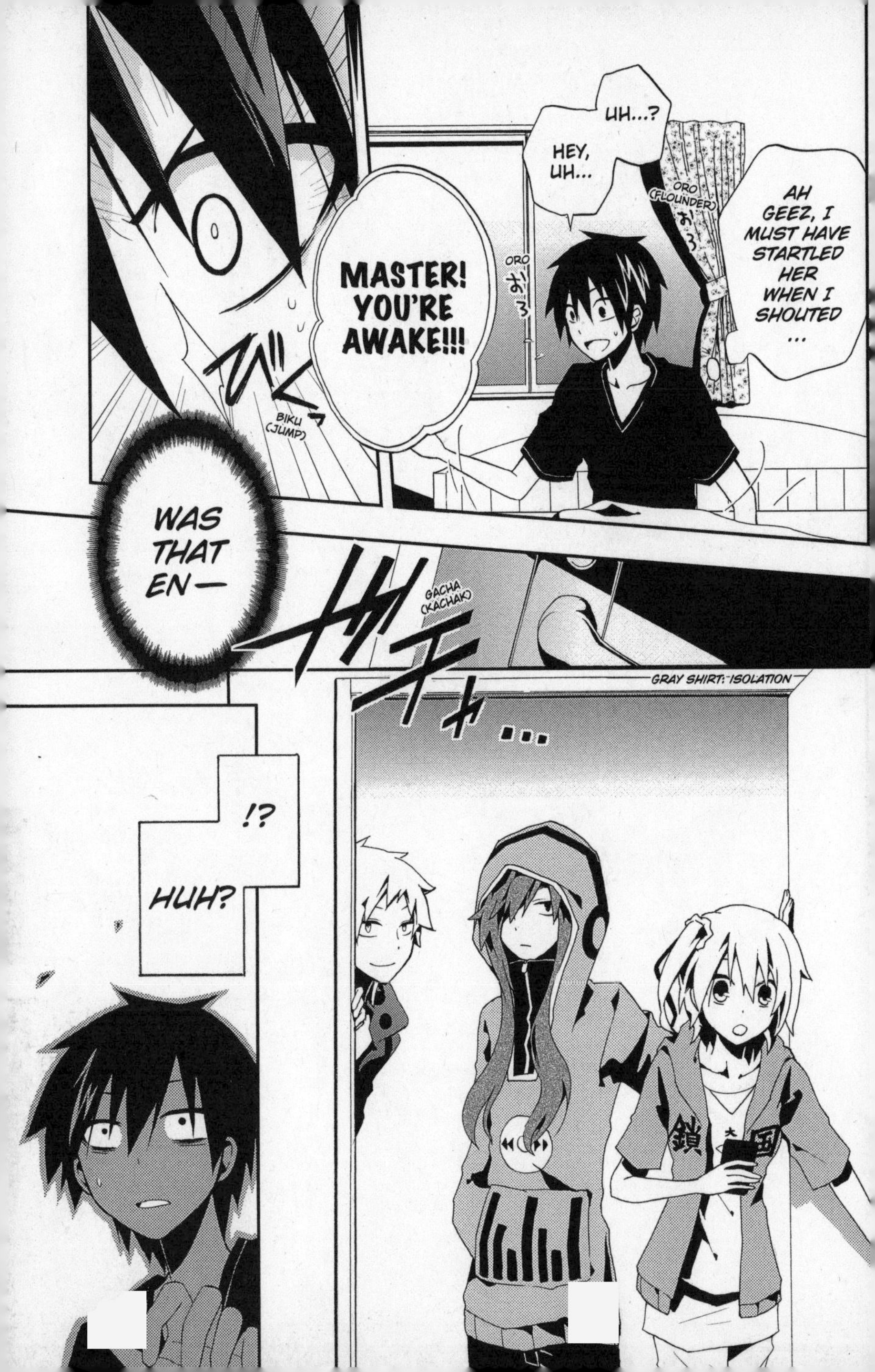
AH GEEZ, I MUST HAVE STARTLED HER WHEN I SHOUTED...
UH...?
HEY, UH...
ORO (FLOUNDER)
ORO
MASTER! YOU'RE AWAKE!!!
BIKU (JUMP)
GACHA (KACHAK)
WAS THAT EN—
GRAY SHIRT: ISOLATION
...
!?
HUH?

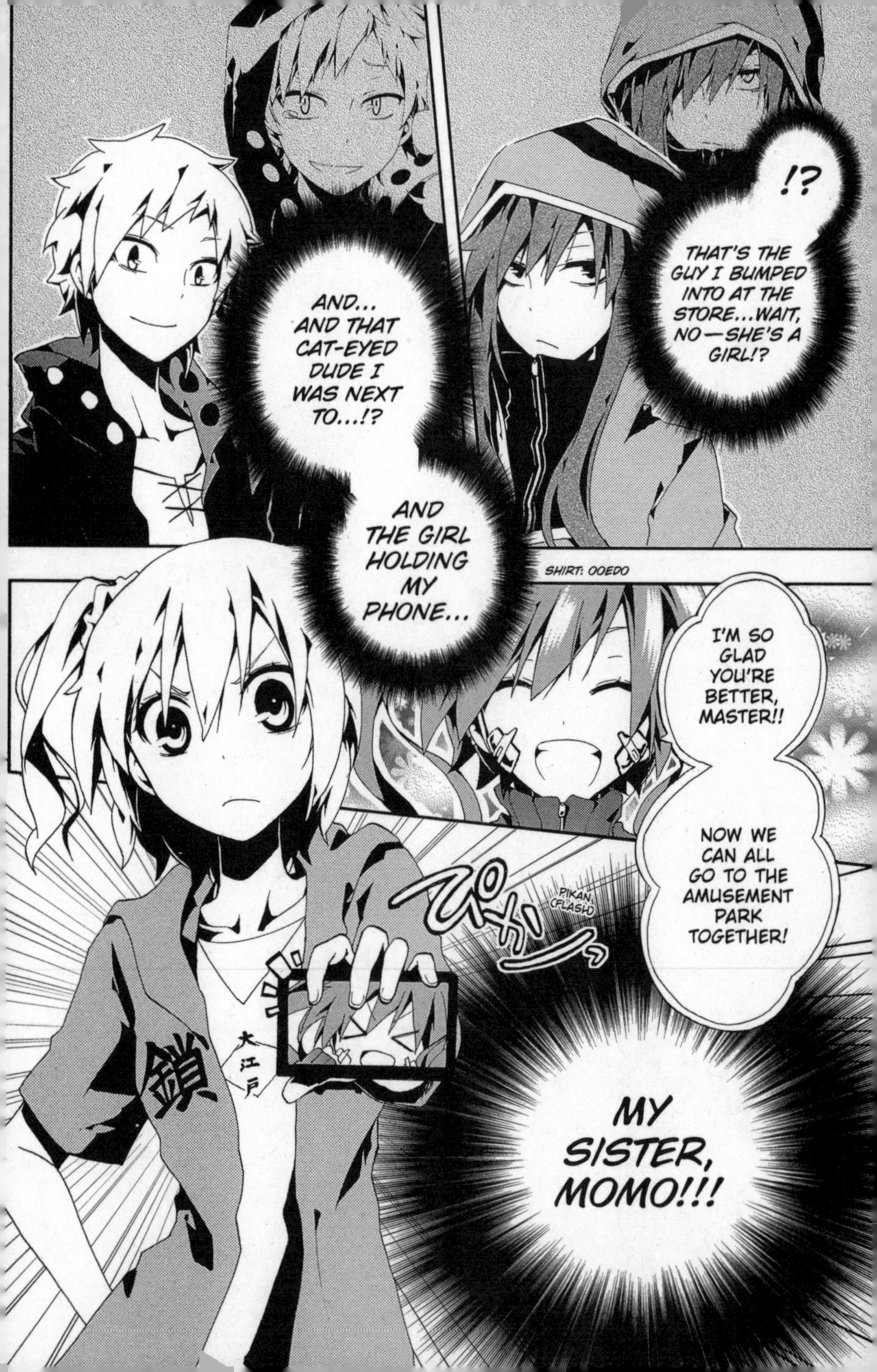
!?
THAT'S THE GUY I BUMPED INTO AT THE STORE...WAIT, NO—SHE'S A GIRL!?
AND... AND THAT CAT-EYED DUDE I WAS NEXT TO...!?
AND THE GIRL HOLDING MY PHONE...
SHIRT: OOEDO
I'M SO GLAD YOU'RE BETTER, MASTER!!
NOW WE CAN ALL GO TO THE AMUSEMENT PARK TOGETHER!
PIKAN (FLASH)
鎖
大江戸
MY SISTER, MOMO!!!

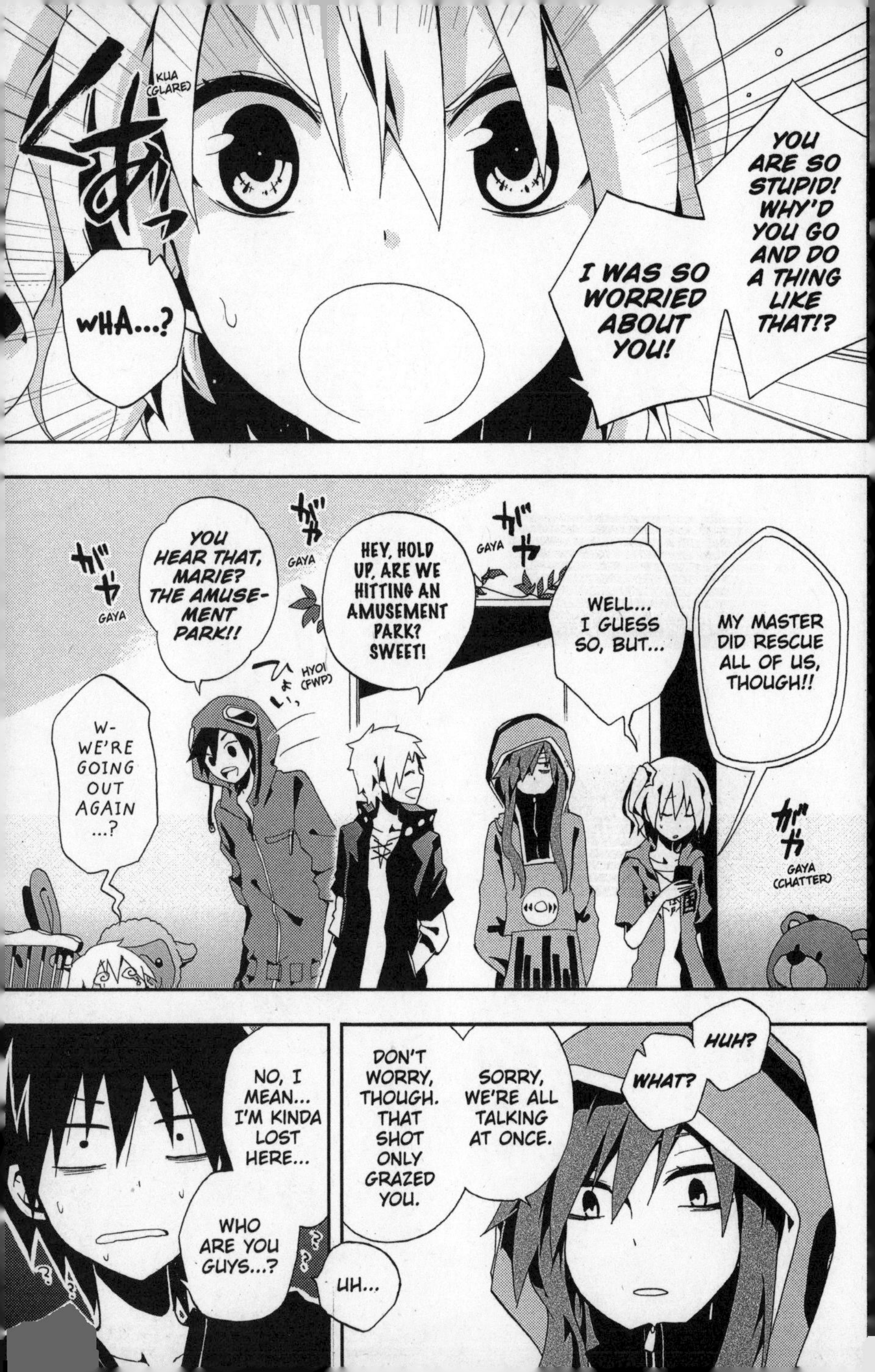
YOU ARE SO STUPID! WHY'D YOU GO AND DO A THING LIKE THAT!?
I WAS SO WORRIED ABOUT YOU!
KUA (GLARE)
WHA...?
GAYA (CHATTER)
MY MASTER DID RESCUE ALL OF US, THOUGH!!
WELL... I GUESS SO, BUT...
GAYA
HEY, HOLD UP, ARE WE HITTING AN AMUSEMENT PARK? SWEET!
GAYA
YOU HEAR THAT, MARIE? THE AMUSE-MENT PARK!!
HYOI (FWP)
GAYA
W-WE'RE GOING OUT AGAIN...?
HUH?
WHAT?
SORRY, WE'RE ALL TALKING AT ONCE.
DON'T WORRY, THOUGH. THAT SHOT ONLY GRAZED YOU.
NO, I MEAN... I'M KINDA LOST HERE...
WHO ARE YOU GUYS...?
UH...

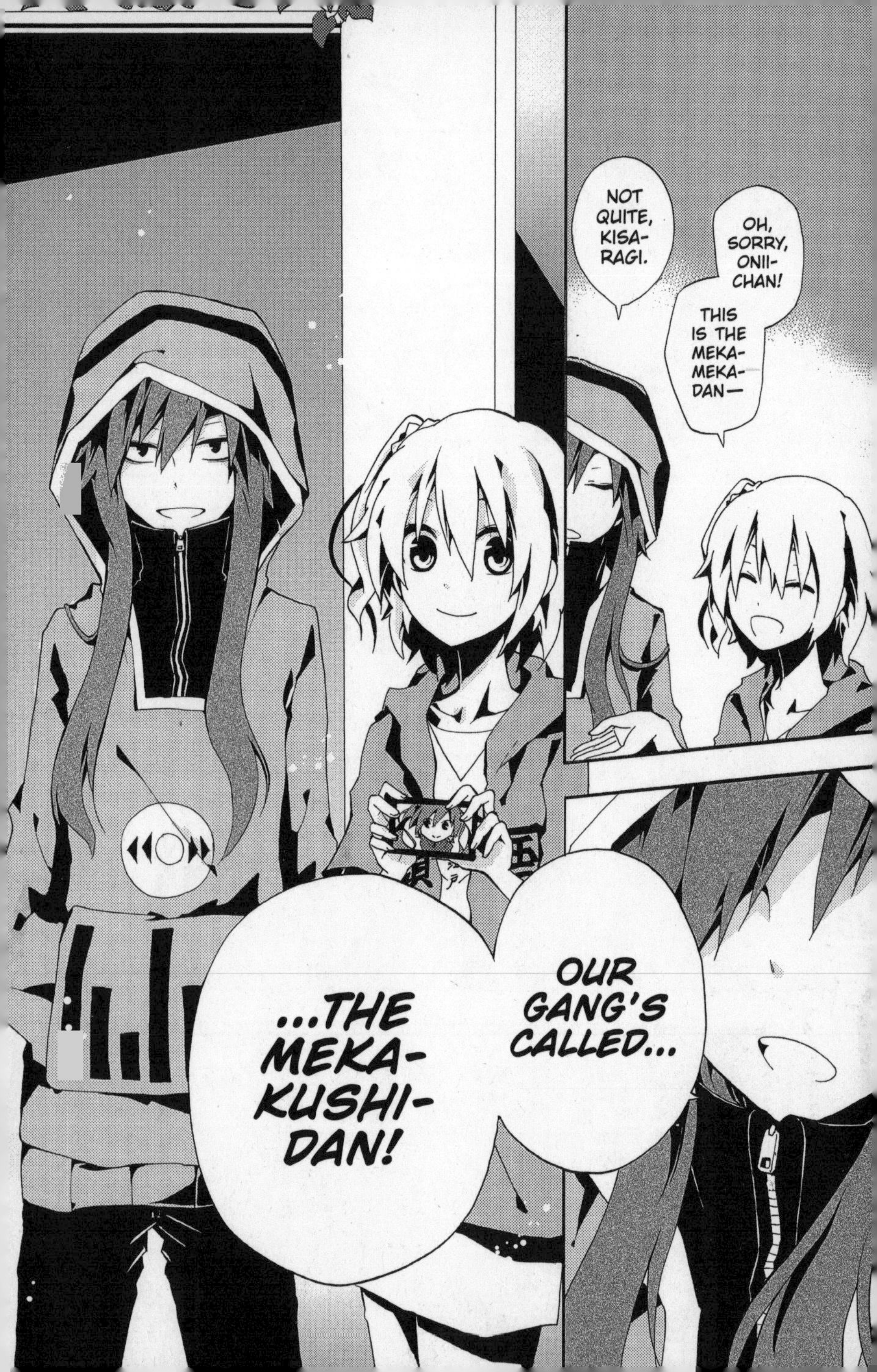
OH, SORRY, ONII-CHAN!
THIS IS THE MEKA-MEKA-DAN—
NOT QUITE, KISA-RAGI.
OUR GANG'S CALLED...
...THE MEKA-KUSHI-DAN!

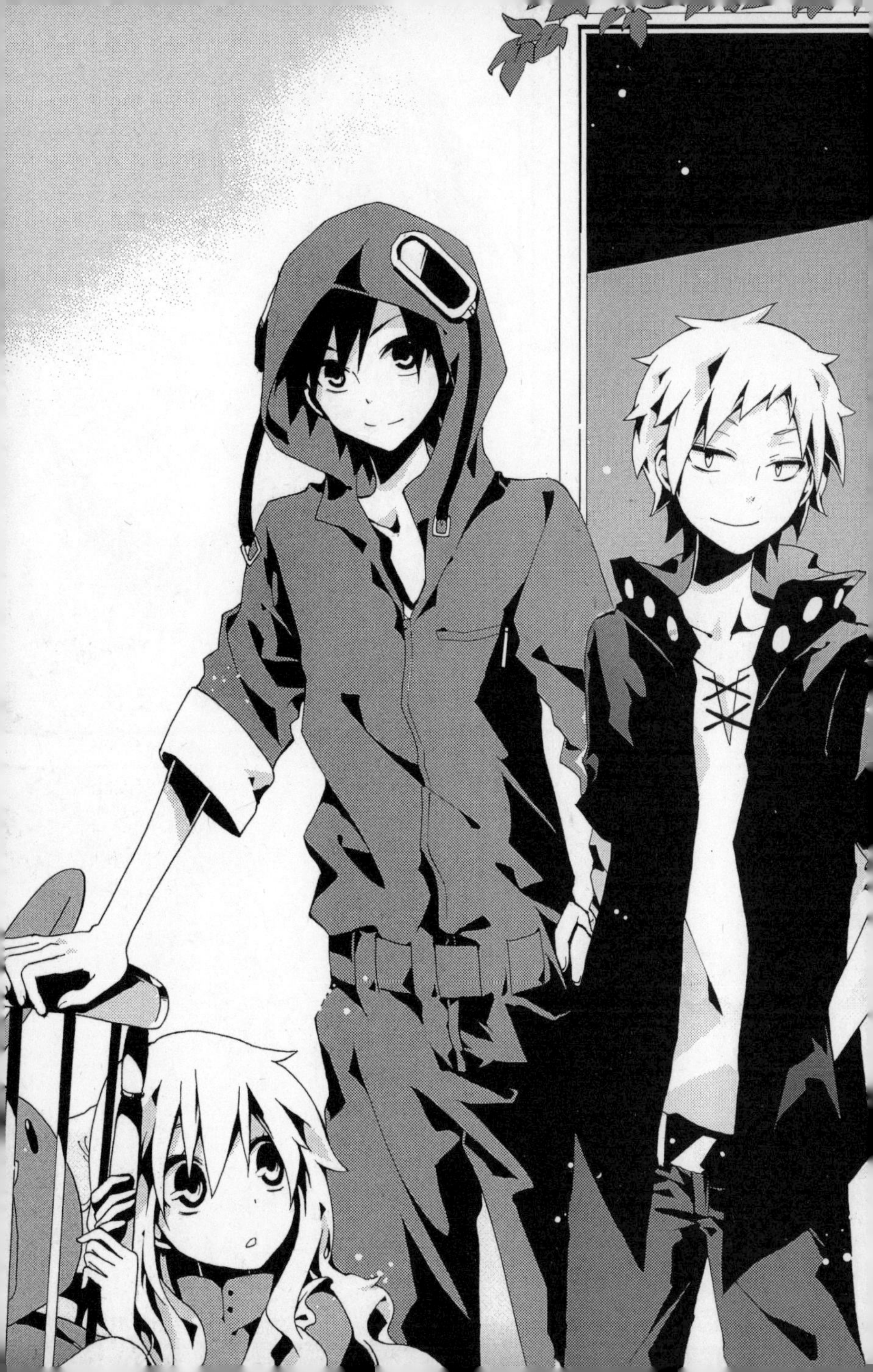

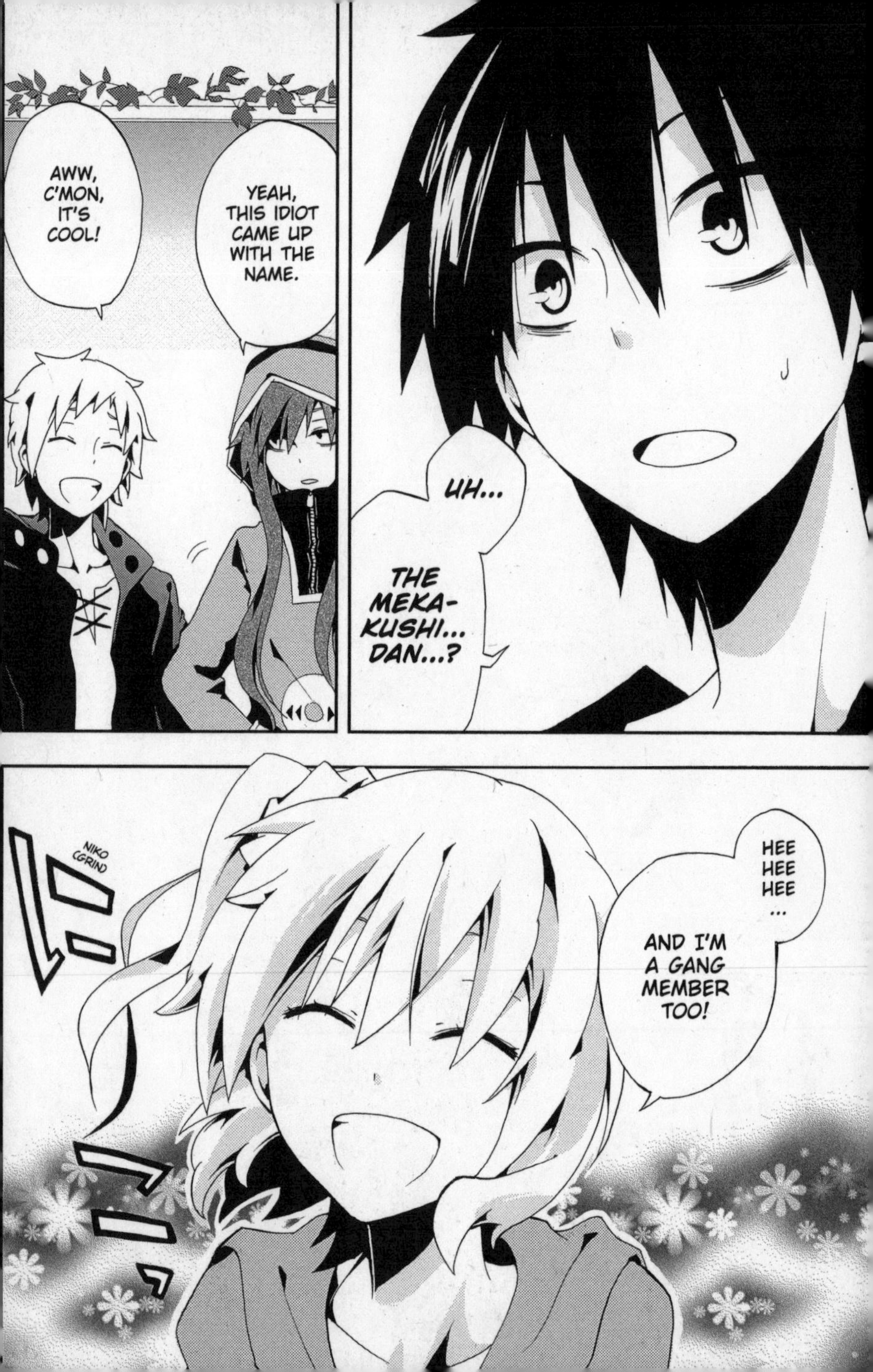
UH...
THE MEKA-KUSHI... DAN...?
YEAH, THIS IDIOT CAME UP WITH THE NAME.
AWW, C'MON, IT'S COOL!
HEE HEE HEE ...
AND I'M A GANG MEMBER TOO!
NIKO (GRIN)

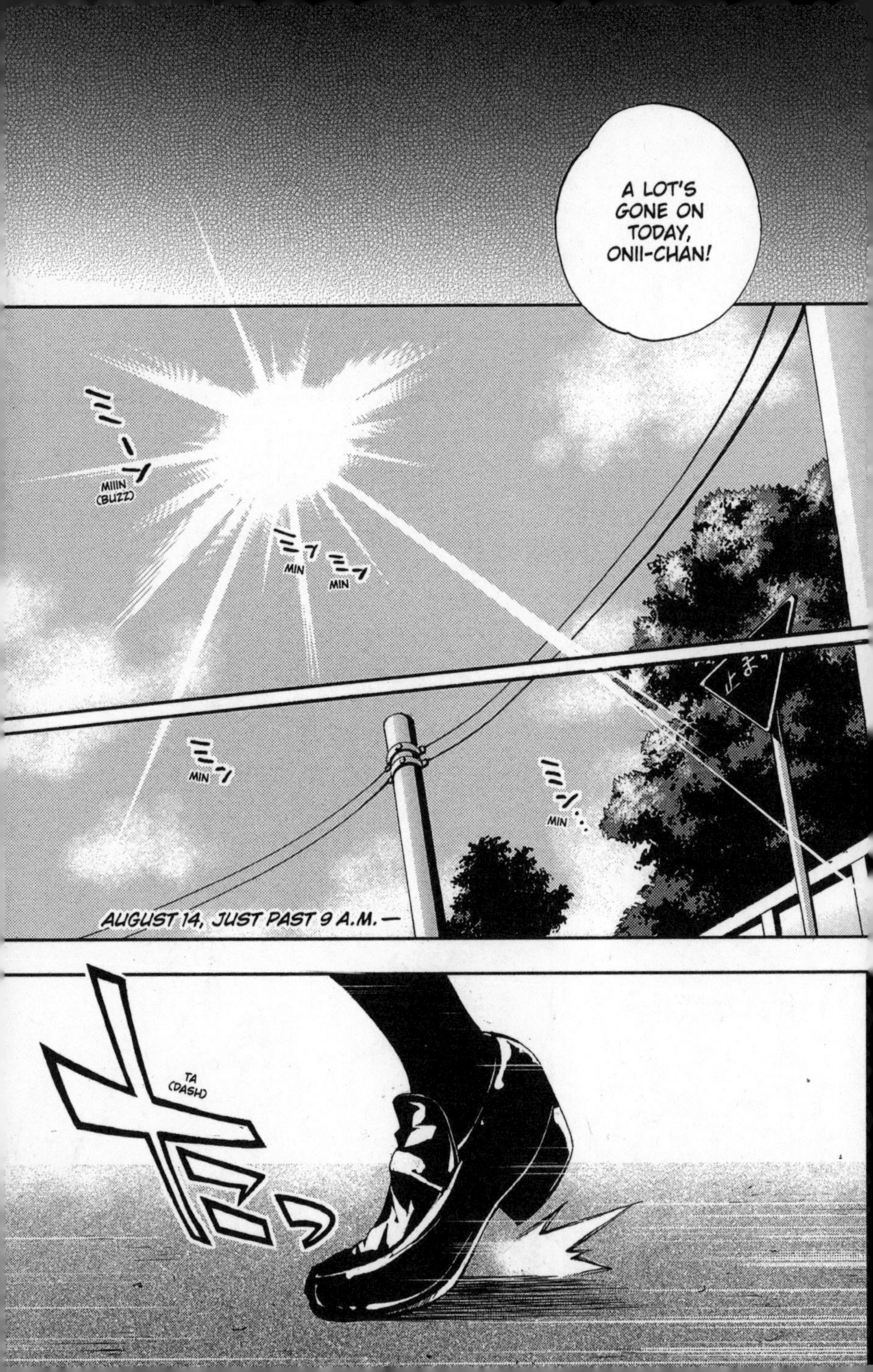
A LOT'S GONE ON TODAY, ONII-CHAN!
MIIIN (BUZZ)
MIN
MIN
MIN
MIN
AUGUST 14, JUST PAST 9 A.M.—
TA (DASH)

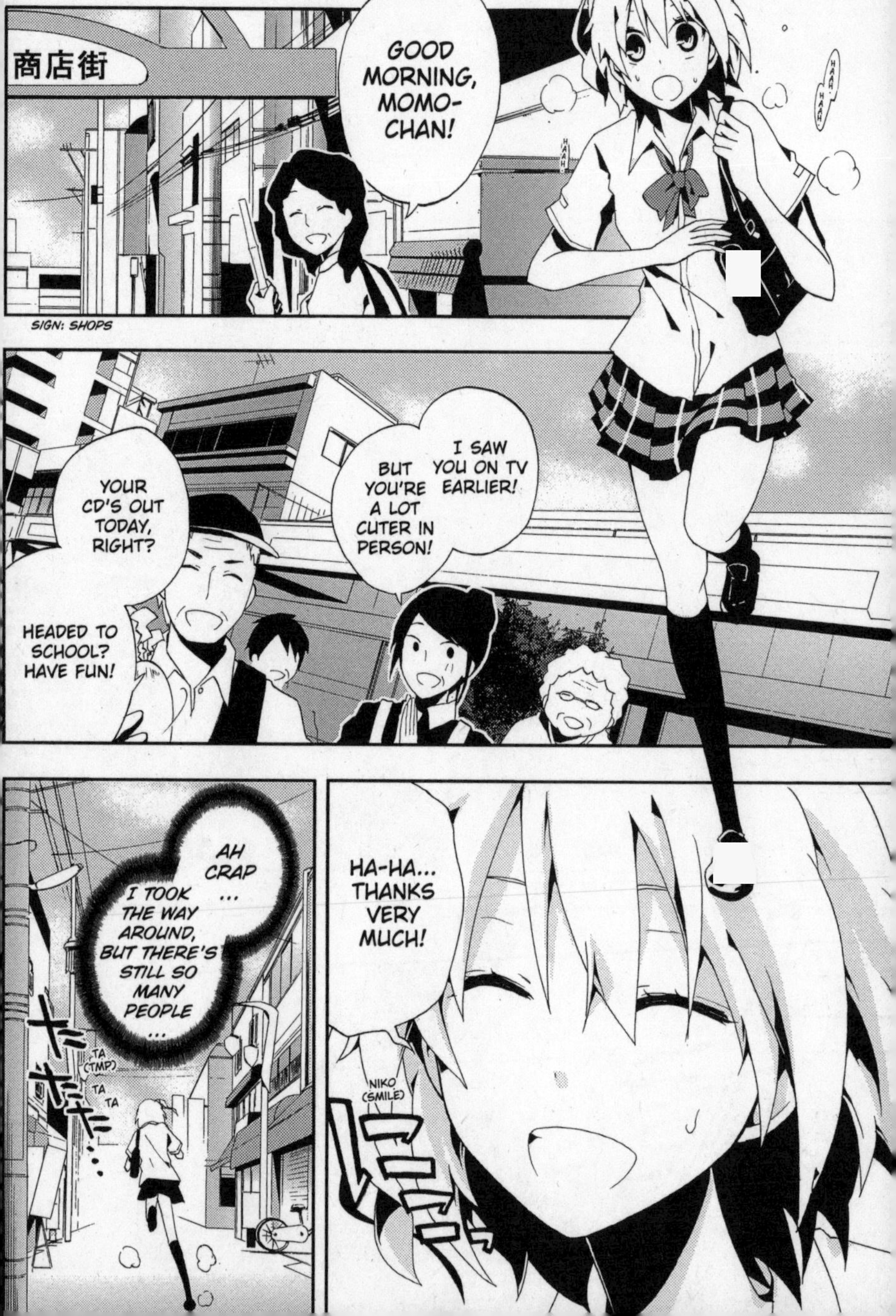
GOOD MORNING, MOMO-CHAN!
HAAH. HAAH.
商店街
SIGN: SHOPS
I SAW YOU ON TV EARLIER!
BUT YOU'RE A LOT CUTER IN PERSON!
YOUR CD'S OUT TODAY, RIGHT?
HEADED TO SCHOOL? HAVE FUN!
HA-HA... THANKS VERY MUCH!
NIKO (SMILE)
AH CRAP... I TOOK THE WAY AROUND, BUT THERE'S STILL SO MANY PEOPLE...
TA (TMP) TA TA

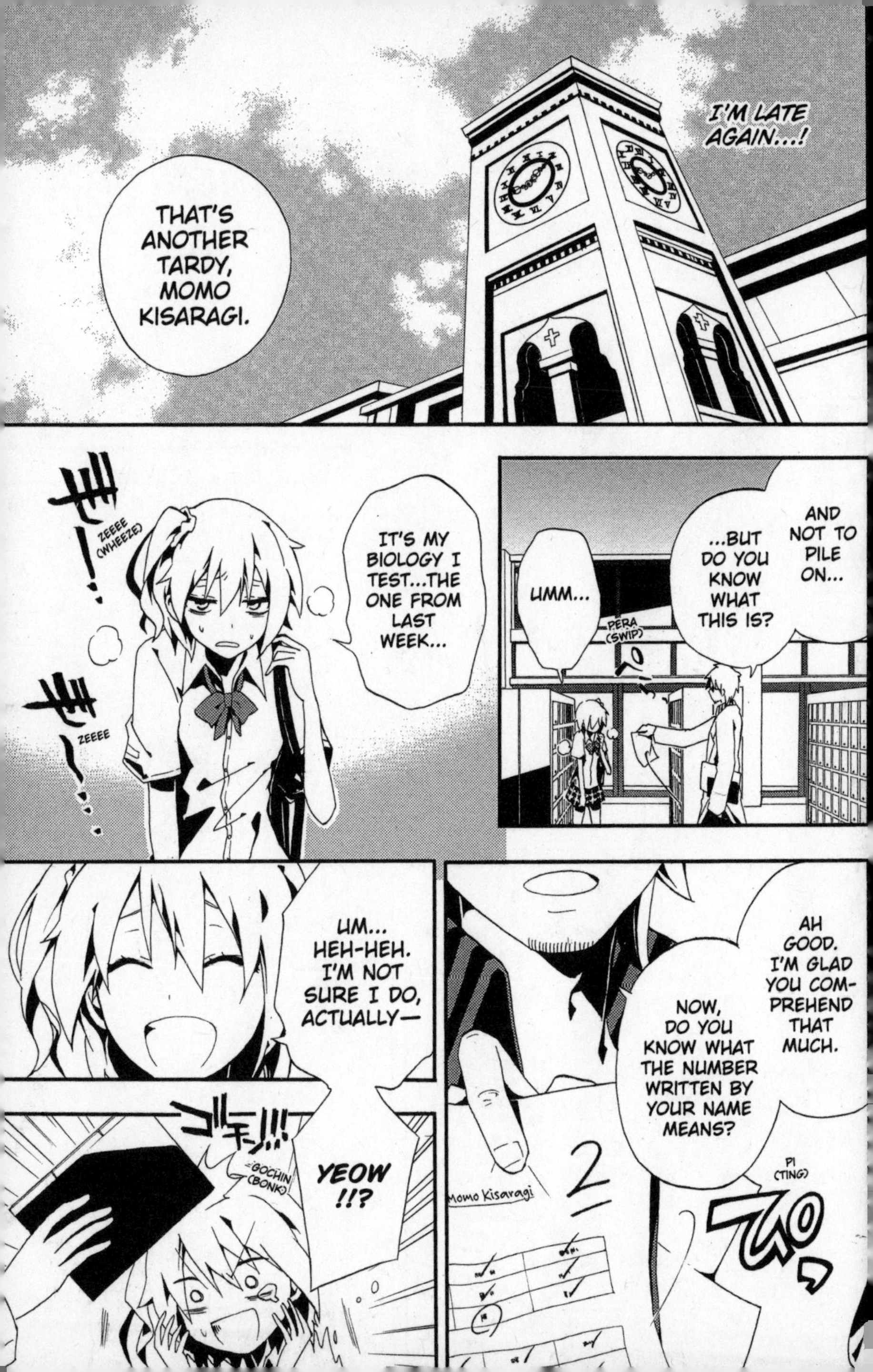
I'M LATE AGAIN...!
THAT'S ANOTHER TARDY, MOMO KISARAGI.
AND NOT TO PILE ON...
...BUT DO YOU KNOW WHAT THIS IS?
PERA (SWIP)
UMM...
IT'S MY BIOLOGY I TEST...THE ONE FROM LAST WEEK...
ZEEEE (WHEEZE)
ZEEEE
AH GOOD. I'M GLAD YOU COMPREHEND THAT MUCH.
NOW, DO YOU KNOW WHAT THE NUMBER WRITTEN BY YOUR NAME MEANS?
PI (TING)
Momo Kisaragi
2
UM... HEH-HEH. I'M NOT SURE I DO, ACTUALLY—
GOCHIN (BONK)
YEOW!!?

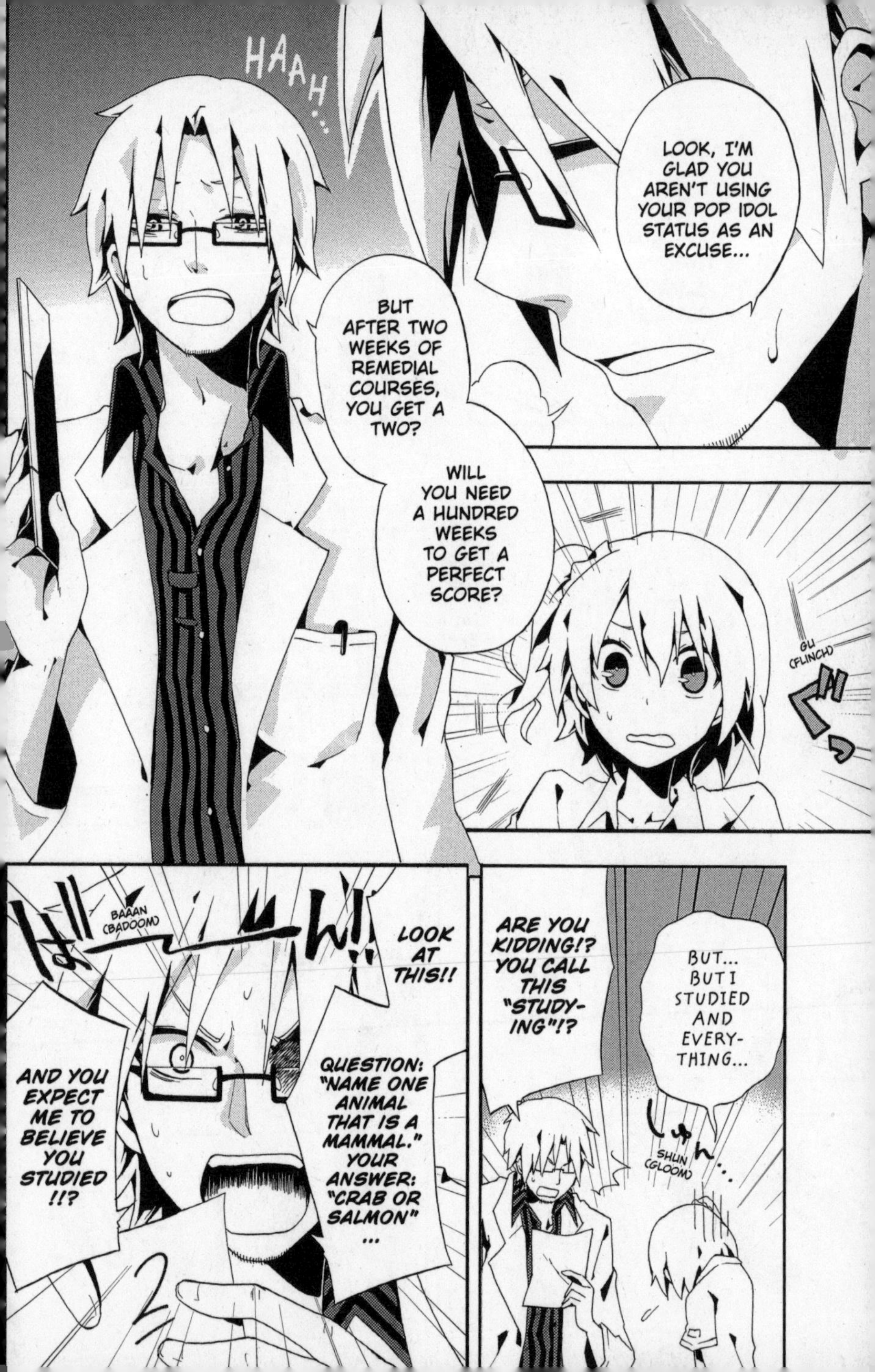
LOOK, I'M GLAD YOU AREN'T USING YOUR POP IDOL STATUS AS AN EXCUSE...
GU (FLINCH)
HAAAH...
BUT AFTER TWO WEEKS OF REMEDIAL COURSES, YOU GET A TWO?
WILL YOU NEED A HUNDRED WEEKS TO GET A PERFECT SCORE?
BUT... BUT I STUDIED AND EVERYTHING...
SHUN (GLOOM)
ARE YOU KIDDING!? YOU CALL THIS "STUDYING"!?
BAAAN (BADOOM)
LOOK AT THIS!!
QUESTION: "NAME ONE ANIMAL THAT IS A MAMMAL." YOUR ANSWER: "CRAB OR SALMON"...
AND YOU EXPECT ME TO BELIEVE YOU STUDIED!!?

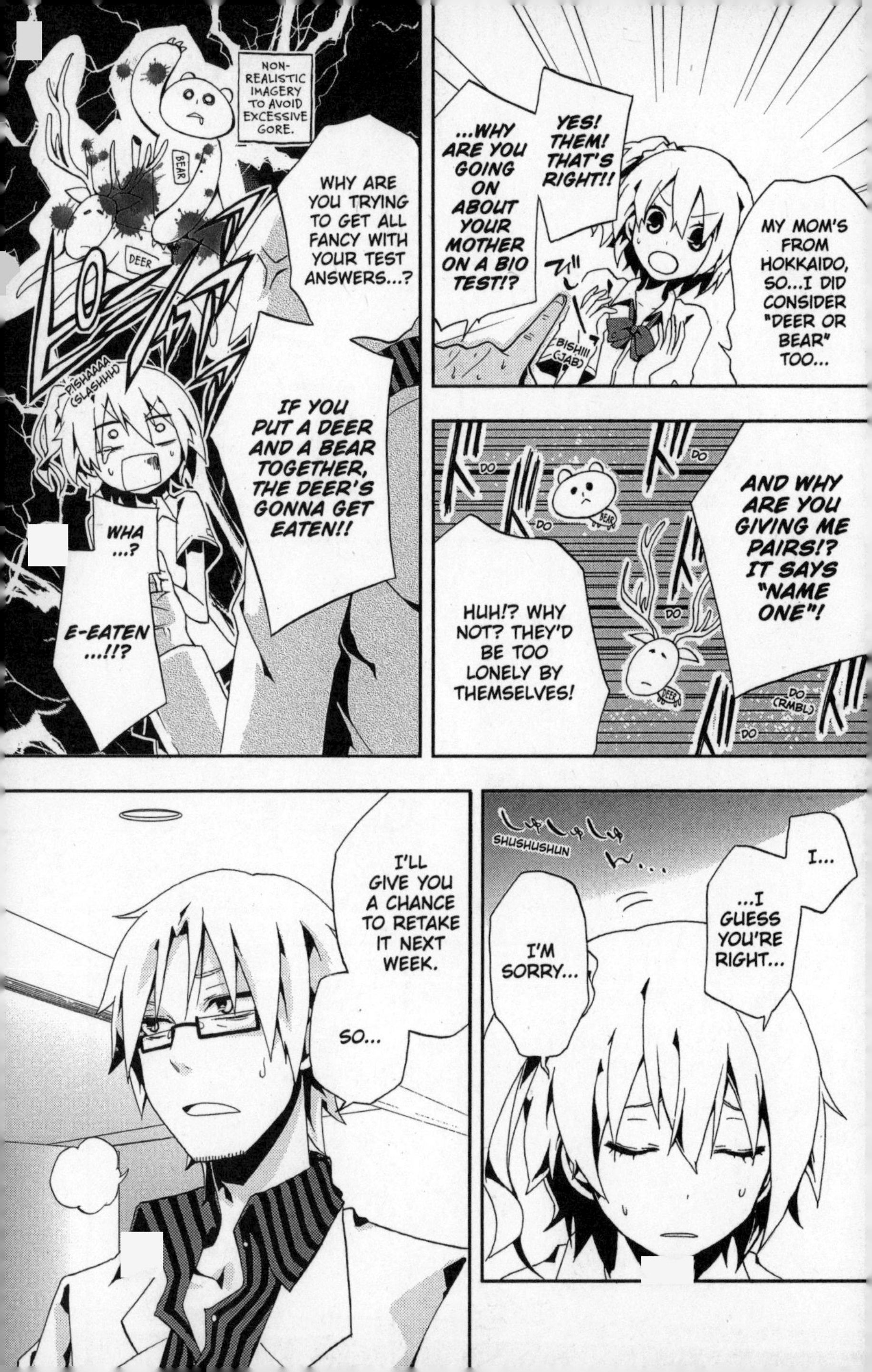
MY MOM'S FROM HOKKAIDO, SO...I DID CONSIDER "DEER OR BEAR" TOO...
YES! THEM! THAT'S RIGHT!!
...WHY ARE YOU GOING ON ABOUT YOUR MOTHER ON A BIO TEST!?
BISHIII (JAB)
AND WHY ARE YOU GIVING ME PAIRS!? IT SAYS "NAME ONE"!
HUH!? WHY NOT? THEY'D BE TOO LONELY BY THEMSELVES!
DO
BEAR
DEER
DO (RMBL)
NON-REALISTIC IMAGERY TO AVOID EXCESSIVE GORE.
WHY ARE YOU TRYING TO GET ALL FANCY WITH YOUR TEST ANSWERS...?
BEAR
DEER
IF YOU PUT A DEER AND A BEAR TOGETHER, THE DEER'S GONNA GET EATEN!!
PISHAAAA (SLASHHH)
WHA ...?
E-EATEN ...!!?
I...
...I GUESS YOU'RE RIGHT...
SHUSHUSHUN
I'M SORRY...
I'LL GIVE YOU A CHANCE TO RETAKE IT NEXT WEEK.
SO...

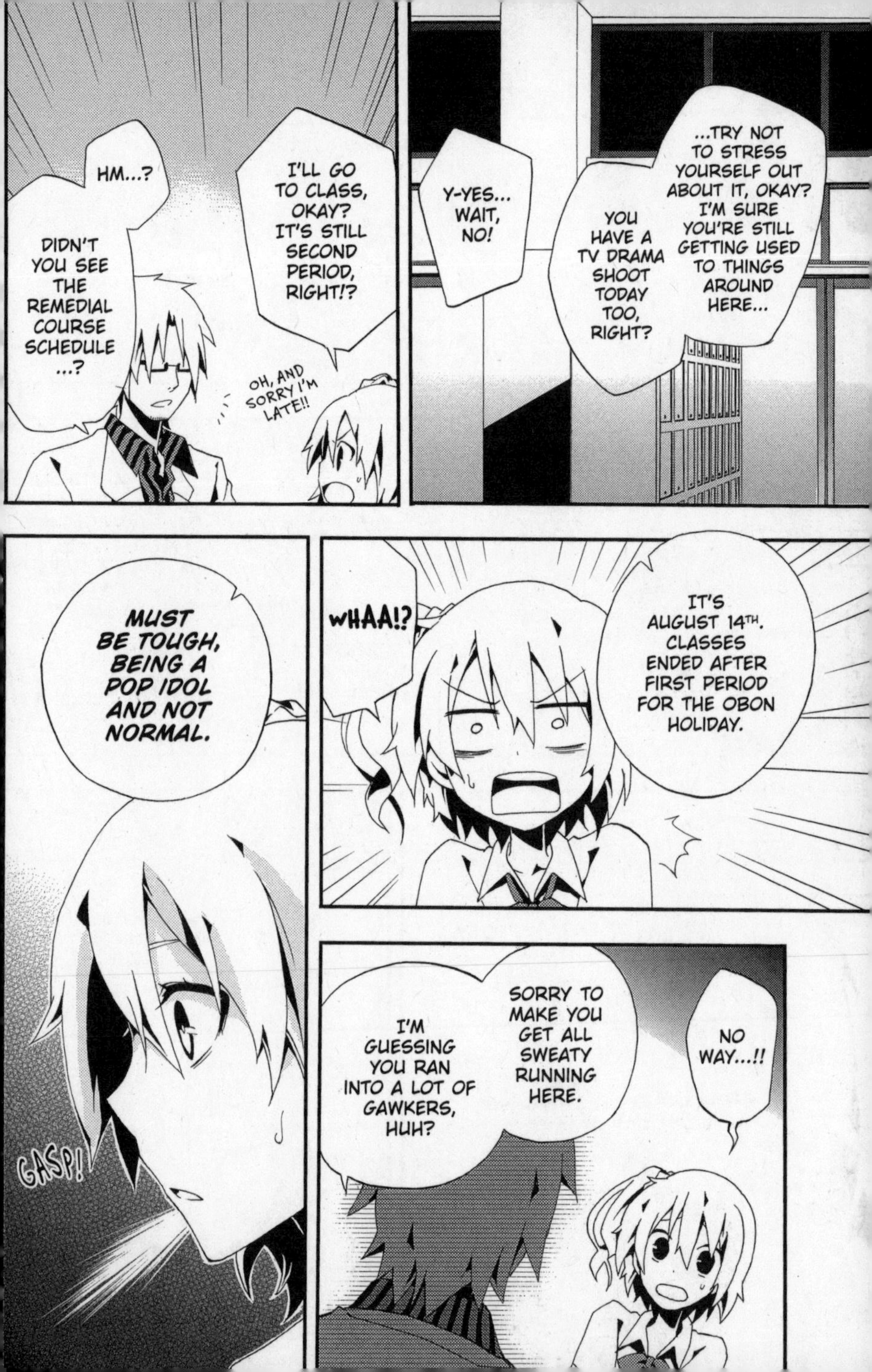

...TRY NOT TO STRESS YOURSELF OUT ABOUT IT, OKAY? I'M SURE YOU'RE STILL GETTING USED TO THINGS AROUND HERE...
YOU HAVE A TV DRAMA SHOOT TODAY TOO, RIGHT?
Y-YES... WAIT, NO!
I'LL GO TO CLASS, OKAY? IT'S STILL SECOND PERIOD, RIGHT!?
OH, AND SORRY I'M LATE!!
HM...?
DIDN'T YOU SEE THE REMEDIAL COURSE SCHEDULE ...?
IT'S AUGUST 14TH. CLASSES ENDED AFTER FIRST PERIOD FOR THE OBON HOLIDAY.
WHAA!?
NO WAY...!!
SORRY TO MAKE YOU GET ALL SWEATY RUNNING HERE.
I'M GUESSING YOU RAN INTO A LOT OF GAWKERS, HUH?
MUST BE TOUGH, BEING A POP IDOL AND NOT NORMAL.
GASP!

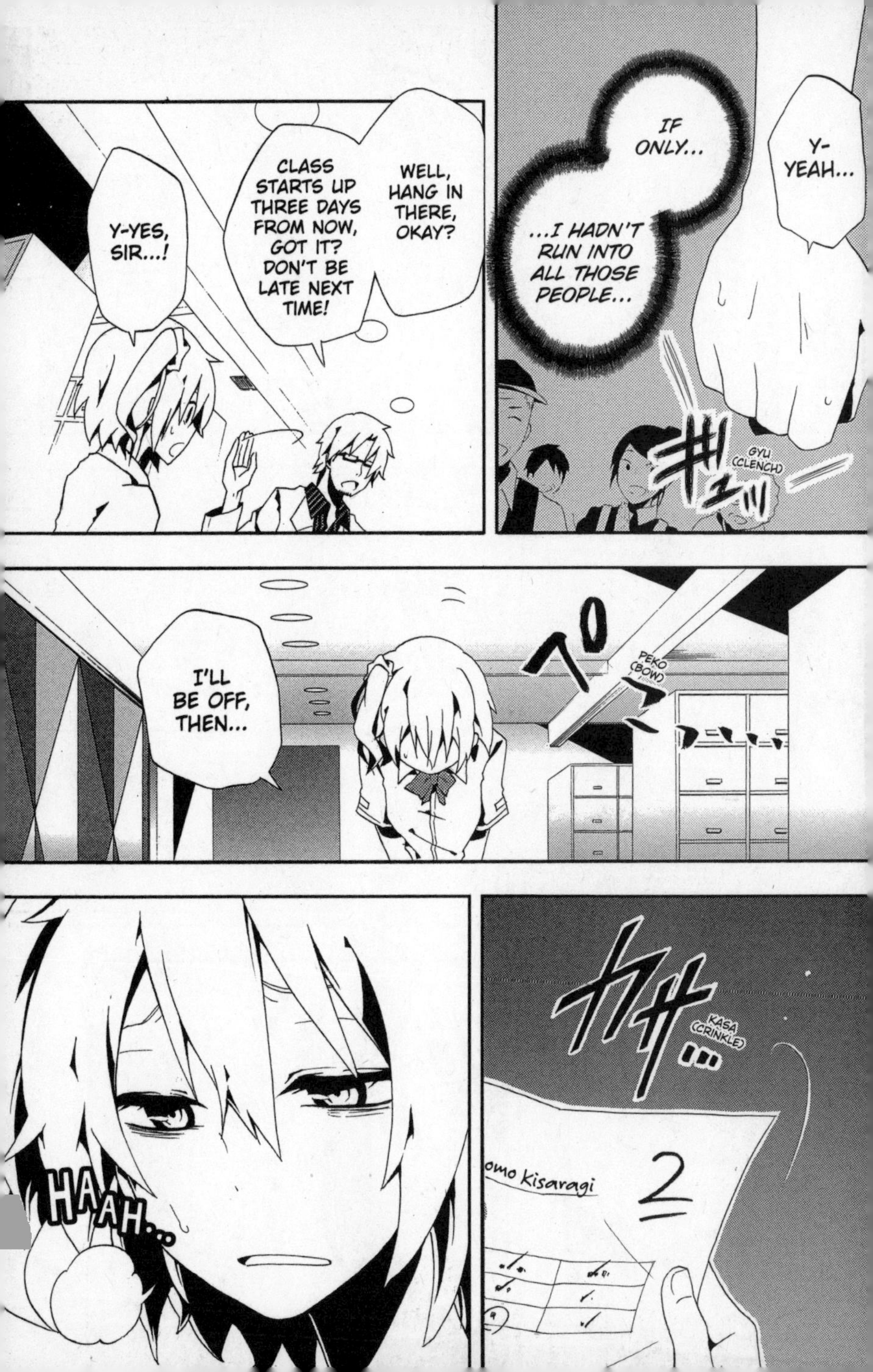
Y-YEAH...
IF ONLY...
...I HADN'T RUN INTO ALL THOSE PEOPLE...
GYU (CLENCH)
WELL, HANG IN THERE, OKAY?
CLASS STARTS UP THREE DAYS FROM NOW, GOT IT? DON'T BE LATE NEXT TIME!
Y-YES, SIR...!
PEKO (BOW)
I'LL BE OFF, THEN...
KASA (CRINKLE)
omo Kisaragi
2
HAAAH...

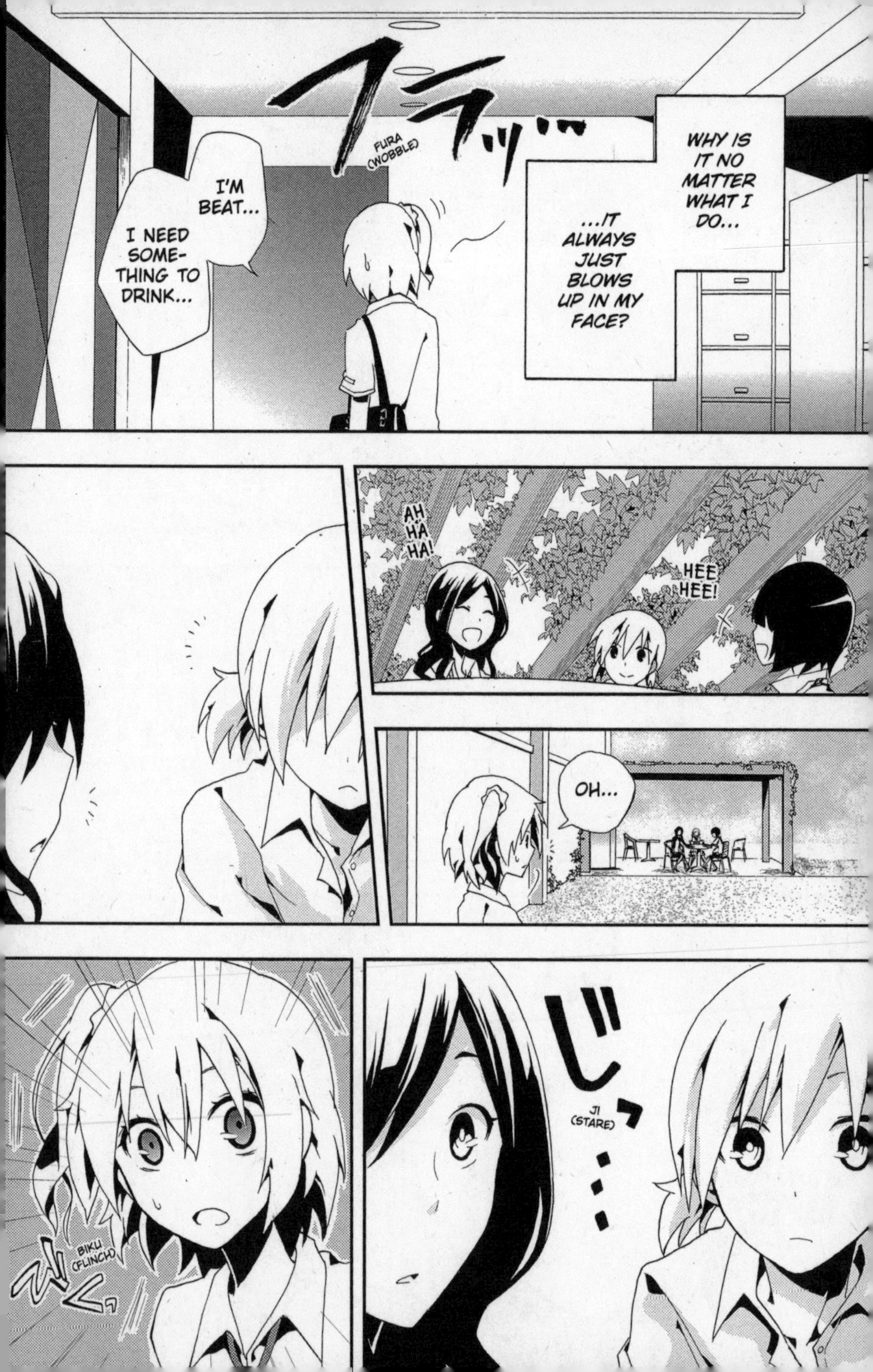
WHY IS IT NO MATTER WHAT I DO... ...IT ALWAYS JUST BLOWS UP IN MY FACE?
FURA (WOBBLE)
I'M BEAT... I NEED SOME-THING TO DRINK...
HEE HEE!
AH HA HA!
OH...
JI (STARE)
BIKU (FLINCH)

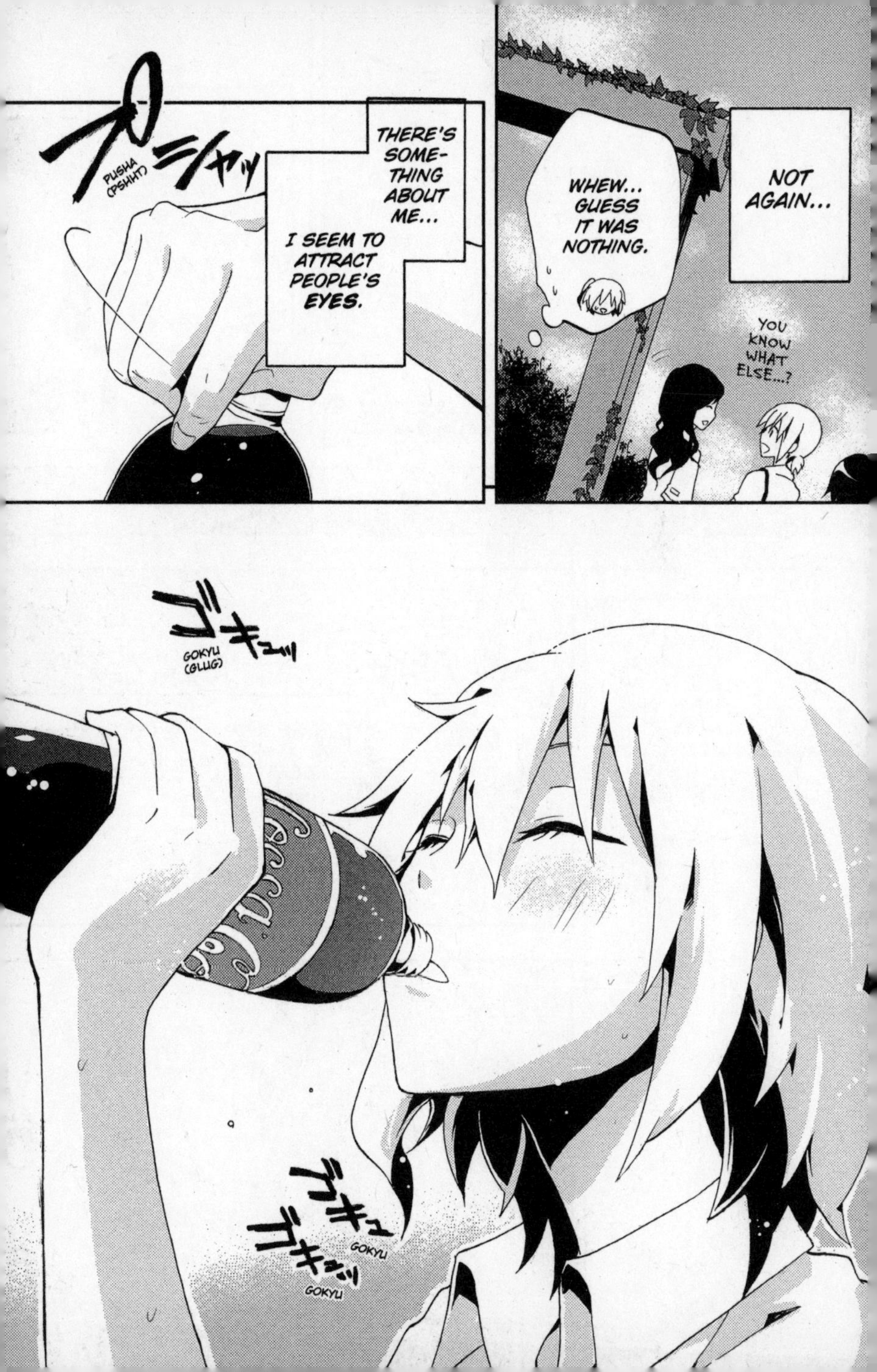
NOT AGAIN...
WHEW... GUESS IT WAS NOTHING.
YOU KNOW WHAT ELSE...?
THERE'S SOMETHING ABOUT ME...
I SEEM TO ATTRACT PEOPLE'S EYES.
PUSHA (PSHHT)
GOKYU (GLUG)
GOKYU
GOKYU

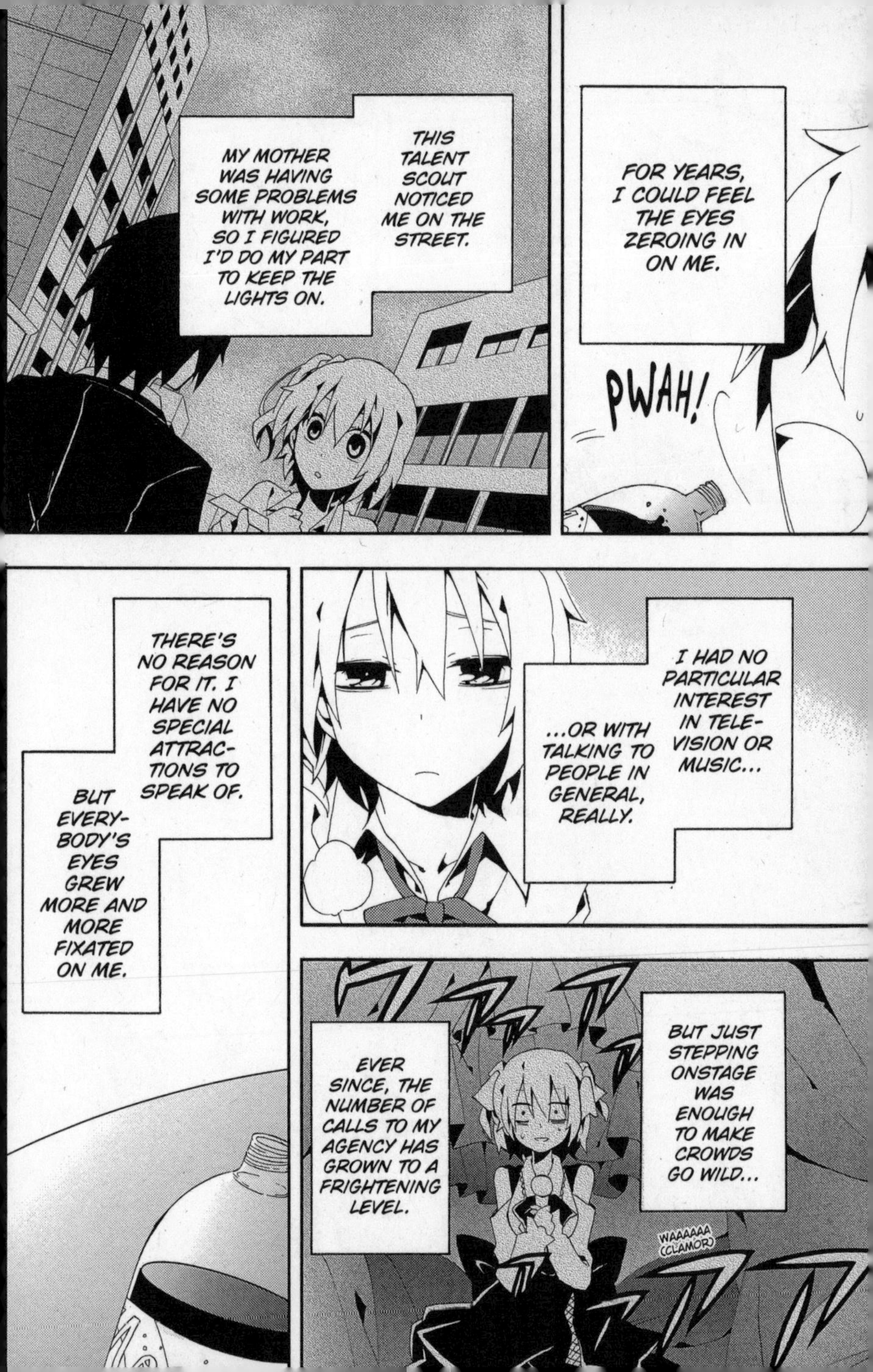
FOR YEARS, I COULD FEEL THE EYES ZEROING IN ON ME.
PWAH!
THIS TALENT SCOUT NOTICED ME ON THE STREET.
MY MOTHER WAS HAVING SOME PROBLEMS WITH WORK, SO I FIGURED I'D DO MY PART TO KEEP THE LIGHTS ON.
I HAD NO PARTICULAR INTEREST IN TELE-VISION OR MUSIC...
...OR WITH TALKING TO PEOPLE IN GENERAL, REALLY.
BUT JUST STEPPING ONSTAGE WAS ENOUGH TO MAKE CROWDS GO WILD...
EVER SINCE, THE NUMBER OF CALLS TO MY AGENCY HAS GROWN TO A FRIGHTENING LEVEL.
WAAAAAA (CLAMOR)
THERE'S NO REASON FOR IT. I HAVE NO SPECIAL ATTRAC-TIONS TO SPEAK OF.
BUT EVERY-BODY'S EYES GREW MORE AND MORE FIXATED ON ME.

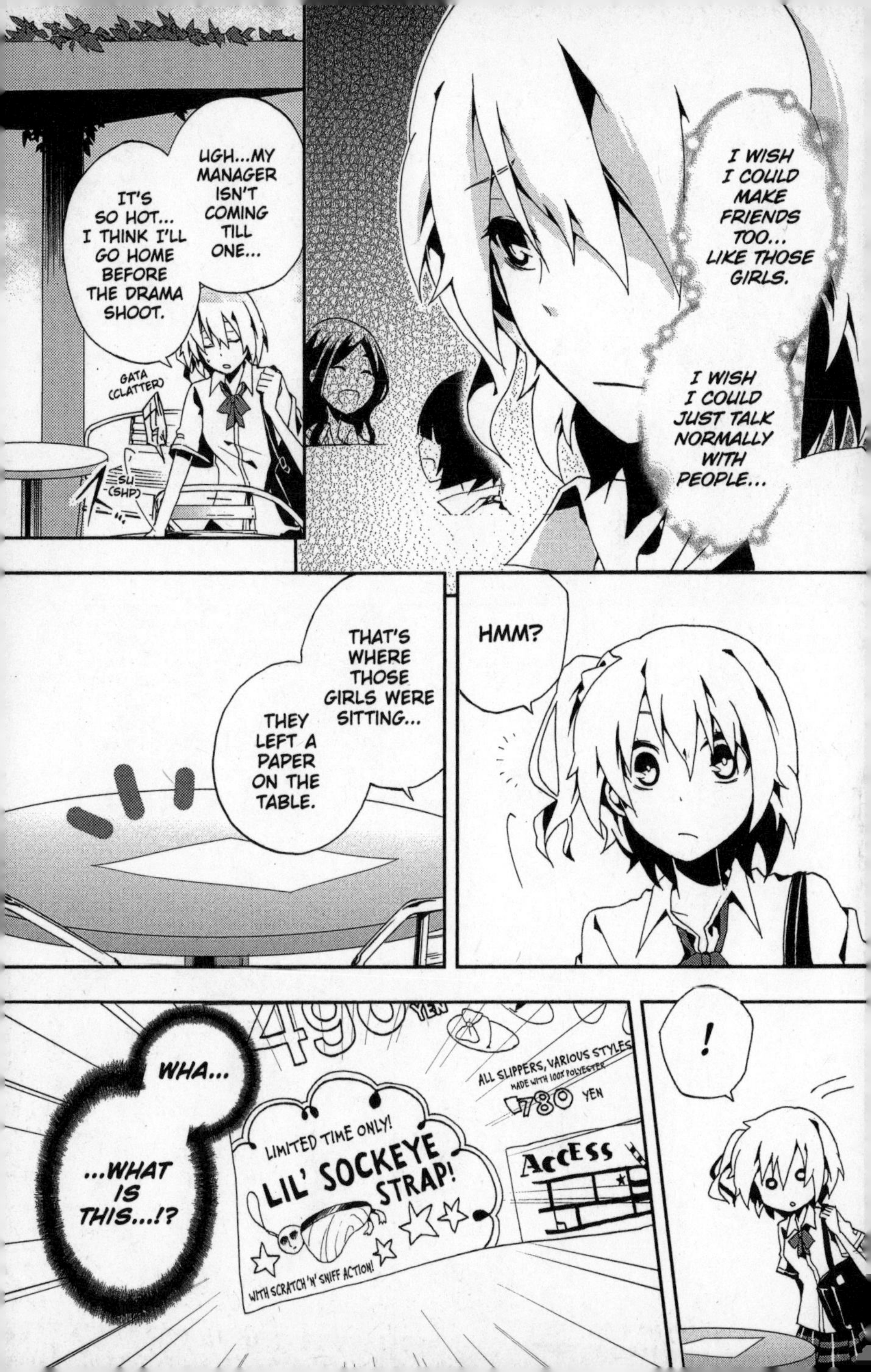
I WISH I COULD MAKE FRIENDS TOO... LIKE THOSE GIRLS.
I WISH I COULD JUST TALK NORMALLY WITH PEOPLE...
UGH...MY MANAGER ISN'T COMING TILL ONE...
IT'S SO HOT... I THINK I'LL GO HOME BEFORE THE DRAMA SHOOT.
GATA (CLATTER)
SU (SHP)
HMM?
THAT'S WHERE THOSE GIRLS WERE SITTING...
THEY LEFT A PAPER ON THE TABLE.
!
WHA...
...WHAT IS THIS...!?
490 YEN
ALL SLIPPERS, VARIOUS STYLES
MADE WITH 100% POLYESTER
780 YEN
LIMITED TIME ONLY!
LIL' SOCKEYE STRAP!
WITH SCRATCH 'N' SNIFF ACTION!
ACCESS

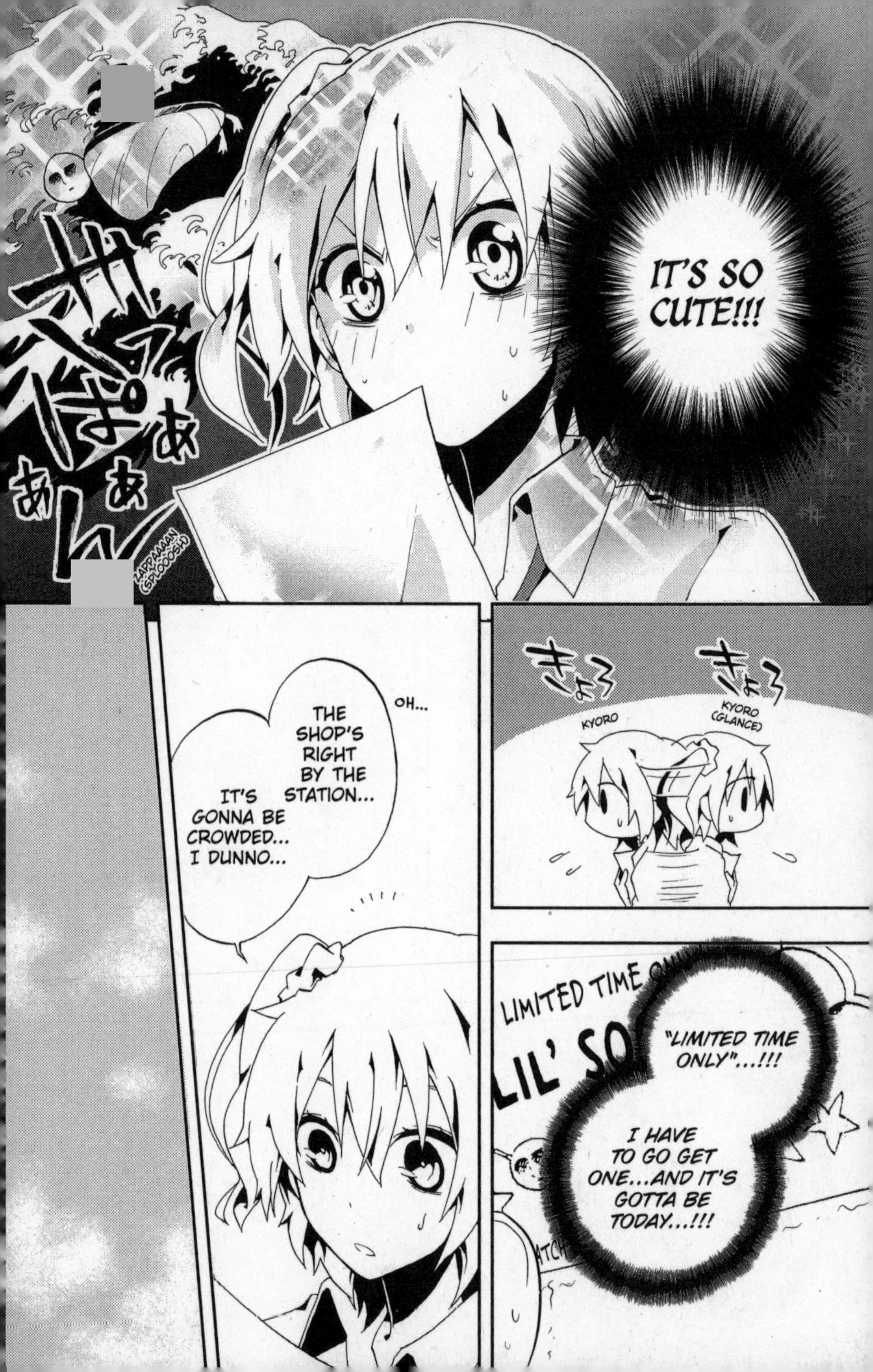
ZAPPAAAAN (SPLOOOSH)
IT'S SO CUTE!!!
きょろ きょろ
KYORO KYORO (GLANCE)
LIMITED TIME
"LIMITED TIME ONLY"...!!!
I HAVE TO GO GET ONE...AND IT'S GOTTA BE TODAY...!!!
OH...
THE SHOP'S RIGHT BY THE STATION... IT'S GONNA BE CROWDED... I DUNNO...

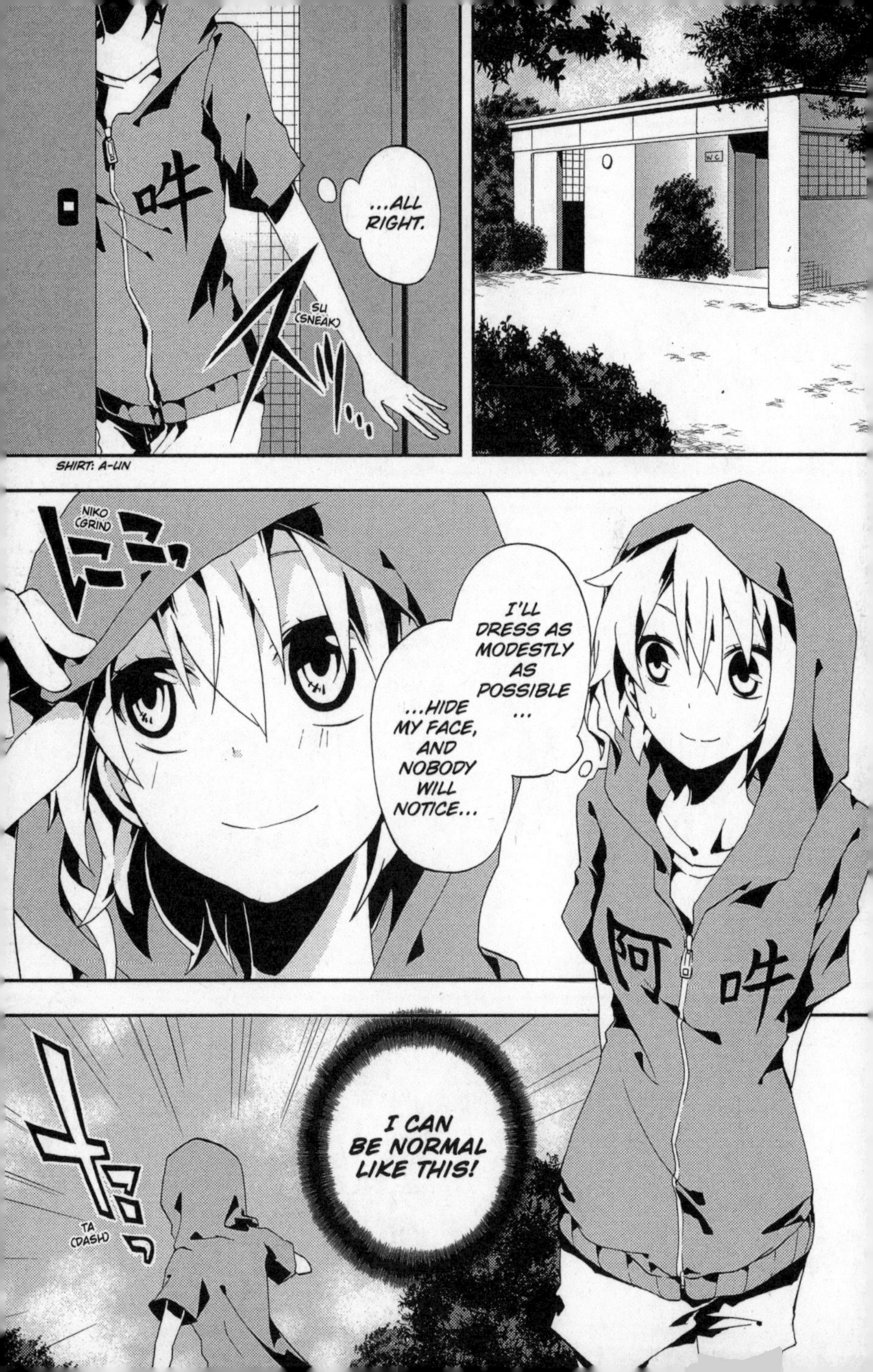
...ALL RIGHT.
SU (SNEAK)
SHIRT: A-UN
I'LL DRESS AS MODESTLY AS POSSIBLE...
...HIDE MY FACE, AND NOBODY WILL NOTICE...
NIKO (GRIN)
I CAN BE NORMAL LIKE THIS!
TA (DASH)

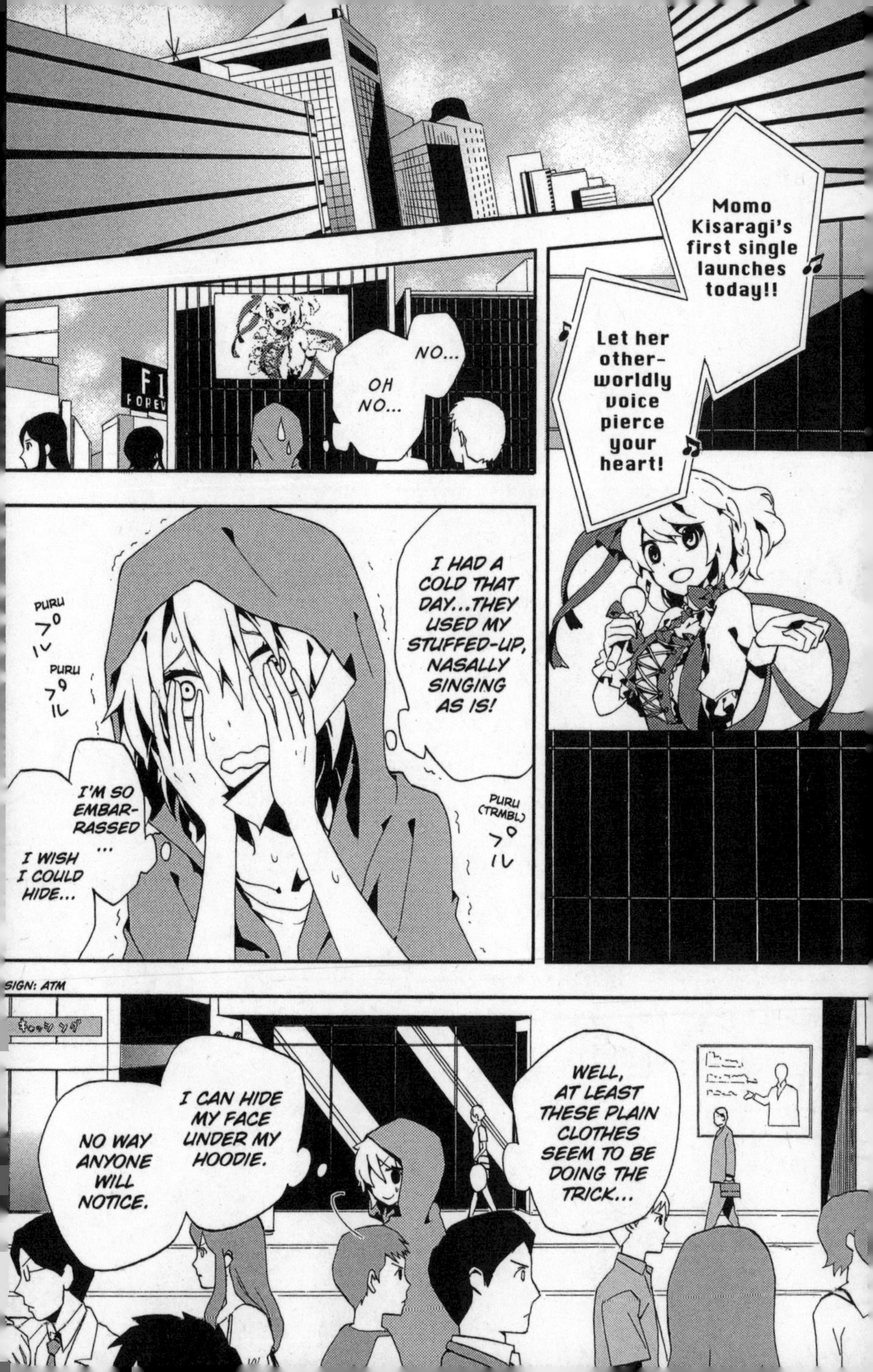
Momo Kisaragi's first single launches today!!
Let her other-worldly voice pierce your heart!
F1 FOREV
NO... OH NO...
I HAD A COLD THAT DAY...THEY USED MY STUFFED-UP, NASALLY SINGING AS IS!
PURU (TRMBL)
PURU
PURU
I'M SO EMBARRASSED... I WISH I COULD HIDE...
SIGN: ATM
WELL, AT LEAST THESE PLAIN CLOTHES SEEM TO BE DOING THE TRICK...
I CAN HIDE MY FACE UNDER MY HOODIE.
NO WAY ANYONE WILL NOTICE.

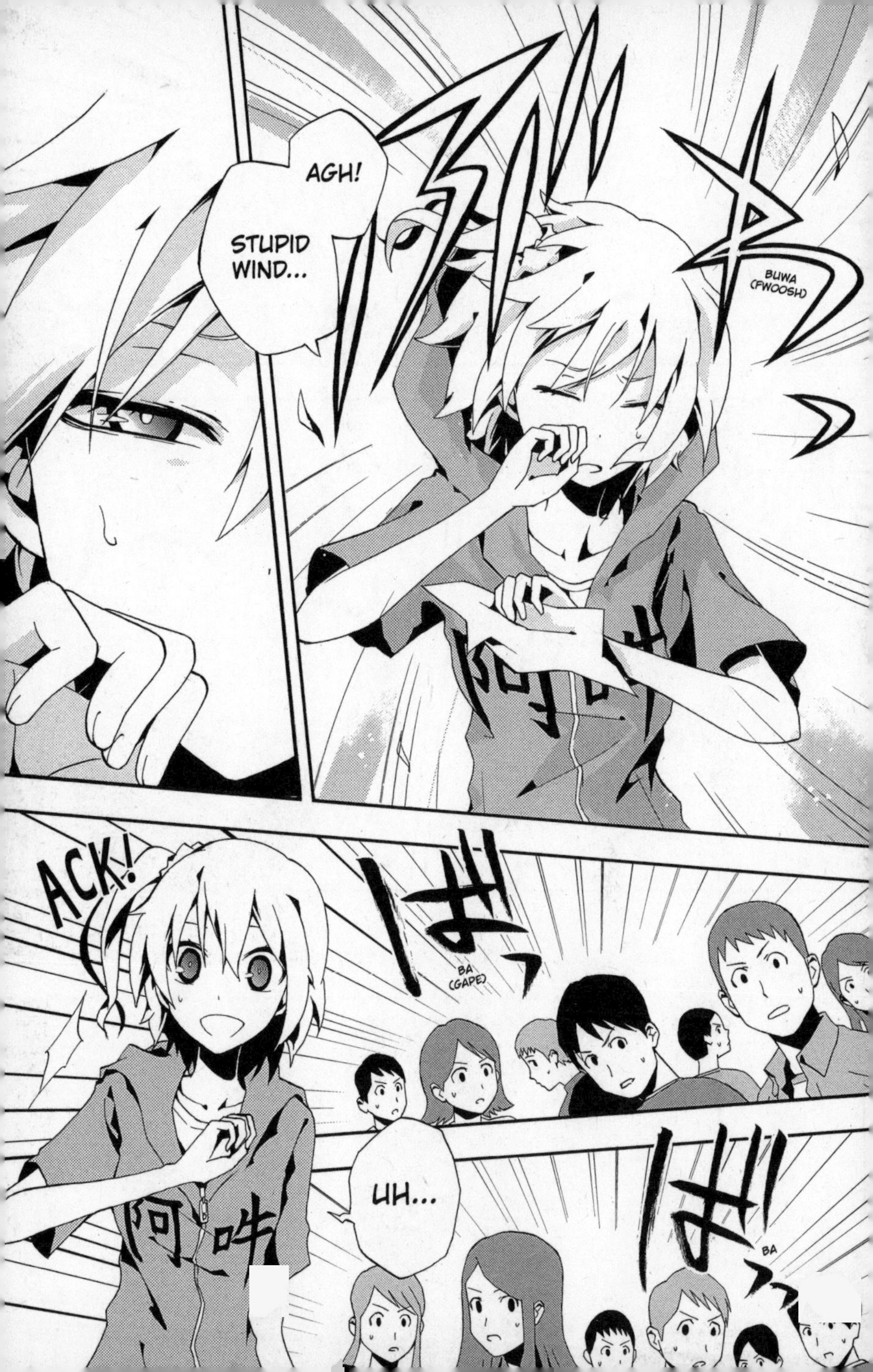
BUWA (FWOOSH)
AGH!
STUPID WIND...
BA (GAPE)
ACK!
BA
UH...
阿吽

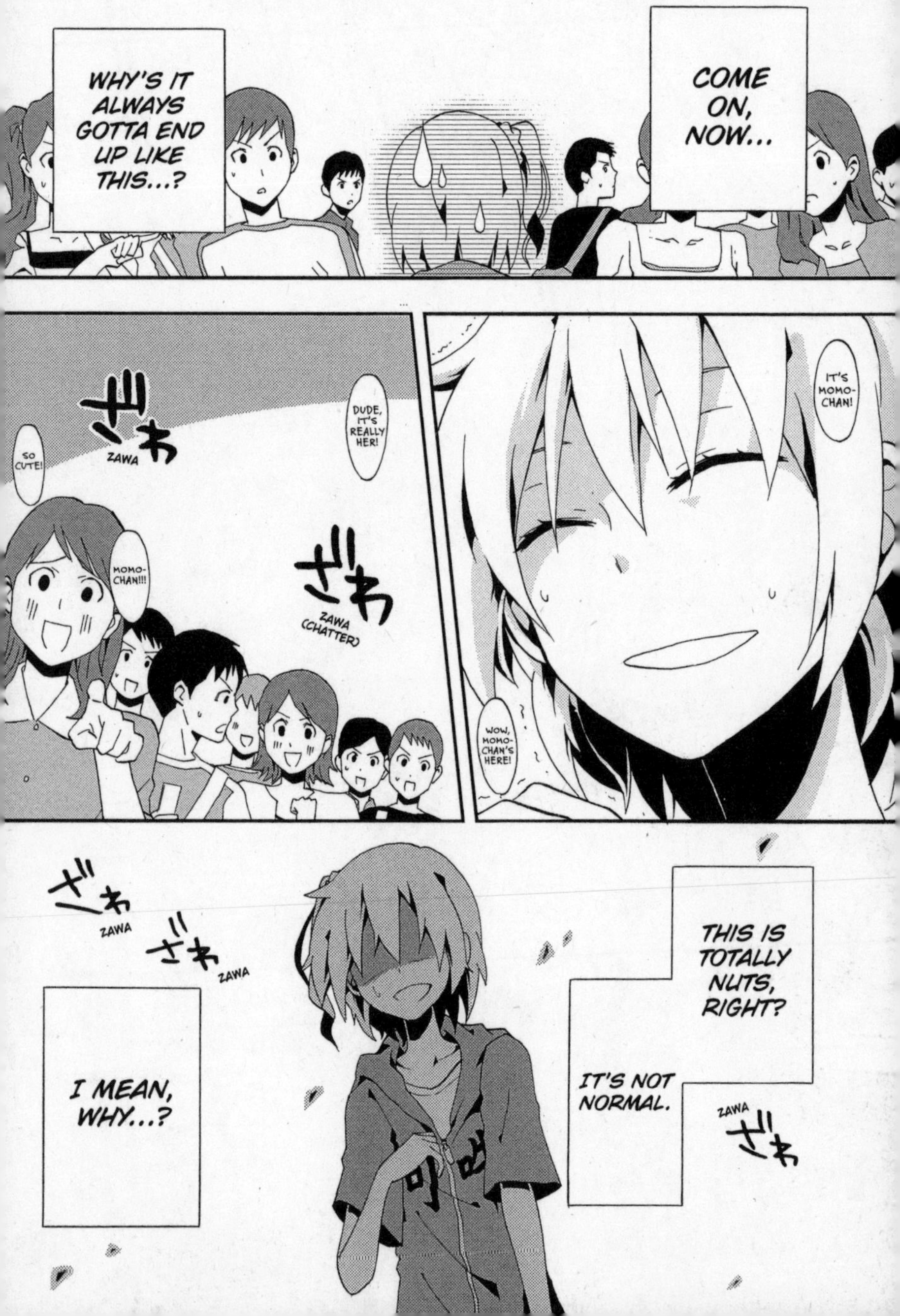
COME ON, NOW...
WHY'S IT ALWAYS GOTTA END UP LIKE THIS...?
IT'S MOMO-CHAN!
WOW, MOMO-CHAN'S HERE!
DUDE, IT'S REALLY HER!
ざわ
ZAWA
SO CUTE!
ざわ
ZAWA (CHATTER)
MOMO-CHAN!!!
THIS IS TOTALLY NUTS, RIGHT?
IT'S NOT NORMAL.
ZAWA
ざわ
ざわ
ZAWA
ざわ
ZAWA
I MEAN, WHY...?

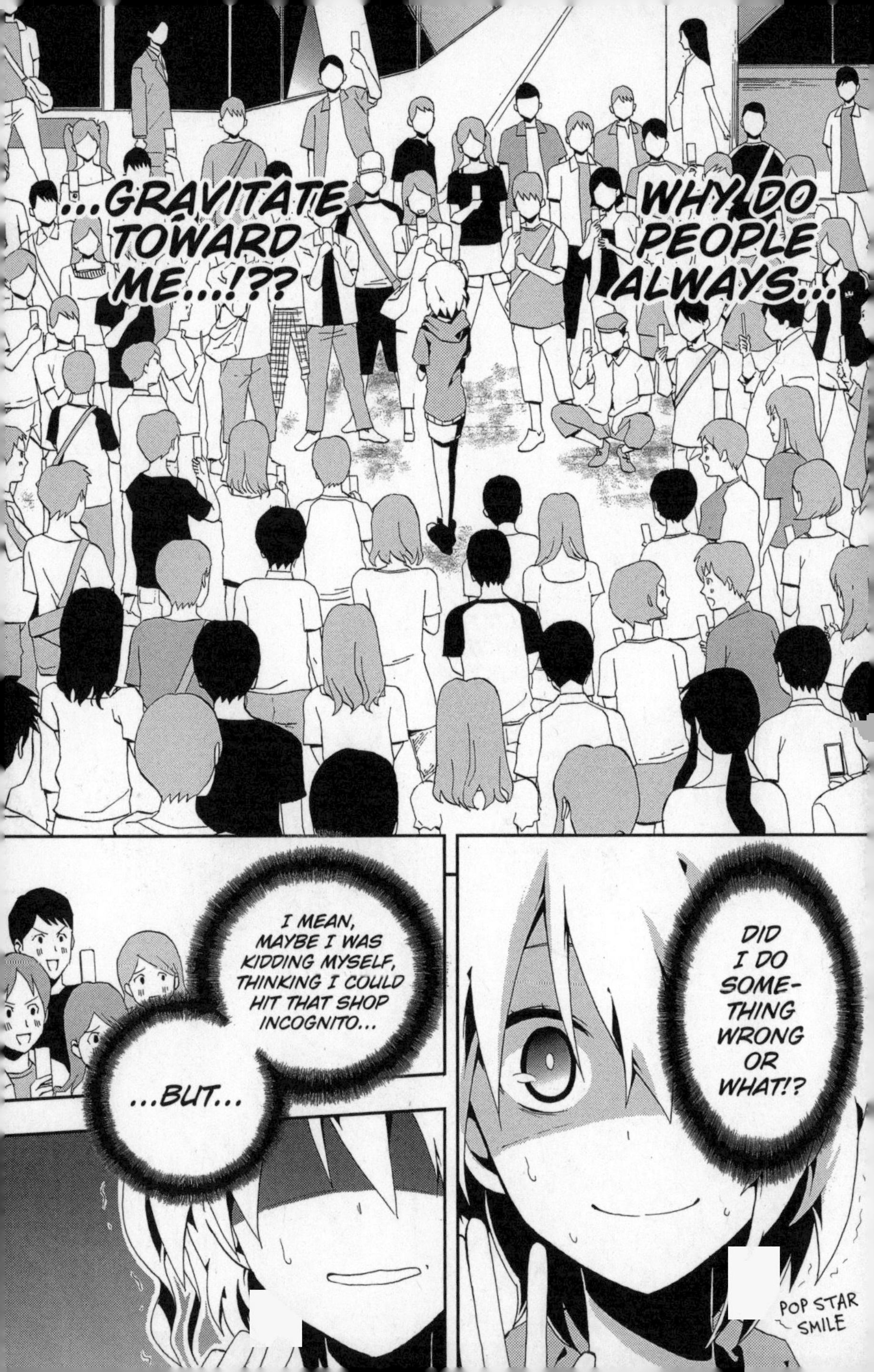
WHY DO PEOPLE ALWAYS...
...GRAVITATE TOWARD ME...!??
DID I DO SOME-THING WRONG OR WHAT!?
POP STAR SMILE
I MEAN, MAYBE I WAS KIDDING MYSELF, THINKING I COULD HIT THAT SHOP INCOGNITO...
...BUT...

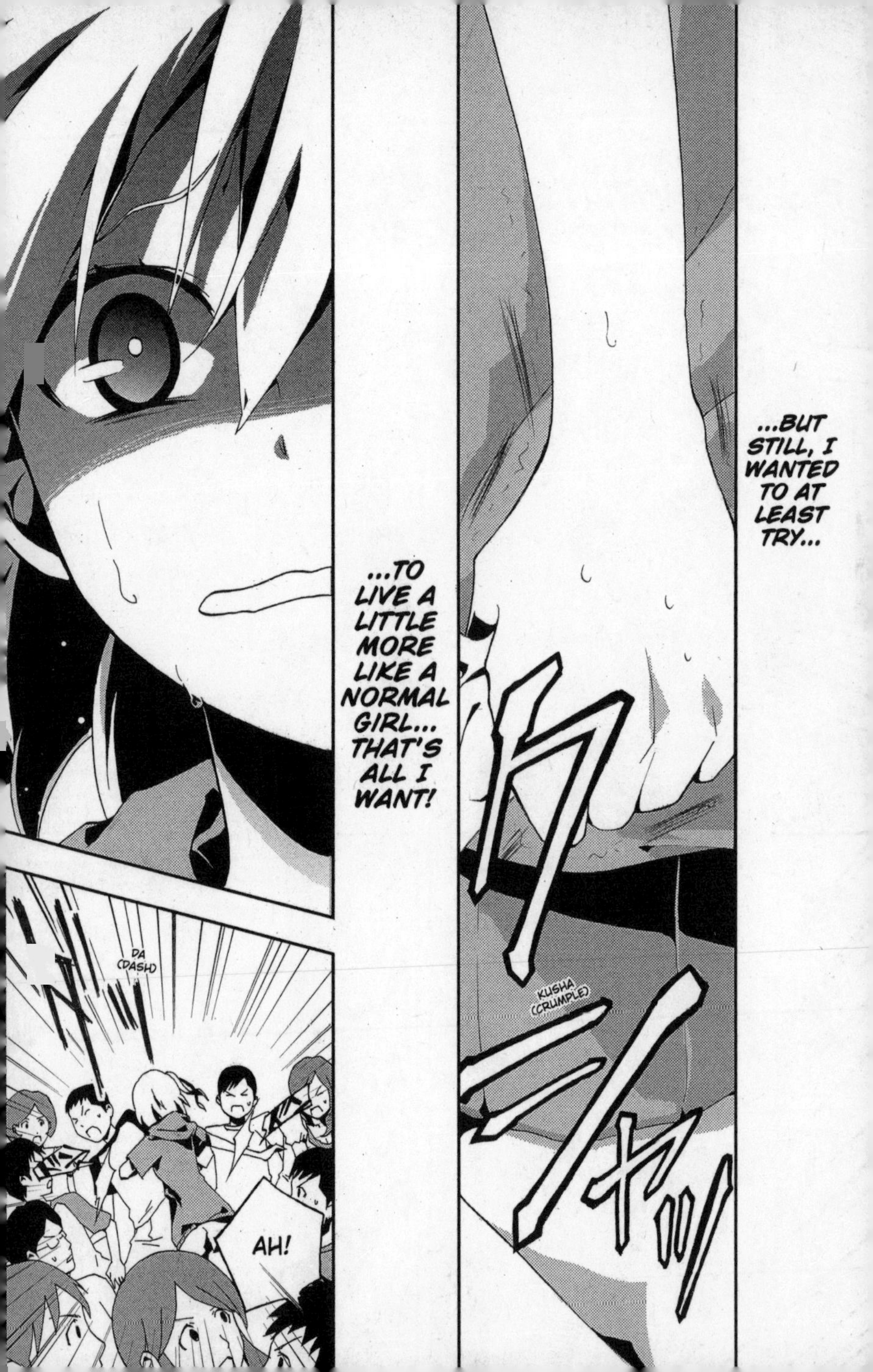
...BUT STILL, I WANTED TO AT LEAST TRY...
KUSHA (CRUMPLE)
...TO LIVE A LITTLE MORE LIKE A NORMAL GIRL... THAT'S ALL I WANT!
DA (DASH)
AH!

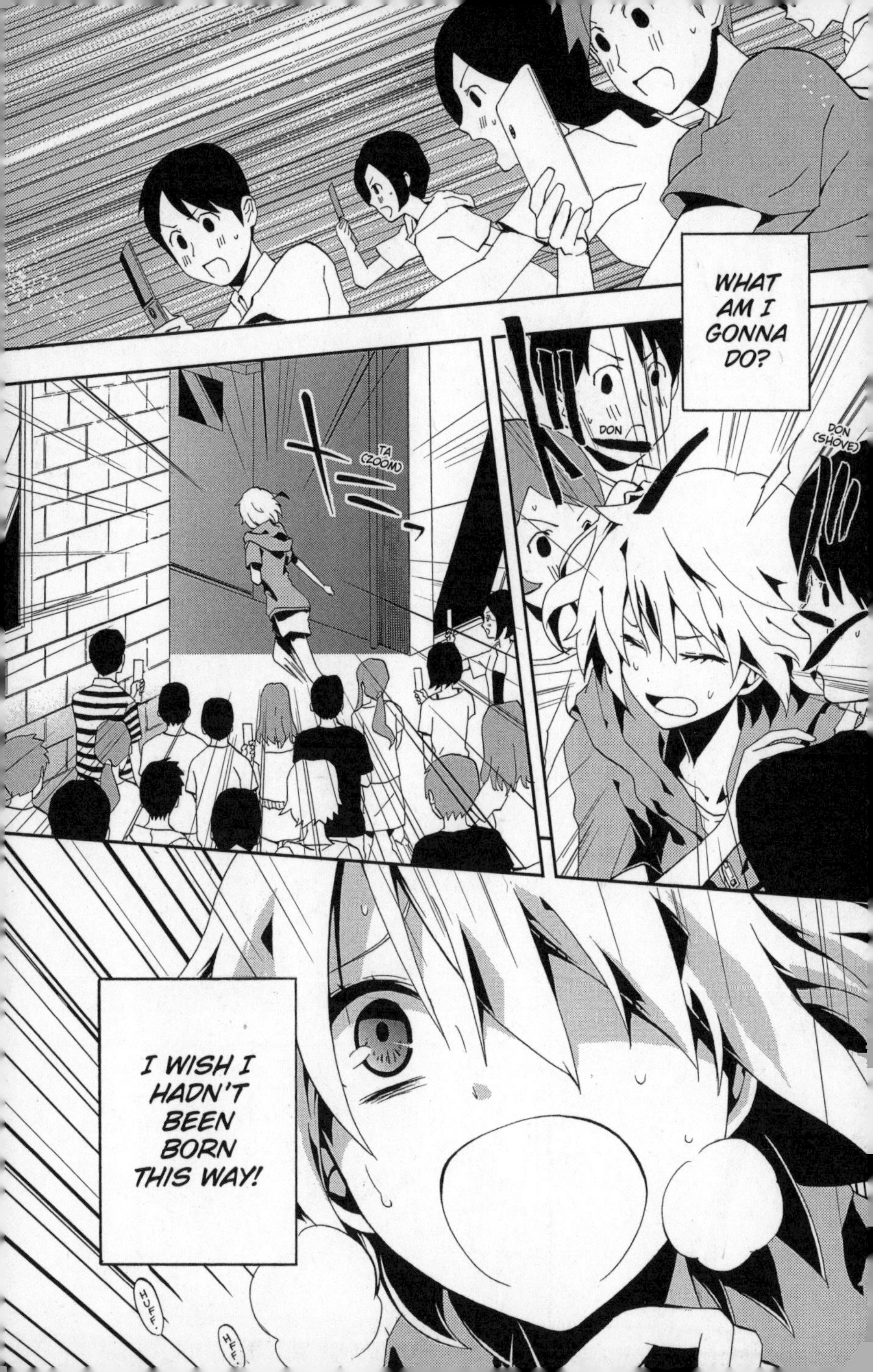
WHAT AM I GONNA DO?
DON (SHOVE)
DON
TA (ZOOM)
I WISH I HADN'T BEEN BORN THIS WAY!
HUFF.
HFF.

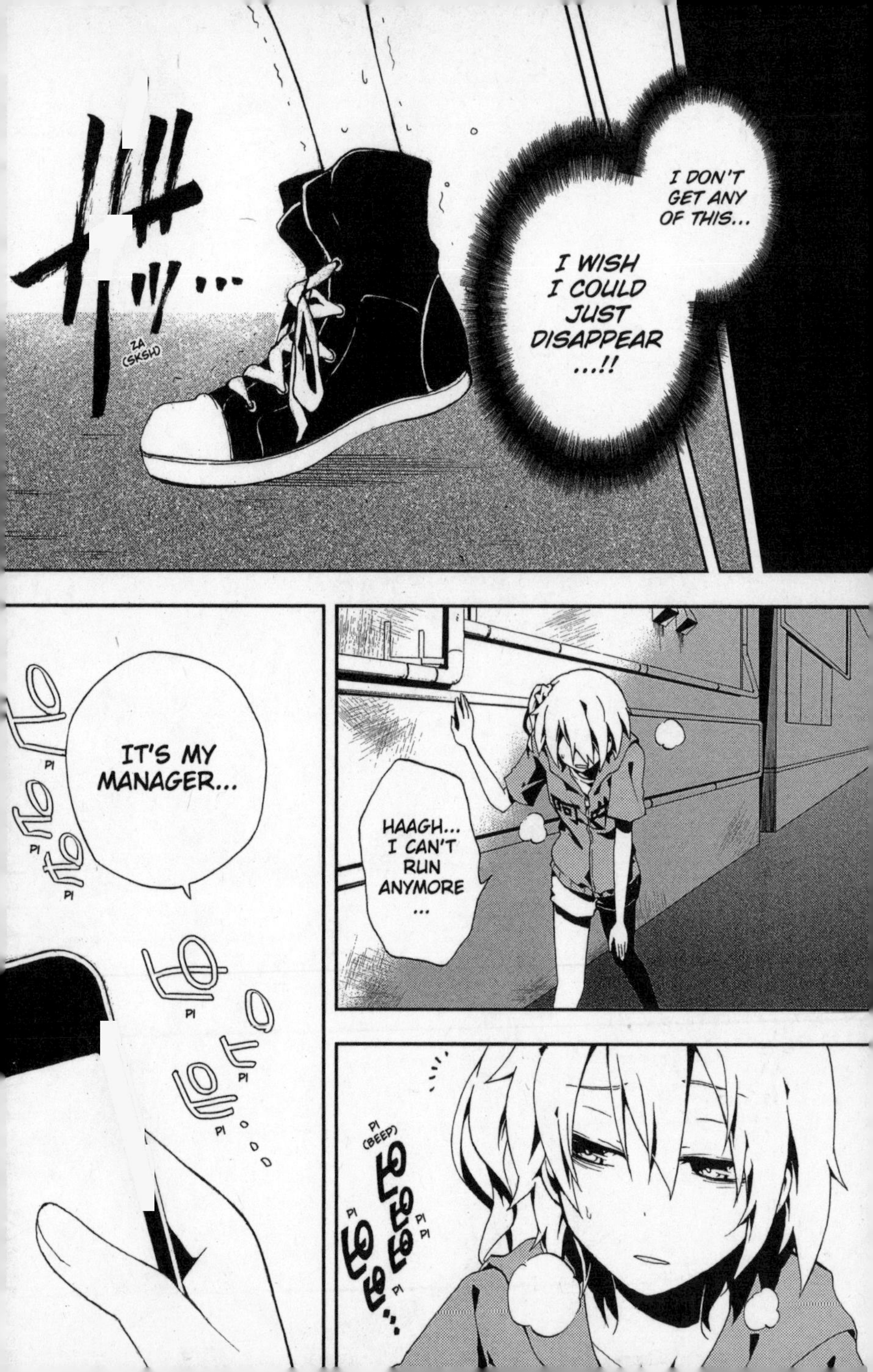
I DON'T GET ANY OF THIS...
I WISH I COULD JUST DISAPPEAR...!!
ZA (SKSH)
HAAGH... I CAN'T RUN ANYMORE...
PI (BEEP)
PI PI PI PI
IT'S MY MANAGER...
PI PI PI
PI PI PI

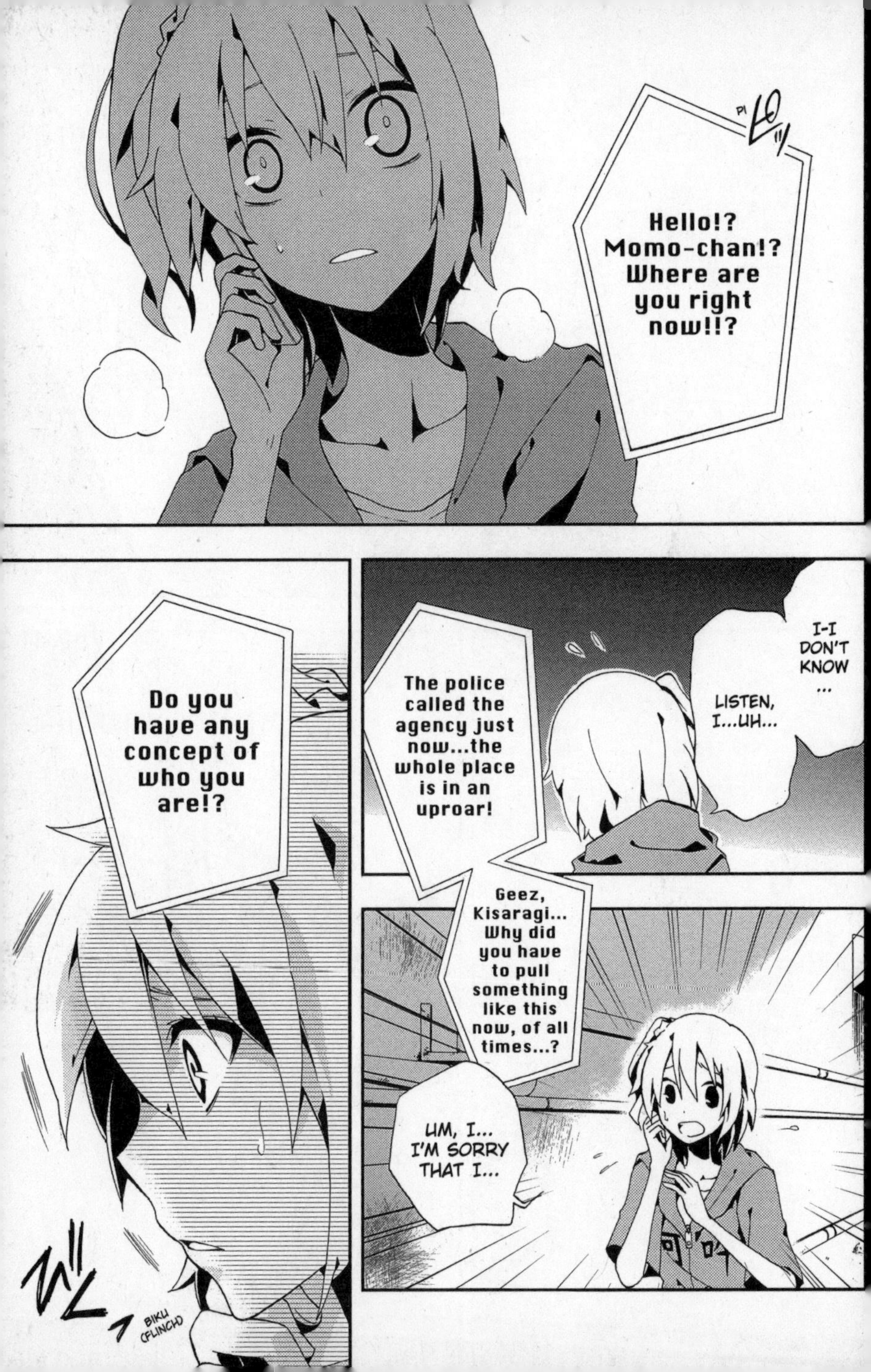
PI
Hello!? Momo-chan!? Where are you right now!!?
I-I DON'T KNOW...
LISTEN, I...UH...
The police called the agency just now...the whole place is in an uproar!
Geez, Kisaragi... Why did you have to pull something like this now, of all times...?
UM, I... I'M SORRY THAT I...
Do you have any concept of who you are!?
BIKU (FLINCH)

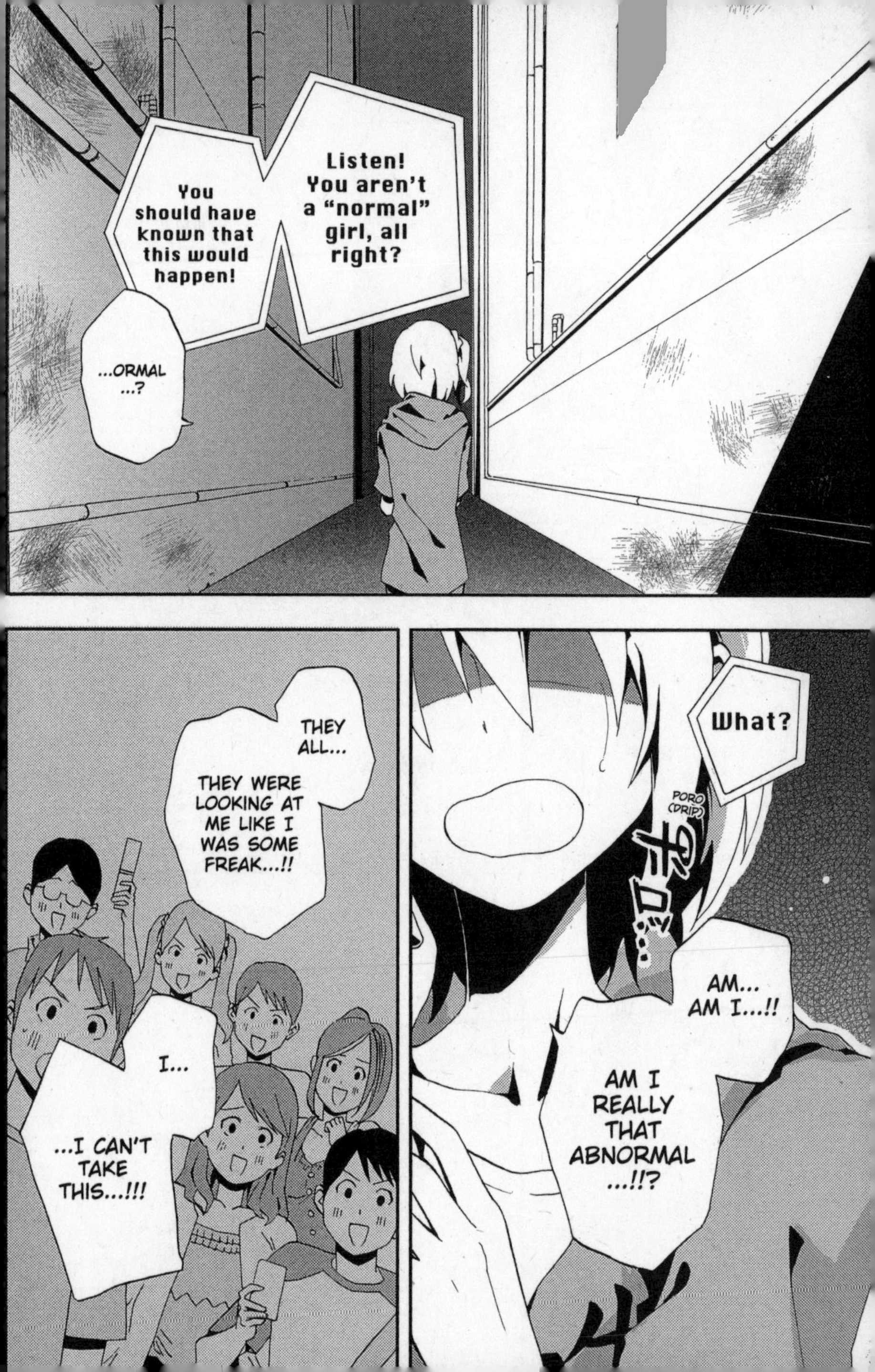
Listen! You aren't a "normal" girl, all right?
You should have known that this would happen!
...ORMAL ...?
What?
PORO (DRIP)
AM... AM I...!!
AM I REALLY THAT ABNORMAL ...!!?
THEY ALL...
THEY WERE LOOKING AT ME LIKE I WAS SOME FREAK...!!
I...
...I CAN'T TAKE THIS...!!!

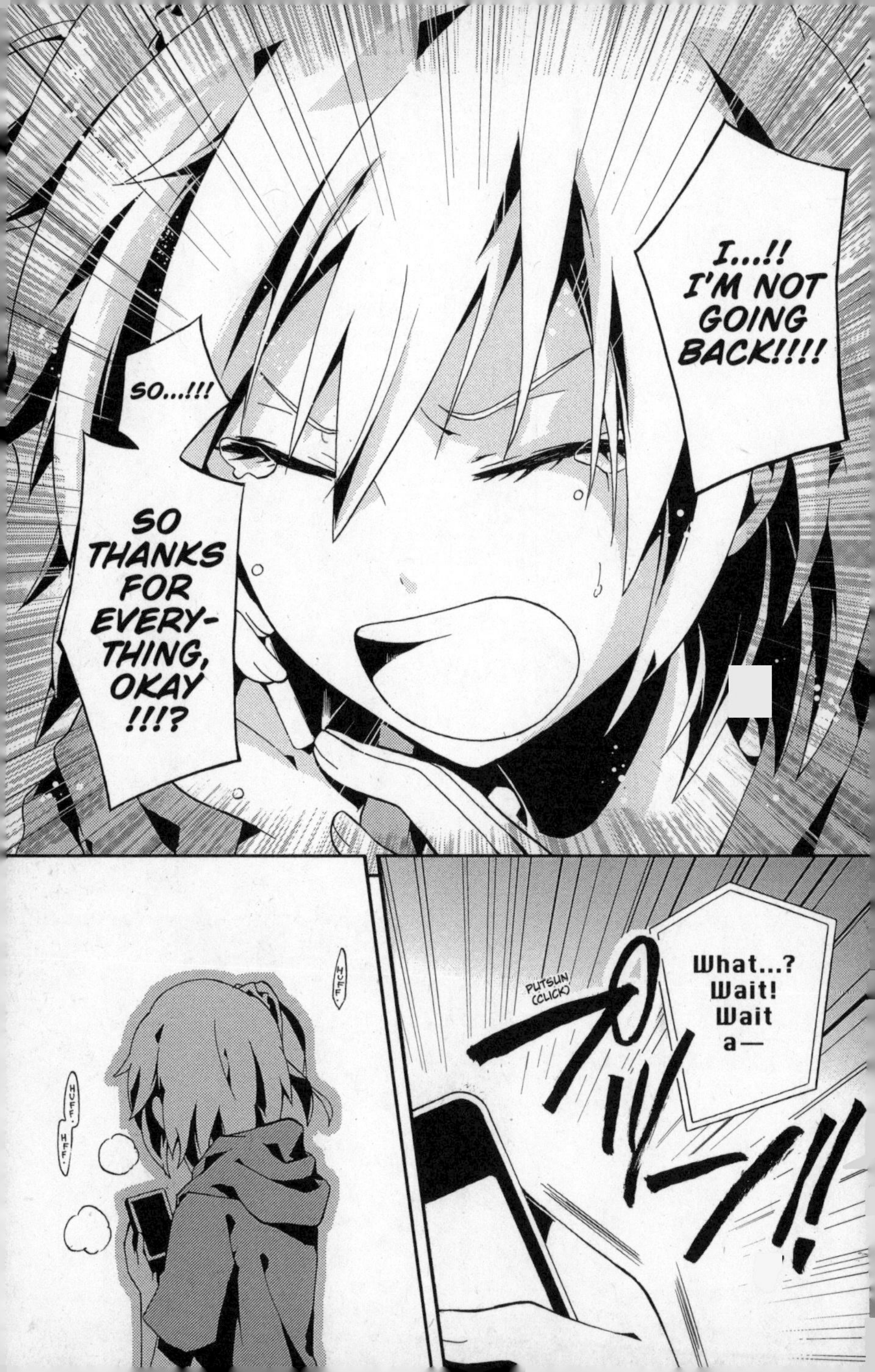
I...!! I'M NOT GOING BACK!!!!
SO...!!!
SO THANKS FOR EVERY-THING, OKAY!!!?
What...? Wait! Wait a—
PUTSUN (CLICK)
HUFF.
HUFF. HFF.

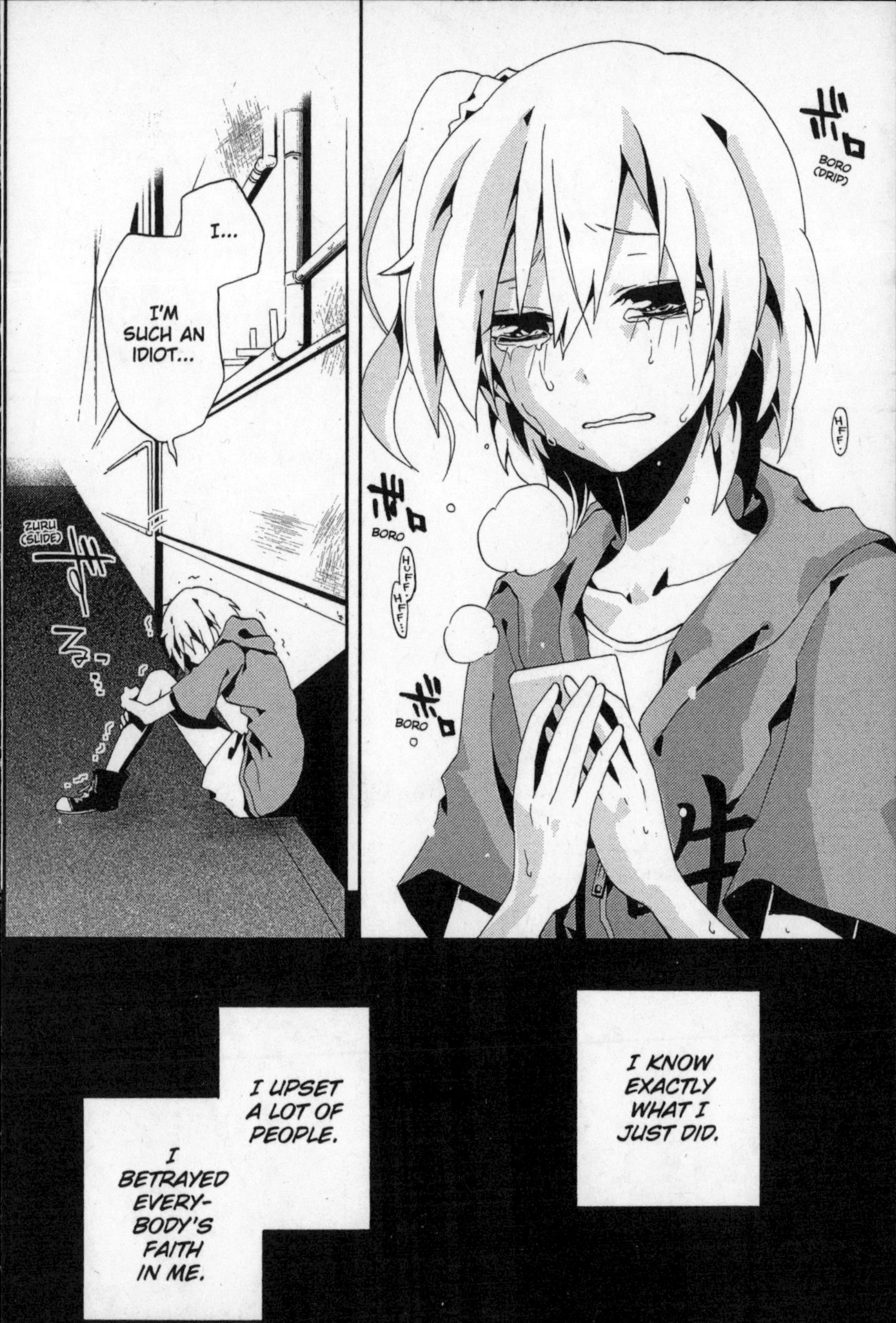
ボロ
BORO (DRIP)
HFF.
ボロ
BORO
HUF HFF...
ボロ
BORO
I...
I'M SUCH AN IDIOT...
ZURU (SLIDE)
I KNOW EXACTLY WHAT I JUST DID.
I UPSET A LOT OF PEOPLE.
I BETRAYED EVERY-BODY'S FAITH IN ME.

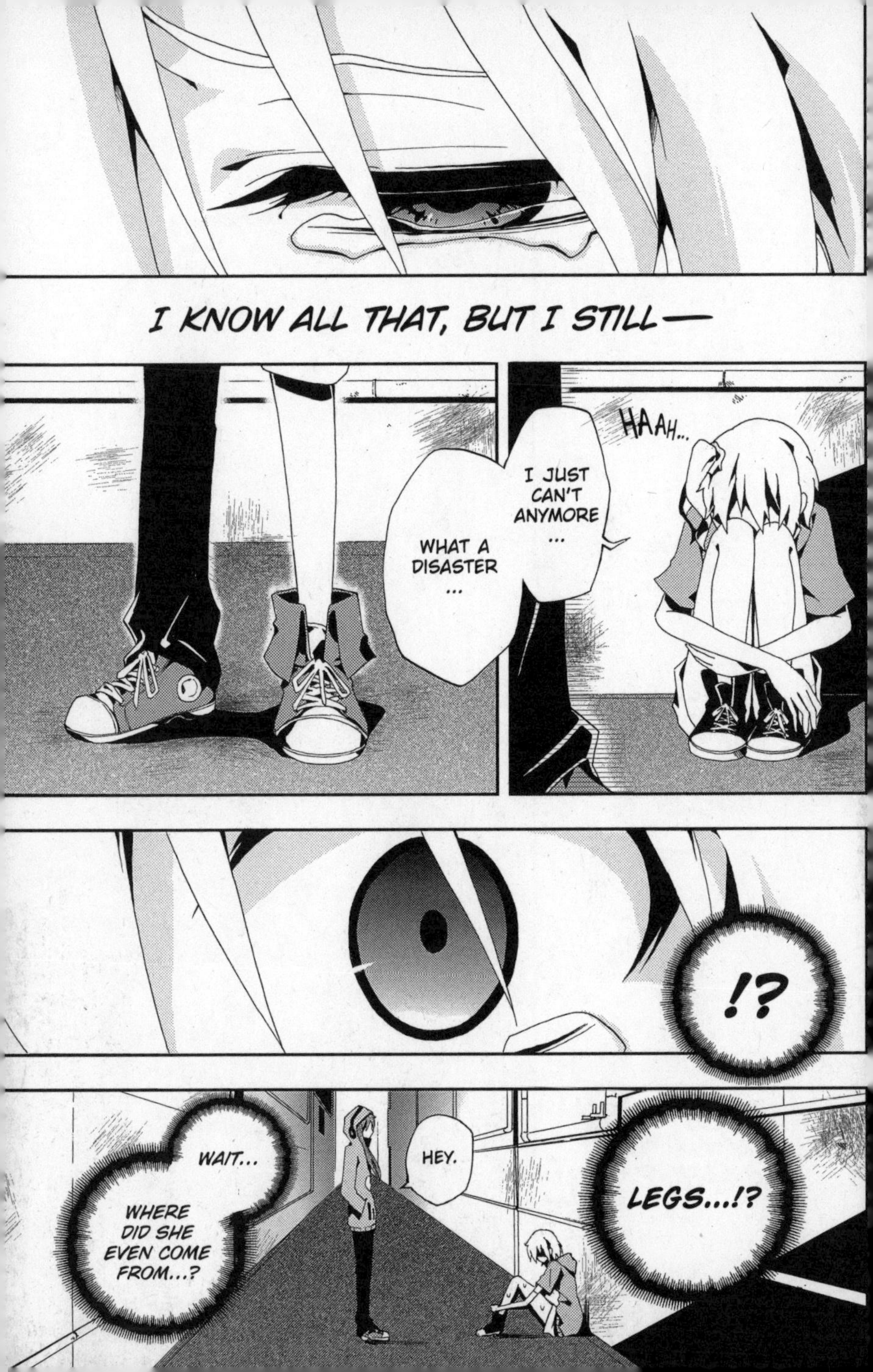
I KNOW ALL THAT, BUT I STILL—
HAAH...
I JUST CAN'T ANYMORE ...
WHAT A DISASTER ...
!?
LEGS...!?
HEY.
WAIT...
WHERE DID SHE EVEN COME FROM...?

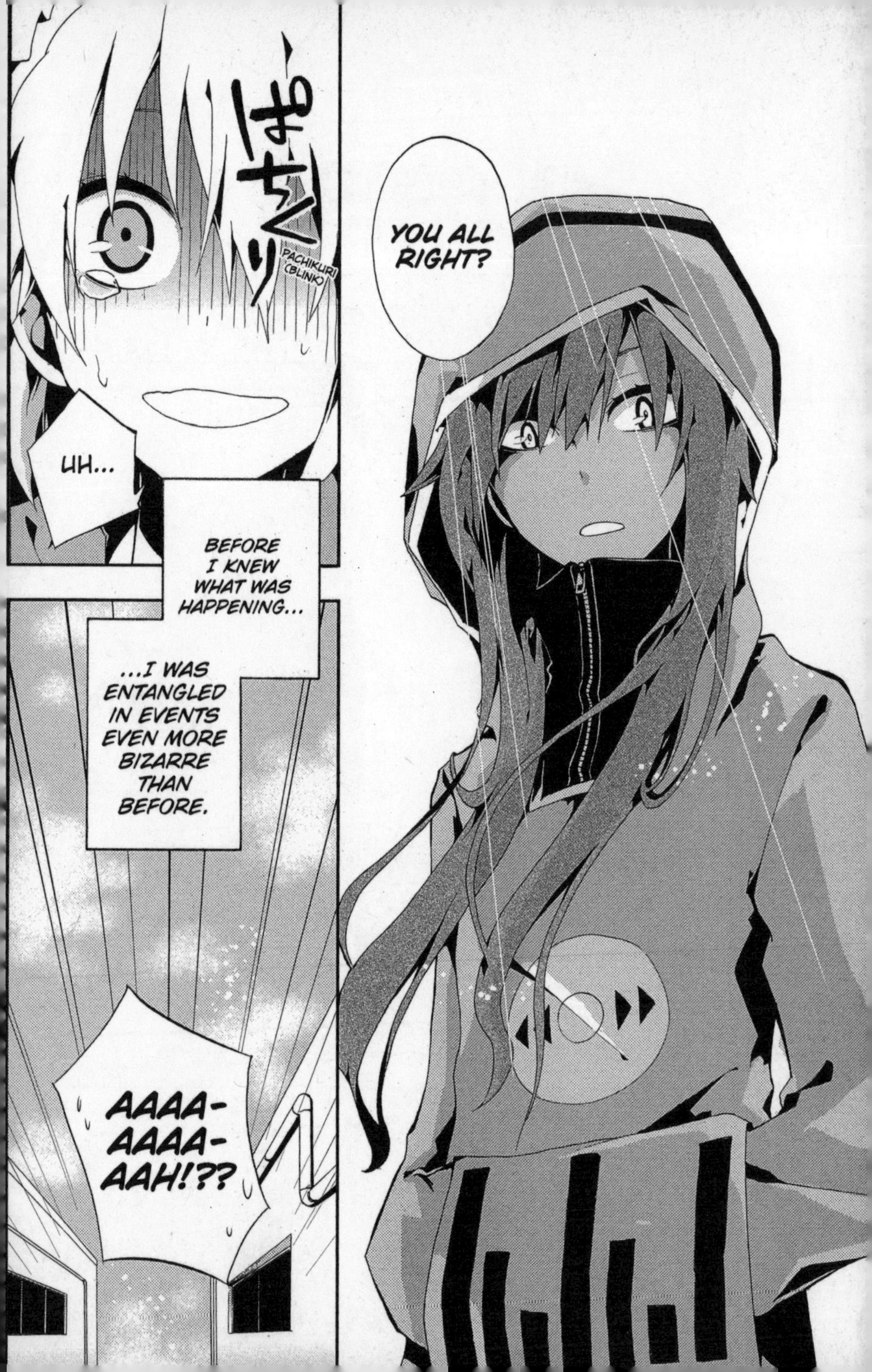
YOU ALL RIGHT?
ぱちくり
PACHIKURI (BLINK)
UH...
BEFORE I KNEW WHAT WAS HAPPENING...
...I WAS ENTANGLED IN EVENTS EVEN MORE BIZARRE THAN BEFORE.
AAAA-AAAA-AAH!??

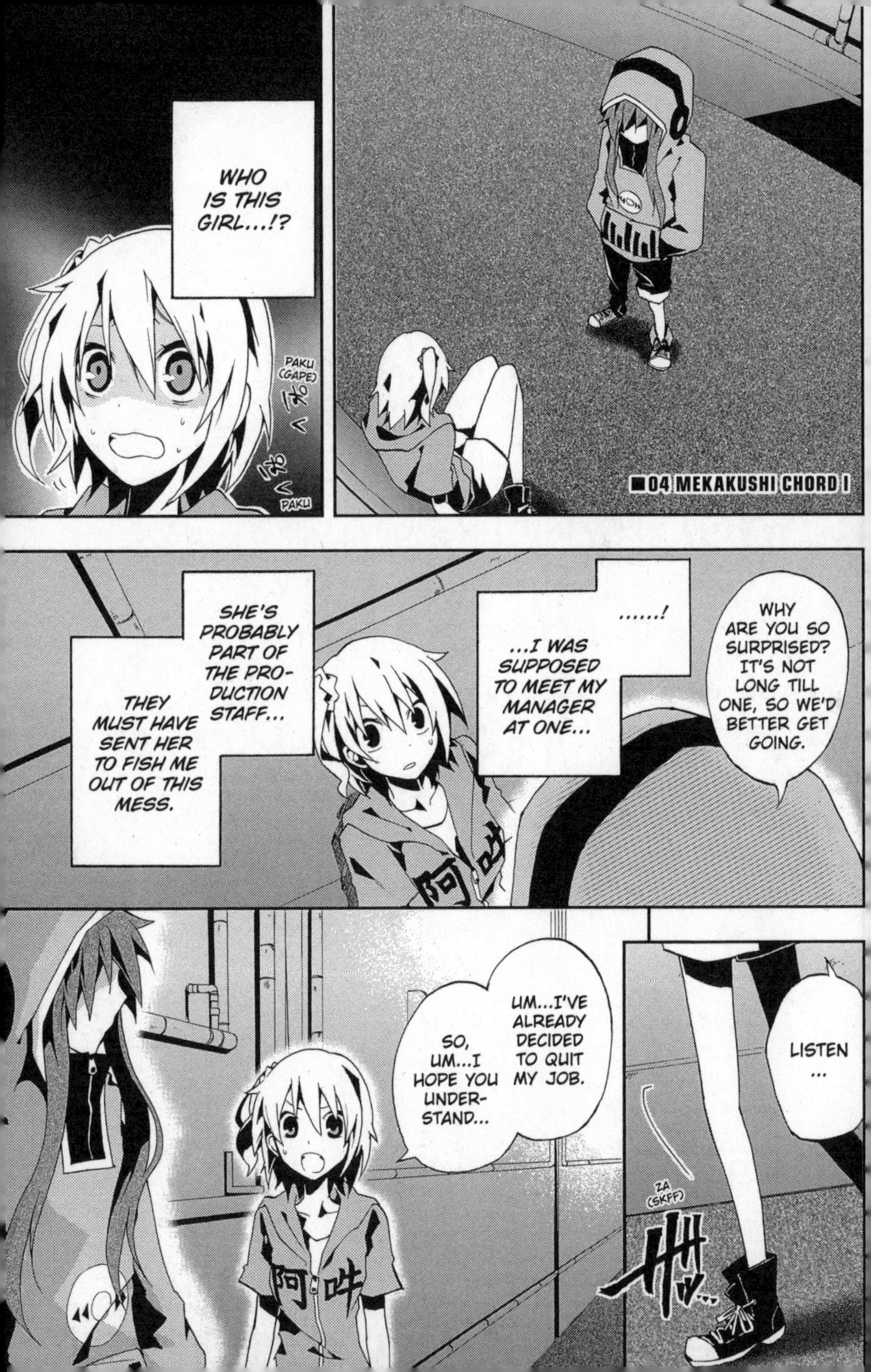
04 MEKAKUSHI CHORD I
WHO IS THIS GIRL...!?
PAKU (GAPE)
PAKU
WHY ARE YOU SO SURPRISED? IT'S NOT LONG TILL ONE, SO WE'D BETTER GET GOING.
......!
...I WAS SUPPOSED TO MEET MY MANAGER AT ONE...
SHE'S PROBABLY PART OF THE PRO-DUCTION STAFF...
THEY MUST HAVE SENT HER TO FISH ME OUT OF THIS MESS.
LISTEN ...
ZA (SKFF)
UM...I'VE ALREADY DECIDED TO QUIT MY JOB.
SO, UM...I HOPE YOU UNDER-STAND...

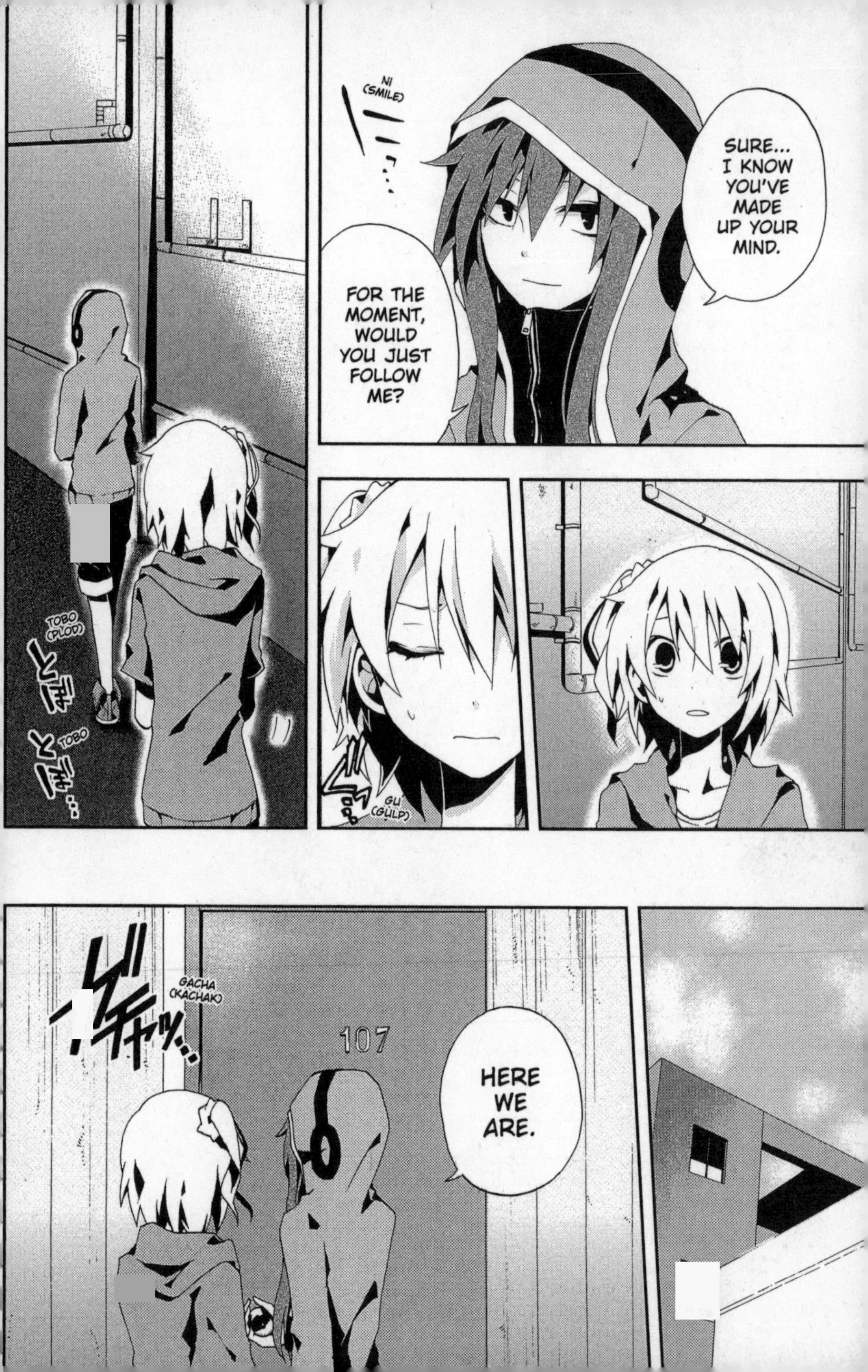
SURE... I KNOW YOU'VE MADE UP YOUR MIND.
NI (SMILE)
FOR THE MOMENT, WOULD YOU JUST FOLLOW ME?
GU (GULP)
TOBO (PLOD)
TOBO
HERE WE ARE.
107
GACHA (KACHAK)

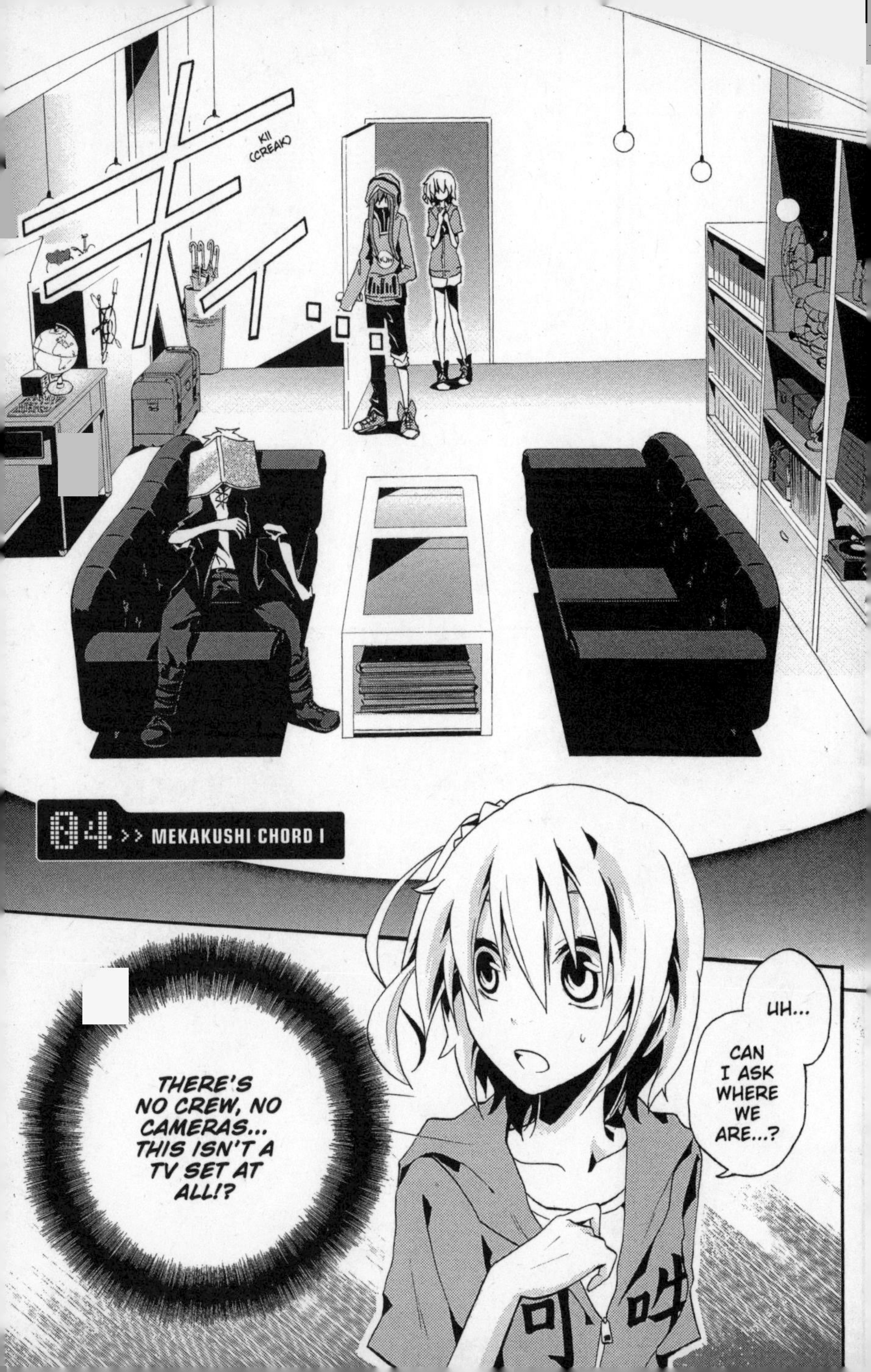
KII (CREAK)
04 >> MEKAKUSHI CHORD I
UH...
CAN I ASK WHERE WE ARE...?
THERE'S NO CREW, NO CAMERAS... THIS ISN'T A TV SET AT ALL!?

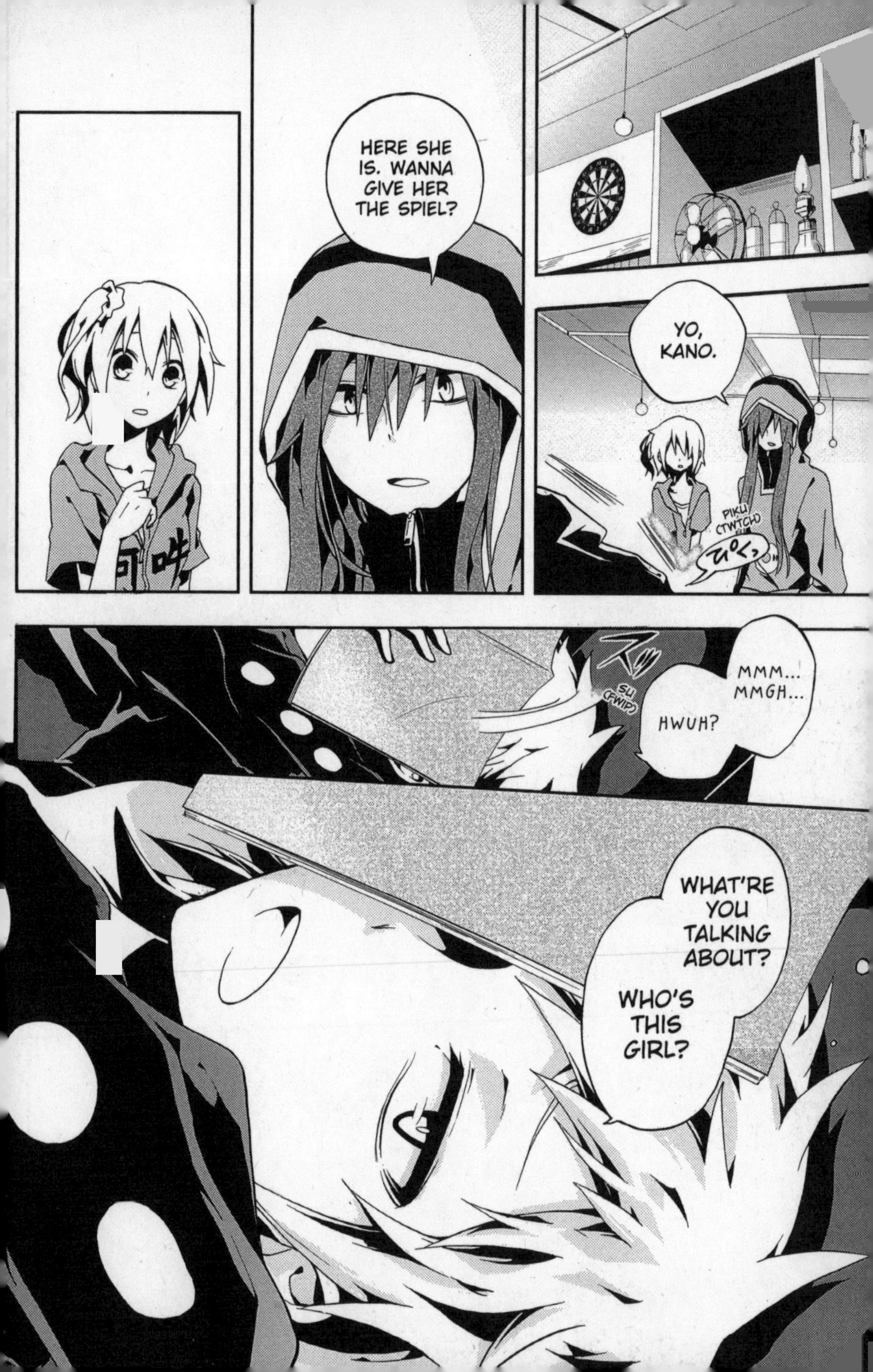
YO, KANO.
PIKU (TWITCH)
ぴくっ
HERE SHE IS. WANNA GIVE HER THE SPIEL?
SU (FWIP)
MMM... MMGH...
HWUH?
WHAT'RE YOU TALKING ABOUT?
WHO'S THIS GIRL?

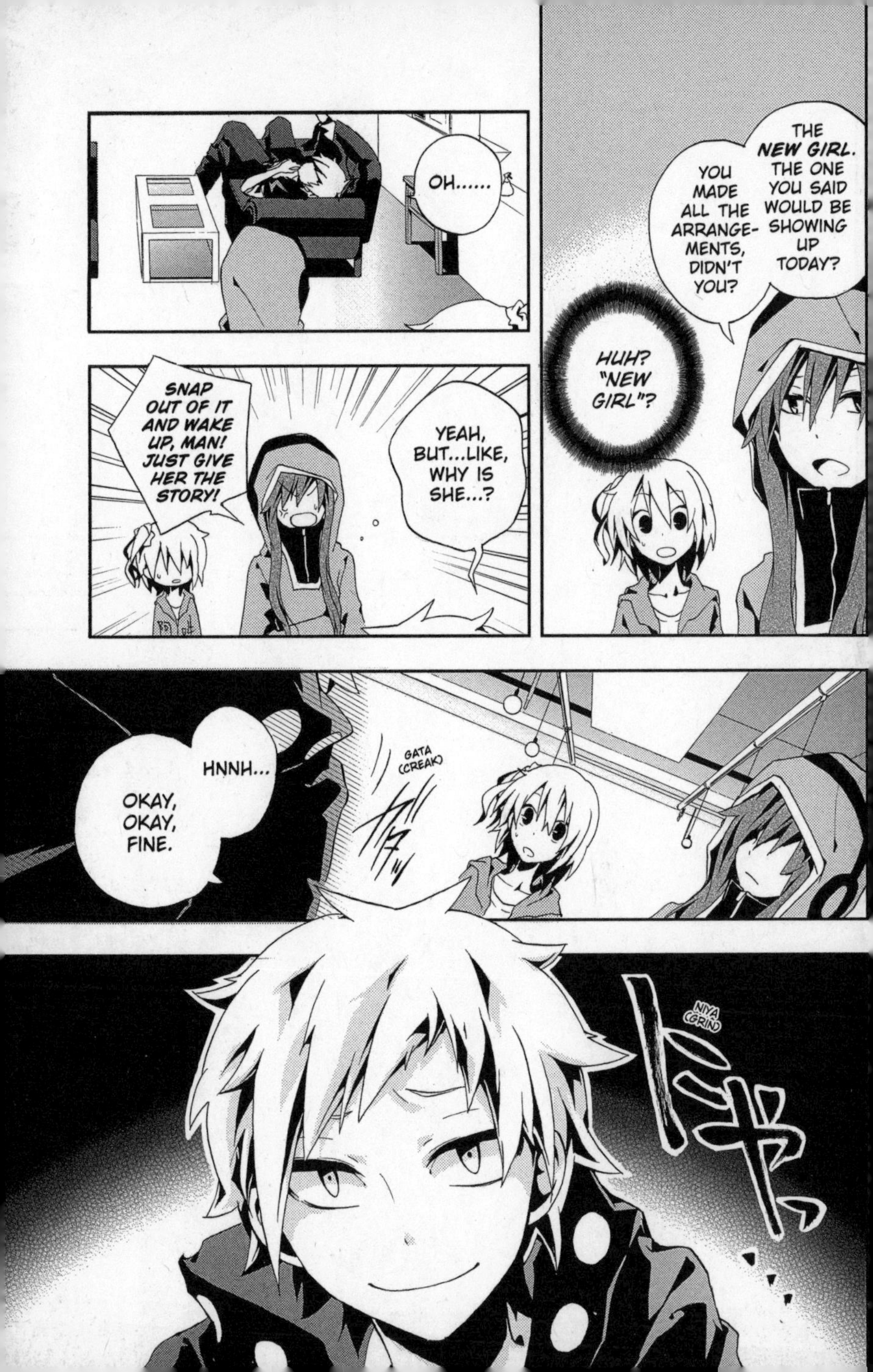
THE NEW GIRL. THE ONE YOU SAID WOULD BE SHOWING UP TODAY?
YOU MADE ALL THE ARRANGEMENTS, DIDN'T YOU?
HUH? "NEW GIRL"?
OH......
YEAH, BUT...LIKE, WHY IS SHE...?
SNAP OUT OF IT AND WAKE UP, MAN! JUST GIVE HER THE STORY!
GATA (CREAK)
HNNH...
OKAY, OKAY, FINE.
NIYA (GRIN)

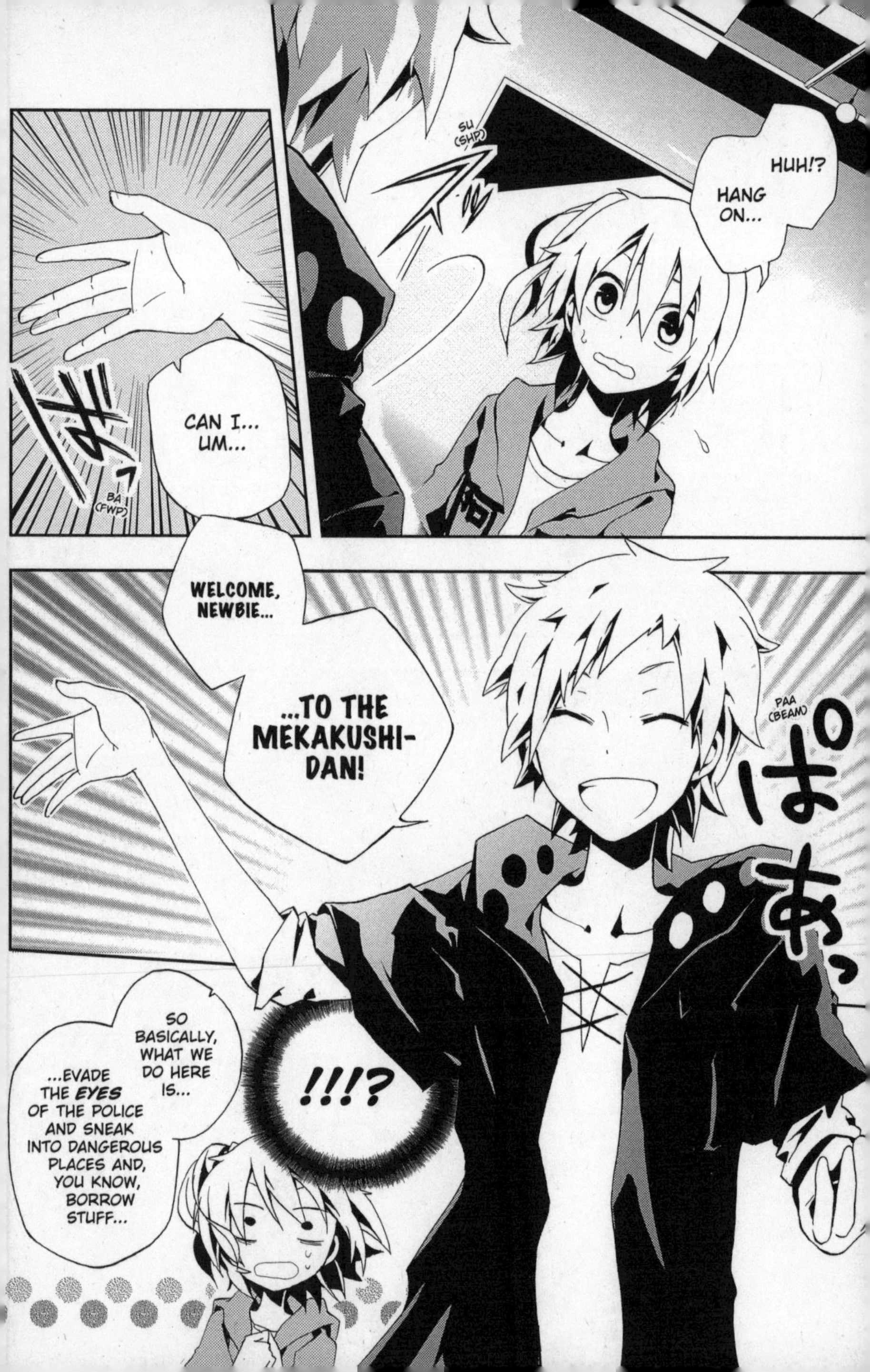
SU (SHP)
HUH!? HANG ON...
CAN I... UM...
BA (FWP)
WELCOME, NEWBIE...
...TO THE MEKAKUSHI-DAN!
PAA (BEAM)
SO BASICALLY, WHAT WE DO HERE IS...
...EVADE THE *EYES* OF THE POLICE AND SNEAK INTO DANGEROUS PLACES AND, YOU KNOW, BORROW STUFF...
!!!?

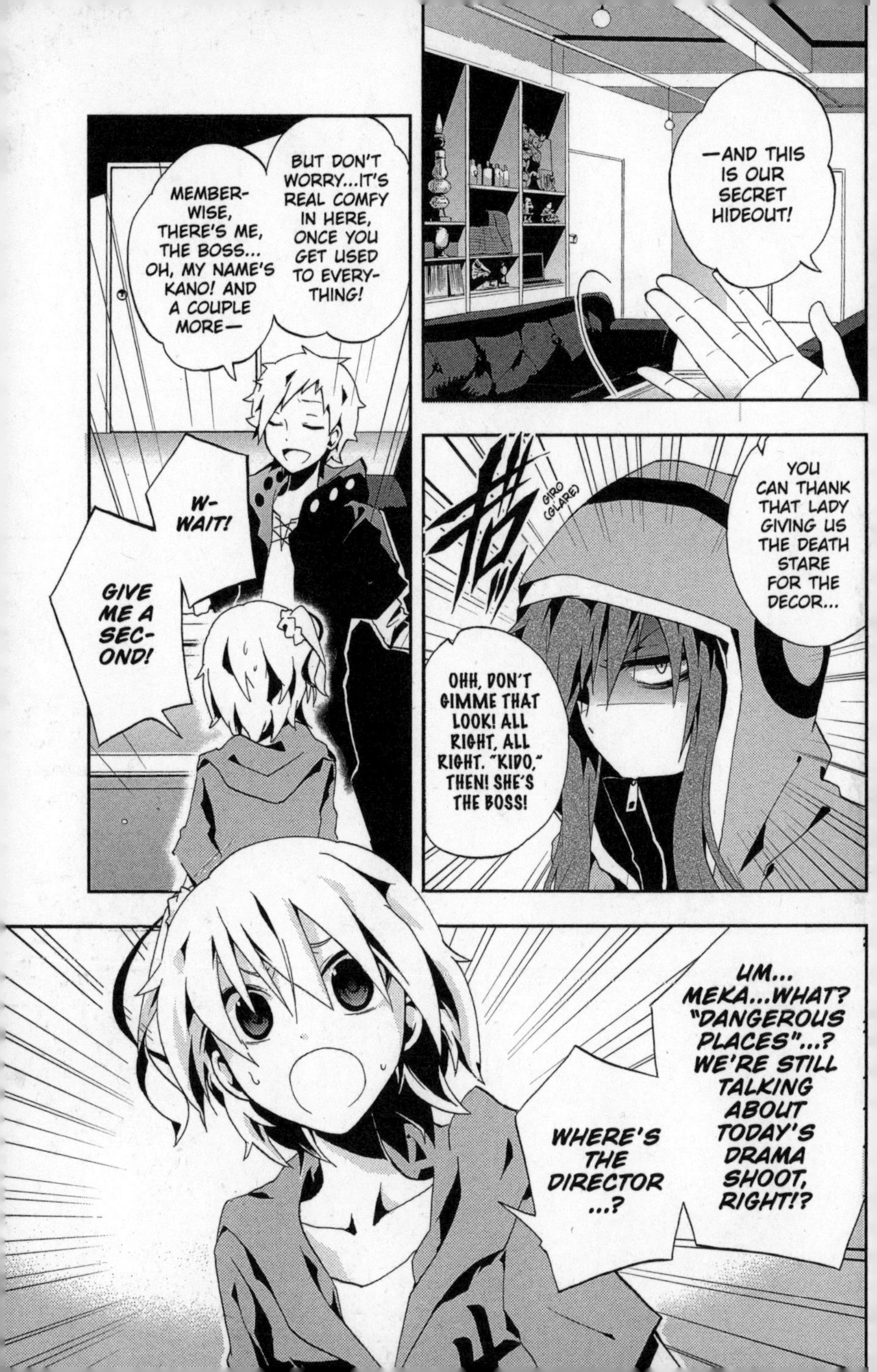
—AND THIS IS OUR SECRET HIDEOUT!
YOU CAN THANK THAT LADY GIVING US THE DEATH STARE FOR THE DECOR...
GIRO (GLARE)
OHH, DON'T GIMME THAT LOOK! ALL RIGHT, ALL RIGHT. "KIDO," THEN! SHE'S THE BOSS!
BUT DON'T WORRY...IT'S REAL COMFY IN HERE, ONCE YOU GET USED TO EVERY-THING!
MEMBER-WISE, THERE'S ME, THE BOSS... OH, MY NAME'S KANO! AND A COUPLE MORE—
W-WAIT!
GIVE ME A SEC-OND!
UM... MEKA...WHAT? "DANGEROUS PLACES"...? WE'RE STILL TALKING ABOUT TODAY'S DRAMA SHOOT, RIGHT!?
WHERE'S THE DIRECTOR ...?

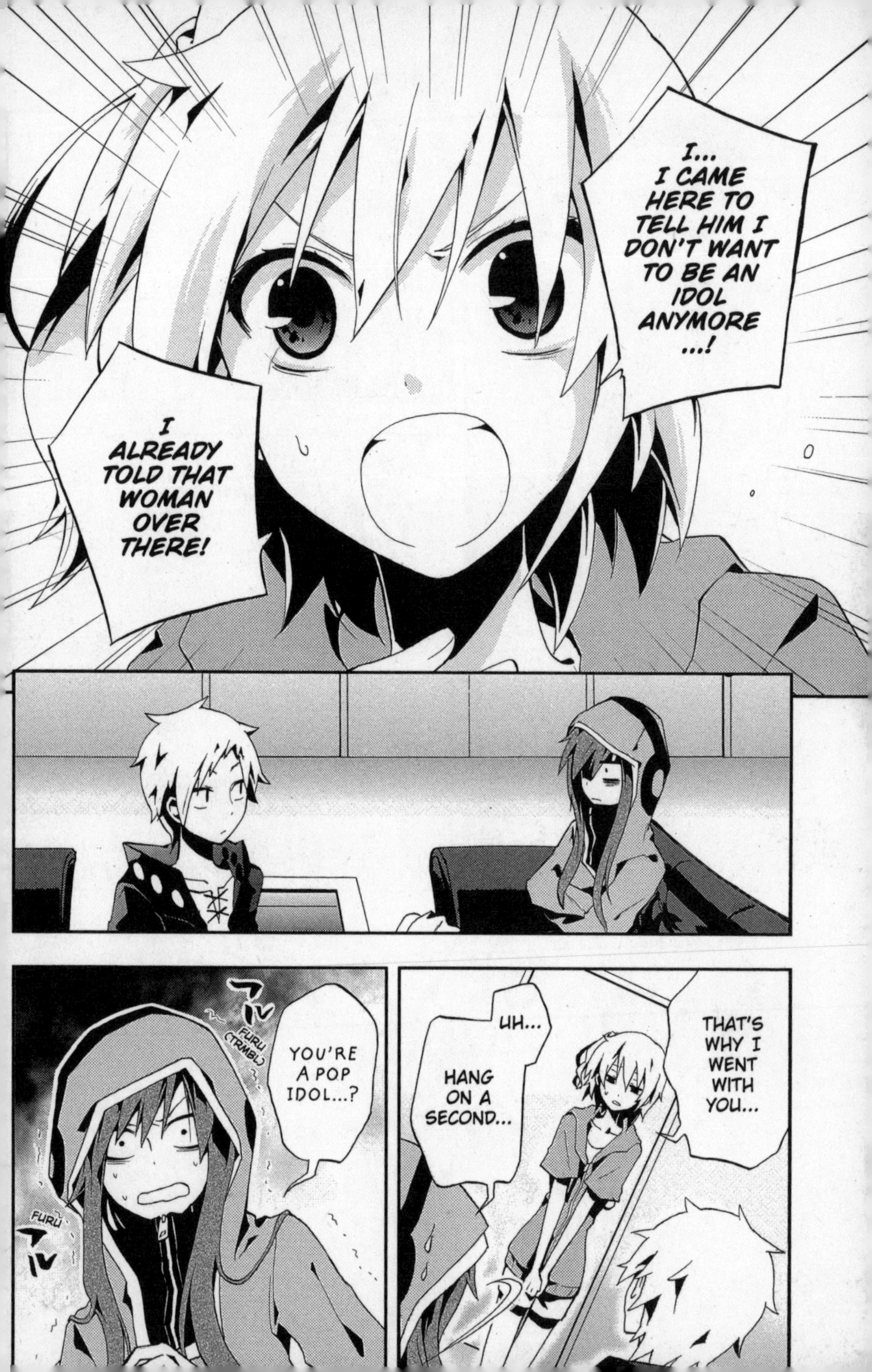
I... I CAME HERE TO TELL HIM I DON'T WANT TO BE AN IDOL ANYMORE ...!
I ALREADY TOLD THAT WOMAN OVER THERE!
THAT'S WHY I WENT WITH YOU...
UH...
HANG ON A SECOND...
FURU (TRMBL)
YOU'RE A POP IDOL...?
FURU

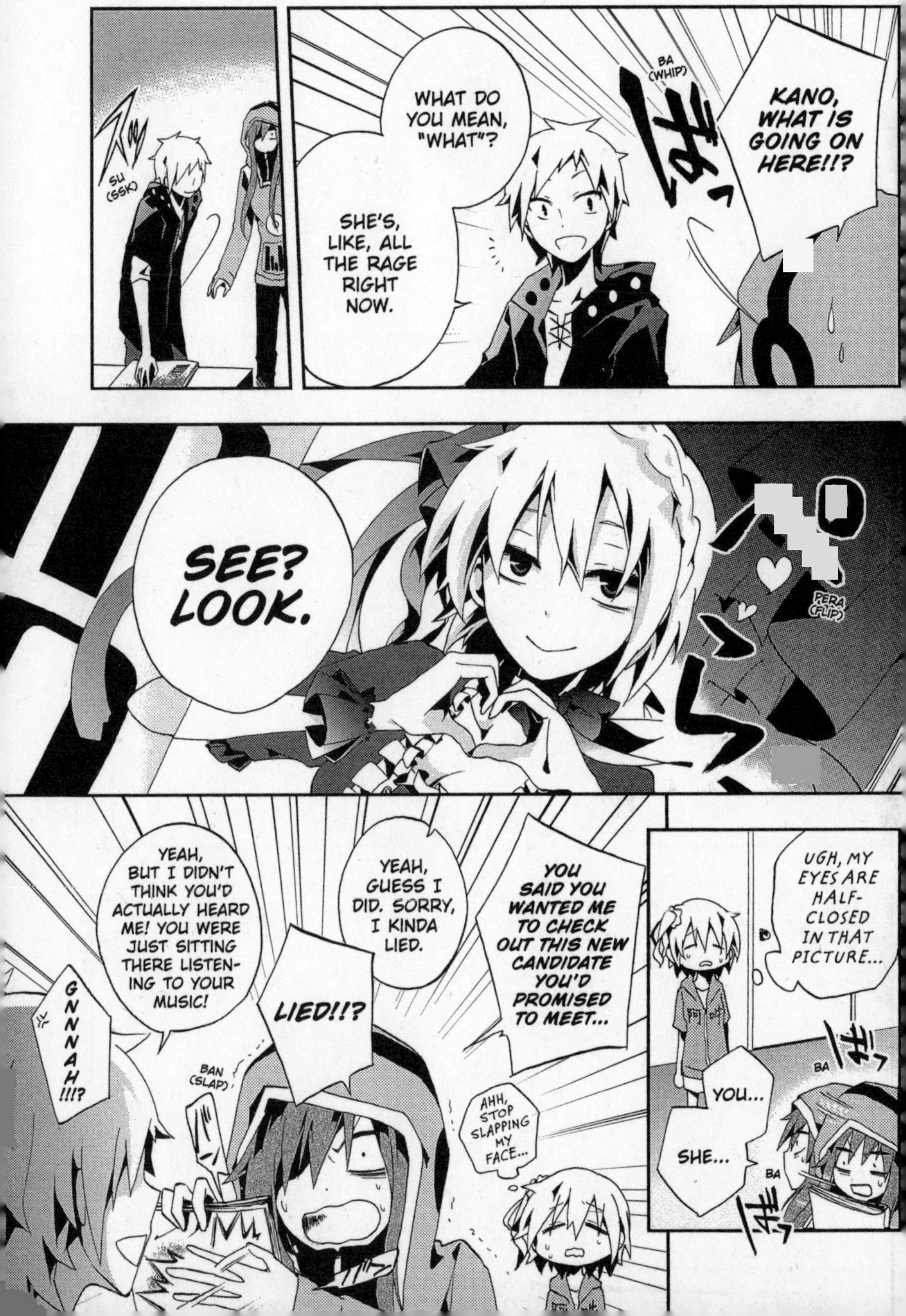
BA (WHIP)
KANO, WHAT IS GOING ON HERE!!?
WHAT DO YOU MEAN, "WHAT"?
SHE'S, LIKE, ALL THE RAGE RIGHT NOW.
SU (SSK)
PERA (FLIP)
SEE? LOOK.
UGH, MY EYES ARE HALF-CLOSED IN THAT PICTURE...
BA
YOU...
SHE...
BA
YOU SAID YOU WANTED ME TO CHECK OUT THIS NEW CANDIDATE YOU'D PROMISED TO MEET...
YEAH, GUESS I DID. SORRY, I KINDA LIED.
LIED!!?
YEAH, BUT I DIDN'T THINK YOU'D ACTUALLY HEARD ME! YOU WERE JUST SITTING THERE LISTENING TO YOUR MUSIC!
AHH, STOP SLAPPING MY FACE...
BAN (SLAP)
GNNNAH!!!?

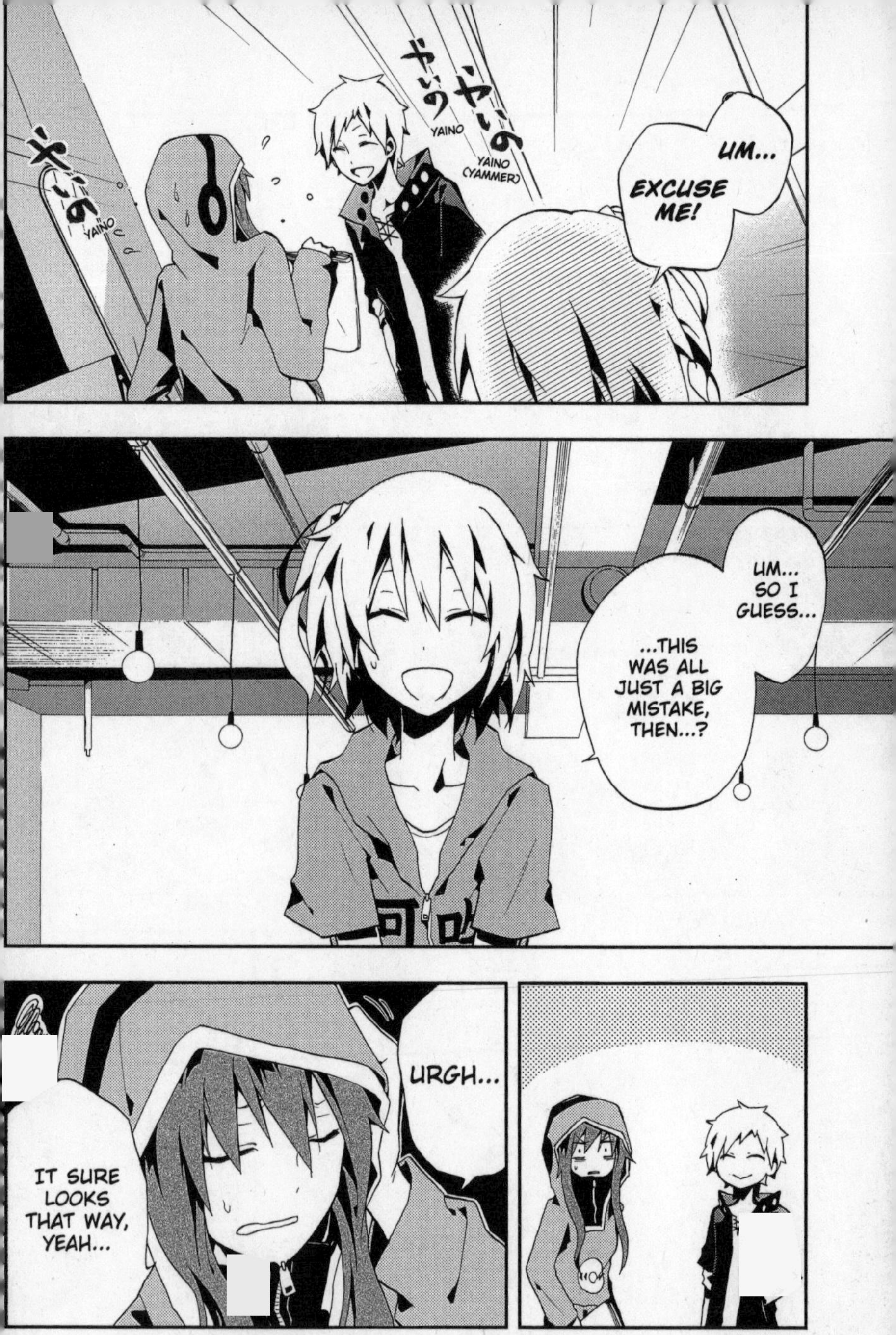

UM... EXCUSE ME!
YAINO (YAMMER)
YAINO
YAINO
UM... SO I GUESS...
...THIS WAS ALL JUST A BIG MISTAKE, THEN...?
URGH...
IT SURE LOOKS THAT WAY, YEAH...

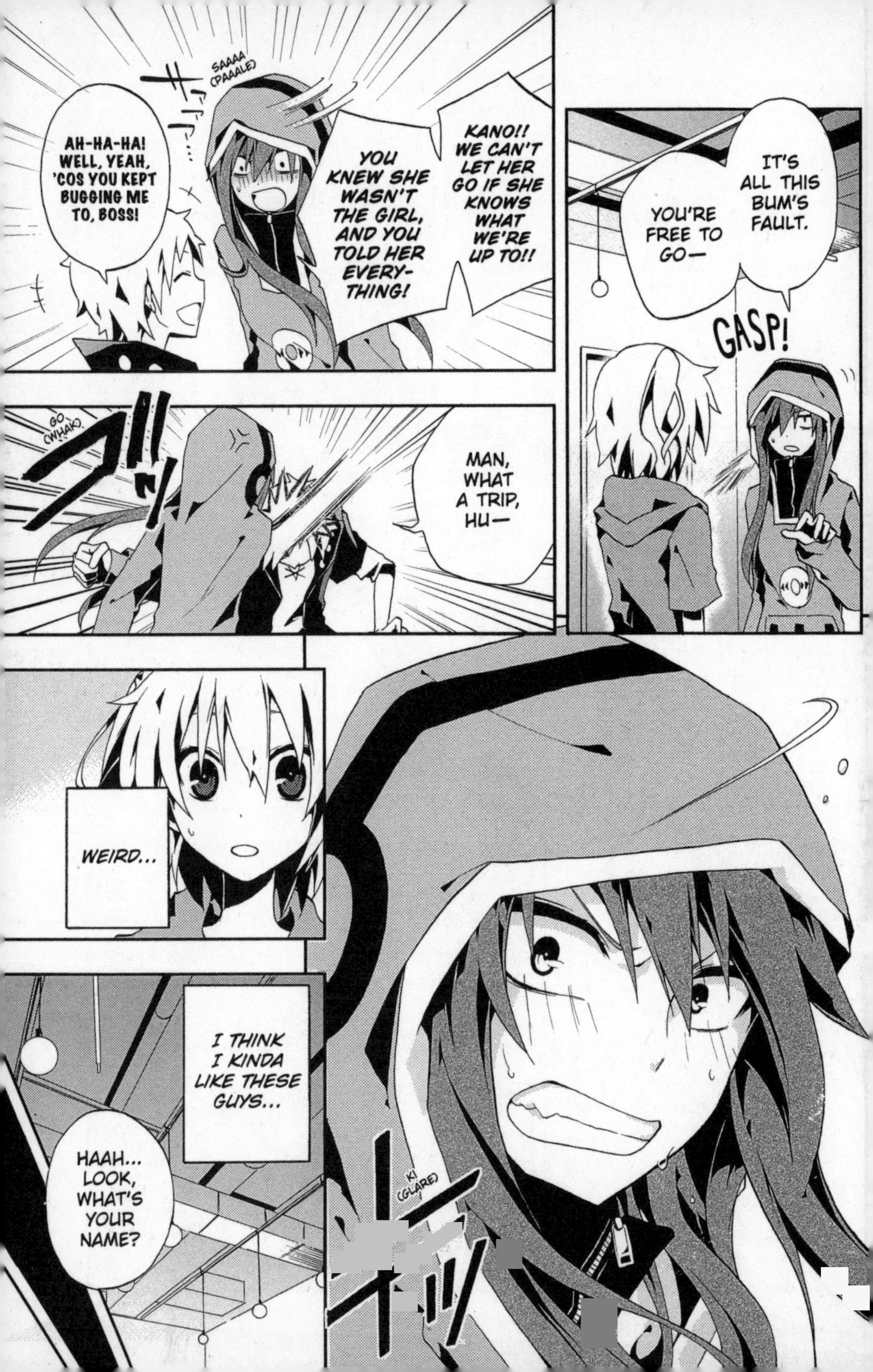
IT'S ALL THIS BUM'S FAULT.
YOU'RE FREE TO GO—
GASP!
KANO!! WE CAN'T LET HER GO IF SHE KNOWS WHAT WE'RE UP TO!!
YOU KNEW SHE WASN'T THE GIRL, AND YOU TOLD HER EVERY-THING!
SAAAA (PAAALE)
AH-HA-HA! WELL, YEAH, 'COS YOU KEPT BUGGING ME TO, BOSS!
MAN, WHAT A TRIP, HU—
GO (WHAK)
KI (GLARE)
WEIRD...
I THINK I KINDA LIKE THESE GUYS...
HAAH... LOOK, WHAT'S YOUR NAME?

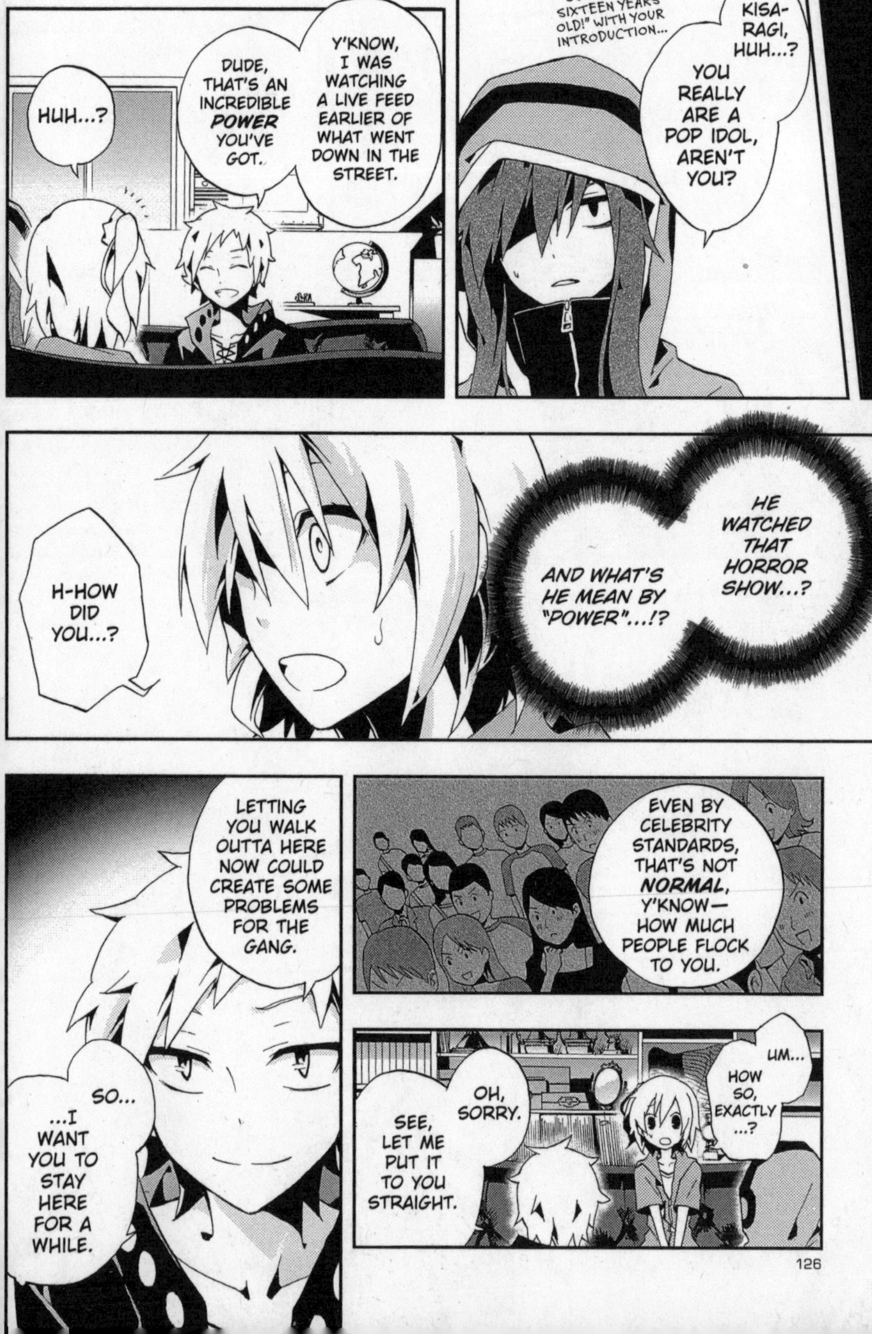
KISA-RAGI, HUH...? YOU REALLY ARE A POP IDOL, AREN'T YOU?
SPELLING OUT "AND I'M SIXTEEN YEARS OLD!" WITH YOUR INTRODUCTION...
Y'KNOW, I WAS WATCHING A LIVE FEED EARLIER OF WHAT WENT DOWN IN THE STREET.
DUDE, THAT'S AN INCREDIBLE **POWER** YOU'VE GOT.
HUH...?
HE WATCHED THAT HORROR SHOW...?
AND WHAT'S HE MEAN BY "POWER"...!?
H-HOW DID YOU...?
EVEN BY CELEBRITY STANDARDS, THAT'S NOT **NORMAL**, Y'KNOW—HOW MUCH PEOPLE FLOCK TO YOU.
UM... HOW SO, EXACTLY...?
OH, SORRY.
SEE, LET ME PUT IT TO YOU STRAIGHT.
LETTING YOU WALK OUTTA HERE NOW COULD CREATE SOME PROBLEMS FOR THE GANG.
SO...
...I WANT YOU TO STAY HERE FOR A WHILE.

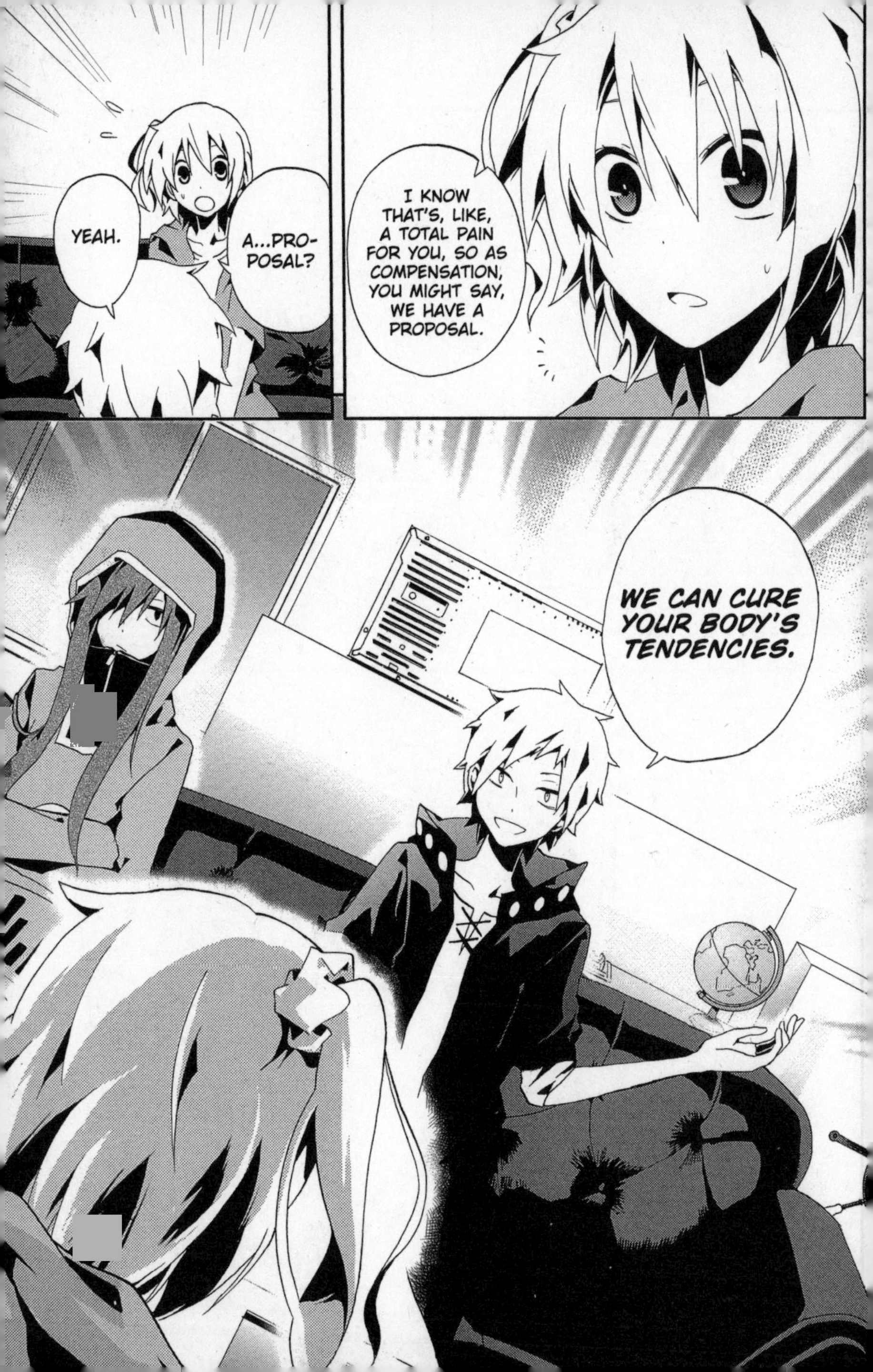
I KNOW THAT'S, LIKE, A TOTAL PAIN FOR YOU, SO AS COMPENSATION, YOU MIGHT SAY, WE HAVE A PROPOSAL.
A...PRO-POSAL?
YEAH.
WE CAN CURE YOUR BODY'S TENDENCIES.

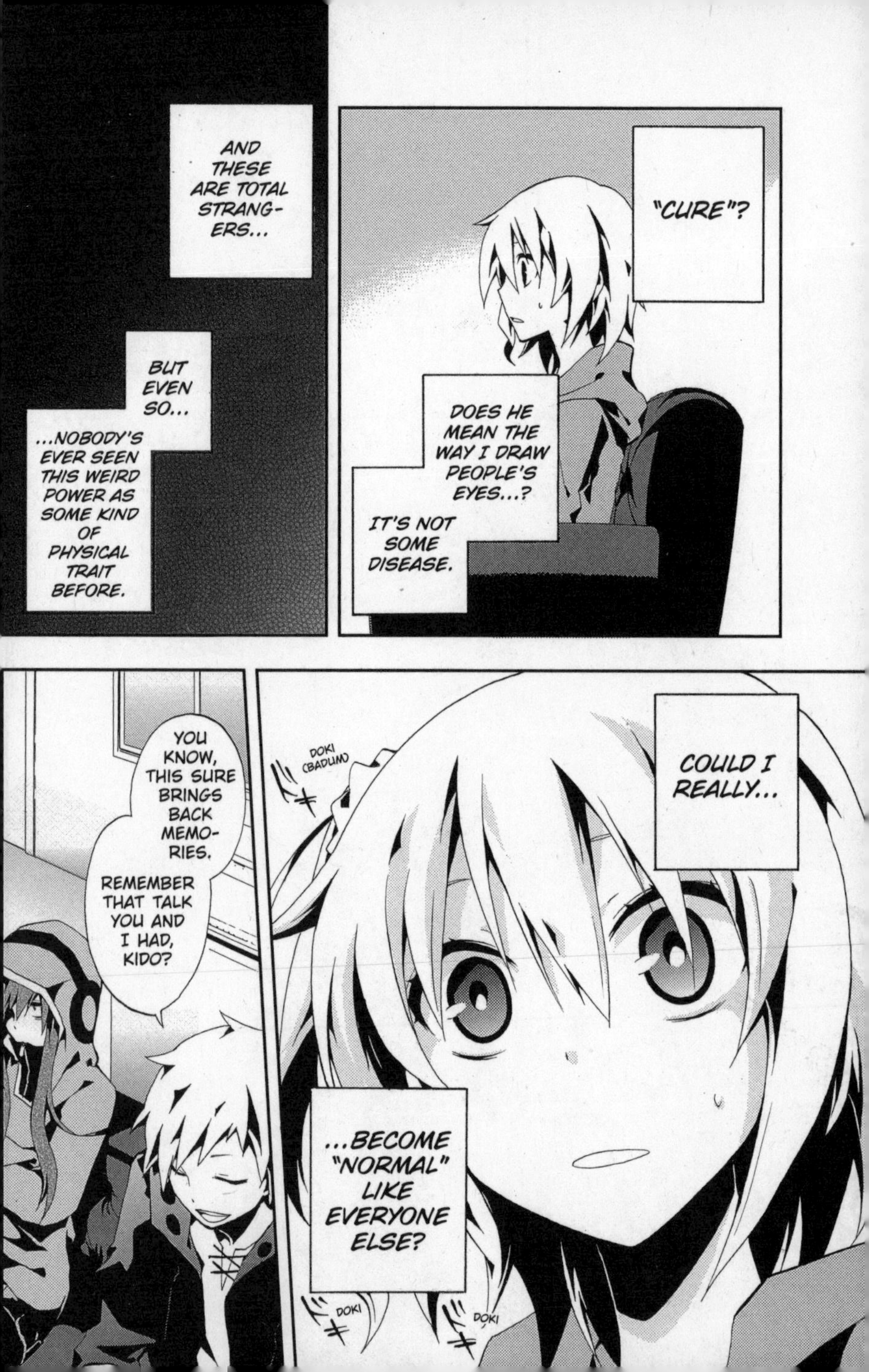
"CURE"?
DOES HE MEAN THE WAY I DRAW PEOPLE'S EYES...?
IT'S NOT SOME DISEASE.
AND THESE ARE TOTAL STRANG-ERS...
BUT EVEN SO...
...NOBODY'S EVER SEEN THIS WEIRD POWER AS SOME KIND OF PHYSICAL TRAIT BEFORE.
COULD I REALLY...
DOKI (BADUM)
...BECOME "NORMAL" LIKE EVERYONE ELSE?
DOKI
DOKI
YOU KNOW, THIS SURE BRINGS BACK MEMO-RIES.
REMEMBER THAT TALK YOU AND I HAD, KIDO?

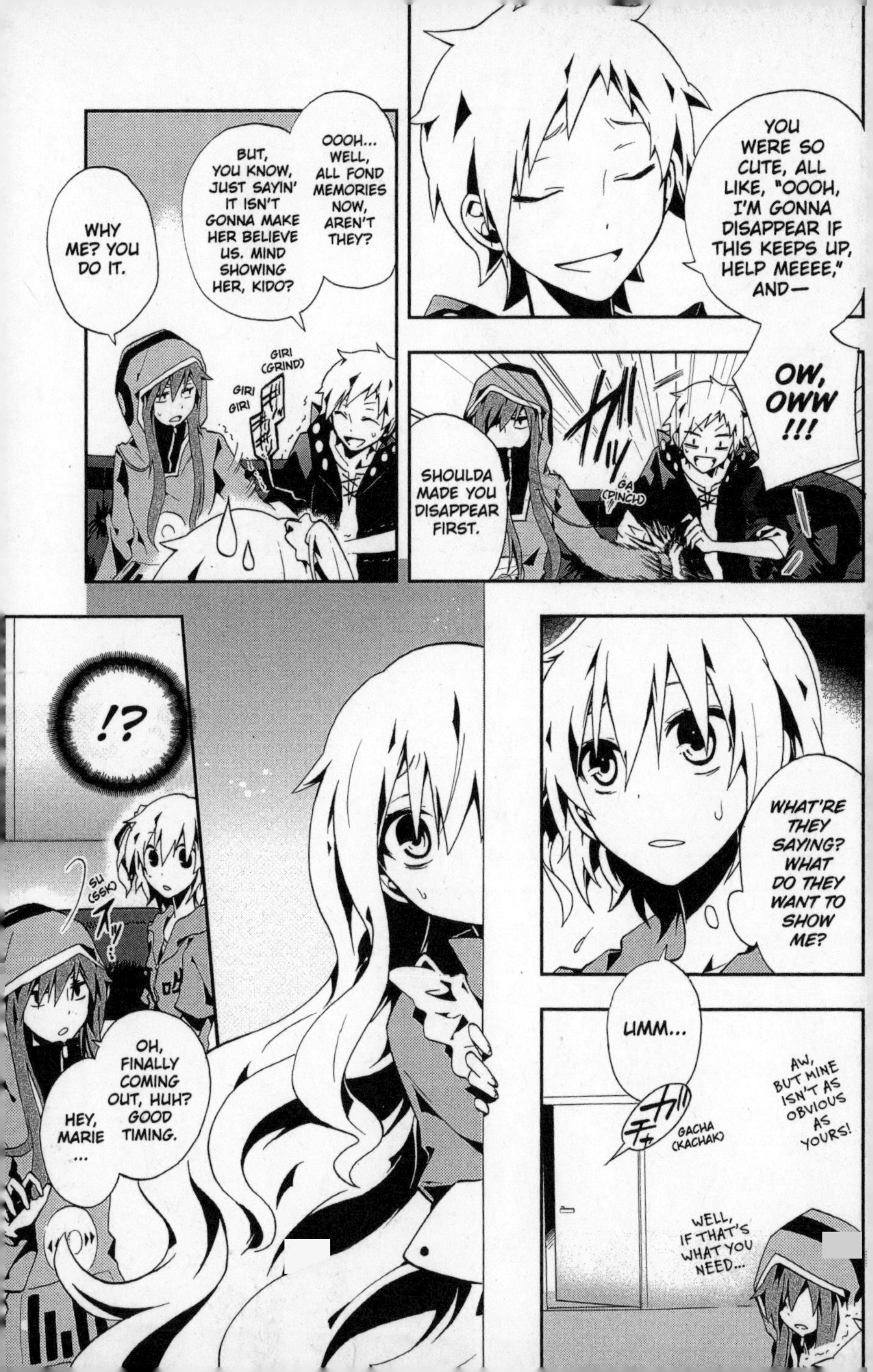
YOU WERE SO CUTE, ALL LIKE, "OOOH, I'M GONNA DISAPPEAR IF THIS KEEPS UP, HELP MEEEE," AND—
OW, OWW!!!
GA (PINCH)
SHOULDA MADE YOU DISAPPEAR FIRST.
OOOH... WELL, ALL FOND MEMORIES NOW, AREN'T THEY?
BUT, YOU KNOW, JUST SAYIN' IT ISN'T GONNA MAKE HER BELIEVE US. MIND SHOWING HER, KIDO?
GIRI (GRIND)
GIRI GIRI
WHY ME? YOU DO IT.
WHAT'RE THEY SAYING? WHAT DO THEY WANT TO SHOW ME?
UMM...
GACHA (KACHAK)
AW, BUT MINE ISN'T AS OBVIOUS AS YOURS!
WELL, IF THAT'S WHAT YOU NEED...
!?
SU (SSK)
OH, FINALLY COMING OUT, HUH? GOOD TIMING.
HEY, MARIE ...

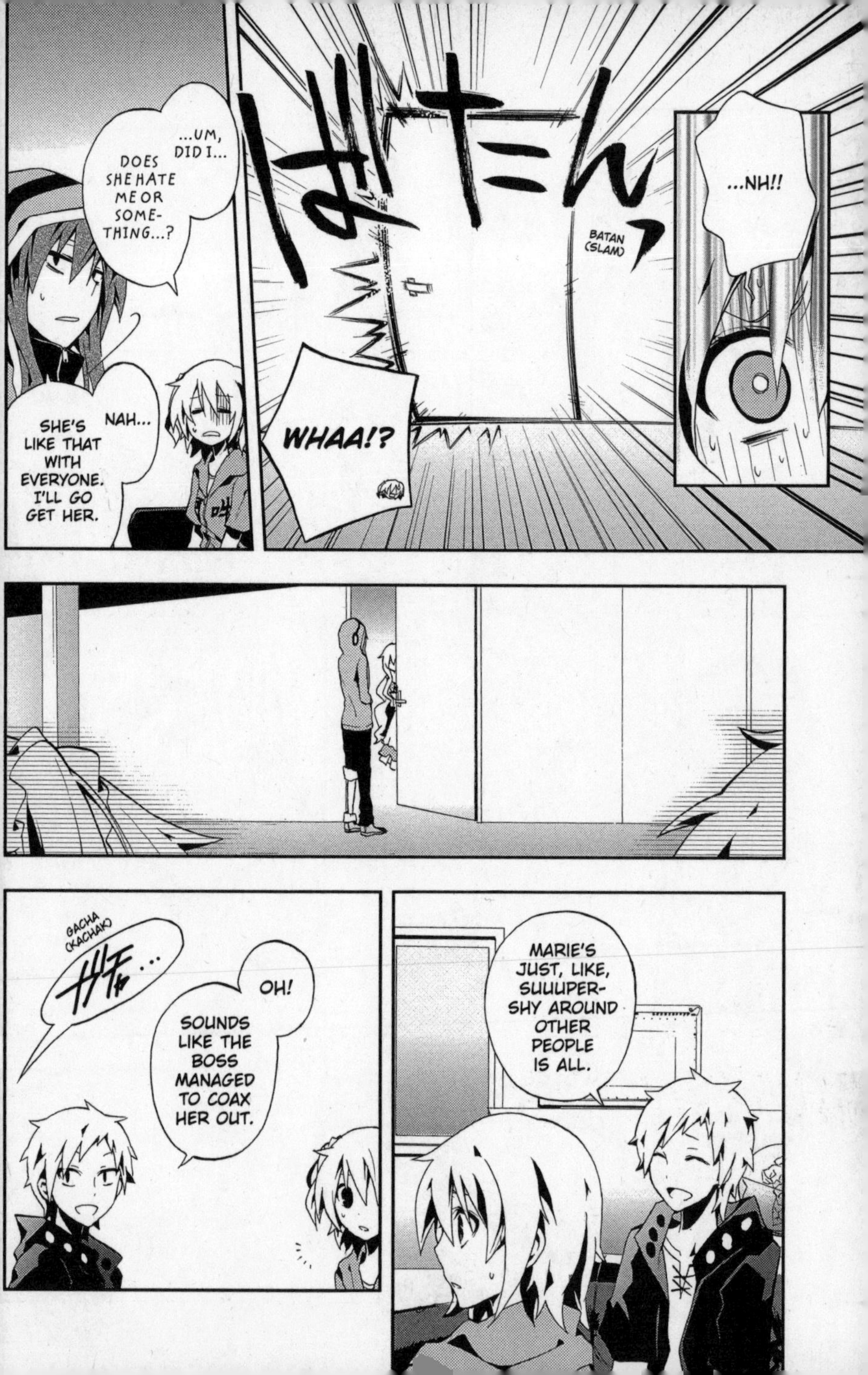
...NH!!
BATAN (SLAM)
WHAA!?
...UM, DID I...
DOES SHE HATE ME OR SOME-THING...?
NAH...
SHE'S LIKE THAT WITH EVERYONE. I'LL GO GET HER.
MARIE'S JUST, LIKE, SUUUPER-SHY AROUND OTHER PEOPLE IS ALL.
GACHA (KACHAK)
OH!
SOUNDS LIKE THE BOSS MANAGED TO COAX HER OUT.

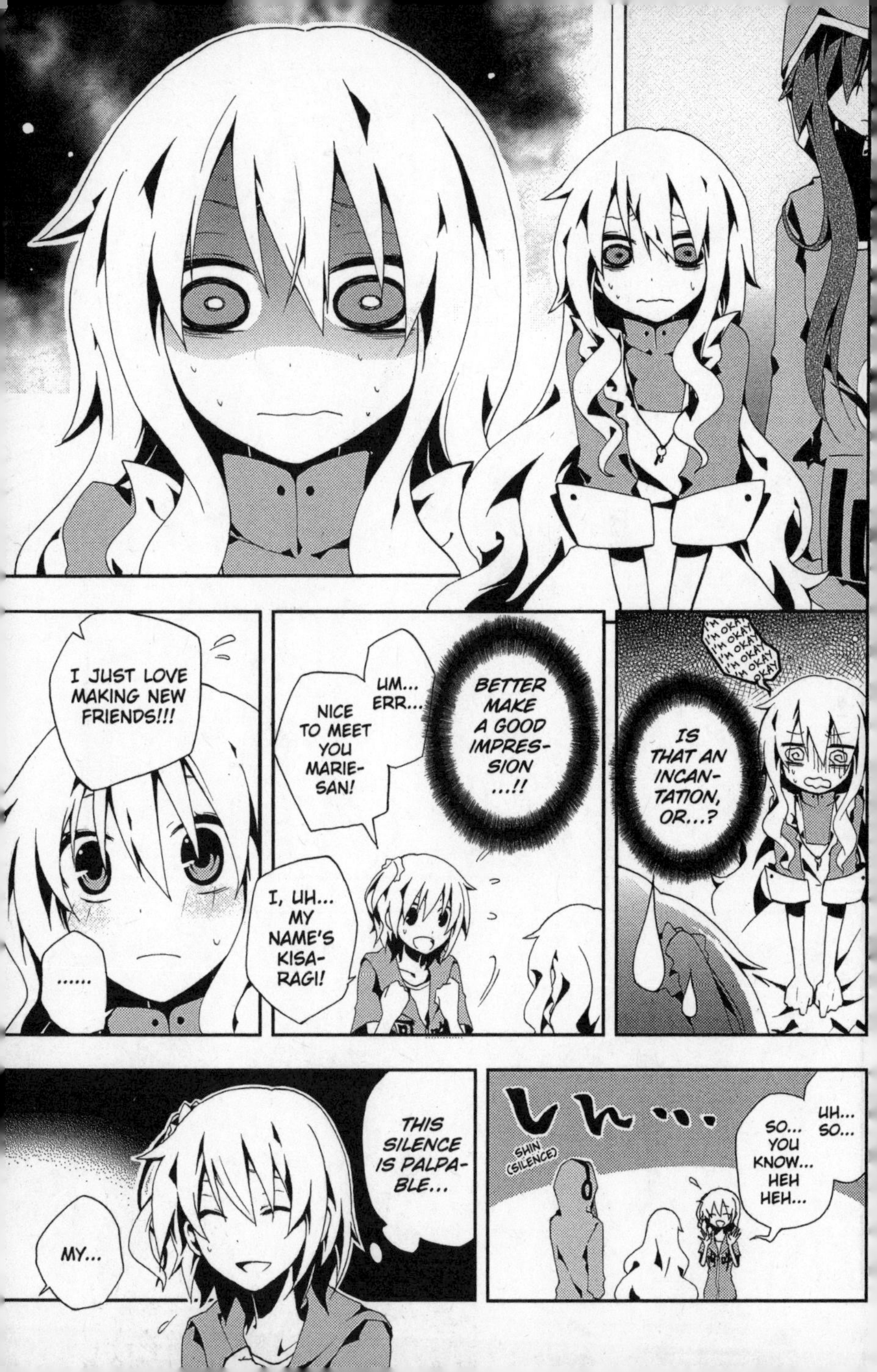
I'M OKAY I'M OKAY I'M OKAY I'M OKAY I'M OKAY
IS THAT AN INCANTATION, OR...?
BETTER MAKE A GOOD IMPRESSION ...!!
UM... ERR...
NICE TO MEET YOU MARIE-SAN!
I, UH... MY NAME'S KISARAGI!
I JUST LOVE MAKING NEW FRIENDS!!!
......
しん…
SHIN (SILENCE)
UH... SO...
SO... YOU KNOW... HEH HEH...
THIS SILENCE IS PALPABLE...
MY...

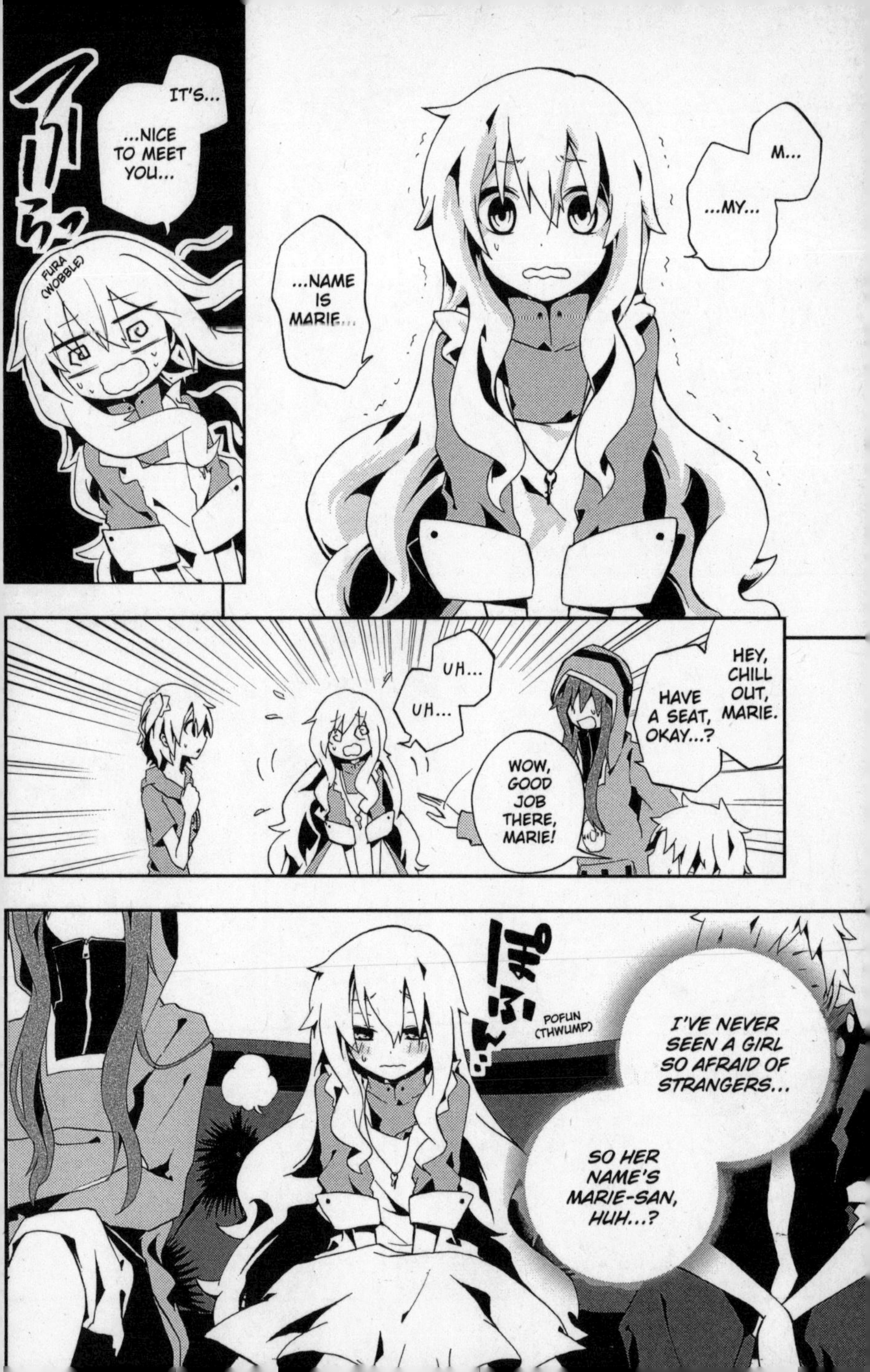
M...
...MY...
...NAME IS MARIE...
IT'S...
...NICE TO MEET YOU...
FURA (WOBBLE)
HEY, CHILL OUT, MARIE.
HAVE A SEAT, OKAY...?
WOW, GOOD JOB THERE, MARIE!
UH...
UH...
I'VE NEVER SEEN A GIRL SO AFRAID OF STRANGERS...
SO HER NAME'S MARIE-SAN, HUH...?
POFUN (THWUMP)

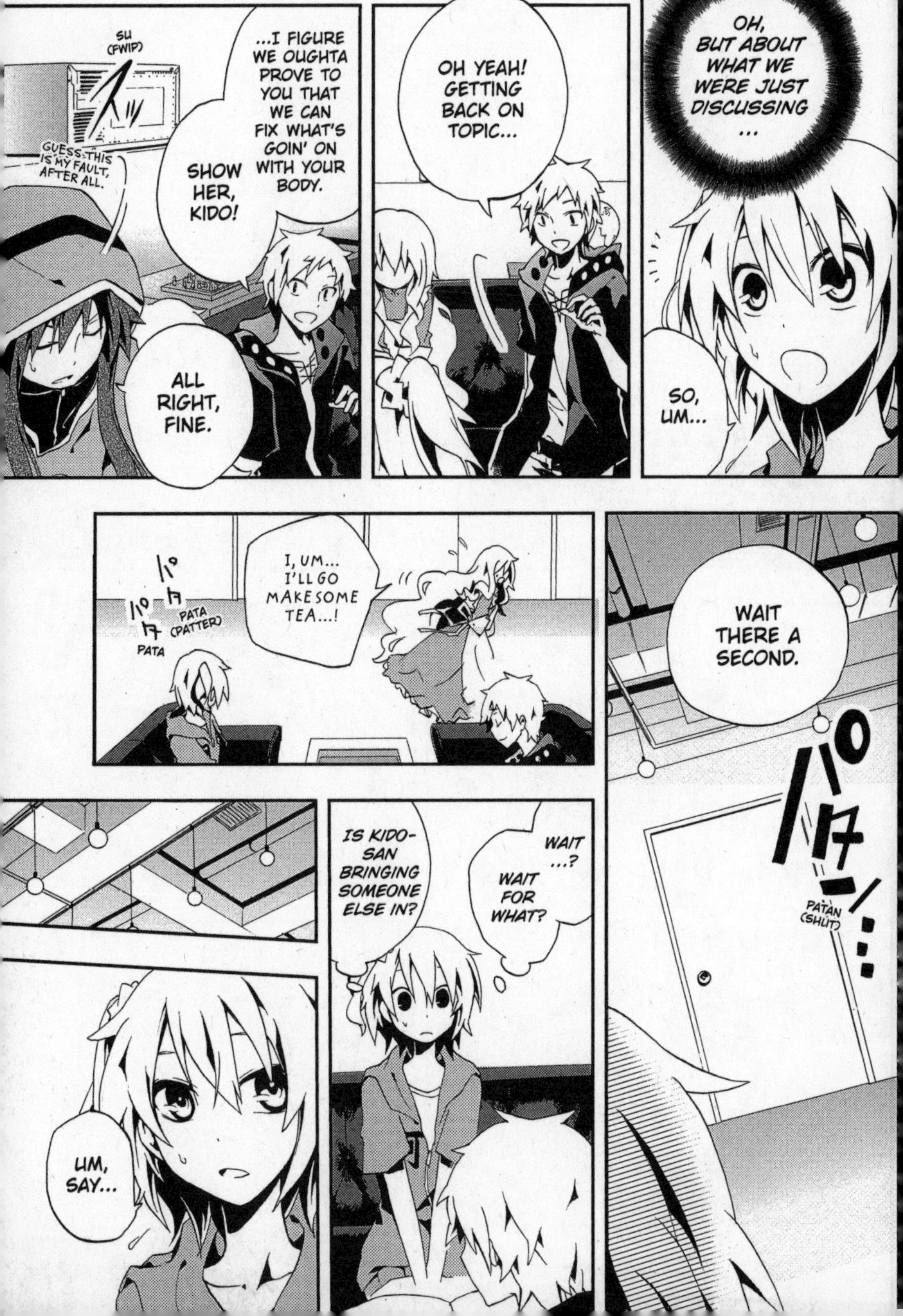
OH, BUT ABOUT WHAT WE WERE JUST DISCUSSING ...
SO, UM...
OH YEAH! GETTING BACK ON TOPIC...
...I FIGURE WE OUGHTA PROVE TO YOU THAT WE CAN FIX WHAT'S GOIN' ON WITH YOUR BODY.
SHOW HER, KIDO!
SU (FWIP)
GUESS THIS IS MY FAULT, AFTER ALL.
ALL RIGHT, FINE.
WAIT THERE A SECOND.
PATAN (SHUT)
I, UM... I'LL GO MAKE SOME TEA...!
PATA PATA (PATTER)
WAIT ...? WAIT FOR WHAT?
IS KIDO-SAN BRINGING SOMEONE ELSE IN?
UM, SAY...

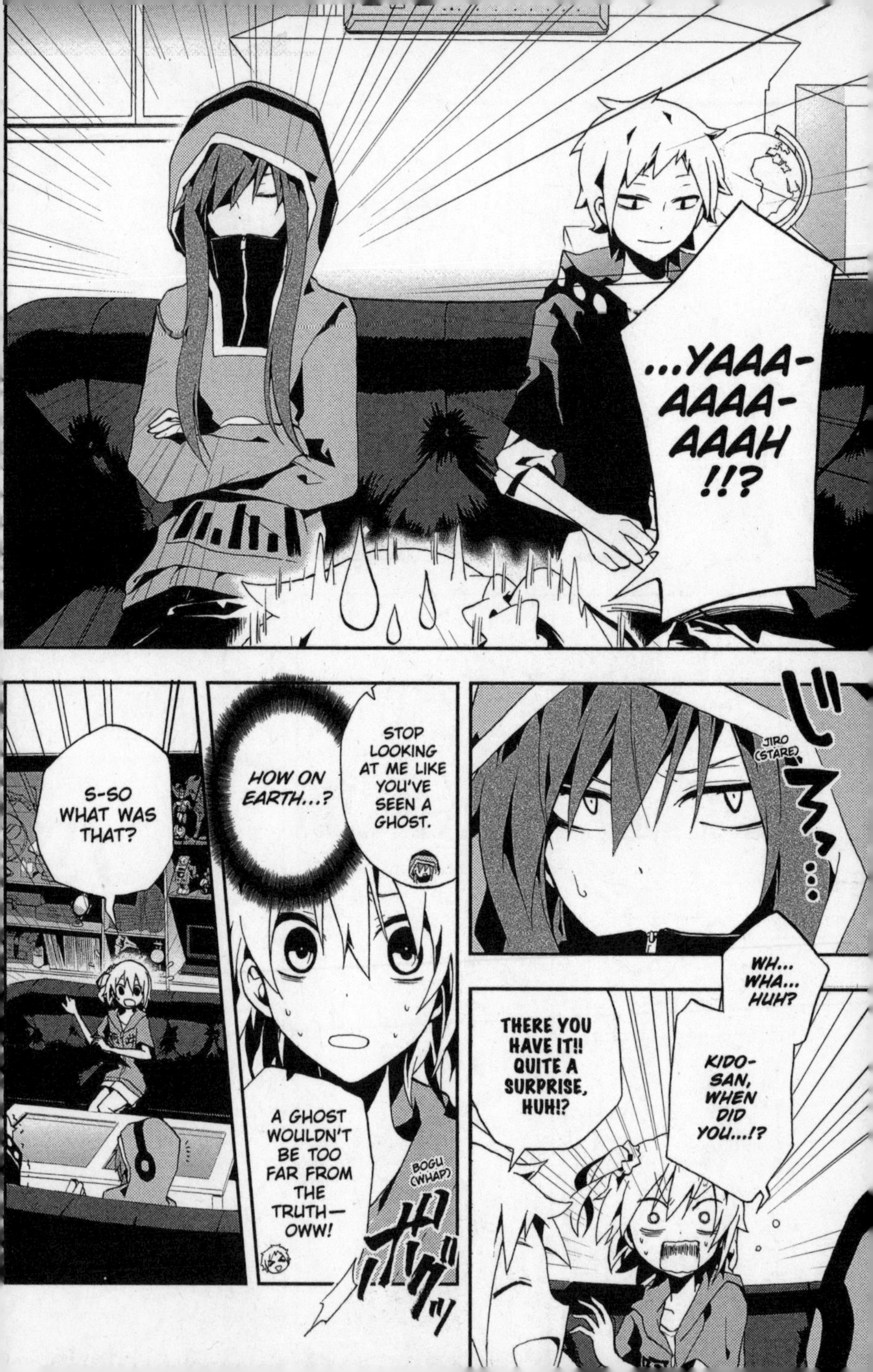
...YAAA-AAAA-AAAH!!?
JIRO (STARE)
WH... WHA... HUH?
KIDO-SAN, WHEN DID YOU...!?
THERE YOU HAVE IT!! QUITE A SURPRISE, HUH!?
STOP LOOKING AT ME LIKE YOU'VE SEEN A GHOST.
HOW ON EARTH...?
A GHOST WOULDN'T BE TOO FAR FROM THE TRUTH— OWW!
BOGU (WHAP)
S-SO WHAT WAS THAT?

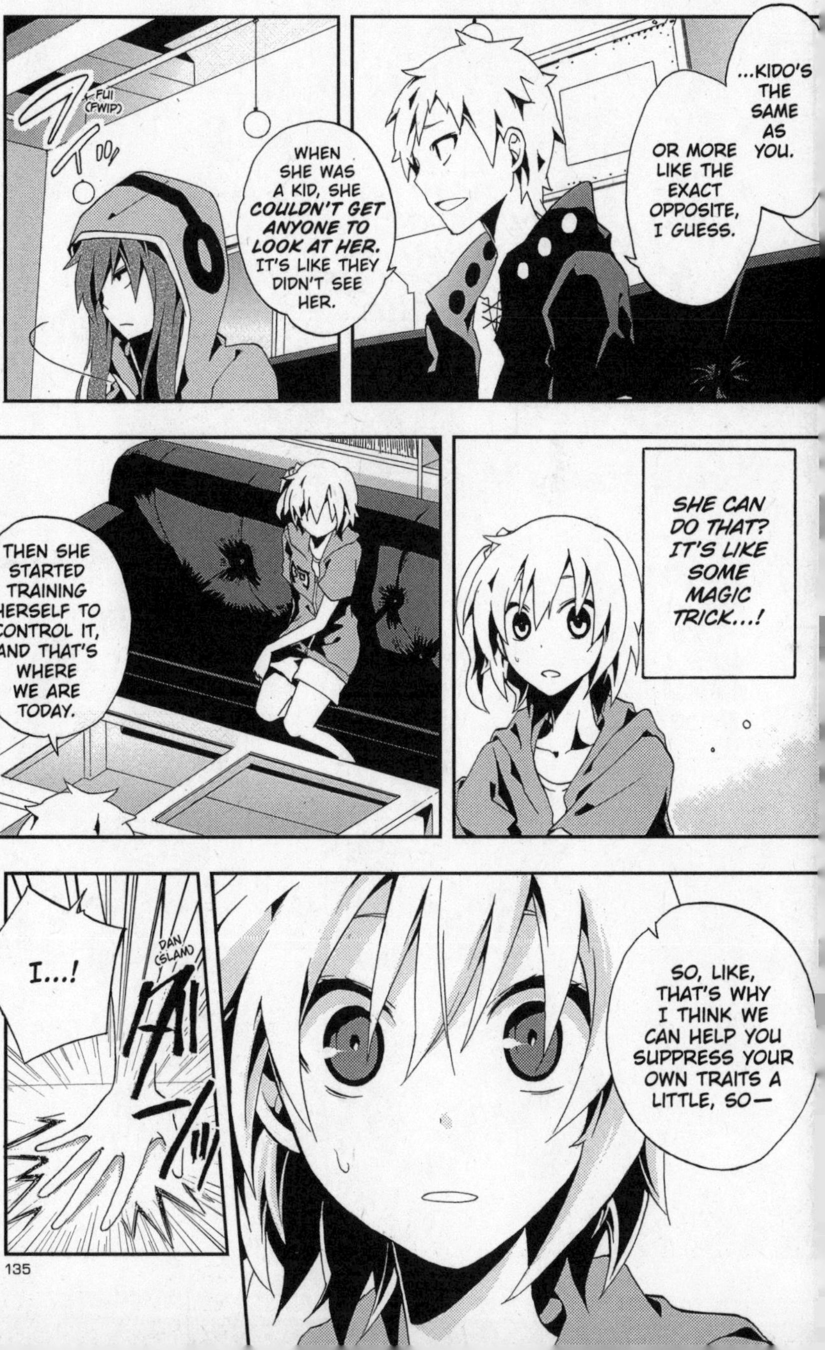
...KIDO'S THE SAME AS YOU.
OR MORE LIKE THE EXACT OPPOSITE, I GUESS.
WHEN SHE WAS A KID, SHE COULDN'T GET ANYONE TO LOOK AT HER. IT'S LIKE THEY DIDN'T SEE HER.
FUI (FWIP)
SHE CAN DO THAT? IT'S LIKE SOME MAGIC TRICK...!
THEN SHE STARTED TRAINING HERSELF TO CONTROL IT, AND THAT'S WHERE WE ARE TODAY.
SO, LIKE, THAT'S WHY I THINK WE CAN HELP YOU SUPPRESS YOUR OWN TRAITS A LITTLE, SO—
DAN (SLAM)
I...!

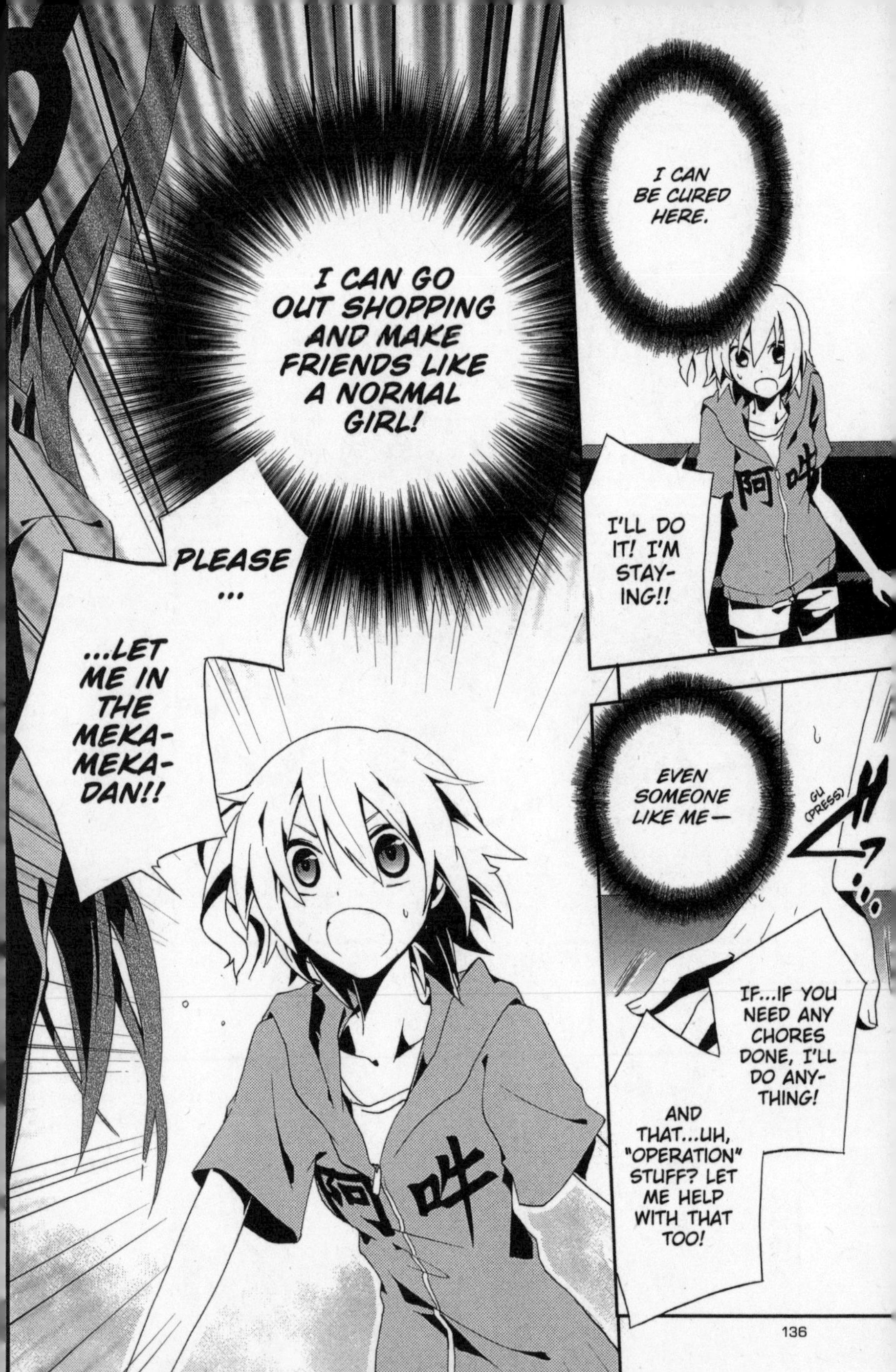
I CAN BE CURED HERE.
I'LL DO IT! I'M STAYING!!
EVEN SOMEONE LIKE ME—
GU (PRESS)
IF...IF YOU NEED ANY CHORES DONE, I'LL DO ANYTHING!
AND THAT...UH, "OPERATION" STUFF? LET ME HELP WITH THAT TOO!
I CAN GO OUT SHOPPING AND MAKE FRIENDS LIKE A NORMAL GIRL!
PLEASE...
...LET ME IN THE MEKA-MEKA-DAN!!

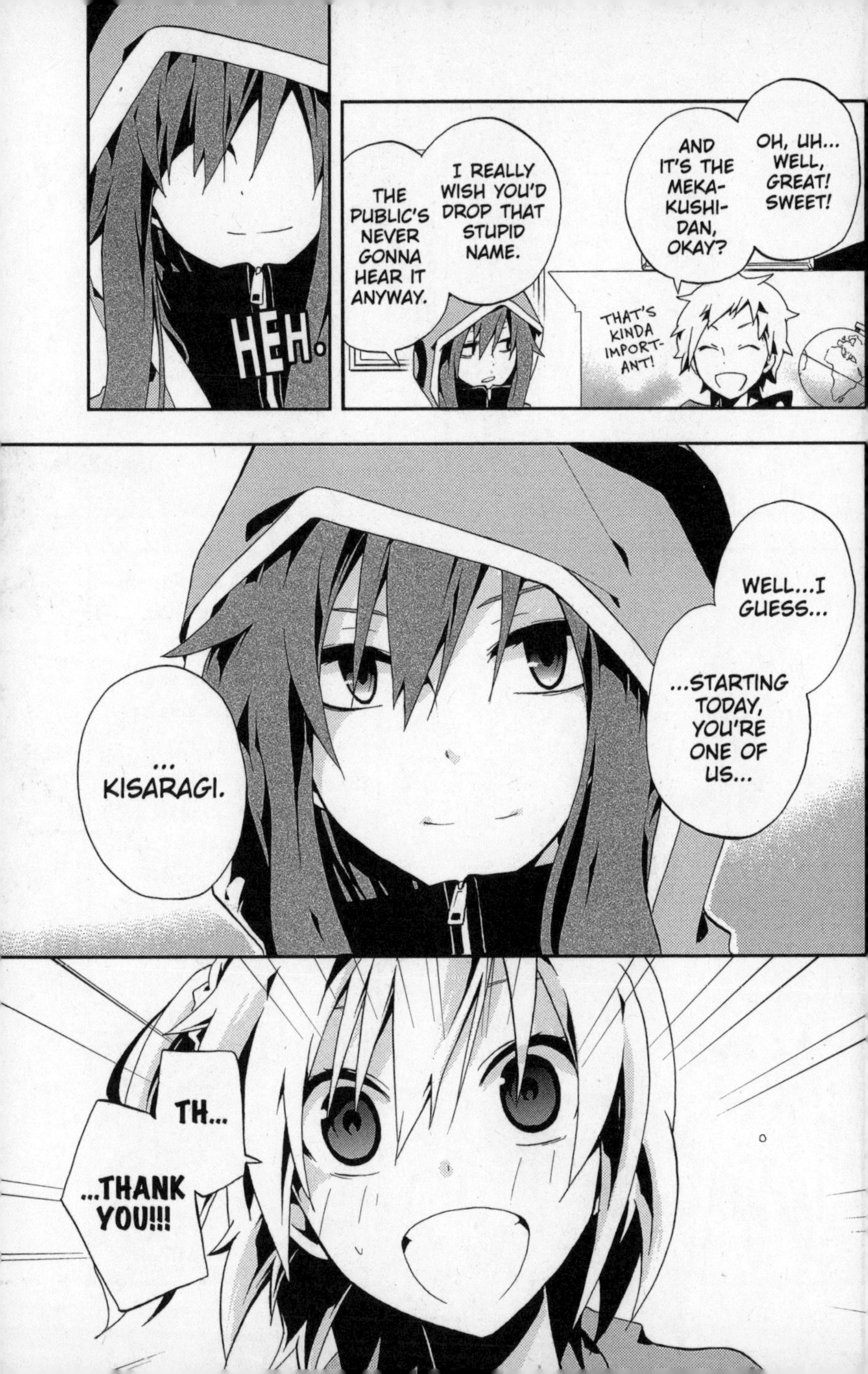
OH, UH... WELL, GREAT! SWEET!
AND IT'S THE MEKA-KUSHI-DAN, OKAY?
THAT'S KINDA IMPORT-ANT!
I REALLY WISH YOU'D DROP THAT STUPID NAME.
THE PUBLIC'S NEVER GONNA HEAR IT ANYWAY.
HEH.
WELL...I GUESS...
...STARTING TODAY, YOU'RE ONE OF US...
... KISARAGI.
TH...
...THANK YOU!!!

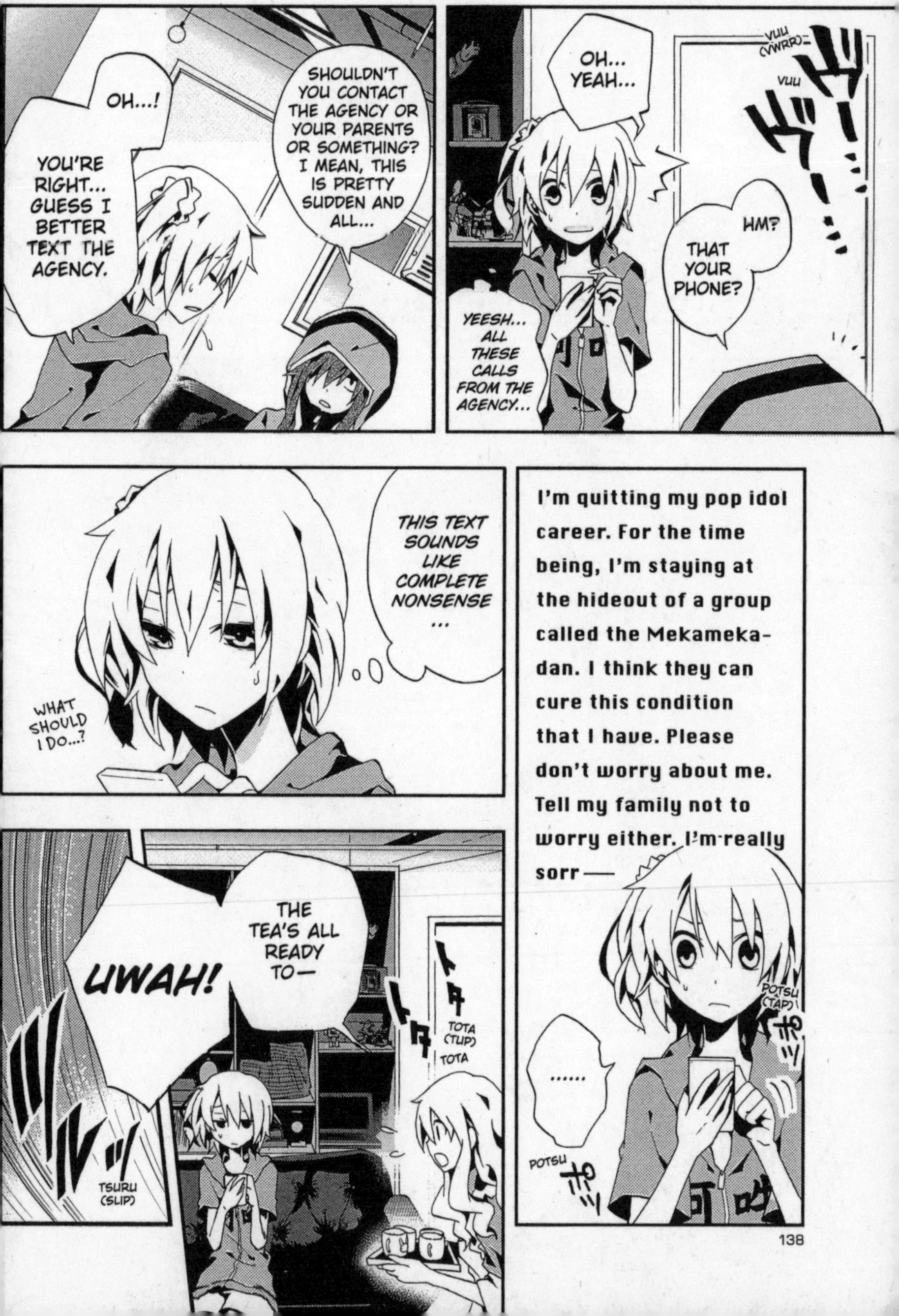
VUU (VWRR)
VUU
OH... YEAH...
HM? THAT YOUR PHONE?
YEESH... ALL THESE CALLS FROM THE AGENCY...
SHOULDN'T YOU CONTACT THE AGENCY OR YOUR PARENTS OR SOMETHING? I MEAN, THIS IS PRETTY SUDDEN AND ALL...
OH...! YOU'RE RIGHT... GUESS I BETTER TEXT THE AGENCY.
I'm quitting my pop idol career. For the time being, I'm staying at the hideout of a group called the Mekameka-dan. I think they can cure this condition that I have. Please don't worry about me. Tell my family not to worry either. I'm really sorr—
POTSU (TAP)
......
POTSU
THIS TEXT SOUNDS LIKE COMPLETE NONSENSE...
WHAT SHOULD I DO...?
THE TEA'S ALL READY TO—
TOTA (TUP)
TOTA
UWAH!
TSURU (SLIP)

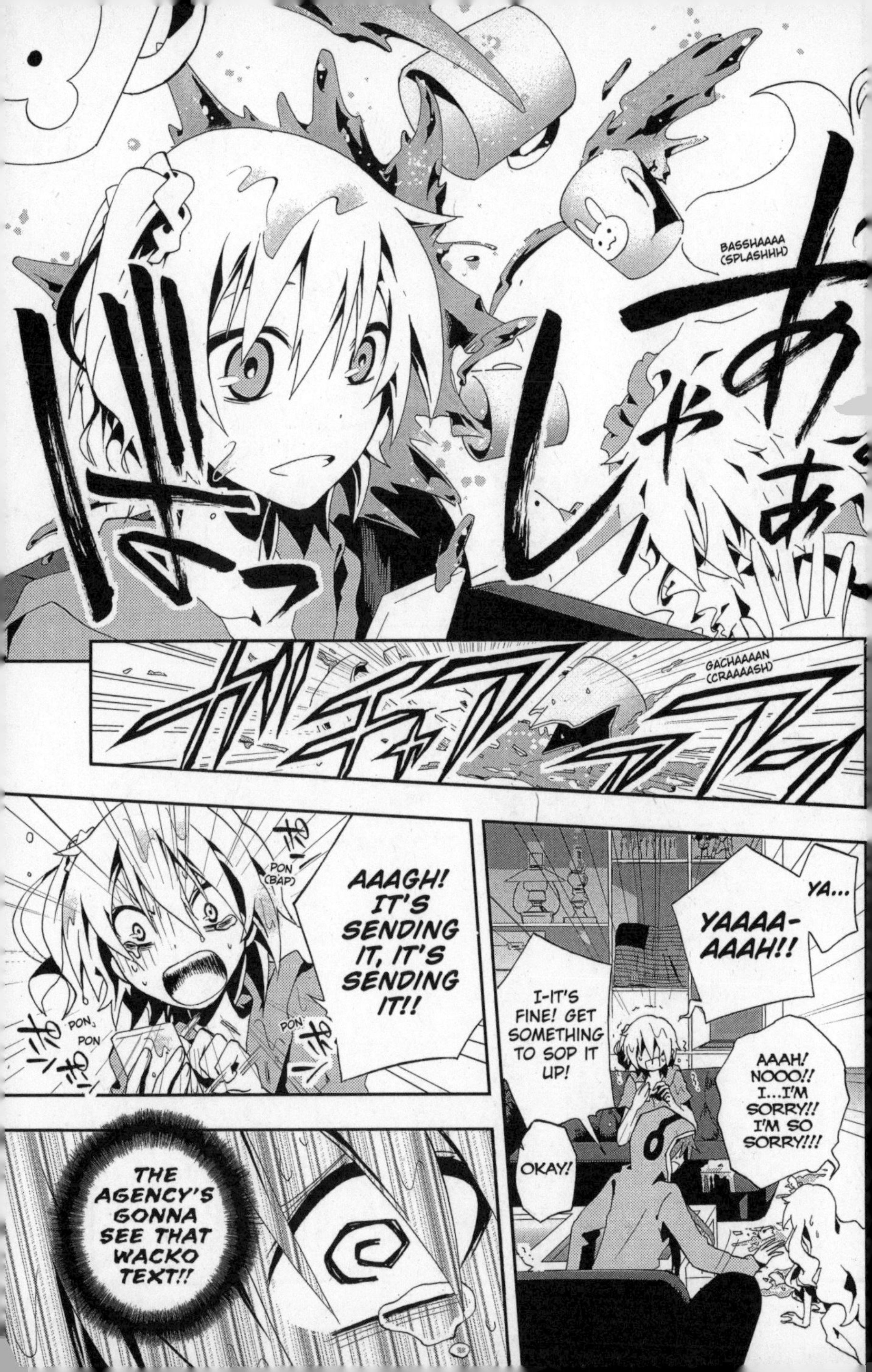
BASSHAAAA (SPLASHHH)
GACHAAAAN (CRAAAASH)
YA...
YAAAA-AAAH!!
AAAH! NOOO!! I...I'M SORRY!! I'M SO SORRY!!!
I-IT'S FINE! GET SOMETHING TO SOP IT UP!
OKAY!
PON (BAP)
AAAGH! IT'S SENDING IT, IT'S SENDING IT!!
PON PON
PON
THE AGENCY'S GONNA SEE THAT WACKO TEXT!!

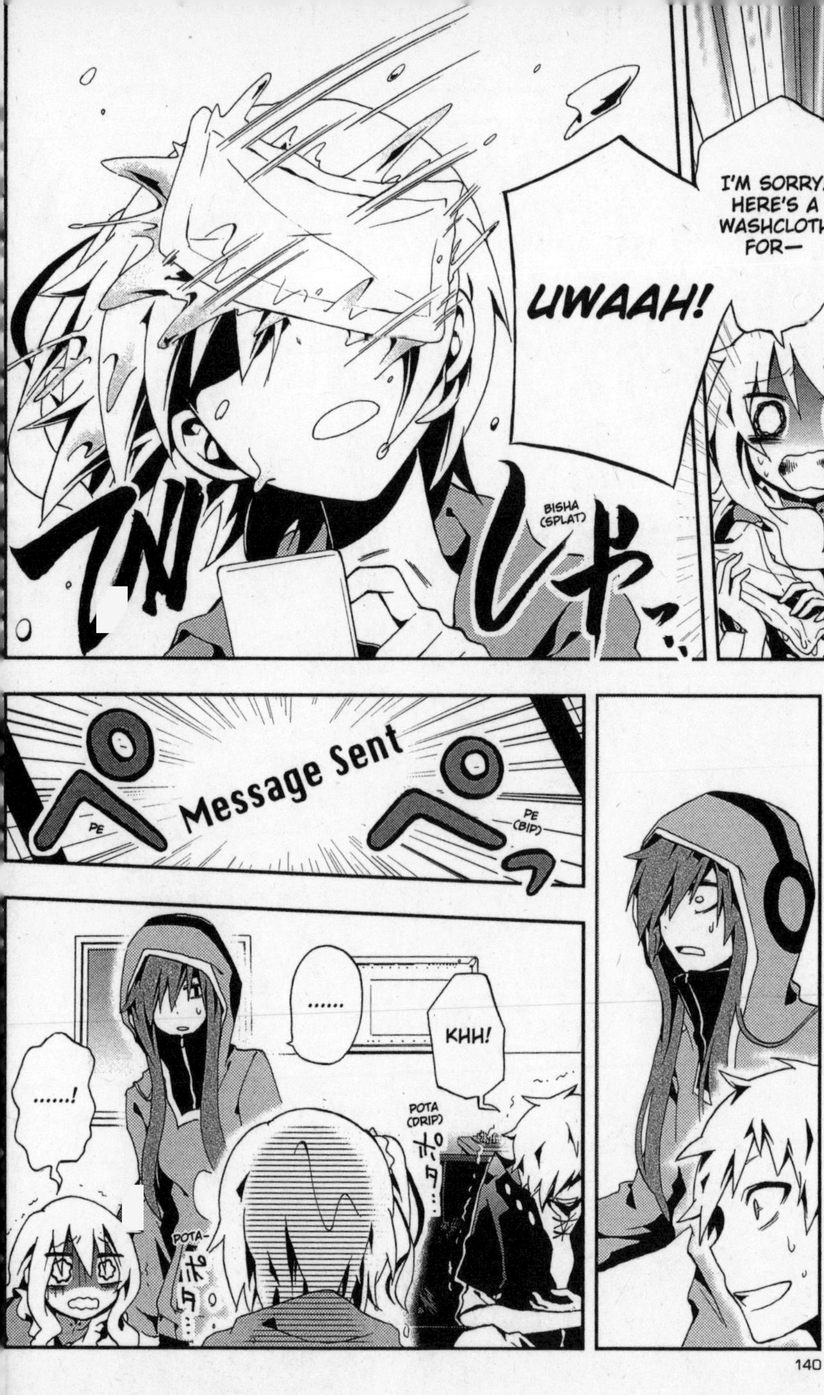
I'M SORRY! HERE'S A WASHCLOTH FOR—
UWAAH!
BISHA (SPLAT)
PE (BIP)
Message Sent
PE
KHH!
……
POTA (DRIP)
……!
POTA-

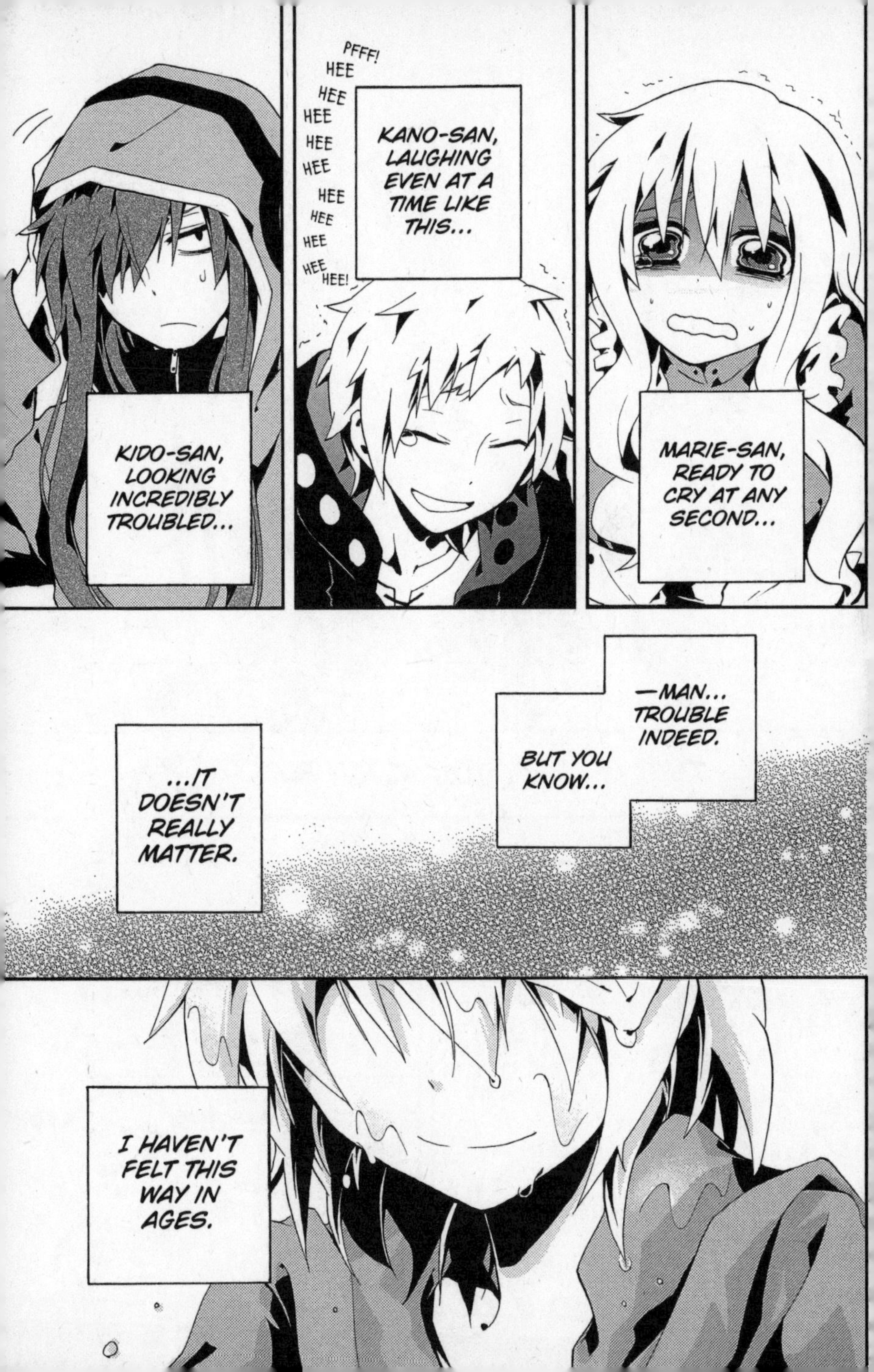
MARIE-SAN, READY TO CRY AT ANY SECOND...
KANO-SAN, LAUGHING EVEN AT A TIME LIKE THIS...
PFFF! HEE HEE HEE HEE HEE HEE HEE HEE HEE HEE!
KIDO-SAN, LOOKING INCREDIBLY TROUBLED...
—MAN... TROUBLE INDEED.
BUT YOU KNOW...
...IT DOESN'T REALLY MATTER.
I HAVEN'T FELT THIS WAY IN AGES.

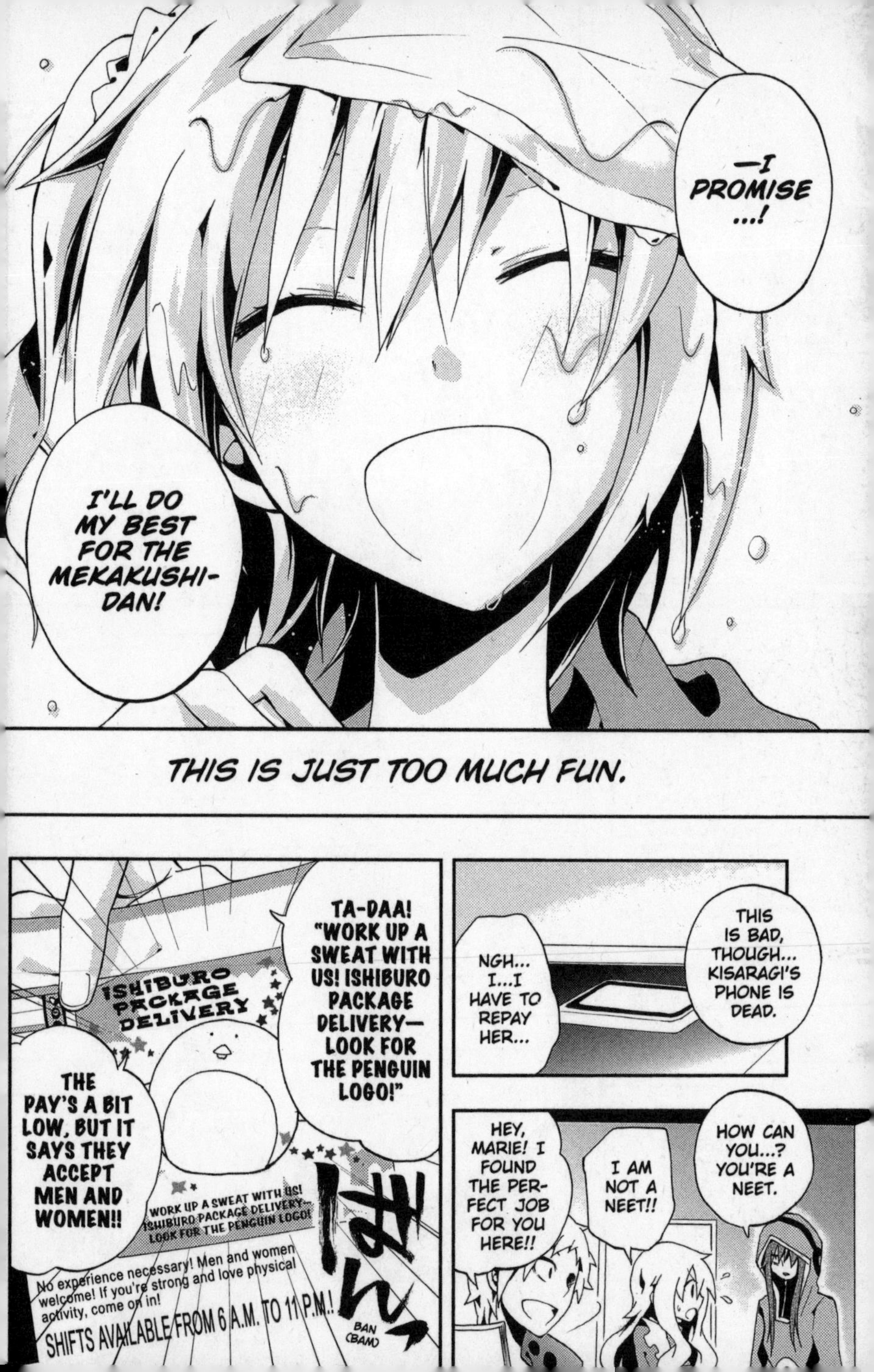
—I PROMISE ...!
I'LL DO MY BEST FOR THE MEKAKUSHI-DAN!
THIS IS JUST TOO MUCH FUN.
THIS IS BAD, THOUGH... KISARAGI'S PHONE IS DEAD.
NGH... I...I HAVE TO REPAY HER...
HOW CAN YOU...? YOU'RE A NEET.
I AM NOT A NEET!!
HEY, MARIE! I FOUND THE PERFECT JOB FOR YOU HERE!!
TA-DAA! "WORK UP A SWEAT WITH US! ISHIBURO PACKAGE DELIVERY—LOOK FOR THE PENGUIN LOGO!"
ISHIBURO PACKAGE DELIVERY
THE PAY'S A BIT LOW, BUT IT SAYS THEY ACCEPT MEN AND WOMEN!!
WORK UP A SWEAT WITH US! ISHIBURO PACKAGE DELIVERY—LOOK FOR THE PENGUIN LOGO!
No experience necessary! Men and women welcome! If you're strong and love physical activity, come on in!
SHIFTS AVAILABLE FROM 6 A.M. TO 11 P.M.!
ばん
BAN (BAM)

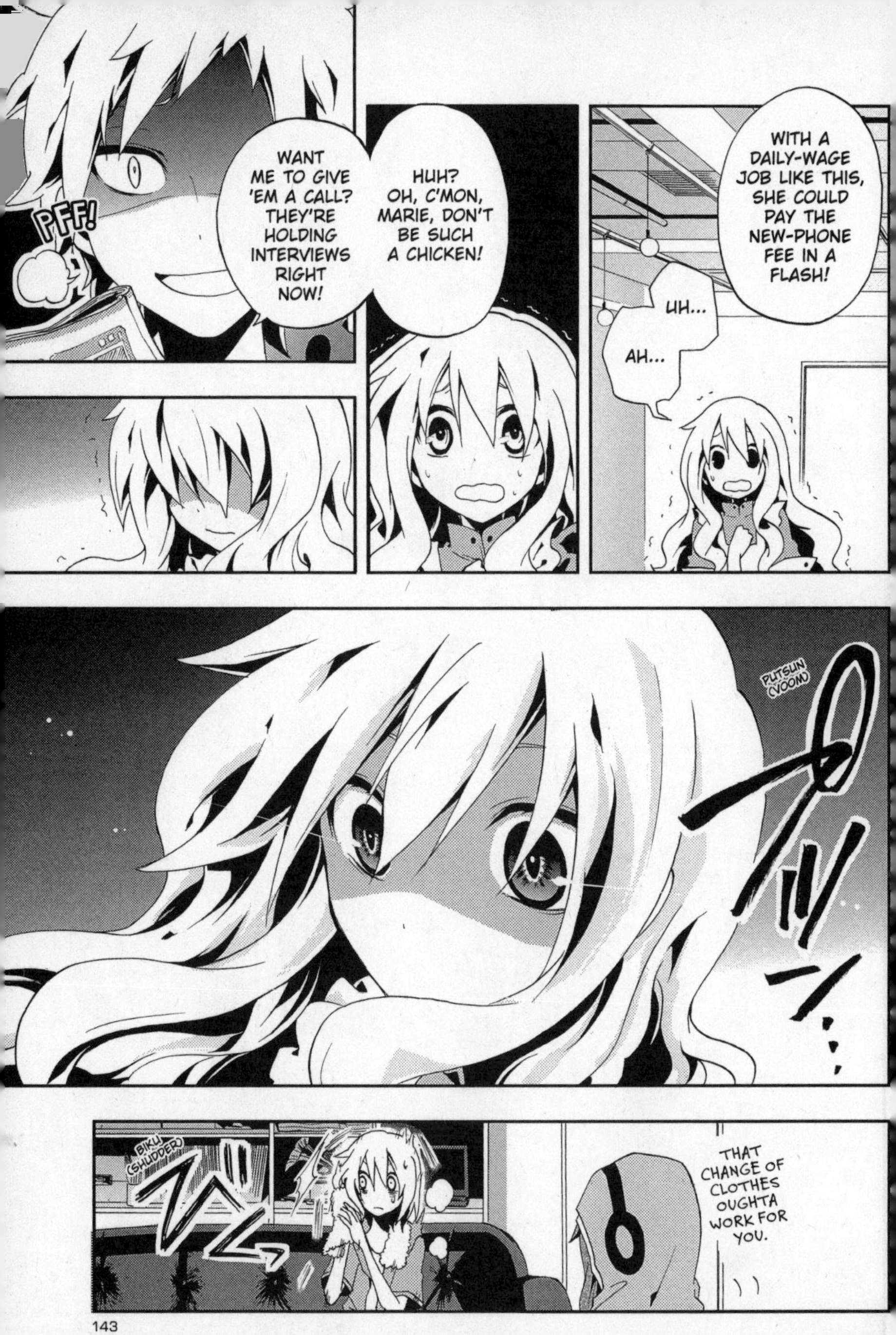
WITH A DAILY-WAGE JOB LIKE THIS, SHE COULD PAY THE NEW-PHONE FEE IN A FLASH!
UH...
AH...
HUH? OH, C'MON, MARIE, DON'T BE SUCH A CHICKEN!
WANT ME TO GIVE 'EM A CALL? THEY'RE HOLDING INTERVIEWS RIGHT NOW!
PFF!
PUTSUN (VOOM)
THAT CHANGE OF CLOTHES OUGHTA WORK FOR YOU.
BIKU (SHUDDER)

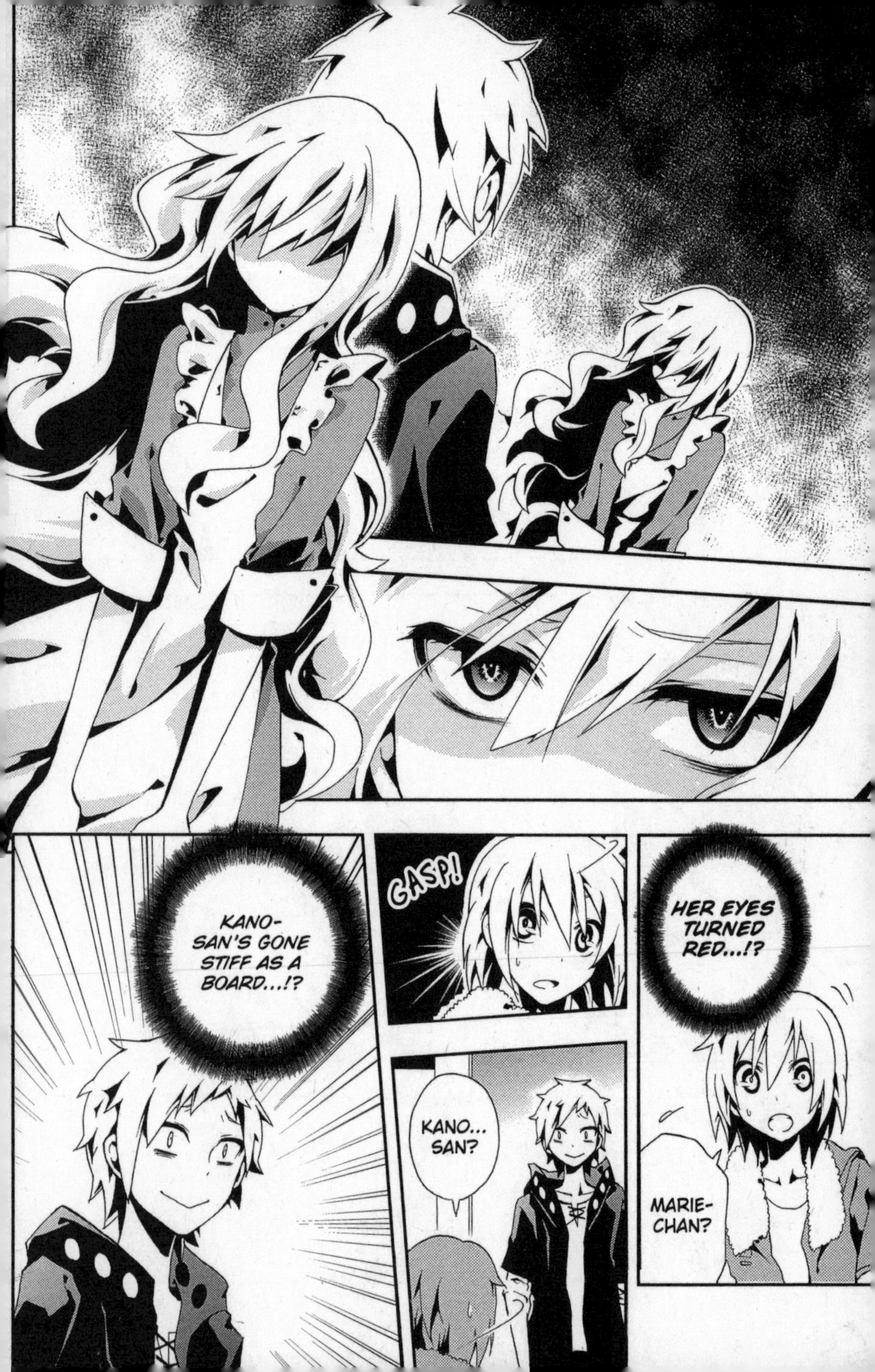
HER EYES TURNED RED...!?
MARIE-CHAN?
GASP!
KANO... SAN?
KANO-SAN'S GONE STIFF AS A BOARD...!?

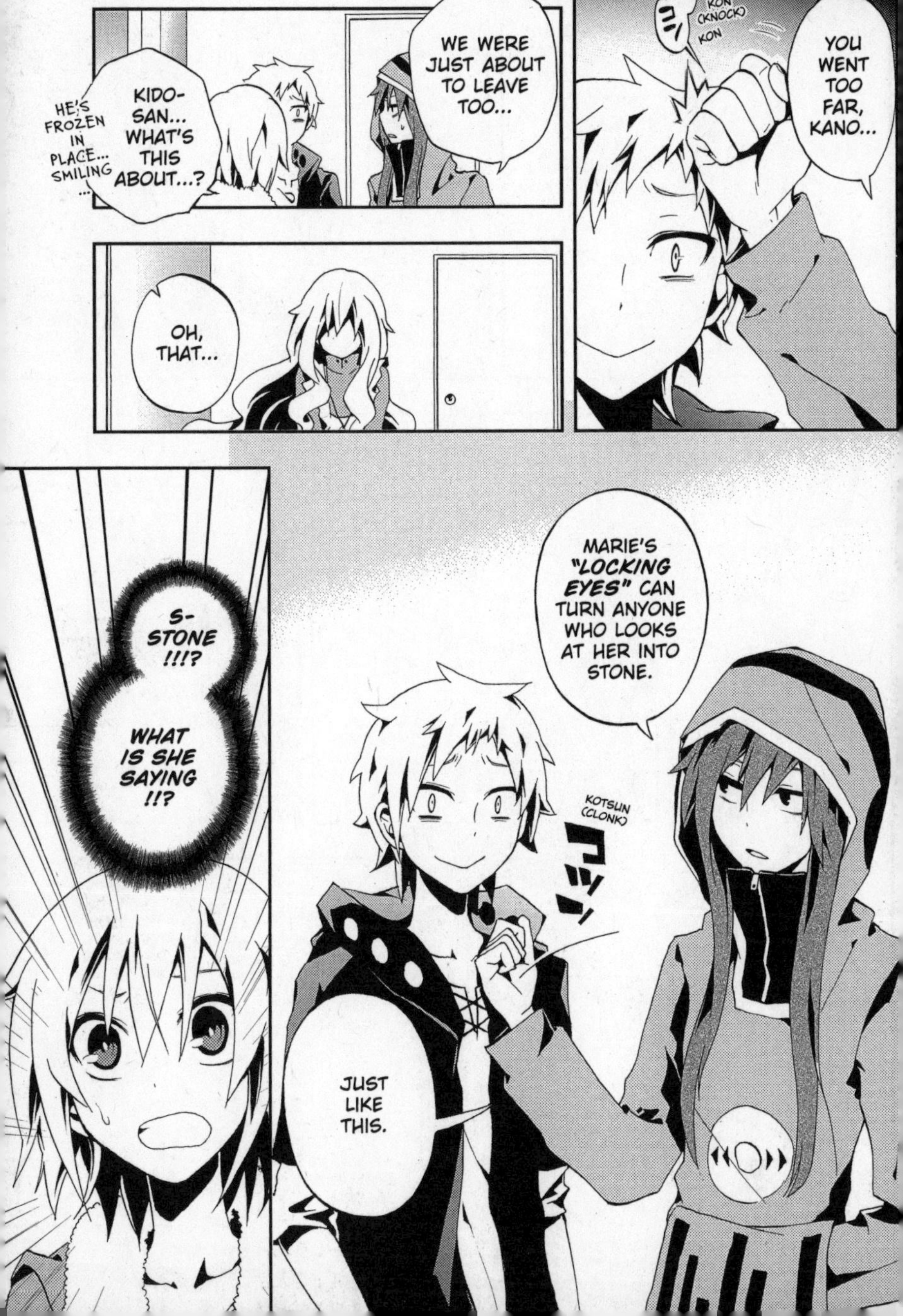

KON (KNOCK) KON
YOU WENT TOO FAR, KANO...
WE WERE JUST ABOUT TO LEAVE TOO...
KIDO-SAN... WHAT'S THIS ABOUT...?
HE'S FROZEN IN PLACE... SMILING ...
OH, THAT...
MARIE'S "LOCKING EYES" CAN TURN ANYONE WHO LOOKS AT HER INTO STONE.
KOTSUN (CLONK)
JUST LIKE THIS.
S-STONE !!!?
WHAT IS SHE SAYING !!?

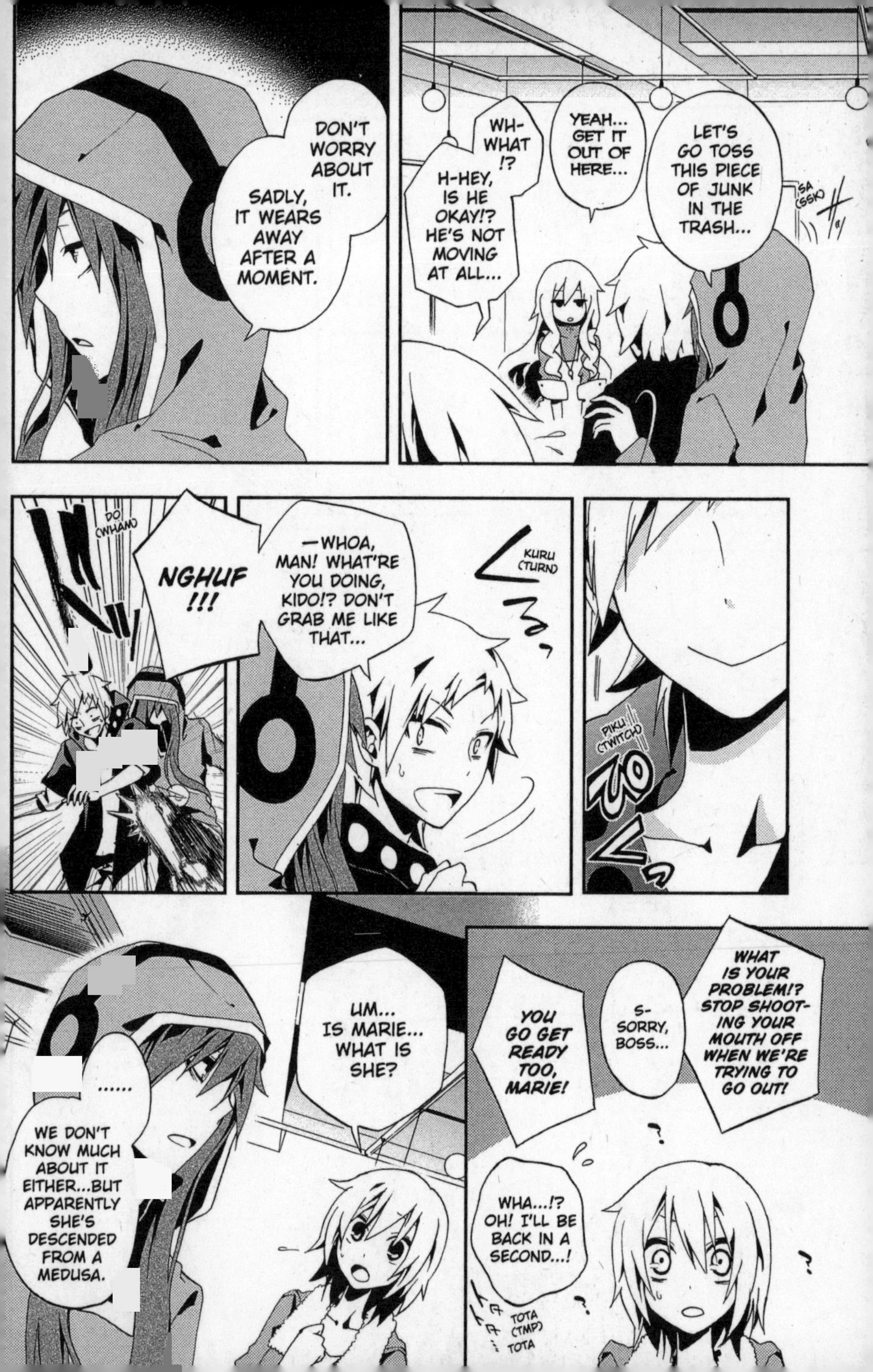

LET'S GO TOSS THIS PIECE OF JUNK IN THE TRASH...
SA (SSK)
YEAH... GET IT OUT OF HERE...
WH-WHAT!?
H-HEY, IS HE OKAY!? HE'S NOT MOVING AT ALL...
DON'T WORRY ABOUT IT.
SADLY, IT WEARS AWAY AFTER A MOMENT.
PIKU (TWITCH)
KURU (TURN)
—WHOA, MAN! WHAT'RE YOU DOING, KIDO!? DON'T GRAB ME LIKE THAT...
NGHUF!!!
DO (WHAM)
WHAT IS YOUR PROBLEM!? STOP SHOOTING YOUR MOUTH OFF WHEN WE'RE TRYING TO GO OUT!
S-SORRY, BOSS...
YOU GO GET READY TOO, MARIE!
WHA...!? OH! I'LL BE BACK IN A SECOND...!
TOTA (TMP) TOTA
UM... IS MARIE... WHAT IS SHE?
......
WE DON'T KNOW MUCH ABOUT IT EITHER...BUT APPARENTLY SHE'S DESCENDED FROM A MEDUSA.

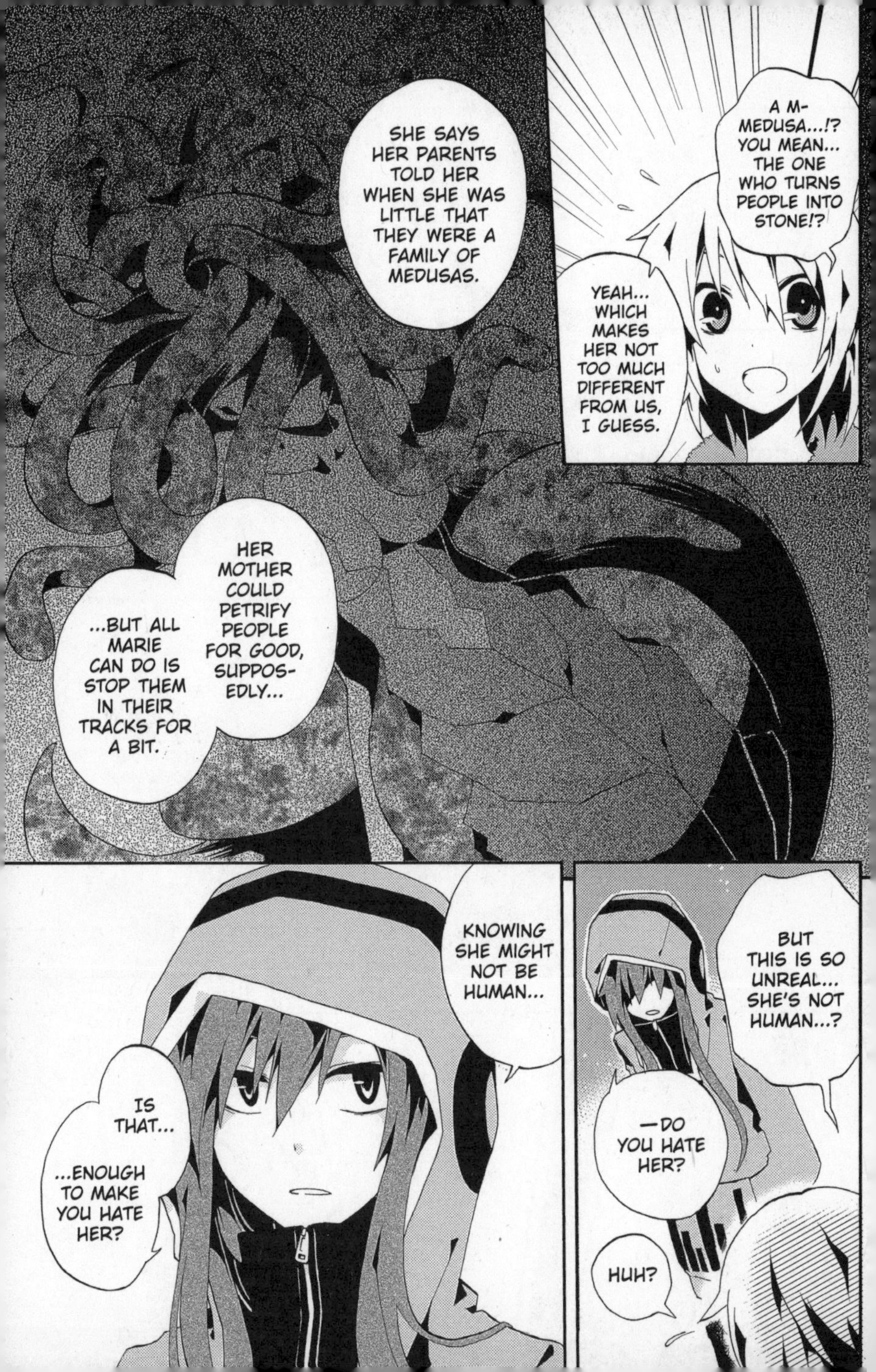
A M-MEDUSA...!? YOU MEAN... THE ONE WHO TURNS PEOPLE INTO STONE!?
YEAH... WHICH MAKES HER NOT TOO MUCH DIFFERENT FROM US, I GUESS.
SHE SAYS HER PARENTS TOLD HER WHEN SHE WAS LITTLE THAT THEY WERE A FAMILY OF MEDUSAS.
HER MOTHER COULD PETRIFY PEOPLE FOR GOOD, SUPPOS-EDLY...
...BUT ALL MARIE CAN DO IS STOP THEM IN THEIR TRACKS FOR A BIT.
BUT THIS IS SO UNREAL... SHE'S NOT HUMAN...?
—DO YOU HATE HER?
HUH?
KNOWING SHE MIGHT NOT BE HUMAN...
IS THAT...
...ENOUGH TO MAKE YOU HATE HER?

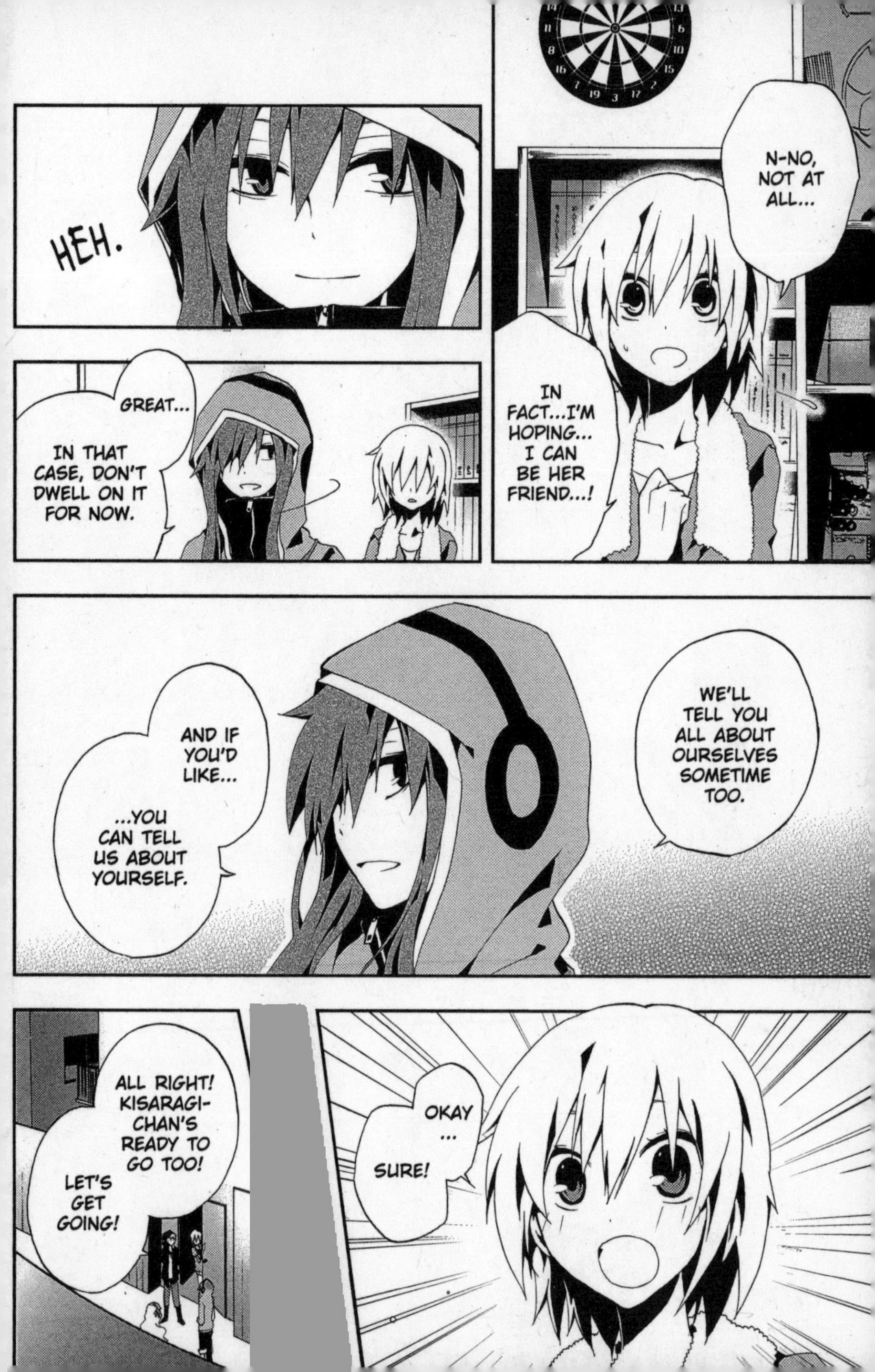
N-NO, NOT AT ALL...
IN FACT...I'M HOPING... I CAN BE HER FRIEND...!
HEH.
GREAT...
IN THAT CASE, DON'T DWELL ON IT FOR NOW.
WE'LL TELL YOU ALL ABOUT OURSELVES SOMETIME TOO.
AND IF YOU'D LIKE...
...YOU CAN TELL US ABOUT YOURSELF.
OKAY... SURE!
ALL RIGHT! KISARAGI-CHAN'S READY TO GO TOO!
LET'S GET GOING!

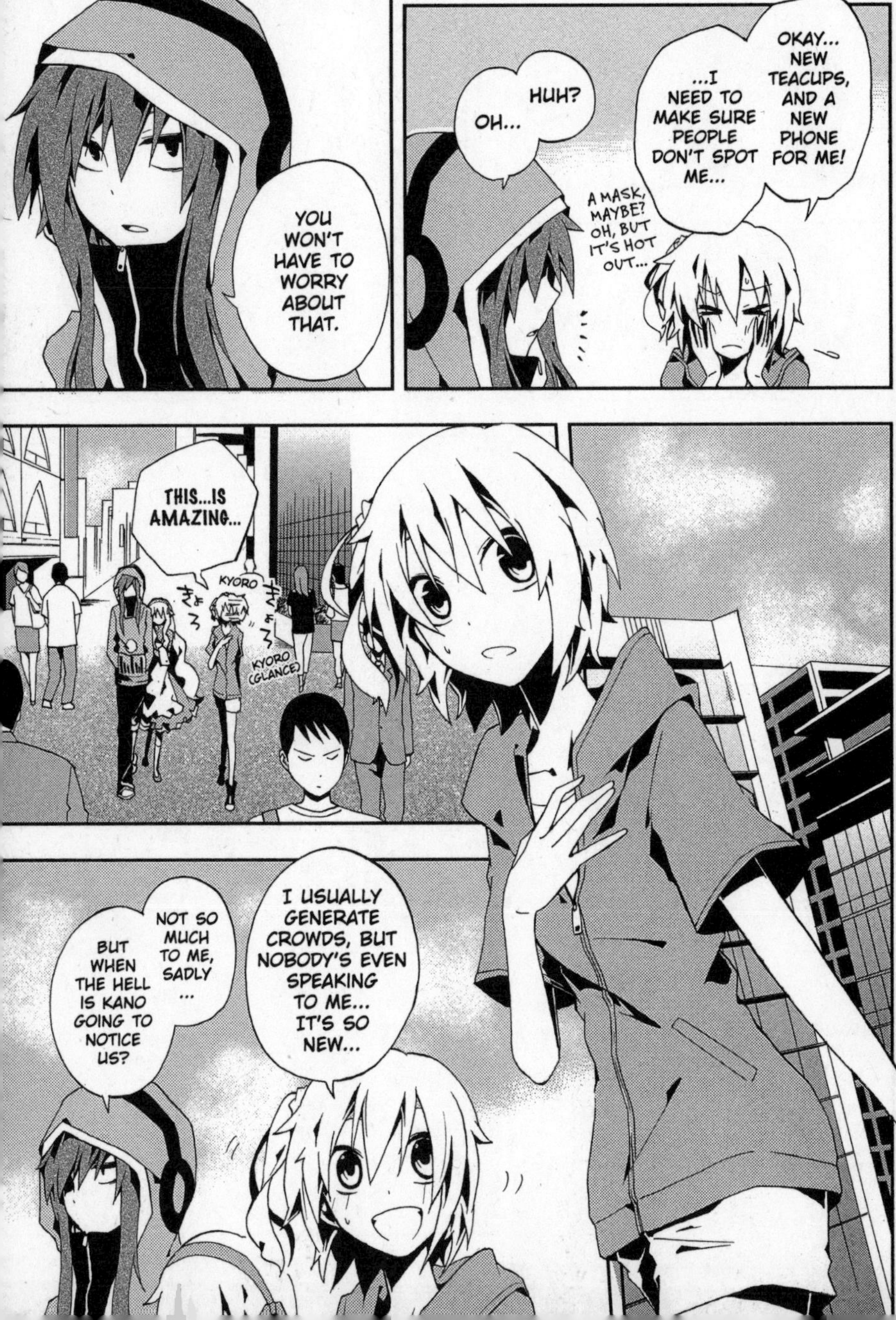
OKAY... NEW TEACUPS, AND A NEW PHONE FOR ME!
...I NEED TO MAKE SURE PEOPLE DON'T SPOT ME...
HUH? OH...
A MASK, MAYBE? OH, BUT IT'S HOT OUT...
YOU WON'T HAVE TO WORRY ABOUT THAT.
KYORO
きょろ
KYORO (GLANCE)
きょろ
THIS...IS AMAZING...
I USUALLY GENERATE CROWDS, BUT NOBODY'S EVEN SPEAKING TO ME... IT'S SO NEW...
NOT SO MUCH TO ME, SADLY...
BUT WHEN THE HELL IS KANO GOING TO NOTICE US?

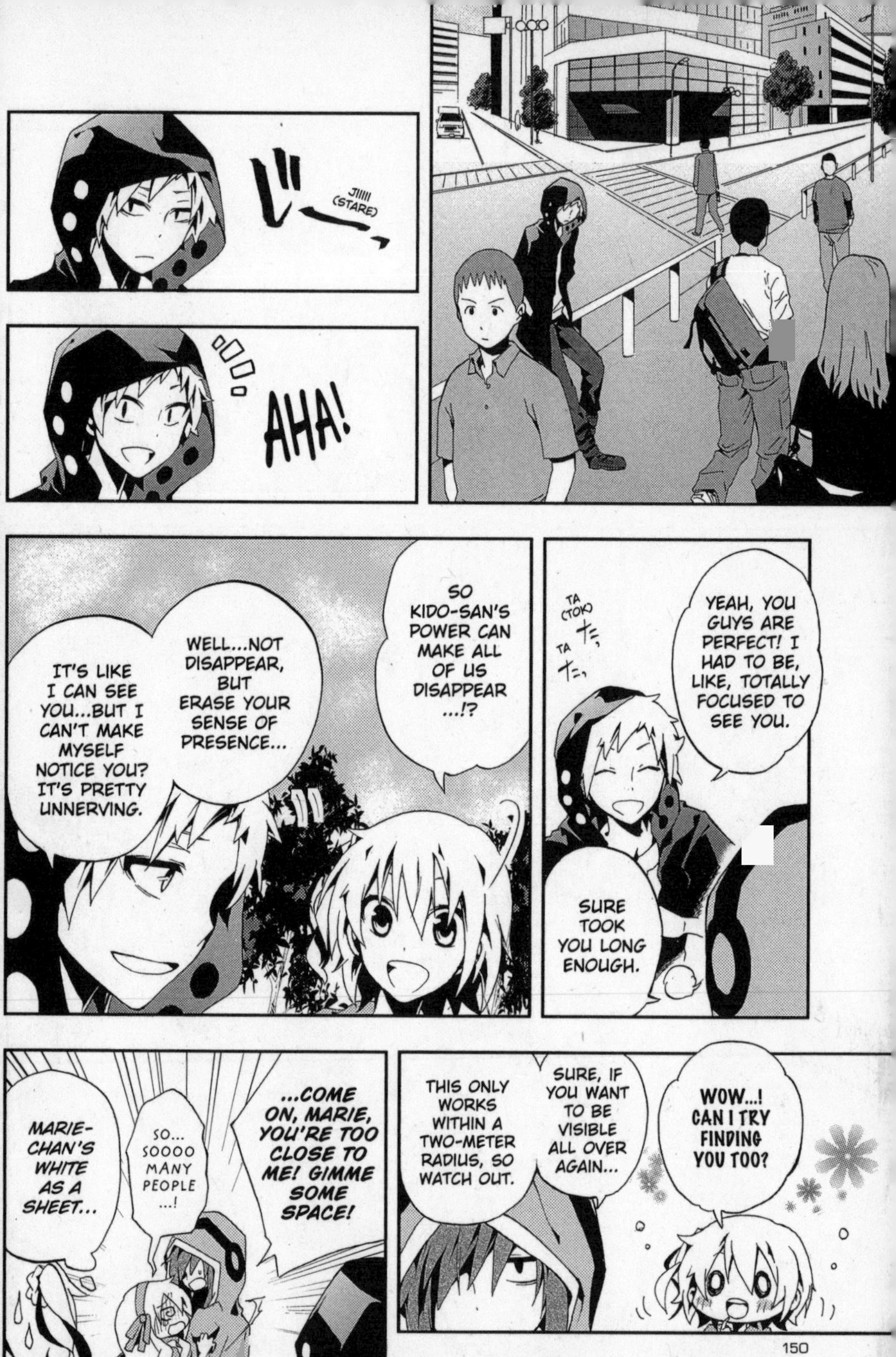
JIIIII (STARE)
AHA!
TA (TOK)
TA
YEAH, YOU GUYS ARE PERFECT! I HAD TO BE, LIKE, TOTALLY FOCUSED TO SEE YOU.
SURE TOOK YOU LONG ENOUGH.
SO KIDO-SAN'S POWER CAN MAKE ALL OF US DISAPPEAR ...!?
WELL...NOT DISAPPEAR, BUT ERASE YOUR SENSE OF PRESENCE...
IT'S LIKE I CAN SEE YOU...BUT I CAN'T MAKE MYSELF NOTICE YOU? IT'S PRETTY UNNERVING.
WOW...! CAN I TRY FINDING YOU TOO?
SURE, IF YOU WANT TO BE VISIBLE ALL OVER AGAIN...
THIS ONLY WORKS WITHIN A TWO-METER RADIUS, SO WATCH OUT.
...COME ON, MARIE, YOU'RE TOO CLOSE TO ME! GIMME SOME SPACE!
SO... SOOOO MANY PEOPLE ...!
MARIE-CHAN'S WHITE AS A SHEET...

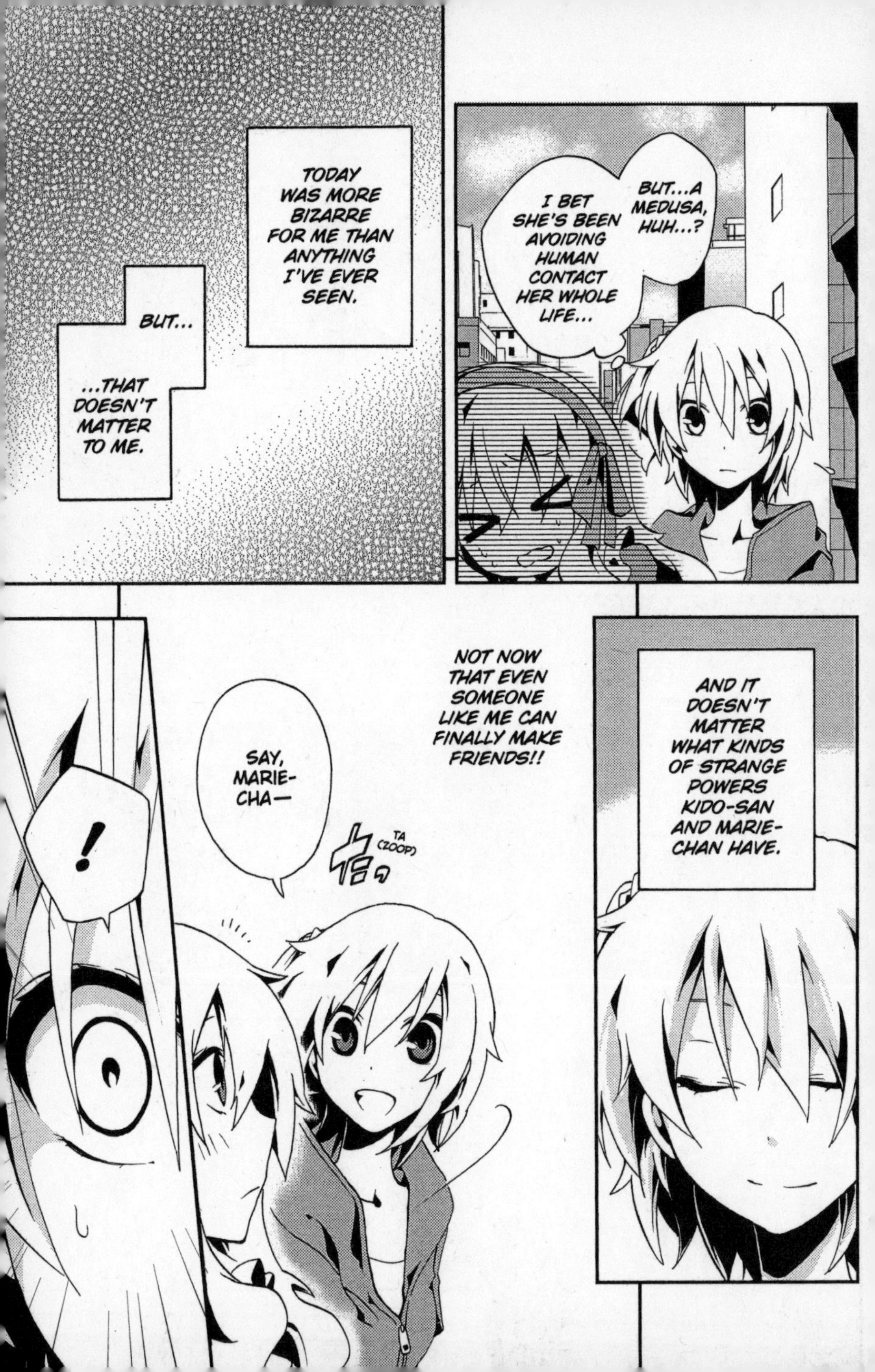
BUT...A MEDUSA, HUH...?
I BET SHE'S BEEN AVOIDING HUMAN CONTACT HER WHOLE LIFE...
TODAY WAS MORE BIZARRE FOR ME THAN ANYTHING I'VE EVER SEEN.
BUT...
...THAT DOESN'T MATTER TO ME.
AND IT DOESN'T MATTER WHAT KINDS OF STRANGE POWERS KIDO-SAN AND MARIE-CHAN HAVE.
NOT NOW THAT EVEN SOMEONE LIKE ME CAN FINALLY MAKE FRIENDS!!
SAY, MARIE-CHA—
TA (ZOOP)
!

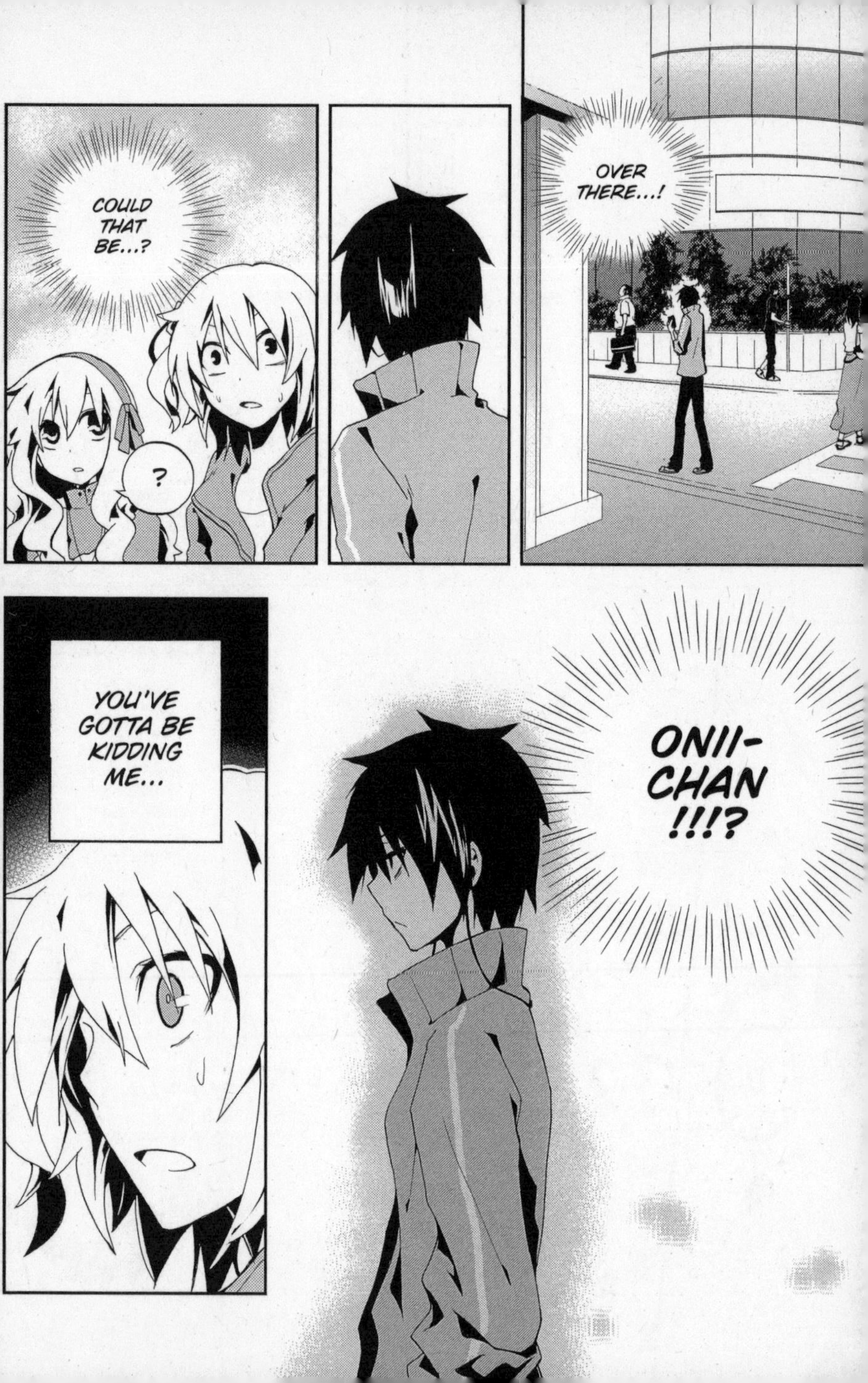
OVER THERE...!
COULD THAT BE...?
?
ONII-CHAN!!!?
YOU'VE GOTTA BE KIDDING ME...

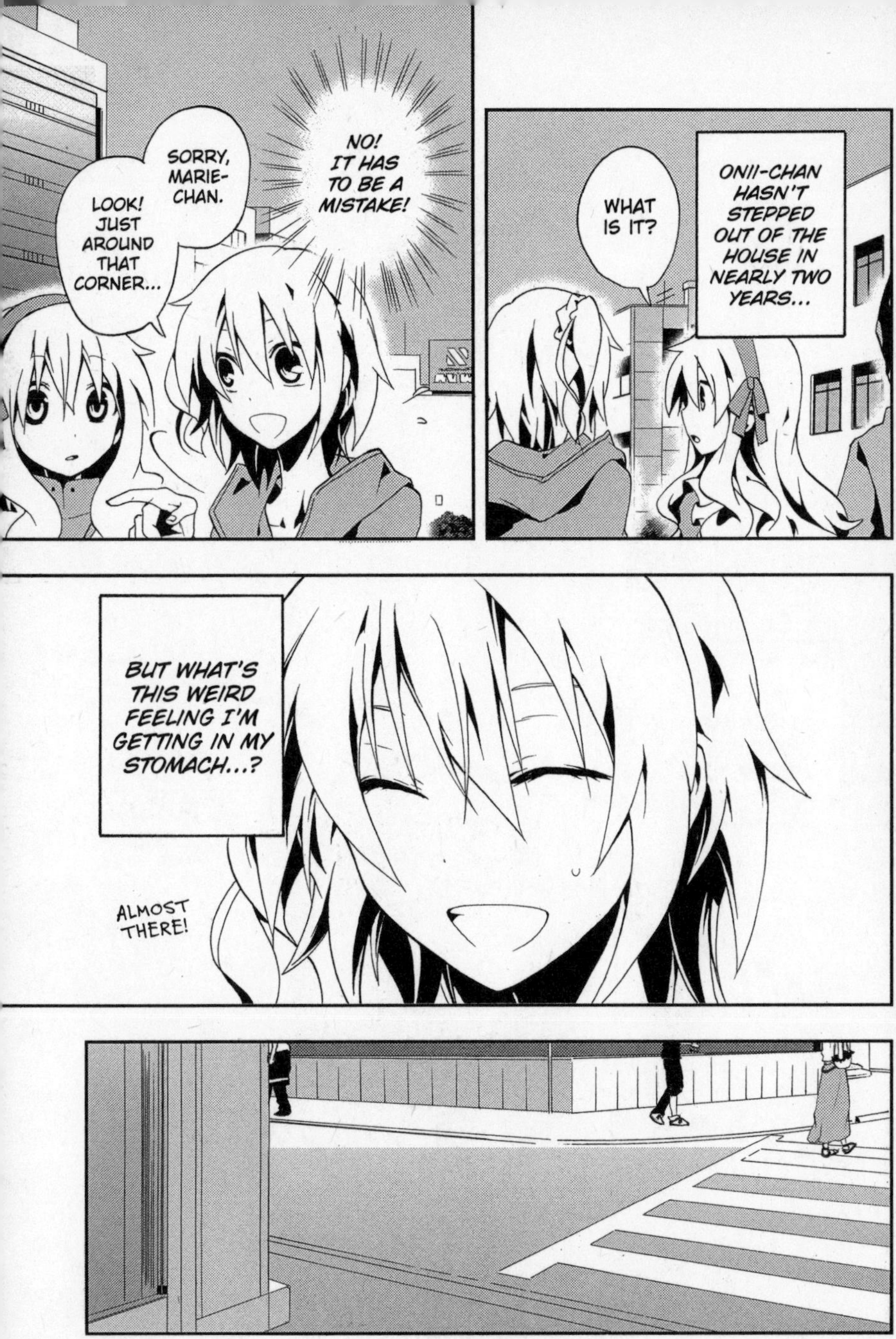
ONII-CHAN HASN'T STEPPED OUT OF THE HOUSE IN NEARLY TWO YEARS...
WHAT IS IT?
NO! IT HAS TO BE A MISTAKE!
SORRY, MARIE-CHAN.
LOOK! JUST AROUND THAT CORNER...
BUT WHAT'S THIS WEIRD FEELING I'M GETTING IN MY STOMACH...?
ALMOST THERE!

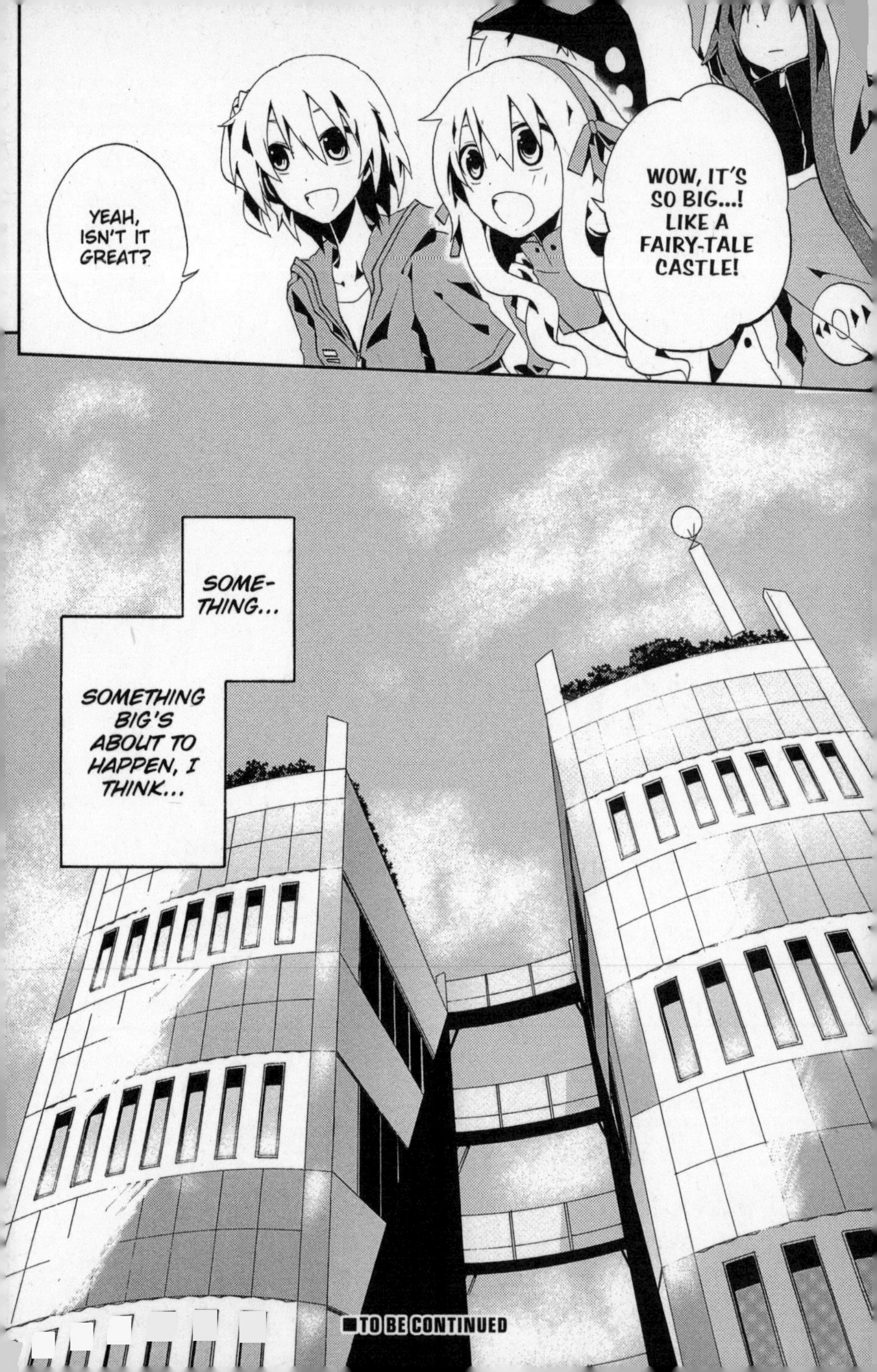
WOW, IT'S SO BIG...! LIKE A FAIRY-TALE CASTLE!
YEAH, ISN'T IT GREAT?
SOME-THING...
SOMETHING BIG'S ABOUT TO HAPPEN, I THINK...
TO BE CONTINUED

THANK YOU FOR READING!

THIS IS MY FIRST REGULAR MANGA GIG, SO I HAD NO IDEA HOW IT WOULD TURN OUT... THERE'S STILL A TON LEFT FOR ME TO LEARN AND GET USED TO, BUT THANKS TO ALL SORTS OF PEOPLE HERE, IT'S BEEN A TON OF FUN TO DRAW!! THANKS SO MUCH TO EVERYONE WHO'S KEPT ON SUPPORTING ME...! I'LL DO MY BEST! AND IT'D BE GREAT IF I GOT TO SEE YOU IN THE NEXT VOLUME TOO!! UNTIL THEN...!

佐藤 まひろ
MAHIRO SATOU

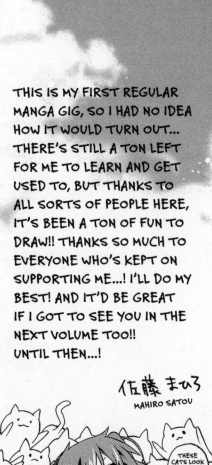

THESE CATS LOOK LIKE MISO-KICHI, HUH? SORRY...!!

I'LL DO MY BEST TO GET BETTER AT DRAWING MANGA, SO THANKS FOR THE SUPPORT!

Congratulations on launching Volume 1 of the manga!

I'm having a blast reading it. I'll try my hardest not to let the manga steal the spotlight from my music and novels, so here's to a fun competition!

Jin

CONGRATULATIONS ON VOLUME 1 OF THE KAGEROU DAZE MANGA!

I'm personally a big fan of Kano when he's drawn by Mahiro-san. Thank you very much for that. I'm looking forward to all the stuff yet to come too. Here's to a wonderful future for all of us.

This is starting to sound like a New Year's card...

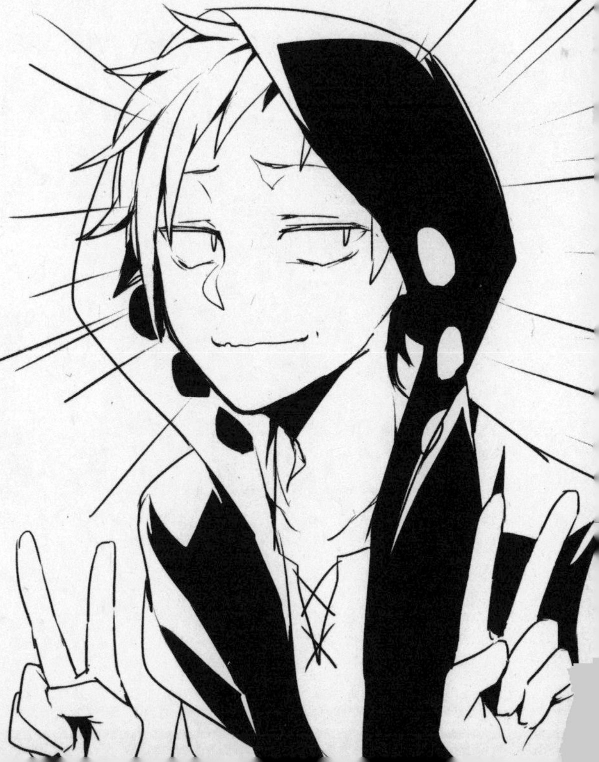

Sidu

(and Kano)

CONGRATS ON THE MANGA LAUNCH!!

@Wannyanpuu-

Congrats on releasing the first volume!! It's like it came out in the blink of an eye...Thanks for all the hard work...! The Kagerou Project characters Mahiro-sensei draws are all so cute, so cool, and so packed with awesome expressions! I get really excited whenever a new character debuts in the magazine!! I can't wait to see how future developments are portrayed in the manga too!

Please keep up the good work!!

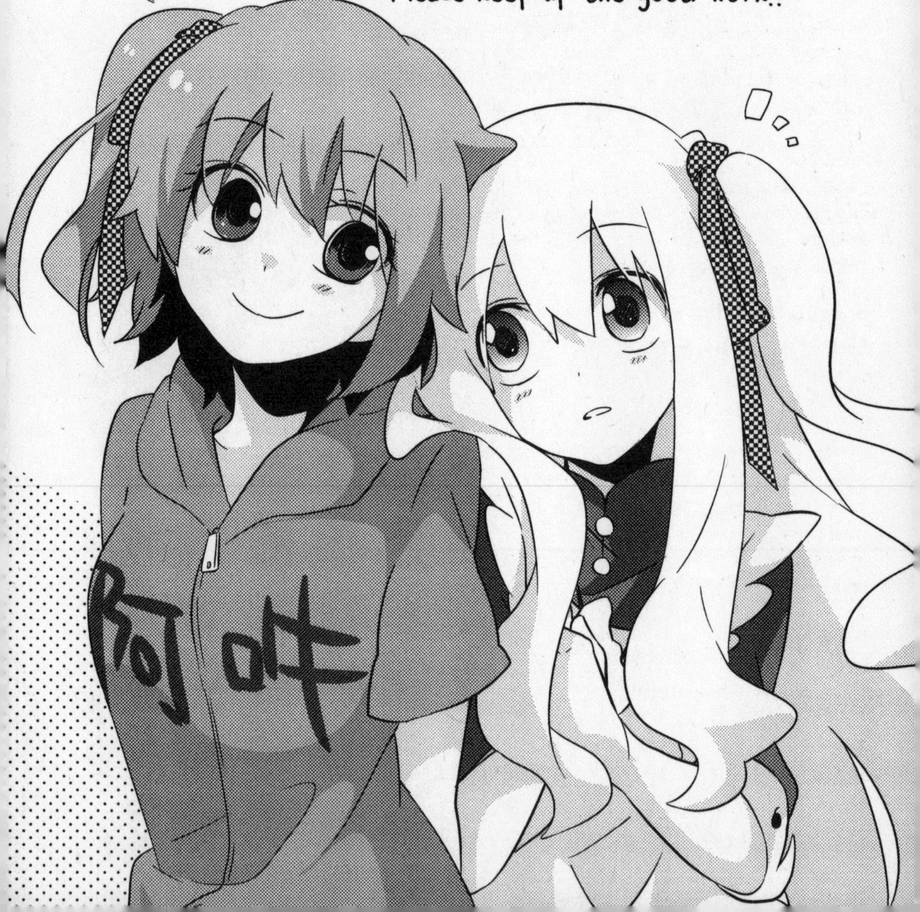

■ TRANSLATION NOTES

Common Honorifics:

no honorific: Indicates familiarity or closeness; if used without permission or reason, addressing someone in this manner would constitute an insult.

-san: The Japanese equivalent of Mr./Mrs./Miss. If a situation calls for politeness, this is the fail-safe honorific.

-kun: Used most often when referring to boys, this indicates affection or familiarity. Occasionally used by older men among their peers, but it may also be used by anyone referring to a person of lower standing.

-chan: An affectionate honorific indicating familiarity used mostly in reference to girls; also used in reference to cute persons or animals of either gender.

-oniisan, onii-san, etc.: Terms used to address an elder brother or brother-like figure.

Chapter Titles:

Each chapter title, as well as the title of this manga, refers to a specific musical composition from JIN (Shizen no Teki-P).

Kagerou means "mirage" or "heat haze." *Jinzou* means "artificial" or "man-made." *Kisaragi* is a poetic term for the second lunar month, but it can also be a surname. Finally, a *mekakushi* is a blindfold, thus *Mekakushi-dan* could be translated as "Blindfold Gang."

PAGE 22
Obon or **Bon** is a three-day festival held in honor of passed relatives and ancestors. Typical Obon events often include visits with family or to family grave sites, a summer festival or carnival, traditional dance and music performances, and a paper lantern-lighting ceremony.

PAGE 64
A-un, the kanji on Momo's hoodie, is the Japanese spelling of the sacred Sanskrit syllable "aum," also known as "om."

PAGE 84
Ooedo, or "Greater Edo," was a high-class term for referring to the cultural and geographic extent of the Japanese capital of Edo (which later became Tokyo).

PAGE 86
Mekameka is a nonsense word. Momo has forgotten the somewhat tongue-twister-y term "Mekakushi-dan."

PAGE 142
NEET stands for "Not in Employment, Education, or Training." It's a nice way of saying "unemployed freeloader."

PAGE 155
Misokichi is a fluffy (and very fat) white cat character created by artist ryuuseee.

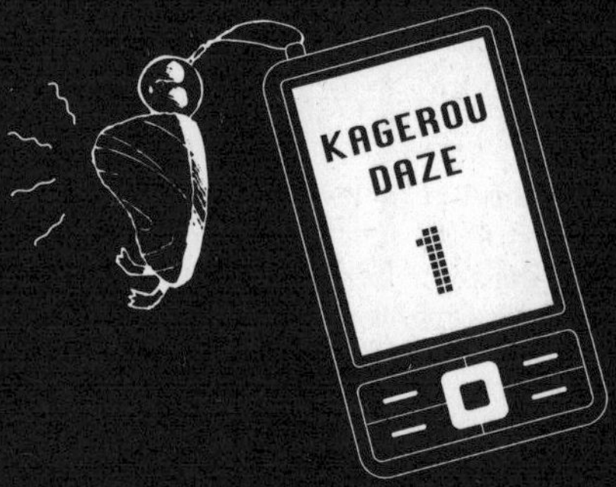
KAGEROU
DAZE
1

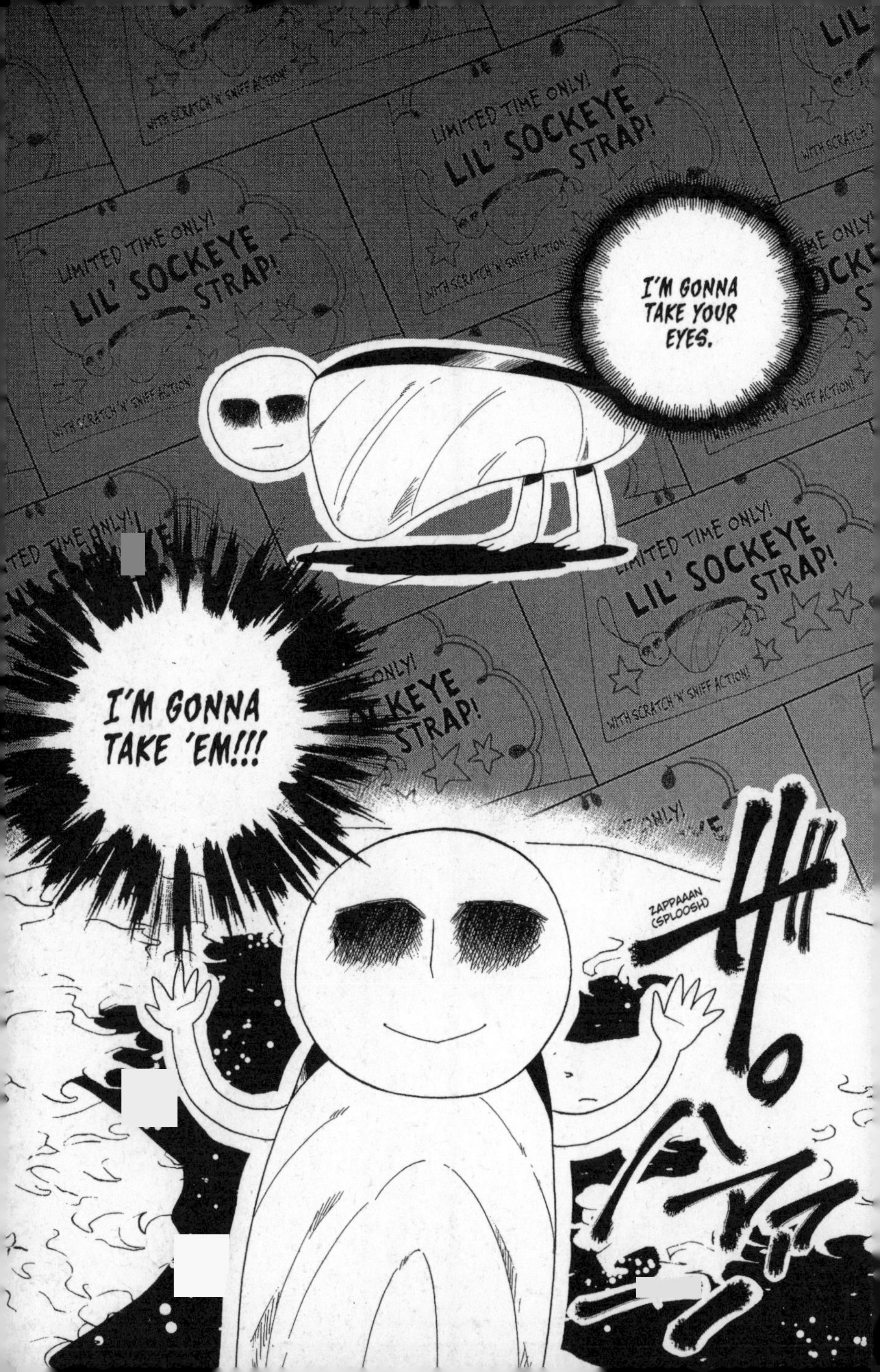
LIMITED TIME ONLY!
LIL' SOCKEYE STRAP!
WITH SCRATCH 'N' SNIFF ACTION!
I'M GONNA TAKE YOUR EYES.
I'M GONNA TAKE 'EM!!!
ZAPPAAAN (SPLOOSH)

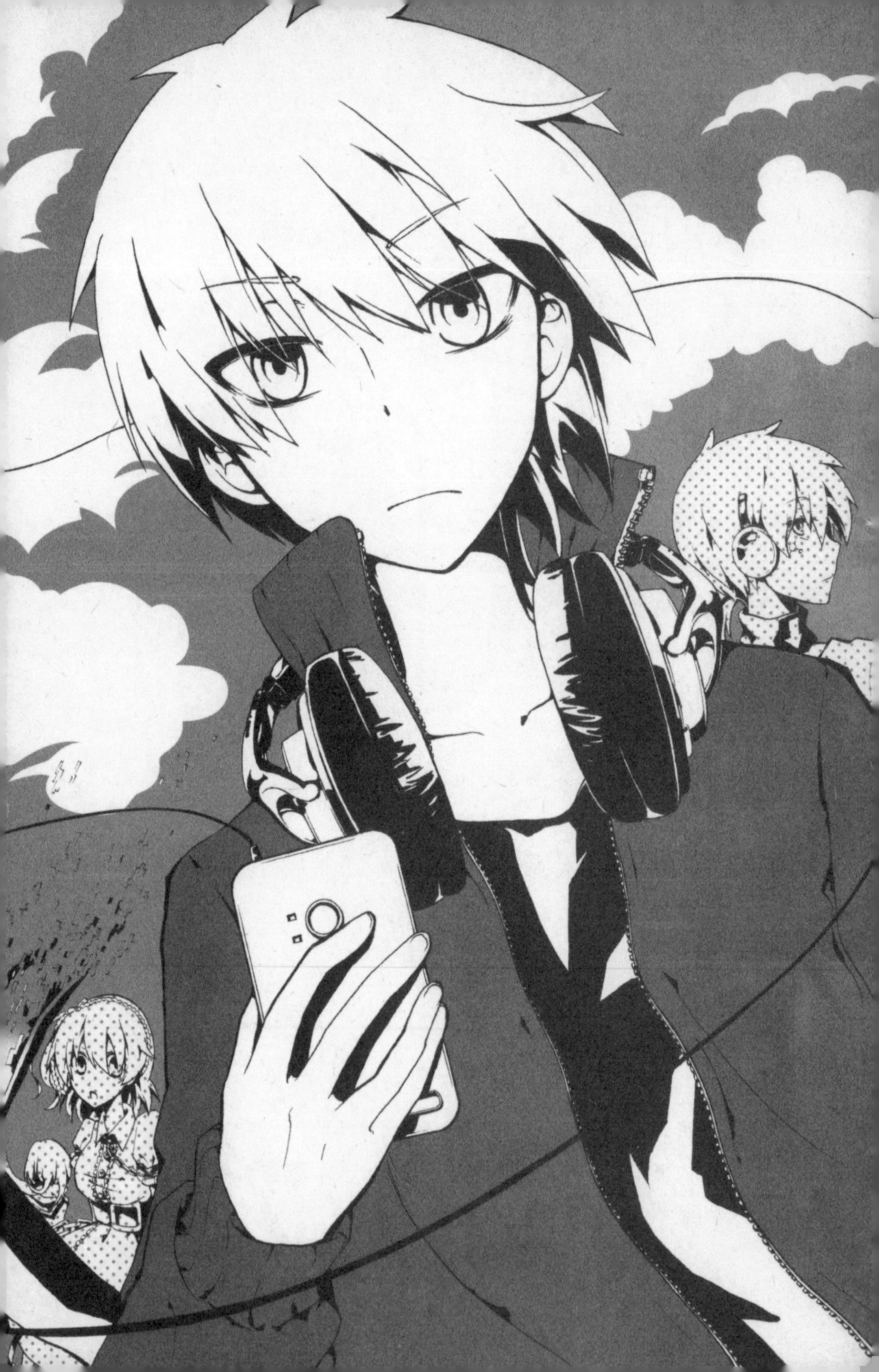

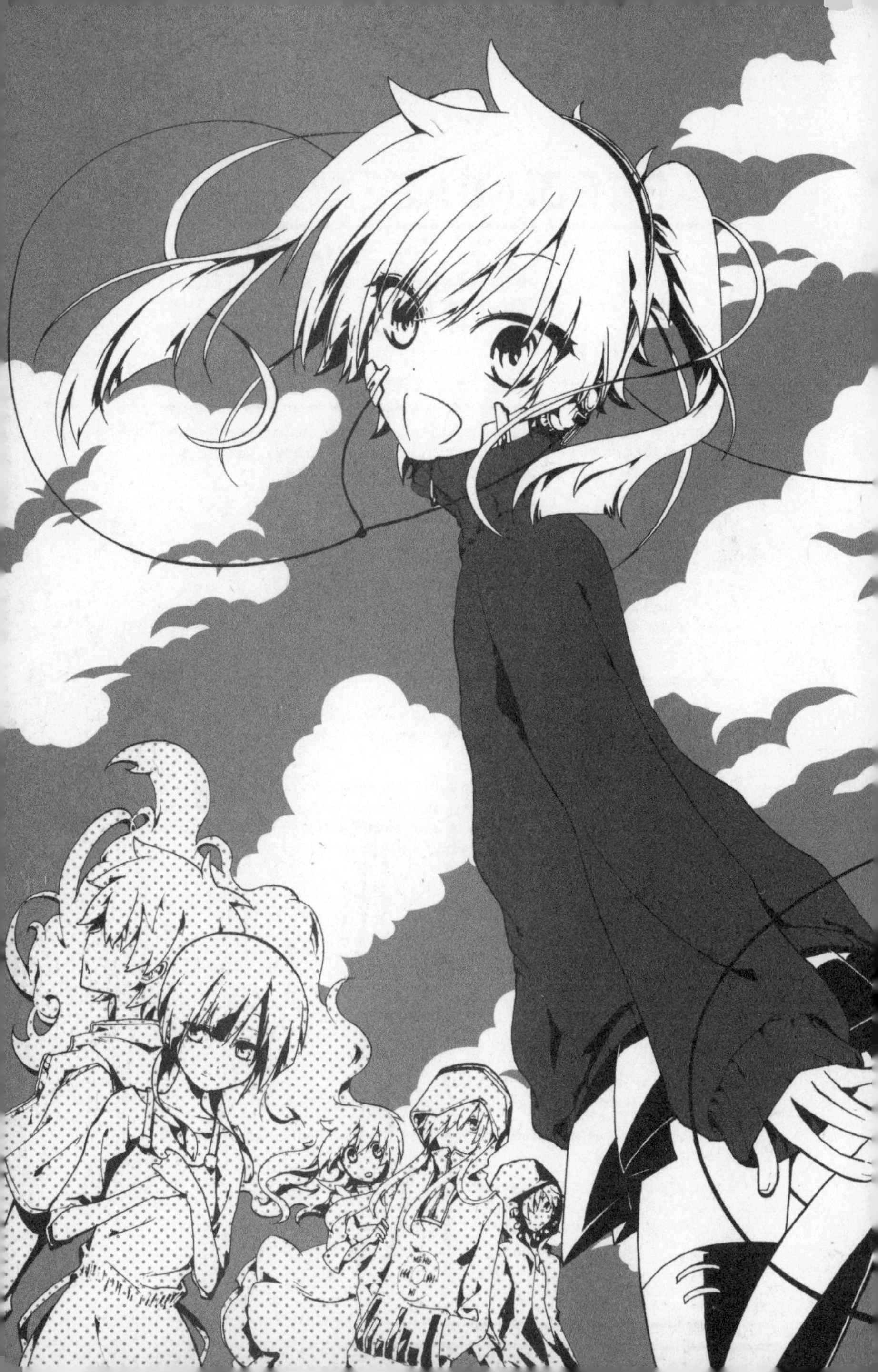

KAGEROU DAZE 01

MAHIRO SATOU
Original Story: JIN (SHIZEN NO TEKI-P)
Character Design: SIDU, WANNYANPUU-

Translation: Kevin Gifford • Lettering: Abigail Blackman

Kagerou Daze
© Mahiro Satou 2012-2015
© KAGEROU PROJECT / 1st PLACE 2012-2015
Edited by MEDIA FACTORY
First published in Japan in 2013 by KADOKAWA CORPORATION.
English translation rights reserved by Yen Press, LLC under the license from KADOKAWA CORPORATION, Tokyo through TUTTLE-MORI AGENCY, Inc., Tokyo.

English translation © 2015 by Yen Press, LLC

Yen Press
1290 Avenue of the Americas
New York, NY 10104

Visit us at yenpress.com
facebook.com/yenpress
twitter.com/yenpress
yenpress.tumblr.com

First Yen Press Edition: April 2015

ISBNs: 978-0-316-25949-1 (paperback)
      978-0-316-34621-4 (ebook)
      978-0-316-34624-5 (app)

10 9 8

BVG

Printed in the United States of America